The Belt and The Road Initiative

Implications for India

The Belt and The Road Initiative

Implications for India

MANISH

PENTAGON PRESS LLP

The Belt and the Road Initiative: Implications for India

Manish

First Published in 2021

ISBN 978-93-90095-36-0

Published by
PENTAGON PRESS LLP
206, Peacock Lane, Shahpur Jat,
New Delhi-110049
Phones: 011-64706243, 26491568
Telefax: 011-26490600
email: rajan@pentagonpress.in
website: www.pentagonpress.in

Printed at Aegean Offset Printers, Greater Noida, U.P.

CONTENTS

FOREWORD

During his first visit to India in September 2014, President Xi Jinping delivered a speech at an event hosted by the Indian Council of World Affairs (ICWA), in which emphasis was laid on the three aspects of India-China cooperation: First, China and India should become closer partners for development and jointly pursue their respective national renewal. Second, China and India should become cooperative partners for growth and jointly promote Asia's prosperity and revitalisation. Third, China and India should become global partners for strategic coordination and work for a more just and equitable international order. Regarding South Asia, President Xi said:

> "A South Asia that enjoys peace, stability, development and prosperity serves the interests of countries and people in the region and of China as well. China wants to live in harmony with all countries in the region and contribute its share to the development of the region. The "Belt" and "Road" initiatives that China has put forward are precisely aimed at strengthening connectivity among countries along the routes of the traditional land and maritime Silk Roads, with a view to achieving common prosperity, complementarity in trade and closer people-to-people ties. China hopes that, propelled by the two "wings" of the "Belt" and the "Road", its economy will take off together with those of South Asian countries.
>
> "China and countries in South Asia are important partners for cooperation. Our cooperation, like a massive treasure long waited to be unearthed, promises great prospects for us. In the next five years, China will work with South Asian countries to increase the bilateral trade to US$ 150 billion and its investment in South Asia to US$ 30 billion and provide US$ 20 billion in concessional facilities to the region. China will expand people-to-people and cultural exchanges with South Asia. It plans to offer 10,000 scholarships, training opportunities for 5,000 people and an exchange and training program for 5,000 youth, and train 5,000 Chinese language teachers for South Asia in

> the next five years. China will work with countries of South Asia to implement the China-South Asia Partnership Initiative for Science and Technology, give full play to the role of China-South Asia Expo, and build new platforms for mutually beneficial cooperation.
>
> "China is the biggest neighbour of South Asia and India is the largest country in South Asia. China is ready to work together with India and make greater contribution to the development of the region so that the three billion people living on both sides of the Himalayas will enjoy peace, friendship, stability and prosperity".

In the decade since the onset of the global financial crisis, infrastructure and connectivity have emerged as key gaps in India's growth story as indeed for other developing and emerging economies. The importance of connectivity and infrastructure projects therefore cannot be overstated. India has cooperated extensively for enhanced connectivity as is evident from its involvement in projects such as INSTC, Chabahar Port Development, India-Myanmar-Thailand Highway Project, Bangladesh-Bhutan-India-Nepal Initiative (BBIN) and Asia-Africa Growth Corridor.

In this context, the Belt and Road Initiative (BRI) assumes importance and provides the broad context for this book. From a Chinese point of view, this is very much of a global project and has to be seen and analysed as such. Equally inevitable from the Indian point of view is the fact that the China Pakistan Economic Corridor is a critical regional component of this global initiative and deeply colours our view and understanding of the BRI.

Over the past decade, China has been seen experimenting with two parallel but contrasting models for its regional and global economic outreach: The Belt and Road Initiative and the Asian Infrastructure Investment Bank (AIIB). The BRI was first announced in September 2013 without any prior transparent consultation/dialogue with prospective partners. Countries were invited to join the project but there was an absence of any serious efforts to build consensus on the main principles and policies governing it. In March 2015, China issued an action plan for the proposed project. India's position on the project and on the CPEC is well known.

Over the years, China has made some adjustments in response to the criticism it has received from various countries but the Indian concerns remain unaddressed. It is important to stress that the main principles of multilateralism, such as good governance, transparency, accountability, concern for ecology, financial responsibility to avoid unsustainable debt burden for countries and a consultative dialogue prior to the establishment of a multilateral institution need to be followed in letter and spirit. In this list, the sovereignty and territorial integrity of other countries ranks at the very top. It is important to investigate and analyse whether China has followed these principles in the context of the BRI. This book makes a significant contribution in this regard.

The second model follows a more consensual approach. The initiative to establish AIIB was put forward by China in October 2013. A dialogue-driven collaborative process was initiated, and took about two years of negotiation and preparation with prospective members before the AIIB was officially launched in January 2016. The Articles of Agreement of AIIB, highlighted its aims to build a rule-based multilateral institution, stressing transparency in planning and implementing projects and accountability for the member-states. India chose to be a founder-member of the AIIB primarily because a dialogue-driven collaborative process was initiated and the main governing principles were agreed to by the members.

There is an obvious contrast in our approaches to the BRI and the AIIB and the contrast reflects the diverse world views that underpin them. Therefore, it is logical to highlight the significance of the AIIB model of consensual initiative over the BRI model of unilateral initiatives. India will obviously continue to engage with consensus-based initiatives from China given that consensual and collaborative engagements allow all members to formulate and shape policy. Similarly, it will shun initiatives that do not conform to the fundamental principles of international engagement.

China is a major country in Asia and our biggest neighbour. Notwithstanding the negative developments of the recent past and continued Chinese continental and maritime assertion, our future relationship with China remains a principal factor not just for India but for the entire region. This also necessitates that scholarship in India remains abreast of changes in China and we analyse and understand developments in that country from the perspective of our own national interest. The two countries have distinct outlooks towards their international engagement and outreach and this means that scholarship and a deep understanding of China and our bilateral interface with it is an essential adjunct to policy formulation. Obviously, such scholarship will have greater value if it is objective and clinical and one step removed from the emotions and polemics associated with day to day developments.

The Indian Council of World Affairs was glad to be associated with the two-day conference organised by the Central University of Gujarat on the Belt and Road Initiative in which a number of scholars and researchers had participated. I am now delighted to see that a conference proceedings volume is ready and this will further expand debate and scholarship on this theme.

23 June 2021

T.C.A. Raghavan
Director-General
Indian Council of World Affairs

ACKNOWLEDGEMENTS

This book is an outcome of a two-day conference on the Belt and Road Initiative (BRI) organised by the School of International Studies, Central University of Gujarat (CUG), Gandhinagar in collaboration with the Indian Council of World Affairs (ICWA), New Delhi. Many authors were participants to this two-day deliberation. I would like to acknowledge their contribution and thank them for giving their chapters for publication subsequently.

I would also thank the CUG and the ICWA for the financial support extended to this project. At a time when the world is debating China's 'rise' and how the BRI could potentially be a challenge for us, it was imperative to understand and develop an Indian response. This book thus is a small contribution aimed towards understanding the various facets of BRI from an Indian standpoint.

I also would put my special thanks to Rajan Arya and Pentagon Press LLP for commissioning this edited volume. My sincere gratitude to the team of young scholars, Aditya Mani, Alok Behera, Anu Sharma, Aparna Tripathi, Prashant Kaushik and every person who has contributed at various stages of the preparation of the manuscript. Needless to mention, the errors are all mine.

MANISH

CONTRIBUTORS

Aditya Mani is Ph.D. Candidate at the Centre for International Politics, School of International Studies, Central University of Gujarat, Gandhinagar.

Ajey Lele is Senior Fellow at the Manohar Parrikar Institute for Defence Studies and Analyses, New Delhi.

Anu Sharma is Ph.D. Candidate at Centre for International Politics, School of International Studies, Central University of Gujarat, Gandhinagar.

Arun Vishwanathan is Associate Professor and Chairperson at Centre for Security Studies, School of National Security Studies, Central University of Gujarat, Gandhinagar.

Atanu Mohapatra is Professor and Chairperson of the Centre for Diaspora Studies at Central University of Gujarat, Gandhinagar.

Baladas Ghoshal is former Professor of Southeast Asia and South-West Pacific Studies and Chairman of the Centre for South and Southeast Asian Studies at Jawaharlal Nehru University, New Delhi.

G.V.C. Naidu is former Professor in Southeast Asian Studies, School of International Studies, School of International Studies, Jawaharlal Nehru University, New Delhi.

Hemant Adlakha is Associate Professor at the Centre for Chinese & South East Asian Studies, School of Language, Literature & Culture Studies, Jawaharlal Nehru University.

Kritika Roy is Student Assistant at the Hertie School Centre for International Security and MIA Candidate 2022 at the Hertie School, Berlin.

Manish is Professor and Dean, School of International Studies, Central University of Gujarat, Gandhinagar.

Oindrilla Dattagupta is an Assistant Professor in Department of Political Science, Vivekanand College for Women, University of Calcutta, Kolkata.

Prashant Kaushik is Assistant Professor, Centre for Chinese Studies, School of Language, Literature and Culture Studies, Central University of Gujarat, Gandhinagar.

Ramakrushna Pradhan is an Assistant Professor in Political Science and International Relations in the Department of Social Science, Fakir Mohan University, Balasore, Odisha, India.

Sanchita Bhattacharya is Research Fellow at Institute for Conflict Management, New Delhi.

Sanjay K. Jha is Professor and Dean , School of National Security Studies , Central University of Gujarat, Gandhinagar.

Shishir Upadhyaya is a former Indian naval officer with a background in operations and intelligence. He is an alumnus of the Defence Services Staff College. He is the author of India's Maritime Strategy: Balancing Regional Ambitions and China.

Sitakanta Mishra is Associate Professor in School of Liberal Studies, Pandit Deendayal Energy University, Gandhinagar.

Sreeradha Datta is Centre Head & Senior Fellow, Neighbourhood Studies, Vivekananda International Foundation (VIF) New Delhi.

Srikanth Kondapalli is Professor, Chinese Studies at Centre for East Asian Studies, School of International Studies, Jawaharlal Nehru University, New Delhi.

Vijay Sakhuja is Former Director National Maritime Foundation, New Delhi.

INTRODUCTION

Manish and Prashant Kaushik

China's rise to great power status perhaps remains one of the most debated themes of the 21st century. The process unleashed by 40 years of unrelenting reform and opening up has surely catapulted China to the centre-stage of the global arena where China is actively participating in the formation of a global order, best reflected through the Belt and the Road Initiative (BRI). The BRI is by far China's largest cross-regional (or cross-continental) initiative in the world today. It runs through Asia, Europe and Africa connecting the world's most economically active region of East Asia with the most developed parts of Europe, and in between sweeping through the vast hinterland of West Asia, North Africa, Central Asia, South Asia and then stretching all the way to encompass Latin America and South America. Symbolizing its larger acceptability, if nothing much, China has signed BRI cooperation documents with 140 countries and 30 international organizations as of January 2021. The initiative is also a giant of initiatives whereby China has already invested about USD 755 billion in BRI countries between 2013 and June 2020, thereby becoming the second largest investing country in the world.[1] BRI investments span the sectors of energy, transport, real estate, metals, agriculture, chemicals, finance, health, entertainment, logistics and others (Nedopil, Christoph 2020). Domestically, the BRI has been enshrined into the CPC constitution following the 19th CPC National Congress in November 2017 as Xi Jinping's pet project and 'China's top-level cooperation initiative' ('国家级顶层合作倡议'). Undoubtedly, the BRI is the most ambitious of Chinese projects launched till date having far-reaching global ramifications and China has heavily invested in it, both in terms of prestige and money.

The need to understand the BRI cannot be overemphasized and any attempt to comprehend it cannot be fruitful without first taking into account its fluid nature. The very fact that the duality of land and water, reflected through the overland Silk Road Economic Belt and the 21st Century Maritime Silk Road, lies at the core of the BRI, making it resemble the fluid duality inherent in Chinese *yin-yang*. This unprecedented and unique combination of the land element with that of the water in an inseparable manner is rooted in China's desire to develop as both a land and a maritime power and ensure its long-term growth in an ever-evolving global scenario. At the other end of the spectrum, the BRI and its corresponding endeavour of building a "community of common destiny" (命运共同体) appear quite ingenious when seen in terms of China's requirements as a "nation-state" and based on imagining itself as a "civilizational state" (Zhang Weiwei, 2014, 2019).[2] As a "nation-state" China continues to exist in an 'anarchic' Hobbesian world and urgently needs a "grand strategy" to explicate its rise and ensure its future growth in the least, whereas the requirement of a normative set of values applicable beyond the limitations of space and time is desirable as a "civilizational state" having huge population, large territory, long history, rich philosophy, unique political culture and a booming economy. Hence, in an overview of the idea of the Silk Road and its relationship with the BRI, China's self-perception as a "civilizational state", and the need and search for a grand strategy as a rising power can prove helpful in understanding the nature of the BRI. On the other hand, an appreciation of the BRI's relationship with its proponent, Chinese president Xi Jinping, could prove helpful in understanding its genesis at a particular point in time. The answers to the questions about the implications of the BRI for India or whether does India have concerns with BRI could only be in the affirmative (Manish et al., 2019; Prashant et al., 2019).

The Idea of the Silk Road and the BRI

> "*We are heirs to two Silk Roads: not the ancient and the modern, but the invented and the reinvented.*"
>
> **—Tamara Chin, 2013 (*Critical Inquiry*/Autumn 2013)**

Ferdinand Freiherr von Richthofen (1833-1905), a German geographer and geologist, first coined the terms "Seidenstraße" and "Seidenstraßen", translated in English as "Silk Road(s)" or "Silk Route(s)", in 1877. Richthofen's exposition on the Silk Road belonged to a multi-volume geological survey of China advocating construction of a commercial railroad linking China with Europe. Richthofen's student, Sven Hedin (1865-1952), played a key role in popularizing the idea of the Silk Road in the first half of the 20th century advocating the "revival of the

Silk Road" as a motorable road from China to Europe, particularly through his best seller titled *The Silk Road* (1936). Both Richthofen and Hedin made Chinese historical accounts essential to modern geographical knowledge and traced the historicity of the Silk Road to the imperial embassy sent by the Han emperor Wudi 汉武帝 (156 BCE–87 BCE) to the region in the west of the Han empire in 138 BCE under Zhang Qian 张骞 (164–114 BCE) to seek help against the raging Huns invading the Han empire from the north (Liu Xinru 2010; Tamara Chin 2013, 2019; Mark Elliott 2019).[3] The term "silk road" never existed in the long tradition of imperial histories in China, but as a neologism 'silk road' became intrinsically tied with the Han dynasty due to accounts of Zhang Qian's embassy in the Han annals. The Han dynasty so thoroughly established what came to be considered "Chinese culture" that "Han 汉" also became a byword for things and people "Chinese", so much so that the largest ethnic group in China forming 92 per cent of the total population is called "Han 汉族" today.

Nonetheless, before the term "Silk Road" (sichou zhi lu 丝绸之路) was "rediscovered" in China in the 1970s, it had a limited circulation with its renditions like "si lu" (丝路) or "sichou zhi lu" (丝绸之路) often appearing within quotation marks or as the "so-called Silk Roads" (Tamara Chin, 2013). But much on the same lines as today when China feels the need to tell the China story well to the world to spread the Chinese voice to showcase the real multifaceted China and to improve its soft power and cultural influence (Xinhua 2016; Reuters 2016; *Guangming Daily* 2018; Ouyang Hui 2019), a China embarking on the process of reform and opening up in 1978 felt the need to project itself to the world, coincidently, exactly after a century when the term "silk road" was first coined in 1877. An apt opportunity came in the form of an offer from the Japan Broadcasting Corporation (NHK) to shoot a documentary in China following the normalization of Sino-Japan relations in 1972. The China Central Television (CCTV) and NHK collaborated through the 1970s to jointly produce a 12-episode documentary named "The Silk Route"《丝绸之路》. It was first aired in Japan in April 1980 and was the earliest audio-visual adaptation of this famous historical phenomenon. Its sequels covering the silk road beyond the borders and seas of China were made and broadcast over the next decade.[4] The person who played an instrumental role in giving permission to NHK to shoot in interior China was none other than the father of China's opening up to the world—Deng Xiaoping. The documentary series not only "introduced China to the rest of the world"[5] at an opportune time when China was emerging from behind the Iron Curtain, but it also worked to consolidate China's claim on the historicity and provenance of the Silk Road.

A lot of water has flowed under the Nanjing Yangtze River bridge since then, and the most remarkable event of our times remains China's emergence, or, as the Chinese leadership believes, "re-emergence", as a great power. How China sees itself as a "long-standing entity" hence assumes immense importance in the present context of an attempt to understand the BRI, more so, because as a modern nation-state, China came into existence over the period of the last hundred years with the Opium Wars with Great Britain serving as a watershed, and as an ancient civilization it existed for several millennia enjoying unparalleled economic prosperity, domestic stability, and political dominance.

China as a Civilizational State and the BRI

Since the beginning of the present century, the very idea of China as an unbounded civilization rooted in a long history and rich culture has gained traction. It found resonance in American sinologist Lucian Pye's description that today's China is not a country but rather a "civilization pretending to be a state". During most of the 20th century, China's long civilizational history was considered as an impediment by numerous Chinese scholars, intellectuals and politicians who blamed a long historical tradition and Confucian heritage as hindering China's march toward modernity. However, today the emphasis in China has shifted to building a "civilizational-state" and seeing China as such, with huge population, large territory, long history, rich philosophy, unique political culture, and a booming economy. This belief is further buttressed by the narrative that the concept of a nation-state rooted in euro-centrism is not suitable for China. The very idea of a nation-state is perceived to be narrow which leads to cultural self-dwarfing in China. Seen through the prism of a nation-state, the concepts and ideas belonging to China tend to become "unique or special" in contrast to those belonging to the West which become "standard" or "universal". Thus, a nation-state is an antithesis of an inclusive and multi-ethnic Chinese civilization. Therefore, the idea of "civilization state" better carries the strong national consciousness inherent in Chinese cultural traditions and could help China find a strong foothold between tradition and modernity. The idea also best assimilates China as a state, nation, and civilization (Zhu Bibo et al., 2020). Moreover, just like the West has made its values universal and rules normative thus giving shape to a "universalism" interpreted and enforced by itself, China also needs to employ the idea of "civilization-state" to make Chinese cultural traditions universal, and express universal concern for the world (Gan Yang, 2008; Sun Xiangchen, 2014; Andrew Grant, 2019).

The means to express universal concern and recast China as a *sui generis* civilization-state that interacts with and enriches and grows from its neighbouring civilizations are best manifested in the theory of the building of a community of common destiny practised through the building of the BRI. The borderless map of the world depicting only the cartography of the BRI totally undermines the idea of a nation-state by ignoring its defining feature—the political boundaries. Such representations of the BRI produced from China depicts a frictionless world of global economic integration centred around China which is no longer a country jealously guarding its borders but a civilization facilitating and leading economic development through a network of belts and roads (Andrew Grant 2019).

The theoretical underpinning to this civilizational endeavour of the BRI is provided by the official expositions on how it is devoted to building a "community of common destiny" (命运共同体). As the man at the helm, Xi Jinping has built upon his predecessor Hu Jintao's promotion of the Confucian-inspired concept of a "harmonious world" (和谐世界), but he promotes the idea of "community of common destiny" while steering clear of the concepts such as *Tian xia* (天下) which were once close to the Chinese dominance in the Confucian cultural sphere in its neighbourhood. No wonder that the scope of this community of common destiny widens and its prominence increases every time Xi Jinping expounds on it. The "new model" of "community of common destiny" is juxtaposed with the "old model" of international relations associated with the West. While the "new model" is premised on promoting harmony and win-win relations, the old model is oriented towards a "clash of civilizations" and governed by "zero-sum" thinking and "Cold War mentality". The very fact that "the community of common destiny" has been written into the CPC constitution as a defining aspect of "Xi Jinping Thought" goes on to show that, as a civilization-state, China is trying to imagine geopolitical relations and interactions in registers quite different from those of nation-states, thereby providing normativeness to the BRI (Jacob Mardell, 2017; Andrew Grant, 2019).

Nation-state and BRI: What, Why, How

That China, as a nation-state itself, must still face a Hobbesian world full of anarchy and other nation-states devoted to self-preservation and safeguarding individual interests is the other side of the coin, equally real like the notion of a "civilization-state" but perhaps demanding a different strategy. Hence, in order to answer questions regarding how and why the world saw the launch of the BRI by a quintessential nation-state like China, it is immensely pertinent to look at the two prominent strands of discourse prevailing in China regarding its quest for a grand strategy and the dichotomy to see and develop itself as a land power or a sea power when Xi Jinping came to power and then juxtapose them with the measures and policies he subsequently adopted.

Chinese Grand Strategy Discourse: *Land Power vs. Sea Power*

In a much-cited article published almost a year before Xi Jinping became the general secretary of the Communist Party of China in 2012, Wang Jisi, then Dean of the School of International Studies at Peking University and one of the top 100 Global Thinkers listed by *Foreign Policy* in 2012, remarked that "China's grand strategy is a field still to be plowed" (Wang Jisi, 2011). As Wang Jisi put it, China's power and influence had outgrown the expectations of even its own leaders and hence it was necessary "for the international community to understand China's strategic thinking and try to forecast how it might evolve according to its interests and its leaders' vision" (Wang Jisi, 2011). Through his intervention, Wang Jisi actually contributed to the research on "Grand Strategy" (大战略研究) in China that had gained currency at the onset of the 21st century.

The backdrop against which Wang Jisi elaborated on China's quest for a grand strategy was formed by a dramatic increase in the Chinese academia's interest in the theories of grand strategy following the rapid and continuous development of China's comprehensive national strength since reform and opening up and China's accession to the World Trade Organisation (WTO) in 2001 which was a watershed moment signifying its "integration" with a globalising world. Much like other watershed moments in Chinese history, when China felt the need to learn from the West, this time around as well numerous works of famous contemporary Western strategic thinkers like Sir Basil Henry Liddell Hart, Paul Michael Kennedy, Edward N. Luttwak, Barry R. Posen, John L. Gaddis, and Williamson Murray among others, began to be translated and introduced in China. Most notable among the Chinese translators of these works was Prof. Shi Yinhong 时殷弘 from the Renmin University in Beijing, China, who led from the front and in collaboration with the Commercial Press 商务印书馆 and the World Affairs Press 世界知识出版社 brought contemporary Western strategic thought closer to Chinese readers (Ge Hanwen, 2018).

Another noteworthy trend was the introduction and publication of works of a Taiwanese scholar, Niu Xianzhong 钮先钟. Niu's works were significant for the comparison, albeit rooted in the Eastern/Chinese experience, conducted between the evolution of the Western strategic (including grand strategy) thinking and China's historical experience. It was against this backdrop of translating and engaging with Western strategic thought that many Chinese scholars started paying attention to erecting China's own theoretical system for a grand strategy (Ge Hanwen, 2018).

Interestingly, much before Alfred Thayer Mahan and Halford J. Mackinder theorized about "sea power" and "geographical pivot" respectively, China had been grappling with the same issues as reflected in Admiral Zheng He's seven sea voyages covering most of the known world between 1405 and 1433 under the Ming dynasty and an abrupt end to which Chinese seafaring was put under the late Ming and Qing dynasties. The debate became much more acute following the Chinese defeat in the Opium Wars by Britain, quintessentially a small island-nation but a big sea power. This strand of Chinese strategic and diplomatic discourse revolving around the dichotomy of whether to consider and develop China as a continental power or a sea power 陆权海权之争 also informed the discourse on China's grand strategy. The debate in Chinese strategic circles was about whether to first "head West" through the land corridor or "go South" through the sea lanes "西进"还是"南下".[6] This debate manifested that, first, the sea power-continental power dichotomy remained the main thinking framework for Chinese scholars to understand China's geopolitical strategy, and, second, this dichotomy was embedded in modern geopolitical imaginations to a large extent, that is, various nation-states compete and confront each other in order to seize a dominant position in the world, the only difference being the ways through sea or land to achieve this position. Third, although there were some voices calling for China to pay equal attention to land and sea simultaneously, there was an utter lack of specific proposals and mechanisms as to how to achieve such an equilibrium (Zeng Xianghong, 2016).

At another level there was a broad consensus in Chinese academia that China could face "hostile feelings and hostile intentions" "敌对情感和敌对意志" in Clausewitzian terms due to its rapid rise which was bound to have a profound impact on the existing international political and economic system, especially the structure of international power dominated by Western countries. Such a consensus was further buttressed by the widespread prevalence of the "China threat" theory. The Western realist international relations theory saw China as an unsatisfied rising power which was bound to challenge the dominant position of the USA and disrupt the international status quo (Wang Jianwei, 2009). China under the Hu-Wen leadership (2003-2013) tried to formulate a response to the "China threat" by advancing the idea of China's "Peaceful Rise".[7] Nonetheless, this formulation came under strong criticism for "peaceful" was seen as a weakening of China's territorial claims, especially vis-à-vis Taiwan, and "rise" (崛起 jué qǐ) was criticised for being too provocative, unfeasible, premature, and going against the sacrosanct dictum of "not to show off one's capability but to keep a low profile," (韬光养晦有所作为) as proposed by Deng Xiaoping. Clearly there was an urgency for the fifth-generation leadership of the CPC led by Xi Jinping and

Li Keqiang to come up with a new paradigm for China's emergence particularly owing to the unique position that China had come to occupy under them.

The uniqueness flowed from several facts like China already becoming the second largest economy in the world but not yet reaching the standards of a "developed" country, and the clamour for China to play a more proactive role in international affairs. China was the world's biggest trading nation and the most important bilateral trade partner of 124 countries all over the world, yet it could hardly count these countries as its friends. China was undergoing urbanisation at breakneck speed but was faced with a huge regional imbalance and income inequality, which regularly led to social unrest and violent protests. China's strategic interests had expanded enormously largely due to its status as a net energy importer but attempts to secure such interests were ending up compounding "the China threat". China also remained the only non-Western Permanent Member of the United Nations Security Council and the only nation that could propose "a new great power relationship" with the USA.

As the newly-appointed general secretary of the Communist Party of China, Xi Jinping was well aware of the above-mentioned urgency and dextrously addressed his domestic audience by reiterating and (re-)emphasizing the idea of the "Chinese Dream" 中国梦. Xi pointed out that China is closest to and confident and capable of realizing the great rejuvenation of the Chinese nation than at any other point in history. However, the road to "transform the blueprint into reality" is a long one. That this long and arduous road was to be called "一带一路" *yidai yilu*[8] was revealed subsequently in Indonesia and Kazakhstan in 2013 where Xi proposed the building of the 21st-century Maritime Silk Road and the Silk Road Economic Belt, respectively. The significance of the BRI in terms of a "grand strategy" was never lost on the Chinese leadership as they saw a concrete implementation mechanism for the Chinese grand strategy in the BRI which had deftly combined the land with the sea in a *yin-yang* manner thus overcoming the limitations of the traditional geopolitical thinking of a separation between land and sea (Zeng Xianghong, 2016). The major question facing the Chinese leadership was to whether to present the BRI as China's grand strategy or not.

Is the BRI China's Grand Strategy?

The strategic nature and significance of the BRI flows, first, from the Chinese leadership's recognition of various domestic problems of industrial overcapacity, corruption, widening gap between rich and poor, regional imbalance, slowing economic growth, and the anxiety that these domestic troubles might combine with foreign factors to affect the stability of the ruling Communist regime as has happened on various occasions in Chinese history when foreign powers like Mongols and Manchus have taken advantage of the domestic unrest to usurp power in China. Second, lessons gleaned from the historical process of the rise and fall of great powers indicated that the fate of late-developing powers like China could either be to break the siege and complete their rise or be strangled by the prevailing hegemon. Obviously breaking the siege to rise continuously would be the preferred choice for any late-developing power like China. Hence, though the official pronouncement by the Chinese government never identifies the BRI as China's grand strategy, as Ye Hailin, deputy director-general at the National Institute of International Strategy of the Chinese Academy of Social Sciences (CASS) puts it, it does not mean that the promotion and implementation of the BRI does not conform to the existing basic strategic theories and laws (Ye Hailin, 2019). In similar vein, Wang Jisi points out in his famous article mentioned above that China needs a grand strategy to serve its domestic priorities and protect its core interests—sovereignty, security, and development—against the messy cluster of threats that the country faces, a grand strategy needs to consider long-term objectives, and requires defining a geostrategic focus (Wang Jisi, 2011).

The BRI seems to fulfil all these preconditions and requirements to qualify itself as a grand strategy. It finds its genesis in the need to further China's economic growth by finding new avenues for its industrial overcapacity and technical know-how. The BRI is honeycombed with China's domestic policies of the development of its western regions 西部大开发 and going-out strategy "走出去战略" of its industries and investment. By creating alternate routes and avenues of importing energy resources, and suggesting the creation of a comprehensive environment for development far advanced than a free trade zone or any other multilateral trading arrangement, strengthening people-to-people exchanges and creating immense goodwill for brand China, BRI not only offers the best protection to Chinese interests but enables them go global. As a long-term endeavour designed to enable China "to realise the great rejuvenation of the Chinese nation" by the middle of the 21st century when the PRC will mark the 100th anniversary of its establishment, the BRI has long-term objectives. In terms of geo-strategic focus, the BRI not only remains focused on China's neighbourhood in Asia but moves beyond to tightly embrace Africa, Europe and even Latin and South America. Evidently, if not the grand strategy itself, the BRI is the closest China could get to a grand strategy.

BRI and the Xi Jinping Era

As an initiative proposed by the Chinese President, Xi Jinping, who is widely held as the most powerful Chinese leader since Mao Zedong, it is pertinent to locate the BRI vis-a-vis its proponents. As mentioned earlier, there was an urgency for Xi Jinping to expound about China's rapid rise following three decades of reform and opening-up, and surely, he did not disappoint. One after another, Xi proposed the Chinese Dream, the BRI, Made in China 2025, China Standards 2035; abolished fixed presidential terms, and enshrined his name in the party constitution as part of the "Xi Jinping Thought on Socialism with Chinese Characteristics for a New Era", an era, of course, most closely identifiable with Xi himself. Xi Jinping is a "princeling"; his father Xi Zhongxun was a CPC veteran who served under Mao and Deng. Moreover, Xi is a child of the Great Proletariat Cultural Revolution (GPCR) and lived in a cave in the village of Liangjiahe, Yanchuan County, Shaanxi province, following his father's purge during the GPCR. Living through the most tumultuous period of recent Chinese history, Xi Jinping gained firsthand experience of the ways in which "power" operates in China and has wielded and exercised it rather well since becoming the core of the fifth-generation Chinese leadership in 2012 (Ananth Krishnan, 2020, 41).

There is no doubt that the BRI is Chinese President Xi Jinping's dream project and is driven by the current development challenge facing China. A cue in this regard could be taken from the historical behaviour of the Chinese leadership whose policy initiatives have been invariably guided by the need to serve China's national interests. Mao signed the Sino-Soviet Friendship Treaty in the 1950s with a view to consolidate state power; whereas the subsequent Sino-Soviet split in the 1960s, normalization of relations with the USA in the 1970s, and reform and opening under Deng in the 1980s, were driven by the need for economic development, and the urge to improve China's international standing, respectively (Heike Holbig et al., 2017).

The BRI also underscores a departure from Deng's dictum of "keeping a low profile" 韬光养晦 for China as Xi Jinping has emphasized that since 1949 China had experienced a "historic rise from standing up (1949-1976) and growing rich (1978-2012) to getting strong (2012 onwards)" (从站起来、富起来到强起来的历史性飞跃) (Heike Holbig et al., 2017). Undoubtedly, Xi's strong China is in the best position to launch and implement a grand initiative like the BRI.

Under Xi Jinping the "principal contradiction of the era" has also undergone a change and has been identified "between unbalanced and inadequate development and the people's ever-growing needs for a better life" "中国特色社会主义进入新时代，我国社会主要矛盾已经转化为人民日益增长的美好生活需要

和不平衡不充分的发展之间的矛盾"[9] thus exerting a profound impact on the work going to be undertaken by the Communist Party of China under the Xi administration. Of course, the BRI is an integral part of this work.

The BRI and India

For the Chinese, the India-China relationship is a "four-in-one" relationship "四位一体" 的关系, namely, relationship between neighbouring countries, major powers, developing countries, and as playing important roles on the multilateral stage (Chen Zonghai, 2012), a relationship that is characterized by the "4Cs" of conflict, competition, coordination and cooperation (Ye Hailin, 2013). Under the BRI schema, India is considered a 'dual status country' (双重身份国家) with access to both the Silk Road Economic Belt and the 21st century Maritime Silk Road (Yang Shu and Wang Shusen, 2019). India is also China's second-biggest neighbour with which it shares a long but disputed border, a significant market for Chinese consumer products, as China's biggest trading partner in South Asia and as a rising power. Hence, in the ideal scheme of things, China would like to see India participate in the BRI bandwagon to ensure its comprehensive success. Nonetheless, given a combination of factors ranging from political, economic, and strategic, such as violation of its territorial sovereignty due to the construction of the China-Pakistan Economic Corridor in Pakistan occupied Kashmir, ever-growing trade deficit and strategic encircling and balancing, India has remained non-committal to the BRI, much to China's dismay.

The biggest point of friction between India and China as regards the BRI remains China's insensitivity towards India's core concerns. The official pronouncements about the BRI uphold it as an open and inclusive initiative apparently involving few, if any, requirements, or restrictions, and propose that it exists in cooperation with, and not against, other international development initiatives. Nonetheless, it seems that the open and inclusive nature of the BRI does not apply to India as its concerns arising out of the violation of its territorial sovereignty in Pakistan occupied Kashmir have never been addressed by China in a serious manner. Hardly any attempt has been made to bring India on board the BRI through consultative mechanisms as has been done at other multilateral platforms like the Asia Infrastructure Investment Bank (AIIB), BRICS, the New Development Bank and even the Shanghai Cooperation Organization (SCO). On the other hand, there are views in China that India should not be convinced to join the BRI, as China is in no position to compromise the CPEC as per Indian requirements of recognition of its sovereignty (Ye Hailin, 2017).

The present volume aims to analyze some of the interconnected, and dynamic developments related to the BRI in the light of India's concerns with the BRI and its implications on India. This volume is divided into six sections. The first part explicates the idea behind and approach of the BRI while maintaining the focus on its implications for India. The second and the most comprehensive part of this volume focuses on India's neighbourhood and minutely investigates various dimensions of the BRI in South Asia having far-reaching implications for regional connectivity and issues of sovereignty in the region. At a time when both India and China are attributing unprecedented significance to their neighbourhood, most of which is common to both, the second section concludes with summing up the ways in which South Asia and India are perceived in China through the BRI prism. The challenges and issues New Delhi faces on account of the BRI in its extended neighbourhood in Central and West Asia are immensely pertinent since India depends on this extended neighbourhood for its energy security. Hence, the third section examines the issues arising in India's extended neighbourhood due to the BRI. Having investigated the land component or the "belt" portion of the BRI in the initial three parts, the fourth section sets its focus on interrogating the maritime "road" part of the BRI underscoring its nature, infrastructure planning and its implications for India. The emergence of China as a tech giant and a major player in technologies such as artificial intelligence (AI), big-data and 5G are illustrative of the tech prowess China has managed to acquire in the last four decades. With the world at the cusp of the next industrial revolution rooted in latest digital technologies, the digital component forms an integral part of the BRI. The fifth section takes stock of BRI connectivity and control hinged on digital technologies with special focus on emerging concerns. The once-in-a-century COVID-19 pandemic has been variously interpreted as a black swan, a black elephant, a gray rhino or even a black jellyfish event (Atanu Biswas, 2020). Having caused unprecedented disruptions in the known world, what impact COVID-19 would have on the BRI is the question addressed in the sixth section of this volume.

Undoubtedly, the objective of these chapters is to develop an Indo-centric understanding of the BRI and also suggest as to how New Delhi could possibly deal with the BRI challenge.

NOTES

1. According to the World Investment Report 2017, foreign direct investment (FDI) outflows from China surged by 44 per cent to 183 billion US dollars making China the second largest investing country in the world for the first time. "UN report: China becomes the second largest investing country", 8 June 2017. Retrieved 4 January 2019 from http://en.people.cn/business/n3/2017/0608/c90778-9225990.html

2. Zhang Weiwei prefers to call China a "civilizational state" and not a "civilization-state", since China has both the characteristics of a "modern nation-state" and "an ancient civilization". Contrary to the idea of Lucian Pye, who famously labelled China as a civilization pretending to be a state, Zhang finds the idea of "civilizational state" more "positively" embodying the two concepts of nation-state and civilization.
3. "The Mission to the West by Zhang Qian", *Selections from the Han Narrative Histories,* https://depts.washington.edu/silkroad/texts/hantxt1.html#zhang
4. "Into the heart of China", http://www.nhk.or.jp/digitalmuseum/nhk50years_en/history/p20/index.html
5. In September 1972, the day after diplomatic relations between China and Japan were restored Chinese Premier Chou Enlai invited reporters to a reception at the Great Hall of the People and sought their support in introducing China to the rest of the world, http://www.nhk.or.jp/digitalmuseum/nhk50years_en/history/p20/index.html
6. The "head west" school was led by academician Wang Jisi 王缉思 of Peking University, whereas the "go South" strategy was propagated by PLA generals like Yang Yi 杨毅 and Luo Yuan 罗援. *Global Times* (2012), "Hong Kong media: Southward vs. Westward Progress: China's Debates its Grand Strategy", 5 November 2012. 环球时报 (2012), 港媒：中国大战略选择有分歧面临南进与西进之争, 2012-11-05. https://m.hqck.net/arc/hqck/jsck/2012/1105/128517.html
7. Zheng Bijian (郑必坚), a CPC polemicist and a former executive vice-president of the Central Committee's Party School, advanced the concept of "Peaceful Rise". At the time of postulating the concept he was the chairman of the China Reform Forum, a CPC—affiliated research unit. Zheng Bijian "China's "Peaceful Rise" to Great-Power Status", *Foreign Affairs*, Vol. 84, No. 5, Sep-Oct, 2005, pp. 18-24. The concept of "Peaceful Rise", while reiterating Deng Xiaoping's three steps of China's development to become a medium-level developed country by 2050, tried to assuage the "China threat "by highlighting that like historical precedents, China will not vie for global domination, it will transcend ideological differences to strive for peace, development, and cooperation with all countries of the world, and will be preoccupied with securing a more comfortable and decent life for its people, all this while following the development path to a peaceful rise."
8. The Chinese switched to the expression "Belt and Road Initiative" (BRI) after the first English translation, namely, "One Belt One Road", encountered numerous misinterpretations. As the focus was too much on the word "one", it was assumed that there is to be only one maritime route and a single land belt, whereas, in reality there are multiple routes. Una Aleksandra (2016) "BRI Instead of OBOR–China Edits the English Name of its Most Ambitious International Project", https://bit.ly/2SU6sZr
9. "The principal contradiction 主要矛盾 has changed four times in the history of the CCP—in 1956, 1969, 1981, and 2017. In the jargon of Sinicised Marxism, one such contradiction characterises each period of social development. By correctly identifying the current contradiction, the CCP is able to adapt to the changing reality of society and thereby further the socialist cause. For the CPC, the Mao era was characterised by the contradiction between the proletariat and the bourgeoisie, and it centred on class struggle. The principal contradiction in the reform era, under Deng, was "between the ever-growing material and cultural needs of the people versus backward social production". (Heike Holbig et al., 2017).

REFERENCES

Ananth Krishnan (2020), *India's China Challenge*, Harper Collins, India.

Andrew Grant (2019), "China's double body: infrastructure routes and the mapping of China's nation-state and civilization-state", *Eurasian Geography and Economics*, 59: 3-4, pp. 378-407.

Atanu Biswas (2020), "Not Black Swan or Grey Rhino: Why Black Jellyfish is the perfect metaphor for the Covid-19 pandemic", 18 May 2020. https://scroll.in/article/961823/not-black-swan-or-grey-rhino-why-black-jellyfish-is-the-perfect-metaphor-for-the-covid-19-pandemic

Chen Zonghai (2012), "The Historical Trend of 60 Years of Sino-Indian Relations and Current Situation—An Analysis Based on the Firsthand Data Mainly from Renmin Daily". *International Forum,* January 2012, Vol. 14, pp. 32-37. 陈宗海 "中印关系 60 年的历史脉络与现实态势", 《国际论坛》 2012 年 1 月第 14 卷 第 1 期.

Gan Yang (2008), From "nation-state" to "civilization-state". 甘阳(2008) "从"民族一国家"走向"文明一国家" ", http://www.aisixiang.com/data/19120.html

Guangming Daily (2018), "To Tell the China Story Well, Let the World Know China Better", 2 September 2018. 光明日报 (2018), "讲好中国故事让世界更好了解中国", 2018-09-02, http://www.xinhuanet.com/politics/2018-09/02/c_1123367300.htm

Heike Holbig, Jean Christopher Mittelstaedt, Yevgen Sautin, and Angela Stanzel (2017), "*China's "New Era" with Xi Jinping characteristics*" 15 December 2017. https://ecfr.eu/publication/chinas_new_era_with_xi_jinping_characteristics7243/

Jacob Mardell (2017), "The 'Community of Common Destiny' in Xi Jinping's New Era" *The Diplomat.* October 25, 2017. https://thediplomat.com/2017/10/the-community-of-common-destiny-in-xi-jinpings-new-era/

Kaushik, Prashant and Mani, Aditya (2019), "The China-Pakistan Corridor and India's Concerns" in Sakhuja, Vijay (2019) ed. *Pentagon Yearbook 2019: South Asia Defence and Strategic Perspective,* Pentagon Press, New Delhi, pp. 85-101.

Liu Xinru (2010), *The Silk Road in World History,* Oxford University Press.

Manish and Kaushik, Prashant (2019), "CPEC, Afghanistan and India's Concerns", *India Quarterly,* 75 (2), pp. 253-261.

Mark Elliott (2019), 13th GDML: The Historical Silk Road & BRI. 14 February. 2019. https://www.youtube.com/watch?v=9hx74OhssQA

Nedopil, Christoph (2020), "Investments in the Belt and Road Initiative"; Beijing, IIGF Green BRI Centre, https://green-bri.org/investments-in-the-belt-and-road-initiative-bri

Ouyang Hui (2019), "Xi Jinping Thought on Telling Well the China Story to the World", February 22, 2019. 欧阳辉(2019) "习近平向世界讲好中国故事的思想", 2019 年 02 月 22 日， http://theory.people.com.cn/n1/2019/0222/c40531-30897581.html

Reuters (2016), "China's Xi urges state media to boost global influence", 19 February 2016, https://www.reuters.com/article/us-china-media-idUSKCN0VS1IF

Sun Xiangchen (2014), "Nation-state, civilization-state and *Tian xia*", *Exploration and Free Views,* 2014.9, 64-71. 孙向晨 (2014) "民族国家、文明国家与天下意识" 《探索与争鸣》, 2014. 9, 64-71.

Tamara Chin (2013), "The Invention of the Silk Road, 1877", *Critical Inquiry,* Vol. 40, No. 1 (Autumn 2013), pp. 194-219.

Tamara Chin (2019), *The Silk Road Idea (1877-1971),* 3 June 2019. https://www.youtube.com/watch?v=7hKbWPcc9J8

Wang Jianwei (2009), "China's Peaceful Rise: A Comparative Study", EAI Fellows Program Working Paper Series No. 19, May 2009.

Wang Jisi (2011), "China's Search for a Grand Strategy: A rising great power finds its way", *Foreign Policy,* March/April 2011.

Xinhua (2016), "President Xi urges new media outlet to "tell China stories well", 31 December 2016, https://www.globaltimes.cn/content/1026592.shtml

Yang Shu and Wang Shusen (2019), "The unique role of the 'dual status' country in the construction of the 'Belt and Road'", 7 January 2019. 杨恕, 王术森 (2019) "双重身份"国家在

"一带一路"建设中的独特作用", 7 January 2019. Retrieved 10 January 2019 fromhttps://www.yidaiyilu.gov.cn/ghsl/gnzjgd/76609.htm

Ye Hailin (2013), "Cooperation, Coordination, Competition and Conflict Coexist in the 21st Century Sino-Indian Relations", *National Humanity History*, Issue 20, 2013, pp. 40-42. 叶海林(2013) "合作、协调、竞争与冲突并存 21 世纪的中印关系"《国家人文历史》, 2013 年第 20 期, 第 40-42 页.

Ye Hailin (2017), "The Modi Administration's "Issue by Issue Diplomacy" Strategy towards China, and Related Attitudes towards the Belt and Road Initiative", *Journal of Contemporary Asia-Pacific Studies*, 2017 (6), pp. 24-47+150-151e 叶海林 (2017), "莫迪政府对华 "问题外交" 策略研究——兼论该视角下印度对 "一带一路"倡议的态度" 《当代亚太》2017 年第6 期,第 24-47 页.

Ye Hailin (2019), "Perceived risks and their prevention in promotion of the Belt and Road Initiative by China", *World Economics and Politics,* No. 10, 2019. 叶海林(2019), "中国推进 "一带一路"倡议的认知风险及其防范",《世界经济与政 治》2019 年第 10 期. .

Zeng Xianghong (2016), "The Belt and Road Initiative" Geopolitical Imagination and Regional Cooperation", *World Economics and Politics,* No. 1, 2016, pp. 46-71. "一带一路"的地缘政治想象与地区合作", 《世界经济与政 治》2016 年第 1 期,第 46-71 页.

Zhang Weiwei (2014),《中国: 一个文明型国家的崛起》, http://theory.people.com.cn/n/2014/0324/c40531-24715709.html

Zhang Weiwei (2019), ""中国, 一个"文明型国家"的崛起" https://www.sohu.com/a/338690651_260616

Zhu Bibo and Zhang Huilong (2020), "Civilizational State: A Theoretical Interpretation of China's National Paradigm", *Thinking,* No. 4, 2020, Vol. 46, pp. 91-97. 朱碧波, 张会龙: "文明国家: 中华国家范式的一种理论阐释" 《思想战线》2020 年第 4 期第 46 卷, 91-97 页.

SECTION I

BRI: Its Idea, Approach and Implications

1

China's Belt and Road Initiative and Implications for India

Srikanth Kondapalli

China, India, and other countries were part of the famed Silk Road of yore involved in the exchange of goods and services, and ideas. Buddhism spread across the Silk Road to a different part of the world. India was part of the old Silk Road with trade and religious linkages. Major trade routes that found their way into the Indian sub-continent include those passing through the Hindu Kush mountains, which also saw a number of invaders, many of whom made India their home. There was also the maritime connection with the Chola Empire extending to the Southeast Asian region and to the southern parts of China. Trade flourished between the east coast of India with ports such as Quanzhou in China. Another connection in ancient times between China and India was through the "Tea Silk Road" through Sichuan, Yunnan and Tibetan regions.[1] With the rise in European colonialism, these routes fell into disuse till China's rise in the past four decades provided them with a new flavour. This chapter traces the developments in the Belt and Road Initiative (BRI), its major areas of focus, vision, and beneficiaries. It then looks at the impact in general at the global and regional levels and the responses thereof. The next section focuses on the BRI and India by outlining interests, developments, and concerns and suggests a few implications for India. It is argued here that the BRI has systemic, structural, and regional implications for India as it is tied with the leadership-related aspects in Asia and the Indo-Pacific region.

The BRI

Since 2013, China has revived the Silk Road in a new avatar of the BRI.[2] During the past seven years since the launch of the BRI, global and regional orders are witnessing major changes with an impact on India as well. The BRI has been hailed as the "project of the century" by none other than President Xi Jinping, who made it a part of the Communist Party's constitution in October 2017. In China, this new-found status in the constitution lends BRI political legitimacy and policy direction for the coming years and decades. President Xi made a speech on 28 August 2018, suggesting that this project does not constitute a process to build a "China Club". Five areas are mentioned in the White Paper on the BRI in 2015 as focus areas of the initiative, viz., policy coordination, connectivity, trade promotion, financial integration, and people-to-people contacts. Six corridors have been identified as part of the BRI, viz., China-Mongolia-Russia, New Eurasian Land Bridge, China-Central and West Asia, Indo-China Peninsula, China-Brazil, and Bangladesh-China-India-Myanmar. That the envelope of the BRI is expanding is suggested by the launching of the Polar Silk Road, Digital Silk Road, Greening BRI, Educational Silk Road and others.

In order to boost its image, it was stated that the areas falling under the influence of the BRI include $ 23 trillion in gross domestic product and 4.4 billion in population. One hundred cooperative agreements were signed with 86 countries, and four main projects have either been completed or in the process of completion, viz., Mombasa-Nairobi railway line, Belgrade-Stara Pazova railway, Khalifa port project in the United Arab Emirates, and Hambantota port in Sri Lanka. Besides, 7,000 cargo trains carried goods to Europe and other regions along 61 railway lines. The Asian Infrastructure Investment Bank (AIIB), which now has 84 members, had released $ 4.2 billion in funding for projects. China's trade with 25 Asian countries increased in 2017 by $ 1.17 trillion suggesting the focus of the BRI in the region. To further imports, China launched an Import Expo at Shanghai in November 2018. China made $ 80 billion in direct investment in non-financial sectors across the BRI and $ 28.9 billion in 82 overseas economic and trade cooperation zones.

The BRI did bring benefits to several countries and within China. Major beneficiaries of the BRI projects are mainly in the infrastructure projects, specifically in Pakistan, Laos, Cambodia, Sri Lanka, Myanmar, Nepal, Central Asian Republics, Russia, Mongolia, Italy, Greece, and Africa. Currently, the following projects have been highlighted as part of the BRI-China-Belarus industrial estate ($ 5 billion); China-Bangladesh bridge and railway project ($ 3.1 billion); Laos railway ($ 5.8 billion); Saudi Arabia refinery ($ 10 billion) and

Colombo city and port ($ 13 billion). The level of cooperation index, developed by the Beijing-based National Informatics Centre, increased with Russia, Kazakhstan, Pakistan, Vietnam, and South Korea while, within China, provinces such as Guangdong, Shandong, Zhejiang, and Shanghai were at the forefront of BRI projects. This also suggests the scope of broad basing the BRI in the coming years.

Impact of the BRI

The BRI has been impacting the global and regional orders by affecting the status quo and ushering in new forms of globalisation.[3] At a time when traditional financial institutions have been shying away from financing infrastructure projects, the BRI has provided alternative forms of financing such projects. It has expanded the circulation of goods and services at a time when global trade figures are either negligible or in negative growth rates.

Several changes in the international system recently have a bearing on the progress of the BRI and global governance. There are a few sets of prospects and challenges in the progress of the BRI. As the global financial crisis intensifies, reflected in the de-globalisation phenomenon in certain quarters, international trade growth has relatively slowed down in the last few years. While the IMF and the World Bank estimate "productive assets" and potential investments of several trillions of dollars, global investors in general are shying away from such investments. The Asian Development Bank (ADB) had estimated over $ 8 trillion requirements for infrastructure projects in Asia alone for the next decade. However, global lending agencies have shied away from such investments or have diverted investments into the Euro Zone crisis. In the light of the above, China's BRI provides one answer to the woes afflicting the global economic situation. Since 2013, over 1,800 projects have been launched as part of the five pillars of BRI, viz., policy coordination, connectivity, trade promotion, financial integration, and people-to-people contacts. As this is a long-term project and connectivity issues do take time for implementation, the progress of the BRI needs to be looked at. Specifically, the investments in hi-tech sectors are higher as compared to connectivity projects. To this extent, the BRI provides for public goods and services for the furtherance of global economic order and governance.

Also, since its launch in 2013 until the Second BRI Summit in 2019, the discourse within China has changed towards a more accommodative approach. Specifically, while the term "unilateral" initiative of China is visible in the beginning, it has become "joint development" or, in the latest form, a "multilateral" drive. This suggests that China has taken into consideration the feelings of many countries and has been willing to change the guiding principles of the BRI towards a more inclusive architecture.

While the BRI is yet to be instituted like the traditional financial institutions such as IMF, World Bank, or the ADB, through its seven long years of work in five connectivities, it has been able to become a model among lending agencies for infrastructure projects. For example, the AIIB, which partly finances Asian infrastructure projects, has today close links with global lending agencies and has, by far, gone through professional considerations in financing projects. To this extent, the AIIB is proving to be a major agency to finance the much-needed infrastructure projects in Asia and beyond. This will have a gradual impact on the global economic governance norms in the near future.

Even though Beijing has denied that the BRI is a "strategy" to position itself at the centre of global and regional orders in the coming decades, and insists that it is only an "initiative",[4] others are not convinced given the scale and importance that the Communist Party of China accords to the BRI. The global responses have been varied in nature.[5] Lack of clear outlining of the motivations behind the BRI has led many major countries in the world to either partly join certain projects of the BRI at a functional level or even oppose the BRI and propose alternative strategies of connectivity.

In the former are countries from the European Union and Japan who see certain BRI projects as lucrative from a financial point of view, while in the latter category are countries such as the USA, India, and others who have opposed many aspects of the BRI. The USA today has been in the forefront of opposing the BRI,[6] even though under the administration of President Barack Obama, the USA had initiated its own Silk Road in 2011 and considered BRI projects as triggering economic interdependencies.[7] The USA also sent a delegation to the first BRI Summit meeting in Beijing in 2017. In the Trump Administration, the following major critical views were expressed on the BRI,[8] viz., that it has promoted predatory financing by extending loans to the recipient countries who were unable to pay back dues for the infrastructure projects; that the sovereignty issues have not been kept in mind while constructing infrastructure projects by China; that most of the contracted projects in the BRI went to the state-owned enterprises of China; that there is no transparency in matters related to the execution of BRI projects and; due environmental security considerations were not made in the BRI projects.

The BRI had triggered other initiatives such as North-South Transit Corridors initiated by Russia and other Central Asian Republics, TAPI (Turkmenistan-Afghanistan-Pakistan-India) pipeline, India's Project Mausam[9] and the recent investments in the Chabahar port in Iran and Sabang in Indonesia as well as the Asia-Africa Growth Corridor (AAGC). The AAGC is an initiative led by think tanks of India, Japan, and Indonesia. A vision document was prepared at a meeting of the Africa Development Bank in Ahmedabad in May 2017, and this was mentioned in the joint statement of the Prime Ministers of India and Japan in November 2016. According to the document, four components are important, viz., development and cooperation projects, quality infrastructure and institutional connectivity enhancing capacities and skills, and people-to-people partnerships. The European Union as well began "sustainable connectivity", and US Secretary of State Pompeo raised a $ 60 billion fund for infrastructure development in the Indo-Pacific region. These initiatives are bound to impact BRI progress in the coming years.[10]

BRI and India

As two "simultaneously rising" countries in Asia—as the official joint statements refer to—India and China are not only concerned about macro-stability issues but also about changes in the regional order. Any new initiative in the region is bound to be weighed carefully by these rising countries not only for the benefits that could accrue to their respective national interests but also to the larger geo-political implications. As mentioned above, at the functional level, China's BRI has five elements—policy coordination, connectivity, trade promotion, financial integration, and people-to-people contacts. On policy coordination, the first time that China reportedly spoke to India on the issue was when its Special Representative, Dai Bingguo, met his Indian counterpart S. S. Menon in February 2014. It was reported that Dai asked Menon to consider joining the maritime aspects of the BRI. However, the joint statements issued by the leaders of the two countries—in September 2014 during President Xi Jinping's India visit or Prime Minister Narendra Modi's visit to Beijing in June 2015—are conspicuous in omitting any mention about the BRI. In the two informal Summit meetings between the leaders at Wuhan in April 2018 and at Chennai in October 2019, no decision was taken concerning the BRI. India also did not send any official delegation to the two BRI summit meetings at Beijing in 2017 and 2019, while it attracted a number of leaders, including from the Indian neighbourhood.[11] This suggests that on policy coordination, there are some differences between the two countries.[12]

On the second aspect, that of connectivity, as the territorial dispute between India and China has not been resolved, this aspect has become tricky. Despite over three decades of talks between officials of the two countries, the 3,488-km-long border between them is yet to be defined, leave alone delimited and demarcated. Periodic border transgressions have only led to the firming up of their respective nationalist positions and some tensions. However, unlike other territorial disputes in the world, the India-China borders are not mined, and hence if the leaderships decide to resolve the dispute, there could be quick prospects for connectivity between the two sides, even though these are mainly mountainous and at times permafrost regions.[13]

The third aspect of the BRI, that of trade promotion, has already been a major plank of bilateral relations since the 1990s. In 2005, both decided to increase the trade volume to over $ 100 billion, although this has not been achieved for various reasons. By 2019, these figures remained over $ 92 billion. Also, trade deficits of over $ 800 billion in favour of China in the last decade have resulted in a nascent trade conflict.

On the fourth aspect of the BRI, financial integration issues are still under discussion. Even though bilateral trade is increasing between the two countries, much of the trade is conducted in US dollars. It was decided to promote trade in regional currencies as part of the BRICS format, but this is yet to materialise between India and China.

On the fifth aspect of people-to-people contacts, in December 2018, China's foreign minister, Wang Yi, visited India in which a "ten pillar" agreement was signed to promote people-to-people contacts including in promoting tourism, youth exchanges, think tank and media forums, recruitment of Chinese language teachers, museum management, and others. While Indian tourist arrivals in China are estimated to be over 2 million, on the other hand, few Chinese think India is their favourite tourist destination.[14]

At the geo-political level, the BRI intends to connect Asia with Europe and Africa with connectivity in the continental and maritime domains. While India has not expressed interest in the continental domains, on the other hand, the proposed Maritime Silk Road passing through the South China Sea and the Indian Ocean has an obvious impact on India. Indeed, China's major interest in approaching India in the BRI project is mainly in the Indian Ocean region, although the latter has not shown any interest in this domain.[15] A former ambassador of China to India, Le Yucheng, had suggested that India's Project Mausam be merged with the Maritime Silk Road of China.[16] This proposal was not accepted by India.

Another area of focus for China has been the Bangladesh-China-India-Myanmar (BCIM) initiative, which was proposed in 1999. Discussions at the "track two" level have been upgraded to track one, although progress on any project implementation is tardy. India officially accepted the BCIM in May 2013 during Premier Li Keqiang's visit to India (and thus preceding the September 2013 speech on the BRI by President Xi Jinping).[17] The 22 May 2015 meeting between Premiers, Modi and Li Keqiang, and the Joint Statement suggested that "The two sides welcomed the progress made in promoting cooperation under the framework of the BCIM (Bangladesh, China, India, and Myanmar) Economic Corridor. Both sides recalled the second meeting of the Joint Study Group of the BCIM Economic Corridor and agreed to continue their respective efforts to implement the understanding reached at the meeting."[18] However, New Delhi was concerned about China's continuing small arms transfers to Indian Northeast rebels and the opening up of the politically fragile Northeast to China's influence. For this reason, even though three high-level official meetings took place on the BCIM, no progress was made except on tourism and transportation networks. China, on the other hand, while including the BCIM Economic Corridor as one of the six corridors of the BRI has, in late 2018, began emphasising a new China-Myanmar Economic Corridor, much akin to the China-Pakistan Economic Corridor—both of which intend to provide maritime access to China through the Bay of Bengal and the Arabian Sea to the Indian Ocean. Since 2008, China had sent over 30 naval contingencies to the Indian Ocean ostensibly to control piracy off the coast of Somalia.[19] It had set up a naval base at Djibouti and has taken hold of the Hambantota port in Sri Lanka and Gwadar port in Pakistan. China is looking for a base at Jiwani in Pakistan. Its submarine visits to the Indian Ocean had alerted India to cooperate with the USA in anti-submarine warfare preparedness. Against this background, India-China equations in the maritime domain have become complex.[20]

Differences are emerging between China and India on the BRI. Firstly, while both India and China are fast-rising countries in Asia, they are still careful in protecting their minimalist foreign policy goals. Both, over a period of time, have expressed concern on any violation by any country on their sovereignty and territorial integrity aspects. China has bound many a country with its "one China" policy of recognising Taiwan and Tibet as part of China. China had utilised veto power at the United Nations Security Council (UNSC) to stall those seen as violating its "one China" policy. In the case of India, many of its leaders have expressed sensitivity on the issue of Kashmir (Jammu & Kashmir and now Jammu & Kashmir and Ladakh Union Territories), which joined the Indian Union in 1947. However, despite Indian sensitivities, China termed the China-Pakistan Economic Corridor (CPEC), that passes through Kashmir, as its "flagship" programme of the BRI in 2014.[21] This has become a contentious issue for India, which had earlier accepted the "one China" policy. Indeed, India's Prime Minister, Narendra Modi, had been categorical in stating that no infrastructure of connectivity project can ignore the sovereignty claims of other countries, with no avail so far from China.[22] Likewise, the Ministry of External Affairs spokesman stated that India objects to the BRI for violating the sovereignty principle with its lack of transparency, unilateralism, debt financing, and environmental issues.[23] While former foreign minister Sushma Swaraj, during her visit to Beijing in January 2015, stated that India is willing to consider 'synergy-based' cooperation[24] such as in the Asian Infrastructure Investment Bank or other areas, the sovereignty aspect remained central to Indian concerns.[25] It was reported that when the Indian side summoned China's Ambassador to New Delhi to explain China's position on sovereignty issues in the region, the latter brushed aside Indian reservations by suggesting that the Silk Road initiative projects in Pakistan are of "commercial" value. Yet, some Indian analysts suggest that China's investments in the disputed territories in the Northern Areas of Kashmir violate one of the key principles of the 28 March 2015 document on the BRI, viz., "mutual respect for each other's sovereignty and territorial integrity".[26]

Implications for India

The implications for India are at two levels—at the global systemic and structural levels of competition for "models of development" and at the neighbourhood levels in South Asia. At the systemic levels, the BRI is being showcased as a global and regional initiative to include Europe, Africa, and Asia but also with projects in South America recently. There is an undercurrent of global competition between China and the USA in a possible power transition globally and regionally. India is thus caught up in this larger picture of geo-politics and geo-strategy. As a rising country, India has its own aspirations. Any endorsement and dependence on China in BRI projects suggest a loss of strategic autonomy for India. It is also not conducive to the Indian model of development based on democracy, free-market economy, and transparency. This is in the light of China suggesting at its 19th party congress in 2017 that the China model will be exported and that its state-owned enterprises will be supported in this drive across the globe. Some Chinese argued that the BRI had unleashed a certain balance of power between China and India. For instance, Zhou Bo suggested that in the light of China's initiatives of CPEC, BCIM, and naval operations in the Indian Ocean Region, India has been shifting towards the "Act East Asia" policy to counter-balance China in the region.[27] This could partly explain India's lukewarm response towards the BRI as it is not clear for the Indian leadership what is at the end of the BRI tunnel and hence the cautious approach towards this initiative. This indicates that more strategic level interactions need to be conducted between the two countries in the future. While there has been a change in Beijing's attitude from terming the BRI from unilateral to that of joint or multilateral efforts, there are no concrete efforts as of now on this change. Hence, India is still considering its policy options.

South Asian Level

China's South Asian connection in the BRI, which is gradually emerging recently, has implications for India. China's assistance to connectivity and infrastructure projects in South Asia have been largely beneficial to China in many ways—as profitable investment destinations in tax-free exclusive industrial zones, garnering assured resources for its domestic industry, opening windows into the South Asian market for its goods on a long-term basis, a favourable balance of payments position, etc. For many South Asian countries as well, these projects provided scope for the expansion of economic development. Such connectivity between China and South Asia or within South Asia with Chinese-aided projects provides for expanding avenues for investment and mutually beneficial outcomes, specifically in the context of lack of capital availability against the backdrop of the Euro Zone crisis, although China's objectives in this regard could be to position itself as a contestant in short to medium-term perspectives and as a dominant player in the region.

While China's overall investments in such projects are minimal and, in fact, seen by many South Asian countries as a reply to offset trade imbalances heavily in favour of Beijing, several reservations were expressed on China's involvement. For instance, in countries like Pakistan, Bangladesh, and Nepal, even as connectivity improved with China's assistance, several reports indicated the flooding of the local markets with cheap Chinese goods, often to the detriment of indigenous cotton textile, jute or leather industries. This has led to an adversarial impact on the balance of payments positions for these countries.

Also, most Chinese investments in infrastructure projects are by state-owned enterprises, and several times the host country had waived the global tendering process to favour the Chinese companies. This had resulted in monopolies and political pressures from Beijing. Again, most of such transactions are not transparent, indicating the rampant corruption or bribery by Chinese companies to local political elites. Sri Lanka, Nepal, Maldives, and others have reported such incidents.

More problematic is that today China insists on protection for its companies in trouble-torn areas of Pakistan, Nepal, Bangladesh, and other South Asian states. This is expected to increase the costs for the host countries in the future, both in terms of the law and order situation as well as any military protection that it entails. In Pakistan, over a division of army troops have been committed for the protection of CPEC projects.

China's forays into South Asian telecommunications and the IT sector could have security implications. The Huawei and ZTE companies of China are operating extensively in India, Pakistan, Sri Lanka, Nepal, Maldives, and other countries. While in the early 1990s and three years ago, India had insisted that these companies desist from using embedded software for possible information-gathering, no such restrictions are in place in other countries. Besides, as telecommunications is emerging as a strategic tool in the 21st century, concerns are expressed, for instance, as witnessed in the 5G bidding process.

Bilateral Level

At the bilateral level, Indian official criticism of the BRI included that the initiative has been unilateral in nature, with China conceiving, directing, and implementing the BRI. In its own experience, as discussed, there was hardly any "policy coordination" between India and China on the BRI with China's State Councillor, Dai Bingguo, mentioning the initiative at a meeting with Indian leaders in February 2014 for the first time—more as an invitation rather than any joint consultations on the subject. Also, there is hardly any scope for Indian participation in the projects with the dominance of China's State-Owned Enterprises bagging almost all projects in BRI construction.

Second, as discussed, Indian criticism is aimed at the violation of sovereignty principles as enshrined in the United Nations Charter, which China itself has been emphasising for several decades. For instance, China did not consult India before plunging into the CPEC, specifically the infrastructure projects passing through India's Kashmir region now under occupation by Pakistan. Such criticism came up from India's highest political levels, with the Prime Minister raising this issue at summit level meetings with his counterpart and also in multilateral institutions such as the Shanghai Cooperation Organisation meeting at Qingdao in June 2018. China's argument that these projects passing through Kashmir are only "commercial" in nature has not cut ice as Beijing deployed over 30,000 "security guards" to protect some of the projects under the CPEC.

Third, India's criticism of the BRI stems from the not so sound financial practices while executing BRI projects. For instance, according to several reports, many of the projects under the BRI have fallen into debt—with the recipient countries unable to pay the loans for the construction projects. Many of the projects are iconic and grand in scale, although the recipient may have no means to pay back the investments due to the slow yield and long gestation periods. Hambantota port, Mombasa port, and others have faced immediate criticism for resulting in "predatory financial practices" from Beijing. The Pakistan Senate as well noted the financial drain on the country with Chinese-built projects at Gwadar and other areas. Pakistan is already reeling under debt and looking for the IMF bailout packages. In the Maldives, leaders like Nasheed have criticised China for the "island grab" in his country. Also, most of the projects have been garnered by China's state-owned enterprises, leaving no room for the entry of other enterprises, including Indian companies. Again, at the South Asian regional levels, China's entry through the BRI has been affecting the "neighbourhood first" policy of the new Indian government since 2014 as China is trying to pull the region into its dependence.[28]

Fourth, environmental issues were raised by the Indian side, given the emphasis in the BRI for thermal powered projects and others. For instance, China has plans to set up over 25 GW projects in the BRI areas. While China had accepted the post-Copenhagen proposals on reducing emissions, such massive coal-fired projects will have drastic implications for the environment. Many such thermal power projects are to be built in the Indian neighbourhood in Sri Lanka, Pakistan, Bangladesh, and others with serious environmental concerns.

Conclusion

China's BRI has been a major project in recent times that originated after the country became the second-largest economy globally and becoming the centre of the trade value chain and displacing Japan in this sphere. As the domestic political discourse shifted from "keeping a low profile" of Deng Xiaoping to "accomplish something" under Xi Jinping, China's international appetite and footprint increased in the BRI form. In the light of the various geo-political and geo-strategic developments regarding the BRI, India has expressed a cautious and balanced approach. New Delhi joined the AIIB as the second-largest stakeholder and for economic development through much-needed infrastructure projects, while opposing the CPEC projects that are seen as violating India's minimalist foreign policy goals. In the light of the BRI push in the South Asian region, India had crafted its own initiatives such as Project Mausam and the Act East Policy or joined other initiatives like the Indo-Pacific or the Asia-Africa Growth Corridor intending to preserve its autonomy at the Asian level even as enhancing its outreach and integration processes with like-minded countries and systems.

NOTES

1. China's Ministry of Commerce considers India's role in the ancient Silk Road as merely that of a "transit point".
   See "印度与"一带一路"的关系" [India and BRI connection] Ministry of Commerce, available at http://history.mofcom.gov.cn/?bandr=ydyydyldgx
2. Two major official documents on the BRI include: "Vision and Actions on Jointly Building Silk Road Economic Belt and 21st-Century Maritime Silk Road", Ministry of Foreign Affairs, March 28, 2015, online available at http://www.fmprc.gov.cn/mfa_eng/zxxx_662805/t1249618.shtml and "Work Together to Build the Silk Road Economic Belt and the 21st Century Maritime Silk Road", Xinhua May 14, 2017, online available at http://news.xinhuanet.com/english/2017-05/14/c_136282982.htm?from=timeline&isappinstalled=1
3. Peng Nian, "U.S. has failed to hamper BRI by seeking to shame it", CGTN, March 24, 2019, online available at https://news.cgtn.com/news/3d3d674d7867544e33457a6333566d54/index.html
4. Coinciding with the launch of the BRI are several other announcements by the Communist Party of China both at its 18th and 19th Party Congresses in 2012 and 2017, respectively, such as China Dream, New Type of International Relations, Community of Shared Destiny, Xi Jinping Thought on Socialism with Chinese Characteristics for a New Era, Two Centennials, a long term plan for Socialist Modernisation by 2050 and the like. In the background of these long-term plans of the CPC, there is a well-grounded view that the BRI is part of the plans of China in this scheme of things. On the grand strategic considerations of China see Jiwoon Baik, "One Belt One Road" and the geopolitics of empire", Inter-Asia Cultural Studies (2019), Vol. 20, No. 3, 358–376 at https://doi.org/10.1080/14649373.2019.1649013
5. Feng Yujun, Alexander Gabuev, Pail Haenle, Ma Bin and Dmitri Trenin, "The Belt and Road Initiative: Views from Washington, Moscow, and Beijing" April 8, 2019, online available at https://carnegietsinghua.org/2019/04/08/belt-and-road-initiative-views-from-washington-moscow-and-beijing-pub-78774
6. Jonathan Hillman, "Five myths about China's Belt and Road Initiative", *Washington Post*, May 31, 2019, online available at https://www.washingtonpost.com/outlook/five-myths/five-myths-about-chinas-belt-and-road-initiative/2019/05/30/d6870958-8223-11e9-bce7-40b4105f7ca0_story.html; Wang Mingjie, "China warns US over BRI criticism", *China Daily* May 10, 2019, online available at http://www.chinadaily.com.cn/a/201905/10/WS5cd54685a3104842260bb06f.html and Xiao Xin, "US criticism of the Belt and Road Initiative only places it at a disadvantage", *The Global Times,* April 23, 2019, online available at http://www.globaltimes.cn/content/1147094.shtml
7. Predating China's BRI, and termed as the New Silk Road, it intended to connect Central and South Asian regions through regional energy markets, trade and transportation networks, customs, business and people-to-people contacts. See "U.S. Support for the New Silk Road" accessed at https://2009-2017.state.gov/p/sca/ci/af/newsilkroad/index.htm
8. See "A Conversation with Ambassador Alice Wells on the China-Pakistan Economic Corridor", The Wilson Centre, November 21, 2019, accessed at https://www.state.gov/a-conversation-with-ambassador-alice-wells-on-the-china-pakistan-economic-corridor/
9. Akhilesh Pillamarri, "Project Mausam: India's Answer to China's 'Maritime Silk Road'", *The Diplomat,* September 18, 2014, accessed at http://thediplomat.com/2014/09/project-mausam-

indias-answer-to-chinas-maritime-silk-road/

10. William C. Pacatte, "Competing to Win - A Coalition Approach to Countering the BRI", CSIS, December 2019, online available at https://csis-prod.s3.amazonaws.com/s3fspublic/publication/191219Pacatte_Countering_BRI_WEB_ FINAL.pdf?ivg8369pub0VTUmhYbJgfbVLTaK4HXL8
11. "两大原因印度再次拒绝一带一路峰会" [Two reasons why India again rejects the BRI summit] April 11, 2019, accessed at https://boxun.com/news/gb/intl/2019/04/201904110831.shtml
12. One Chinese writer, after reviewing Indian policies towards the BRI, stated that India is using this issue as a "bargaining tool". See "印度对"一带一路"态度研究" [A study on India's attitude towards the BRI] 印度洋经济体研究 (2018), No. 2, March 15, 2019, accessed at http://www.cciee.org.cn/Detail.aspx?newsId=16280&TId=231 ; On the other hand, Lan Jianxue believes that policy coordination between the two countries could emerge. See "一带一路"倡议的基本原则、内容及其对中印关系的影响" [The basic principles and content of the BRI and their impact on China-India relations] October 31, 2019, at http://www.ciis.org.cn/2019-10/31/content_40942711.html
13. However, there is a glimmer of possibility according to the following report, "印度拟用列城两项目应对 "一带一路"" [India plans to use the two Leh projects to address the BRI], May 24, 2018, accessed at https://www.imsilkroad.com/tags/%E4%B8%80%E5%B8%A6%E4%B8%80%E8%B7%AF%E4%B8%8E%E5%8D%B0%E5%BA%A6
14. On all the above "five connectivities", however, Wang Dehua argued that there will be progress in the future and that India will join the BRI for "pragmatic cooperation". See Wang Dehua, "印度迟早加入"一带一路"" [Sooner or later India will join the BRI] March 27, 2018, at https://opinion.huanqiu.com/article/9CaKrnK74XB
15. According to Ge Cheng, despite China's offer of "win-win" outcomes and "seeking common ground" on the BRI in the Indian Ocean, India has not been cooperative. See Ge Cheng, "中国与印度携手"一带一路"：前景与挑战" [China Collaborate With India Under "The Belt And Road": Prospects and Challenges] accessed at https://www.ydylcn.com/skwx_ydyl/bookdetail?SiteID=1&ID=6775285
16. See "H.E. Ambassador Le Yucheng's address at the Media and Think Tank Reception" March 4, 2015, at http://www.fmprc.gov.cn/mfa_eng/wjb_663304/zwjg_665342/zwbd_665378/t1242679.shtml; See also Wei Wei, "Reviving the Silk Road—Connecting India, China and Entire Asia", *The Economic Times,* April 14, 2014, accessed at Ministry of Foreign Affairs http://www.fmprc.gov.cn/mfa_eng/wjb_663304/zwjg_665342/zwbd_665378/t1146648.shtml
17. See Yang Siling, "一带一路": 印度的回应及对策" [The One Belt and One Road Strategy: India's Response and Countermeasures] 亚非纵横, No. 6 (2014) pp. 51-60.
18. "Joint Statement between the People's Republic of China and the Republic of India" May 22, 2015, accessed at http://www.china.org.cn/chinese/2015-05/22/content_35634382.htm
19. Xu Ke, "印度洋的海盗威胁与中国的印度洋战略" [The Threat of Maritime Piracy in the Indian Ocean and China's Indian Ocean Strategy] WSšN—xvz, No. 1 (2011), pp. 2-13.
20. Xu Juan and Wei Ling, "印度对 21 世纪"海上丝绸之路"倡议的认知*" [India's Perception of 21st Century Maritime Silk Road] 南亚研究季刊, Vol. 3, No. 158 (2014), pp. 1-6.
21. See Siegfried Wolf, *The China-Pakistan Economic Corridor of the Belt and Road Initiative – Concept, Context and Assessment* (Springer, 2019).
22. China's foreign ministry spokesman denied China violating India's sovereignty and termed these as "commercial" in nature. See "中国对印参与"一带一路"有耐心" [China has patience with India's participation in the "Belt and Road Initiative"] 参考消息网, April 17, 2019, online available at http://column.cankaoxiaoxi.com/2019/0417/2377591.shtml

23. "Official Spokesperson's response to a query on media reports regarding possible cooperation with China on OBOR/BRI", April 5, 2018, accessed at https://www.mea.gov.in/media-briefings.htm?dtl/29768/Official+Spokespersons+response+ to+a+ query+ on+ media+ reports+ regarding+possible+cooperation+with+China+on+OBORBRI; See also the reply of the Minister of State for External Affairs to the Lok Sabha at "Question No.849, One Belt and One Road Initiative" June 26, 2019, online available at https://mea.gov.in/lok sabha.htm?dtl/31484/ QUESTION+NO849+ONE+BELT+AND+ONE+ROAD+INITIATIVE
24. Sutirtho Patranobis, "Sushma Swaraj lays silk road for PM Modi's China visit in May", *The Hindustan Times,* February 1, 2015, online available at http://www.hindustantimes.com/india-news/india-committed-to-settle-boundary-row-early-swaraj-tells-china/article1-1312494.aspx
25. "China eyes consensus with India on building new silk road", *China Daily*, September 18, 2014, online available at http://www.chinadaily.com.cn/world/2014xisco/2014-09/18/content_18623473.htm and Ananth Krishnan, "China wants India to play key role in 'Silk Road' plan", *The Hindu,* August 10, 2014, online available at http://www.thehindu.com/news/international/world/china-wants-india-to-play-key-role-in-silk-road-plan/article6301227.ece and Ananth Krishnan, "China asks India to put aside 'Maritime Silk Road' concerns" *India Today*, February 12, 2015, at http://indiatoday.intoday.in/story/china-india-asean-sushma-swaraj-maritime-silk-road-concerns/1/418576.html
26. At one time China also accused India of violating its sovereignty claims in the South China Sea when an Indian company was involved in drilling for energy resources in the Vietnam-held areas of the region. However, the South China Sea case is different as there are a number of claimants, besides the July 2016 judgement of the Permanent Court of Arbitration overruling any "historical claims" to the artificial reefs in the region. In the case of Jammu and Kashmir, nether the Pakistani nor Chinese constitution has any provisions regarding Kashmir, while the Indian Constitution specially mentions the Instruments of Accession in 1947.
27. Zhou Bo, "China goes West and India acts East", April 27, 2015, accessed at http://www.china.org.cn/opinion/2015-04/27/content_35428900.htm
28. On the "neighbourhood first" policy of India since 2014, see Chen Lijun, "印度的南亚战略及其对"一带一路"国际合作的影响" [India's South Asia strategy and its impact on the BRI international cooperation], April 2, 2018, accessed at http://www.aisixiang.com/data/109257.html

2

India's Strategic Response to China's Belt and Road Initiative

Baladas Ghoshal

Introduction

No other issue in recent diplomatic history has received so much attention and responses, both positive and negative, as China's Belt and Road Initiative (BRI), a multifaceted economic, diplomatic, and geopolitical undertaking that has earned many sobriquets and nomenclatures from the "New Silk Road" to "One Belt One Road".[1] The BRI is an ambitious and dream project of China's paramount leader, Xi Jinping, who is now presiding over China's US$ 10 trillion economy, with a spending of nearly US$ 150 billion a year, in the 68 countries that have signed up to the initiative. As many as 120 countries, including 29 at the top leadership level, attended the inaugural of the Initiative, underlining President Xi Jinping's description of this being the "project of the century".[2] With such massive infrastructure and connectivity projects, unparalleled in history, China is attempting not only to gain political and strategic influence over the host countries through its economic offensive but also impose a Sino-centric regional and global order, based on might over rules. Such a project will automatically impinge on India's security interests and its vision of an open, inclusive, consultative, cooperative, collaborative, and rule-based regional order, and therefore calls for a strategic response and an alternative narrative to Beijing's BRI in collaboration with like-minded countries and those who do not subscribe to the hegemonic world view.

Proposed in 2013, the BRI envisages a US$ 1.3 trillion Chinese-led investment program that aims to create a web of infrastructure, including roads, railways, telecommunications, energy pipelines, and ports, to enhance economic interconnectivity and facilitate development across Eurasia, East Africa, and Asia. The project has two primary components: the overland Silk Road Economic Belt (SREB), and the sea-based Maritime Silk Road (MSR), together forming the "belt" and "road".[3] A project of unprecedented geographical and financial scope, SREB encompasses the New Eurasia Land Bridge and five economic corridors: China-Mongolia-Russia; China-Central Asia-West Asia; China-Pakistan; the China-Indochina peninsula; and Bangladesh-China-India-Myanmar, which New Delhi has refused to be part of. Rail and road connectivity, along with hydrocarbon pipeline networks, will link these corridors. The MSR is focused on developing key ports that connect to these land-based routes.[4]

The BRI is driven extensively by strong economic motivations, including exporting productive capacity, investing in foreign exchange reserves, securing stable energy supplies, and promoting development in China's vast but relatively backward western region. President Xi Jinping's speech to the BRI forum in Beijing in May 2017 linked the BRI to China's foreign policy goals of mutual development and aimed to 'generate strong momentum for building a human community of a shared future.' President Xi, in his speech, also mentioned the BRI in terms of "peace and co-operation", "openness and inclusiveness", "mutual learning," and "mutual benefit". In fact, BRI projects are likely to increase Beijing's economic and political leverage as a financier. As against Beijing's claims, the China-established multilateral Asian Infrastructure Investment Bank (AIIB), together with almost $ 40 billion, will fund the BRI projects, yet the vast majority of funding has come from China's giant state-owned investment banks. The shortage of funds and capital faced by most nations worldwide to carry forward their economic potentials to promote the development and building infrastructures, and the availability of Chinese financial largesse to fund this much-needed infrastructure investment has attracted attention from many prospective partner nations. Additionally, the minimal political conditionalities associated with Chinese finance make it more prospective as compared to the International Monetary Fund (IMF), the World Bank, the Asian Development Bank, etc. Most state-owned Chinese companies are least concerned about the nature of domestic politics in a host country.

Through the BRI, China wants "to productively use its enormous, $ 3 trillion capital reserves, internationalize the renminbi, and deal with structural issues as its economy navigates the so-called 'new normal' of lower growth".[5] It aims to utilize its idle industrial capacity and safeguard jobs in key industries such as steel and cement, deriving political dividends for the government. The Chinese Communist Party's legitimacy rests on maintaining economic growth and improving people's standard of living. Through extensive pipeline networks, it will also ensure the country's energy security through diversification of its energy sources by accessing Russian, Central Asian, and Iranian hydrocarbon resources. China has invested in constructing pipelines through Gwadar in Pakistan to Xinjiang, and coastal Myanmar to Yunnan. Through this, China is trying to diversify its sea lanes of communication for energy supplies and trying to evade the vulnerability related to energy supply at maritime choke-points in the Straits of Malacca and the South China Sea.

Furthermore, the Chinese Navy's blue-water capability will be enhanced through the establishment of port facilities in the Indian Ocean, keeping vulnerable critical sea lines of communication open for maritime energy supplies from West Asia. Also, through BRI plans, the primary objective is to reduce the ability of the US Navy to blockade China's energy supply routes during any conflict scenario.

Through the BRI, President Xi Jinping is visualizing the realization of the 'Chinese dream'[6]. The BRI was included in the Chinese constitution in October 2017, signalling the push to ensure that this vision is realised. Most analysts on China are more or less unanimous on the BRI being an integral part of Xi Jinping positioning himself at the centre of the party and at the centre of China. According to Merriden Varrall, Director, Lowy Institute's East Asia program, "Xi Jinping put his label on a bunch of things that already existed to try to create a legacy for himself out of something already there. Now with it being enshrined in the party constitution..., he's achieved his stamp on China's rejuvenation.... It's about bringing China out of its century of humiliation and regaining what it sees as its proper place in the world. So, it has political, economic, and symbolic components, as well as international strategic components".[7] It is clear that the BRI, being the focal point of Xi's legitimacy and legacy, will be a political imperative for the Chinese government and businesses to be involved in. Additionally, the BRI is largely becoming "a division one, grade A priority" for all levels of the Chinese government, according to an Australian analyst on China.[8] Definitely, it is going to shape China's engagement and investment with the world for years to come.

Indian Response to the BRI

Indian response to the BRI has been to reject it based on sovereignty and procedural, and leadership issues. The China-Pakistan Economic Corridor (CPEC), a significant BRI project, connects China's Xinjiang province with Pakistan's Balochistan province, further connecting to its deep sea port, Gwadar, in the Arabian Sea.[9] This route provides China overland access to the Arabian Sea. Also, this route is not vulnerable to US maritime power, unlike China's east coast sea lanes. A sum of US$ 54 billion of infrastructure is planned for this stretch.[10]

The corridor runs through the contested territory of Gilgit-Baltistan in Pakistan-occupied Kashmir. Despite Chinese foreign minister Wang Yi's assertion that the corridor "will be sensitive to the comfort level of other parties",[11] no satisfactory response from Beijing has been received that addresses the issues raised by New Delhi vis-à-vis the CPEC. India has time and again made its position clear that China cannot ignore New Delhi's concerns related to its territorial integrity. One of the Modi government's earliest steps to counter the BRI was the then External Affairs Minister, Sushma Swaraj, making it clear to her Chinese counterpart, Wang Yi. She said that India's "One China" policy must be congruent to China's "One India" policy, and the Chinese government must be sensitive to India's claims in Pakistan-Occupied Kashmir.[12] In February 2020, India's External Affairs, Minister S. Jaishankar, also conveyed New Delhi's concerns to Beijing about their activities in the region illegally occupied by Pakistan. Along with it, New Delhi also asked them to cease such activities, as the connectivity initiatives must be based on universally recognized international norms of openness, transparency, and financial responsibility and must be pursued in a manner that respects sovereignty, equality, and the territorial integrity of other nations.

Along with India, the USA and Japan also subscribe to the above principles. The India-USA Joint Statement, 'Prosperity through Partnership', released in June 2017 called upon all nations to support the bolstering of regional economic connectivity through transparent development of infrastructure and the use of responsible debt financing practices while ensuring respect for sovereignty and territorial integrity, the rule of law and the environment.[13] As per some media reports, the likely deployment of 30,000 Chinese 'security personnel' to protect projects along the CPEC, in addition to 15,000 troops from the Pakistan army, make the situation alarming for India.[14] Moreover, in the maritime domain, China is set to increase the number of its marine corps from 20,000 to one lakh at the strategic Gwadar port and in the military base of Djibouti.[15] In recent years, China has moved aggressively to increase its power projection capabilities through its navy's rapid modernization and has increased its military spending. The standoff on Demchok and Chumar (2014) and Doklam (2017) following Chinese incursions have drawn concern from the Indian leadership. Therefore, India has crafted a strategy on the CPEC in particular and generally on the BRI, based on a careful assessment of geopolitics and economics.

India's Dual Strategy to Address BRI's Challenges

India's response to the BRI has found expression in two major strategies. Firstly, to highlight the unilateral nature of such a venture having a multinational focus. The possibilities of debt-entrapment with Ukraine, Zimbabwe, Cambodia, and Sri Lanka also are a matter of concern. Secondly, the other strategy related to India's own connectivity projects with the countries of South and Southeast Asia.

The fact that the BRI is essentially a Chinese project sans any consultation with others was articulated first by the then Foreign Secretary, S. Jaishankar, in 2015, "Where we are concerned, this is a national Chinese initiative. The Chinese devised it, created a blueprint. It was not an international initiative they discussed with the world, with countries that are interested or affected by it.... A national initiative is devised with national interests; it is not incumbent on others to buy it. Where we stand is that if this is something on which they want a larger buy-in, then they need to have larger discussions, and those have not happened".[16] China's aggressive pursuit of the BRI in India's neighbouring states like Pakistan, Sri Lanka, Bangladesh, Nepal, and the Maldives automatically raised suspicion in the minds of the Indian policymakers about Beijing's intent in using its economic power to promote its geopolitical designs in undermining India's security interests in the region. He further expressed this concern more eloquently in the 2016 Raisina Dialogue, "The interactive dynamic between strategic interests and connectivity initiatives—a universal proposition—is on particular display in our continent...we cannot be impervious to the reality that others may see connectivity as an exercise in hardwiring that influences choices. This should be discouraged, because, particularly in the absence of agreed security architecture in Asia, it could give rise to unnecessary competitiveness".[17]

Furthermore, he added, "Connectivity should diffuse national rivalries, not add to regional tensions...if we seek a multipolar world, the right way to begin is to create a multipolar Asia. Nothing could foster that more than open-minded consultation on the future of connectivity".[18] Inaugurating the Raisina Dialogue in 2017, Prime Minister Narendra Modi sternly stated that "Connectivity in itself cannot override or undermine the sovereignty of other nations." India has steadfastly stood against the BRI even in the SCO summit, where Prime Minister Modi said, "Connectivity with the neighbourhood is India's priority. We welcome connectivity projects that are sustainable, efficient, and respect territorial integrity and sovereignty of the countries".[19] He further added that India's commitment to connectivity projects is reflected in its involvement in the International North-South Transport Corridor (INSTC), development of Chabahar port, and the Ashgabat Agreement.

India's Alternative Connectivity Narrative

To give substance and meaning to India's Act East policy, New Delhi should improve its connectivity endeavours with its extended neighbourhood. To achieve this, New Delhi is striving with ASEAN countries on multiple connectivity projects. One of the flagship projects for land connectivity between ASEAN countries and India is the India-Myanmar-Thailand Trilateral Highway that connects the three countries from Moreh in India to Mae Sot in Thailand to Bagan in Myanmar. It was first proposed in 2002. India decided to further extend the Trilateral Highway to Cambodia and Vietnam at the Commemorative Summit between ASEAN and India in 2012. However, the project's progress has been quite lethargic due to lack of institutional and financial support from the three countries.

Another project is the Kaladan Multi-Modal Transit Transport Project (KMMTTP) that aims to develop connectivity over land and water to seek an alternative route through Myanmar. It will connect the eastern Indian seaport of Kolkata with Sittwe seaport in Rakhine State, Myanmar, by sea. In Myanmar, it will then link Sittwe port to Paletwavia, the Kaladan riverboat route further by road to Mizoram State in Northeast India. The project includes a waterway component of 158 km on the Kaladan River and a road component of 109 km. The project includes constructing an integrated port and inland water transport (IWT) terminal at Sittwe, the development of a navigational channel along the Kaladan River from Sittwe to Paletwa, and the construction of a highway trans-shipment terminal at Paletwa. Furthermore, this project also envisages the construction of six IWT barges—each of 300 ton capacity—for cargo transportation between Sittwe and Paletwa.

The project was originally scheduled to be completed by 2014 but was delayed due to numerous reasons, some beyond its control.[20] The biggest hurdle has been the acquisition of land for the construction of road projects. This has become a difficult task to achieve due to the increased demands of compensation by landowners in the Mizoram sector.[21] Even with the delay, it was expected to be operational by 2019-2020 as all components of the project have been completed, except the under construction Zorinpui-Paletwa road. However, it may take another three years to complete.[22] With the project missing its deadline, the Parliamentary Standing Committee on Home Affairs has expressed its displeasure over the physical progress of the road component, saying it is "not at all satisfactory." It further indicated the "failure of proper planning, monitoring and supervision". Definitely, this project is an "integral" part of India's Act East Policy and will contribute to economic development in the whole region. Therefore, the delays in this project should be addressed soon, and the project should be completed at the earliest so that the "connectivity woes" of the Northeast are resolved.[23] There is an urgent need to ensure that no further delay occurs in the completion of the project for India to maintain its credibility in its neighbourhood.

The delays were also caused by Myanmar's side as well. In Myanmar, the construction and dredging of Sittwe Port on the mouth of the Kaladan River in Rakhine State and the river terminal at Paletwa have been completed. In April 2018, after years of delay, the construction of the 109-km road between Zorinpui and Paletwa was also started by a New Delhi-based firm. The Myanmar government was hesitant to begin work since the highway would pass through some areas where a rebel group called the Arakan Army has a presence. Since 2017 conflict has increased in the northern areas of Rakhine State, with the Myanmar Army launching a fresh offensive. In October 2018, both the countries signed an MoU, which agreed to facilitate the movement of project personnel, construction material, and equipment to expedite work on the highway.[24] The MoU also laid down that a port operator would be appointed, which would enable the Sittwe Port and the infrastructure at Paletwa to be used commercially for the development of the surrounding areas.

Another initiative is India and ASEAN signing the ASEAN-India Maritime Transport Cooperation Agreement. It will enhance cooperation and communication, eliminate barriers that affect maritime transport, and establish a regional maritime transport framework system. Furthermore, the India, Myanmar, and Thailand Motor Vehicles Agreement (IMT MVA) also needs to be finalized for free movement of cargo, passenger, and personal vehicles along roads linking these countries. Additionally, projects such as a railway link between New Delhi and Hanoi; the Mekong-India Economic Corridor (MIEC) connecting South and Southeast Asia; and Stilwell road and Dawei deep-sea port in Myanmar are also under consideration. The MIEC involves the integration of four Mekong countries—Vietnam, Myanmar, Thailand, and Cambodia—along with India. It will connect Ho Chi Minh City, Dawei, Bangkok, and Phnom Penh with Chennai. Once constructed, this corridor can reduce the transit distance between India and ASEAN countries.

In lieu of these projects, India must remove all the bottlenecks to bring the project to completion. It is also crucial for New Delhi to establish itself as a significant player in the Indo-Pacific region. This will also help in boosting trade and tourism between India and Southeast Asian nations. India, in the past, has announced a Line of Credit of $ 1 billion to encourage such connectivity projects between India and ASEAN, and a Project Development Fund of 5 billion rupees ($ 78 million) to promote manufacturing hubs in Cambodia, Laos, Myanmar, and Vietnam.

Bangladesh, Bhutan, India, and Nepal (BBIN)

The BBIN is another project that links India with its immediate neighbours in Southeast Asia to explore its great potentials and promote connectivity and economic development in India's Northeastern region. It meets through an official representation of member-states to formulate, implement, and review quadrilateral agreements across areas such as water resources management, connectivity of power, transport, and infrastructure. India has been a vital member of the Bangladesh-Bhutan-India-Nepal (BBIN) connectivity project, mainly to show that South Asian countries favour regional connectivity. At the same time, Pakistan's role in spoiling the diplomatic efforts of the physical integration of the SAARC grouping can be highlighted.

The BBIN Motor Vehicle Act (BBIN-MVA) was conceived at the 18th SAARC Summit in Kathmandu. This was done chiefly because of Pakistan's intransigence in failing the SAARC motor vehicle act. The BBIN MVA was signed in June 2015. The agreement will permit member-states to ply their vehicles in each other's territory for cargo and passenger transportation, including third-country transport and personal vehicles. This will require that every vehicle have an electronic permit to enter another country's territory, with significant border security arrangements between the nations. Under this system, cargo vehicles will be tracked electronically with the permits to be issued online and sent electronically to all land ports. SAARC, comprising Afghanistan, Bangladesh, Bhutan, India, the Maldives, Nepal, Pakistan, and Sri Lanka, traded among

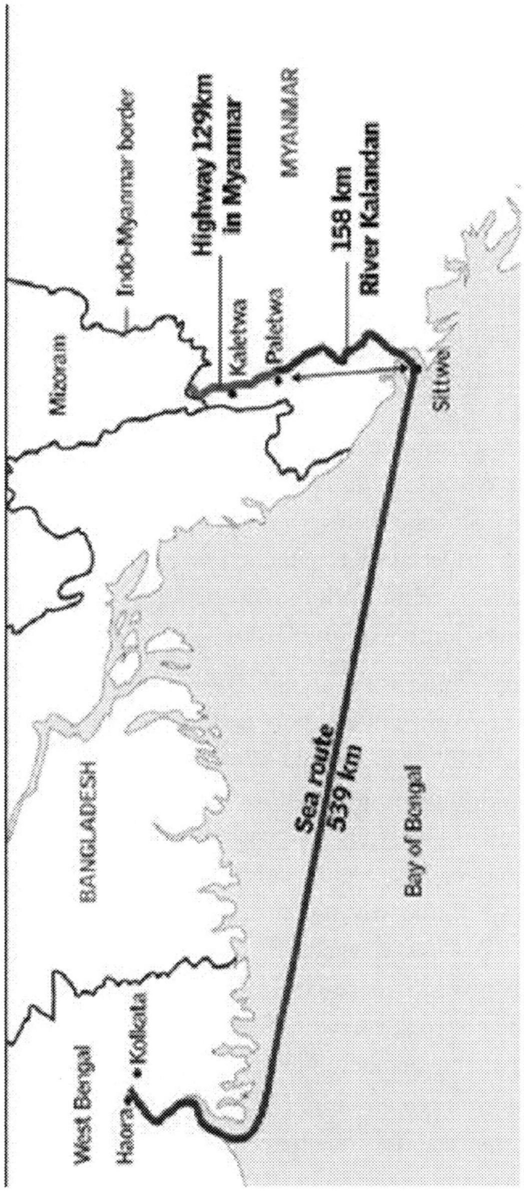

Map of Kaladan Multi-modal transit transport project. Available at Google images

themselves goods and services worth $ 20 billion in 2013-14, a 12.36 per cent increase since 2018-2019.[25]

While the BBIN sought to impel the sub-region's latent socio-economic potential, harnessing disparate stages of development to augment each other, over the years, its objectives expanded to incorporate land and port connectivity. The formation worked toward economic synergy through arterial channels of trade and cross-border initiatives. For instance, to link West Bengal and the remote Northeastern states through Bangladesh by rail, highway, and maritime corridors, alongside north-south transport routes that span Nepal, Bhutan, and Indian hill states to northern Bay of Bengal ports. These grids would then bridge extraneous regions throughout member-states and further eastward. With the accession of the Maldives and Sri Lanka to SASEC in March 2014, notions of quadripartite integration appeared subsumed or rendered dormant. The November 2014 Kathmandu Summit saw the endorsement of an accord on land transport by regional states, apart from one country's reservations causing it to fall through. The subsequent Summit Declaration reiterated sub-regional steps as contributory to wider connectedness. A framework for co-operation was subsequently drawn, with the first quaternary Joint Working Group (JWG) meeting in January 2015.

Another aspect of "connectivity" includes the seamless electrical grids, apart from mutual access to road, rail, air, port infrastructure, and ease of travel. In such a scenario, the BBIN-MVA would allow buses and private vehicles with BBIN permits to travel unobstructed without any border hindrances. Although manifestly of economic intent, the diplomatic weight accorded to this structure as opposed to alternatives in a region considered least integrated was seen to connote purpose beyond interwoven commerce.[26] The first cargo truck to take advantage of BBIN-MVA was flagged off from Kolkata on 1 November 2015. The truck travelled 640 km to reach Agartala via Dhaka. In August 2016, Bangladesh despatched a truck carrying garments from Dhaka to New Delhi as part of a trial run of the agreement. The truck received an electronic permit to enter Indian territory through an online web-based system. Instead of having to undergo customs clearance and formalities, the truck was fitted with an electronic seal with a GPS tracking device. The truck was then inspected for custom clearance at New Delhi rather than at the border.

This MVA agreement will come into force after all the four member nations ratify it. Bangladesh, India, and Nepal have done so. However, Bhutan has not ratified the agreement due to a concern about the number of vehicles entering its territory. An existing bilateral agreement between Bhutan and India already permits seamless vehicle movement between the two countries. Therefore, Bhutan's decision not to ratify the BBIN MVA would only affect its trade with Nepal and Bangladesh.[27] The Bhutanese government requested the other BBIN members to proceed with the agreement and clarified that it would attempt to ratify the MVA after the country held general elections in 2018. India approved $ 1.08 billion for construction and upgradation of 558 km of roads that join Bangladesh, Bhutan, and Nepal. The project will receive 50 per cent funding from the Asian Development Bank. The project is scheduled to be completed by 2018. The road project will cover West Bengal and Manipur on the Indian side, as of now. The project includes, among others, an upgrade of the 122-km Siliguri-Mirik-Darjeeling ($ 15 million) and the widening of the 60-km National Highway-35 (Kolkata-Bangaon) on the border with Bangladesh ($ 130 million). It also includes a new 123-km road to connect with Diamond Harbour, Kolkata, at a cost of $ 250 million. Apart from this, two highways are also proposed in Manipur—115-km Ukhrul-Tolloi-Tadubi (worth $ 230 million) and a 138-km split, four-lane road between the Kohima-Kedima-Kring-Imphal section of National Highway-39 (worth $ 280 million).[28] It is estimated that this project will increase regional trade by 60 per cent. Investments in hard infrastructure such as roads, bridges, and border facilities must also be scaled up, particularly in Bangladesh. However, the BBIN countries are yet to connect through a comprehensive trade facilitation and connectivity measure due to several logistical handicaps. One of the most severe barriers is that trade in the region involves a high number of procedures and documents in all three BBIN corridors, including multiple and complex obligations and compliances to product standards with countries to align customs procedures and recognise each other's services. To meet global, regional and sub-regional obligations, BBIN countries need enhanced trade facilitation measures. In the face of slow movements in trade facilitation, rather than focusing on trade and investment agreements, issues such as connectivity, water resources management, and energy have received increased attention.

India is considering a series of projects aimed at strengthening the links between South Asia and Southeast Asia. Proposals under consideration also include mega cross-border air connectivity projects, along with power and energy initiatives. Dhaka-Chennai-Colombo air connectivity, Chittagong-Kolkata-Colombo shipping connectivity, Bangladesh-North Bengal rail link, Bangladesh-Bhutan internet cables through India, a trade route connecting Nakugaon land port in Bangladesh to Gayleyphug in Bhutan via India, are a few. The BBIN MVA will complement the proposed BIMSTEC MVA having all multi-modal features connecting Sri Lanka with other countries of BIMSTEC through air or sea. BIMSTEC is also mulling connectivity through cruise liners to promote tourism and coastal shipping between member-states. This will facilitate India's Bay of Bengal outreach, complementing its Indian Ocean Region strategy. Connectivity through trans-border rivers among BIMSTEC member-states is also on the cards beginning with the direct sea movement of containerised cargo between India and Bangladesh, which has reduced shipping time from 30-40 days to not more than 10 days. The two states are linked by cross-border buses and trains, in addition to movement of cargo over rivers. Additionally, old rail links are being revived and new routes being added between India and Bangladesh.

The trilateral hydropower cooperation among Bangladesh, India, and Bhutan is another project to discuss in this regard. India had earlier agreed to facilitate the import of electricity to Bangladesh from hydro projects in Nepal. The MoU between NTPC Vidyut Vyapar Nigam Limited and Bangladesh Power Development Board for the supply of 500 MW hydropower from the 900 MW Upper Karnali hydropower plant in Nepal was signed during the visit of Prime Minister Sheikh Hasina to India in April 2017. At present, there are two interconnections through which 660 MW of power is transferred from India to Bangladesh. The state-run Indian firm plans to set up a 1,320 MW coal-fired thermal power plant at Rampal in Bangladesh, and several private players are also setting up power stations in the neighbouring country. India will construct a 135-km long pipeline from Assam to supply oil to Bangladesh following an agreement signed in October 2017. ONGC Videsh Ltd. has acquired two shallow-water blocks in Bangladesh—SS-04 and SS-09—in a 50:50 consortium with Oil India Limited, and is carrying out exploration in them. Other regional efforts are also in the offing, including the Bay of Bengal Industrial Growth Belt, a joint effort of Japan and Bangladesh.[29] "Maritime connectivity is crucial for the BIMSTEC region owing to its geography as well as geostrategic requirements."[30]

India's Initiatives in Leh-Ladakh

In May 2018, Prime Minister Narendra Modi inaugurated the Rs. 6,809 crore Zoji-La tunnel project in Jammu and Kashmir's Leh, kick-starting the work for India's longest tunnel and Asia's longest and strategic bi-directional tunnel, which will provide all-weather connectivity between Jammu and Kashmir's Srinagar, Kargil and Leh. The project will be finished within five years. "It (tunnel) will lead to all-round economic and socio-cultural integration of these regions. It also has immense strategic importance," Modi said.[31] The government approved the construction of the tunnel in the state keeping in mind that Srinagar, Kargil, and Leh remain cut-off from the rest of the world due to heavy snowfall during winters (December to April). The project will reduce the time taken to cross the Zoji La pass from the present three-and-a-half hours to just 15 minutes. The Zojila tunnel will be the longest bi-directional tunnel in Asia. Its construction period will be five years because of a challenging terrain where in some areas; the temperature dips to minus 45 degrees Celsius. The tunnel will be an engineering marvel as the first of its kind in such a geographical area. The pass is situated at an altitude of 11,578 feet on the Srinagar-Kargil-Leh National Highway and remains closed during winters due to heavy snowfall, which cuts off the Ladakh region from Kashmir. Leh is currently connected to mainland India by two main roads—first through the Zoji La pass from Srinagar and second through the Rohtang Pass from Manali. Both these highways are extremely popular biking and driving routes for enthusiasts during summer months. However, they only provide fragile connectivity and are blocked during the harsh winter months. The new Zoji La tunnel is likely to boost tourism in the region and also provide a better means to improve the local economy.

Defence forces have to face a hard time ensuring supplies to border posts during winters. This pass is most strategic for the entire Kargil sector, which has seen intrusion and war in the past. The project aims to construct a 14.15-km-long two-lane bi-directional single tube tunnel with a parallel 14.2-km-long egress tunnel excluding approaches between Baltal and Minamarg in the state.[32] P. Stobdan argues that with the completion of this strategic tunnel, Leh will get all-weather and snow-free road connectivity that will enable traffic to move swiftly and safely between Kashmir and Ladakh. The project would enormously boost local developmental activities, including employment generation and local businesses, by better linking Ladakh to the regional market besides increasing tourist traffic round the year to Ladakh. This will also help defence forces that face a hard time ensuring supplies to border posts during winters.

In addition to this, the government has now turned its focus on building a major high-elevation all-weather, snow-free rail axis to connect Ladakh with the rest of the country. The decks are being cleared to build two types of railway links for Leh–Bilaspur-Manali-Leh and Srinagar-Kargil-Leh. The move comes with the commitment to catch up with the rapid infrastructure growth in neighbouring China. The Leh rail network will have enormous strategic significance for boosting India's defence capabilities and preparedness, enhancing the communication network both along the China border and the border with Pakistan occupied Kashmir (PoK). According to Stobdan, Ladakh's connectivity is critical in the light of China's OBOR. It would eventually help enhance people-to-people connectivity so as to leverage the common heritage of the state, especially to explore the potentials of pilgrim tourism in all three regions of the state—Jammu, Kashmir, and Ladakh. An alternate route to Kailash Mansarovar through Demchok that will be safer, dependable, and shorter would become a reality if relations with China improve.

Connectivity would also help the country optimise Ladakh's strategic advantage as a pivot to accessing Central Asia, China, Russia, and Mongolia for political, trade, and commercial ties. This is critical in the context of counterpoising China's BRI, including the CPEC that passes in the close vicinity of Ladakh. Clearly, the Chinese forays into Gilgit-Baltistan, albeit on the pretext of the CPEC, could have adverse implications on Ladakh in the longer term. After completing railway projects in neighbouring Tibet and Xinjiang, the Chinese are planning to have trains penetrating the Karakoram mountains. "India needs a counter-plan, and it is for the prime minister to set the stage for exploring Ladakh's strategic value as a gateway for gaining direct access to Tarim Basin and the Tibetan plateau. Through this, both Kashmir and Ladakh can once again be brought to the centre-stage to become the economic and cultural hubs of India's connectivity to the north."[33] He further suggests that India's engagement with Eurasia has become critical. With India becoming a member of the Shanghai Cooperation Organization (SCO), its stakes in Central Asia will increase. Here, connectivity to Ladakh could offer a bigger strategic perspective and a historic opportunity for India to physically connect with China, Eurasia, Europe, and beyond, which could be the kernel not only for broader change but also beneficial to India's strategic outreach to the north.

Initiatives by NDA Government

Sagarmala Project

The Sagarmala Project is a strategic ₹ 8.5 trillion investment initiative of the Government of India entailing the setting up of new mega ports, modernization of India's existing ports, development of 14 Coastal Employment Zones (CEZs) and Coastal Employment Units, enhancement of port connectivity via road, rail, multi-modal logistics parks, pipelines and waterways and promote coastal community development, resulting in boosting merchandise exports by US$ 110 billion, and generation of around 10,000,000 direct and indirect jobs. It has become the flagship programme of the Ministry of Shipping to promote port-led development in the country by harnessing India's 7,500-km-long coastline, 14,500 km of potentially navigable waterways, and strategic locations on key international maritime trade routes. Sagarmala aims to modernize India's ports so that port-led development can be augmented, and coastlines can be developed to contribute to India's growth. It also aims for "transforming the existing ports into modern world-class ports and integrate the development of the ports, the industrial clusters and hinterland, and efficient evacuation systems through road, rail, inland and coastal waterways resulting in ports becoming the drivers of economic activity in coastal areas".[34] It is both an enabler and beneficiary of other key Government of India schemes, such as Make in India, Bharat Mala, Dedicated Freight Corridors, Industrial Corridors, Start-up India and Stand-up India.

In 2003, then PM Vajpayee proposed Project Sagarmala with the following features: (1) Set up Sagarmala Development Authority (Similar to National Highway Authority of India); (2) Funding via maritime development cess (5 paise per kg on cargo); (3) to improve ports, shipping industry, inland water transport, coastal shipping; and (4) PPP and FDI to gather more investment.

The Sagarmala project was shelved in 2004 when the UPA came to power. Anyway, the fact is that India's port infrastructure is in a bad shape and needs urgent upgrading. Without efficient ports and waterways systems, trade will not grow between two regions. The ASEAN-India Maritime Connectivity Report"[35] published by the ASEAN-India Centre at Research and Information System for Developing Countries in 2014, points out that in the list of top 25 ports by container volume, ASEAN countries have seven while India has only one. The introduction of the "Sagarmala" project by Prime Minister Narendra Modi, whereby India plans to invest in port infrastructure for improved integration and connectivity through the sea aims to improve India's maritime infrastructure by modernizing existing major and minor ports of India and setting up new ports. The prime objective of the Sagarmala project is to promote port-led direct and indirect development and provide infrastructure to transport goods to and from ports quickly, efficiently, and cost-effectively. Therefore, the Sagarmala Project shall, among other things, aim to develop access to new development regions with intermodal solutions and promote the optimum modal split, enhanced connectivity with the main economic centres, and beyond through expansion of rail, inland water, coastal and road services. The Sagarmala initiative will address challenges by focusing on three pillars of development, namely, (i) Supporting and enabling port-led development through appropriate policy and institutional interventions and providing for an institutional framework for ensuring inter-agency and ministries/departments/states' collaboration for integrated development, (ii) Port infrastructure enhancement, including modernization and setting up of new ports, and (iii) Efficient evacuation to and from the hinterland.

The Sagarmala Project, therefore, intends to achieve the broad objectives of enhancing the capacity of major and non-major ports and modernizing them to make them efficient, thereby enabling them to become drivers of port-led economic development, optimizing the use of existing and future transport assets, and developing new lines/linkages for transport (including roads, rail, inland waterways, and coastal routes), setting up of logistics hubs, and establishment of industries and manufacturing centres to be served by ports in EXIM and domestic trade. In addition to strengthening the port and evacuation infrastructure, it also aims to simplify procedures used at ports for cargo movement and promote usage of electronic channels for information exchange leading to quick, efficient, hassle-free, and seamless cargo movement. Presently Indian ports handle more than 90 per cent of India's total EXIM trade volume. However, the current proportion of merchandise trade in the Gross Domestic Product (GDP) of India is only 42 per cent, whereas, for some developed countries and regions in the world such as Germany and the European Union, it is 75 per cent and 70 per cent, respectively. Therefore, there is a great scope to increase the share of merchandising trade in India's GDP. With the Union Government's 'Make in India' initiative, the share of merchandise trade in India's GDP is expected to increase and approach levels achieved in developed countries. India lags far behind in ports and logistics infrastructure. Against a share of 9 per cent of railways and 6 per cent of roads in the GDP, the share of ports is only 1 per cent. Besides, high logistics costs make Indian exports uncompetitive. Among Indian states, Gujarat has been a pioneer in adopting a port-led development strategy with significant results. While in the 1980s the state grew at only 5.08 per cent per year (National average was 5.47 per cent), this accelerated to 8.15 per cent per annum in the 1990s (All India average, 6.98

per cent) and subsequently to more than 10 per cent per annum, substantially benefitting from the port-led development model.[36]

The growth of India's maritime sector is constrained due to many developmental, procedural, and policy-related challenges, namely, the involvement of multiple agencies in the development of infrastructure to promote industrialization, trade, tourism, and transportation; the presence of a dual institutional structure that has led to the development of major and non-major ports as separate, unconnected entities; lack of requisite infrastructure for evacuation from major and non-major ports leading to sub-optimal transport modal mix; limited hinterland linkages that increases the cost of transportation and cargo movement; limited development of centres for manufacturing and urban and economic activities in the hinterland; low penetration of coastal and inland shipping in India, limited mechanization and procedural bottlenecks and lack of scale, deep draft and other facilities at various ports in India.

An illustrative list of the kind of development projects that could be undertaken in the Sagarmala initiative is (i) Port-led industrialization; (ii) Port-based urbanization; (iii) Port-based and coastal tourism and recreational activities; (iv) Short sea shipping, coastal shipping, and inland waterways transportation; (v) Shipbuilding, ship repair and ship recycling; (vi) Logistics parks, warehousing, maritime zones/services; (vii) Integration with hinterland hubs; (viii) Offshore storage and drilling platforms; (ix) Specialization of ports in certain economic activities such as energy, containers, chemicals, coal, agro products, etc.; (x) Offshore renewable energy projects with base ports for installations; and (xi) Modernizing existing ports and development of new ports. This strategy incorporates both aspects of port-led development, viz., port-led direct development and port-led indirect development.

Composition	*Role*
Chaired by Minister of Shipping	Overall policy guidance
Cabinet Ministers from concerned ministries	High-level coordination
Chief Ministers/Minister(s) in charge of ports of maritime states	Approve the national perspective plan
	Review various aspects of planning
	Review & guidance for implementation

Asia-Africa Growth Corridor

The Asia-Africa Growth Corridor or AAGC is an economic cooperation agreement between India, Japan, and multiple African countries.[37] India, on 25

May 2017, launched a vision document for the Asia-Africa Growth Corridor or AAGC at the African Development Bank meeting in Gujarat. The Research and Information System for Developing Countries (RIS), New Delhi, the Economic Research Institute for ASEAN and East Asia (ERIA), Jakarta, and Institute of Developing Economies (IDE-JETRO), Tokyo, have developed the Vision Document based on consultations with Asian and African think-tanks.[38] It aims for Indo-Japanese collaboration to develop quality infrastructure in Africa, complemented by digital connectivity, which would undertake the realization of the idea of creating a free and open Indo-Pacific region. The AAGC will prioritize development projects in health and pharmaceuticals, agriculture and agro-processing, disaster management, and skill enhancement. The connectivity aspects of the AAGC will be supplemented with quality infrastructure.[39]

Unlike OBOR, or the BRI (Belt and Road Initiative), which entails the development of both land (new economic belt) and ocean (marine silk road) corridors, the AAGC will essentially be a sea corridor linking Africa with India and other countries of South-East Asia and Oceania by rediscovering ancient sea-routes and creating new sea corridors that will link ports in Jamnagar (Gujarat) with Djibouti in the Gulf of Eden and similarly the ports of Mombasa and Zanzibar will be connected to ports near Madurai; Kolkata will be linked to Sittwe port in Myanmar.[40] "The AAGC would consist of four main components: development and cooperation projects, quality infrastructure and institutional connectivity, capacity and skill enhancement, and people-to-people partnerships. These four components, as well as four elements or four pillars, are complementary to promote growth and all-round development in both the continents," the document said.[41]

According to the vision document, many fields of collaboration were laid out. Digital connectivity will also support the growth of innovative technology and services between Asia and Africa. According to people involved in the project, there is scope for Asia to share its experiences of growth and development with Africa. It consists of five remarkable aspects. They are: (a) effective mobilization of financial resources; (b) their alignment with socio-economic development and development strategies of partner countries and regions; (c) application of high-quality standards in terms of compliance with international standards established to mitigate environmental and social impact; (d) provision of quality of infrastructure taking into account aspects of economic efficiency and durability, inclusiveness, safety and disaster-resilience, sustainability as well as convenience and amenities; and (e) contribution to local society and the economy.[42]

A novel form of bilateral co-operation is the Asia-Africa Growth Corridor (AAGC), which started with India and Japan and then expanded to ASEAN and Africa, wherein India and Japan are attempting to create a counter-model to the Chinese BRI in the Indian Ocean and its coastal states.[43] India believes that the security of the Indian Ocean is the primary responsibility of the littoral states and has been promoting the idea of a security provider since 2009 by supporting the efforts and capacity building of the littoral states. In the face of China's increased presence, India has intensified its military co-operation with the island states of Mauritius, Seychelles, the Maldives, and Comoros. In 2014, the Modi government created the Mausam project as a counterweight to the BRI, and since 2015, PM Modi has been promoting the SAGAR (Security and Growth for All in the Region) concept. Together, they offer a new approach to regional cooperation and connectivity, which is non-assertive and peaceful as it leverages its cultural interactions with the region and thus a benevolent alternative to the BRI. The AAGC proposes regional connectivity on a state-to-state level, like major railroad projects linking Delhi to Hanoi that fit within the interest of Southeast Asia to diversify trade and ties. On the state level, the decisions of both the leaderships to build a high-speed rail network project between Ahmedabad and Mumbai has inspired a new approach to major infrastructure cooperation as countries seeking to employ their citizens also want friendly interest rates on their loans. Investing in strategic infrastructure projects such as ports, rails, and telecommunications would find receptive customers in countries seeking to minimize their dependence on individual trading partners. Such cooperation is more sustainable as, unlike BRI, the AAGC infrastructure projects will provide local employment, thus garnering greater regional support for their vision.

The AAGC is commonly portrayed as a response to China's Belt and Road Initiative (BRI). The vision, however, has to be viewed on the back of decades of cooperation amongst two of Asia's largest democracies, both seeking an alignment of interests, be it under democratic security cooperation or Japanese Prime Minister Shinzo Abe's 2006 notion of an Asian 'Arc of Freedom and Prosperity.' During the 2006 visit, Abe reiterated his interest in a maritime security diamond of democracies led in cooperation with Australia and the USA, and once more underlined India and Japan's heavy dependence on a free and open Indo-Pacific region. Though conceived by democratic countries, "democracy" within the AAGC may just refer to the multilateral nature of the project itself, as many countries that form part of this corridor may not even practise democracy in their internal politics. Nevertheless, increased connectivity and investment in businesses through private-public partnerships will bring prosperity to individuals across the regions.

While there are structural hurdles within Japan and India that need to be addressed, their vision of a multilateral Asian and African Growth Corridor has the potential to provide states with an attractive new framework that increases regional economic growth and protects state-sovereignty. Investing in strategic infrastructure projects such as ports, rails, and telecommunications would find receptive customers in countries seeking to minimize their dependence on individual trading partners. A classic example of this is Japan setting up hospitals in a number of countries in the region and how Japanese soft power can ensure a more permanent Japanese presence without fostering local perceptions of foreign control. Japan's high skills and capital and India's own size and experience with economic development can be matched to address key challenges to developing key technologies—be they in pharmacology or solar energy—on a mass scale. With close links in ASEAN, India is widely seen as a benevolent power, and via its cultural and religious ties to Diaspora populations, India has a strong advantage in promoting trade. A strong commitment from Japan and India regarding infrastructure and technology exchanges may go far in bridging the wide economic and geostrategic gaps across the regions.

International North-South Transport Corridor

The International North-South Transport Corridor (INSTC) is a 7,200-km-long multi-mode network of ship, rail, and road routes for moving freight between India, Iran, Afghanistan, Armenia, Azerbaijan, Russia, Central Asia, and Europe. The corridor's objective is to increase trade connectivity between major cities such as Mumbai, Moscow, Teheran, Baku, Bandar Abbas, Astrakhan, Bandar Anzali, etc. Dry runs of two routes were conducted in 2014, the first was Mumbai to Baku via Bandar Abbas, and the second was Mumbai to Astrakhan via Bandar Abbas, Teheran, and Bandar Anzali. The objective of the study was to identify and address key bottlenecks. The results showed that transport costs were reduced by "$ 2,500 per 15 tons of cargo". Other routes under consideration include Kazakhstan and Turkmenistan. This will also synchronize with the Ashgabat Agreement, a multimodal transport agreement signed by India (2018), Oman (2011), Iran (2011), Turkmenistan (2011), Uzbekistan (2011), Kazakhstan (2015), and Pakistan (2016). This is for creating an international transport and transit corridor facilitating transportation of goods between Central Asia and the Persian Gulf.

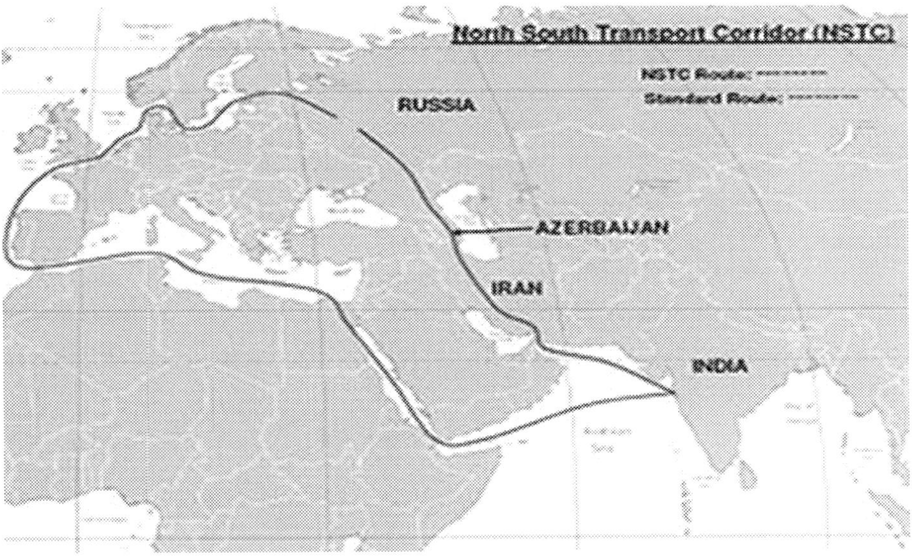

INSTC is basically a new trilateral project, which Russia, Iran, and India have promulgated since 2015.[44] The Corridor, which begins at the Iranian port of Chabahar, is supposed to give India access to Afghanistan, Central Asia, and Russia. In May 2016, the Indian Government allocated $ 500 million for developing Chabahar. The port city is only about 70 km from the Pakistani port of Gwadar, where China's "New Silk Road" and "Maritime Silk Road" meet. In late October 2017, India shipped its first load of wheat to Afghanistan via Chabahar. The Corridor should advance Indian-Afghan trade in the coming years. India has historically enjoyed good relations with Afghanistan. However, because they do not share a border, their physical detachment presents a logistical dilemma. Since 2001, India has taken on many sizable infrastructure projects in its development assistance program in Afghanistan. One of these projects is the Zaranj-Delaram Highway, a 135-mile long highway that connects Zaranj in Nimruz province, near the Iranian border, with Delaram in neighbouring Farah province, and the Afghan-Iranian border with the Kandahar-Herat highway in Delaram.[45] The Zaranj-Delaram highway connects Chabahar Port on the Gulf of Oman to the 1,300-mile Afghanistan Ring Road. It connects 16 of the country's 34 provinces, stretching from Herat, Mazar-i-Sharif, Kabul, Ghazni, and Kandahar and Tajikistan's Gorno-Badakhshan. The highway creates a north-south transport corridor linking the Indian sub-continent and landlocked Central Asia. The new infrastructure enables Afghanistan to access the Arabian Sea through Iran and raises its potential to stimulate more investment from trade with outside powers like India. The port will provide India access to Central Asia, and India's investment will yield immediate strategic gain. On 6 May 6 2015, New Delhi and Tehran signed a memorandum of understanding worth $ 195 million to secure India's participation in the development of Chabahar Port. The port allows India, the world's fourth-largest energy consumer, to access Iran's crude oil reserves of over 150 billion barrels and 1,187 trillion cubic feet of gas reserves. It also allows India access to the added energy resources in Central Asia, where Kazakhstan and Turkmenistan possess 30 billion barrels of oil and 265 trillion cubic feet gas reserves, respectively, and Kazakhstan holds 679,300 tons of uranium and more than 37,000 million short tons of recoverable coal reserves. India is also in discussion with Japans and the USA to pool resources and coordinate approaches to sustainable infrastructure development in the Indo-Pacific.

Conclusion

Managing time and mobilization of resources are essential indices in assessing the success of any foreign policy outreach. If India can manage these two with effective implementation of its promised projects and mobilization of resources with support from other stakeholders, its non-assertive, collaborative, benign, and sustainable approach can offer a benevolent alternative narrative to the hidden agenda of the BRI. For that to happen, India has to put an institutional framework in place so that all its projects can be implemented and completed in time. New Delhi needs to boost India's own civilian maritime infrastructure, which has become terribly creaky and utterly inadequate for a country so dependent on the seas for its economic life. Furthermore, it has to ramp up its capabilities to take up major maritime projects in other countries, as China has done through its BRI initiatives. New Delhi, as of now, does not have the capacity or a policy framework to bid for and execute major infrastructure projects in the Indian Ocean littoral. It indeed has the capability, but it has to be translated into the capacity to execute. For integration and coordination, there is again a need for an apex body that can be a bridge between different agencies involved in India's connectivity projects.

NOTES

1. First mentioned by Mr. Xi in speeches in 2013, the BRI's import has suffered a bit from its confusing branding. Initially referred to as 'One Belt, One Road (OBOR)', the name was changed in 2017 due to confusion related to the fact that 'belt' refers to land routes (as Ancient Silk Road) and that 'road' refers to shipping lanes extending from East Asia to West Asia.
2. According to a 2016 Price Waterhouse Coopers (PWC) report, the countries that had signed up for BRI were mostly small states bordering China. They comprised almost half the world's population and around 30 per cent of the global economy; geographical area mandating infrastructure investment of around US$ 5 trillion. However, countries like India and Australia are among the conspicuous holdouts.

3. According to James Laurenceson, Deputy Director, Australia-China Relations Institute, UTS, "This is what China says it is. It's about improving connectivity across five areas: better infrastructure, policy coordination, freer trade, freer investment and enhancing people to people links as well..." See "What is China's Belt and Road initiative", Available online at https://www.sbs.com.au/news/explainer/what-chinas-belt-and-road-initiative. Accessed 10 June. 2018.
4. "The Belt and Road Initiative", Accessed 12 June 2018, Online available at http://english.gov.cn/beltAndRoad/.
5. Benjamin Habib and Viktor Faulknor, "The Belt and Road Initiative: China's vision for globalisation, Beijing-style," *Myanmar Times,* 19 May 2017. Available online at https://www.mmtimes.com/opinion/26067-the-belt-and-road-initiative-china-s-vision-for-globalisation-beijing-style.html. Accessed on 30 May 2017.
6. The Chinese Dream is a term popularized after 2013 within Chinese society that describes a set of personal and national ethics and ideals. It is extensively used by journalists, government officials and activists to describe the role of the individual in Chinese society as well as the goals of the Chinese nation. President Xi began promoting the phrase as a slogan in a visit to the National Museum of China in November 2012 after assuming power. Since then, there has been widespread usage of this phrase in official announcements and in the essence of political ideology under his leadership. According to President Xi, young people should "dare to dream, work assiduously to fulfil the dreams and contribute to the revitalization of the nation". CCP's theoretical journal *Qiushi* describes the Chinese Dream as about Chinese prosperity, collective effort, socialism, and national glory. Available online at *https://chinacopyrightandmedia.wordpress.com/2013/05/06/the-chinese-dream-infuses-socialism-with-chinese-characteristics-with-new-energy/.* —"Xi Jinping and the Chinese Dream," *The Economist,* 4 May 2013, also available in https://www.economist.com/leaders/2013/05/04/xi-jinping-and-the-chinese-dream. Accessed on 15 June 2018.
7. Quoted in Merriden Varrall, "Chinese World Views and China's Foreign Policy," Lowy Institute, 26 November 2015. Online available at https://www.lowyinstitute.org/publications/chinese-worldviews-and-china-s-foreign-policy. Accessed 12 January 2016.
8. Nick Bisley in Kelsey Munro's, "What is the Belt and Road Initiative?" *Special Broadcasting Service,* Australian TV channel, 10 November 2017. Online available at https://www.sbs.com.au/news/explainer/what-chinas-belt-and-road-initiative. Accessed on 12 November 2018.
9. See "China-Pakistan Economic Corridor: Opportunities and Risks," Report No. 297/Asia, 29 June 2018, Online available at https://www.crisisgroup.org/asia/south-asia/pakistan/297-china-pakistan-economic-corridor-opportunities-and-risks. Accessed on 2 October 2018.
10. See Sudha Ramchandran, "China-Pakistan Economic Corridor: Road to Riches?' *China Brief,* 31 July 2015, No. 15, Online available at https://jamestown.org/program/china-pakistan-economic-corridor-road-to-riches/ Accessed on 20 August 2015.
11. "China's Belt and Road initiatives not solo, but symphony," *Xinhua,* 8 March 2015, Online available at http://www.chinadaily.com.cn/business/2015-03/08/content_19750844.htm. Accessed 20 September 2018. According to Chinese Foreign Minister Wang Yi, "If I may use a musical metaphor, the initiatives are not China's solo, but a symphony performed by all relevant countries." He further added that in advancing the BRI initiatives, China will carry out equal-footed consultation and respect the choice of other countries.
12. Srikanth Kondapalli, "Why India is not part of the Belt and Road Initiative summit," *The Indian Express,* 15 May 2017, Online available at https://indianexpress.com/article/opinion/why-india-is-not-part-of-the-belt-and-road-initiative-summit-465615. Accessed 17 May 2017.
13. Dipanjan Roy Choudhuri, "China-Pakistan Economic Corridor is Illegal: India," *The Economic Times,* 6 February 2020, Online available at https://economictimes.indiatimes.com/news/

defence/china-pakistan-economic-corridor-is-illegal-india/articleshow/73974996.cms. Accessed 7 February, 2020.

14. P. K. Singh, "China-Pakistan Economic Corridor: Connecting the Dots," The United Service Institution of India, New Delhi, Online available at http://usiofindia.org/Article/?pub=Journal&pubno=608&ano=2946. Accessed 8 September 2018.
15. See Joint Statement, US and India: Prosperity Through Partnership, Ministry of External Affairs, Government of India, 27 June 2017, Online available at https://mea.gov.in/bilateral documents.htm?dtl/28560/United_States_and_India_Prosperity_Through_Partnership. Accessed 2 July 2017.
16. Harsh V. Pant & Ritika Passi, *India's Response to China's Belt and Road Initiative: A Policy in Motion*, Project Muse, Asia Policy, National Bureau of Asian Research, No. 24, July 2017, Online available at https://muse.jhu.edu/article/666558/pdf. Accessed 27 July 2017.
17. Anirban Bhaumik, "India opposed to China's One-Belt-One-Road," *Deccan Herald*, 3 March 2016, Online available at https://www.deccanherald.com/content/532353/india-opposed-chinas-one-belt.html. Accessed 4 September 2018.
18. Ibid.
19. See "At Asian Summit SCO, India Refuses to Back China's Belt and Road Project," NDTV, 3 June 2018, Online available at https://www.ndtv.com/india-news/at-asian-summit-sco-india-refuses-to-back-chinas-belt-and-road-initiative-1865295. Accessed 4 June 2018.
20. There are a number of reasons attributed to the slow progress to multiple factors. Extensive rainy season has been identified as the primary cause which has hindered completion of this project. Added to this, the remoteness of the region in Mizoram, lack of availability of labour force, delay in the supply of fuel, spare parts, etc., are the other factors that negatively affect this project. The erratic situation due to these factors has led to an increase in the outlay of the budget from Rs. 507 crore to Rs. 1,011 crore. The possibility of another revision of the budget cannot be ruled out given the current delay and the existing circumstances. Read more at Rajeev Bhattacharyya, "Slow progress mars Mizoram-Myanmar Kaladan project as India misses deadline for road third time in a row," *First Post*, 31 December 2018, Online available at https://www.firstpost.com/india/slow-progress-mars-mizoram-myanmar-kaladan-project-as-india-misses-deadline-for-road-third-time-in-a-row-5817371.html. Accessed 4 January 2019.
21. In January 2020, the Lawngtlai District Land Owners' Association, an umbrella association of landowners in Lawngtlai district, moved court in order to stall the two constructing agencies related to payment of compensation amounting to more than Rs. 50 crore. Read more at Henry L. Khojol, "Kaladan Multi-Modal Transit Transport Project yet to get green nod," *East Mojo*, 28 February 2020, Online available at https://www.eastmojo.com/mizoram/2020/02/28/kaladan-multi-modal-transit-transport-project-yet-to-get-green-nod. Accessed 3 May 2020.
22. Shemin Joy, "Key 'Act East' Project on creating shipping corridor misses deadline," *Deccan Herald*, 10 March 2020, Online available at https://www.deccanherald.com/national/key-act-east-project-on-creating-shipping-corridor-misses-deadline-812316.html. Accessed 15 March 2020.
23. Ibid. The Inland Waterways Authority of India is the project development consultant for the waterways component and IRCON Infrastructure Services Ltd are the project management consultants for the road component. The 158-km waterway component was awarded to Essar Projects (India) Ltd. in 2010. The originally approved works were completed in May 2017. Following this, a port operator has been appointed for operation and maintenance of the waterways component in February 2020. The port has been handed over to the Myanmar Government. The road component was allocated to a joint venture of M/s EPIL and M/s C&C Construction Ltd in March 2017.
24. Rajeev Bhattacharya, "Slow progress mars Mizoram-Myanmar Kaladan project as India misses

deadline for road third time in a row," *Firstpost*, 31 December 2018, Online available at https://www.firstpost.com/india/slow-progress-mars-mizoram-myanmar-kaladan-project-as-india-misses-deadline-for-road-third-time-in-a-row-5817371.html Accessed 4 January 2019.

25. See SAARC Group on Statistics, Online available at http://www.saarcstat.org/db/trade_stat/saarc_exports_by_month. Accessed 3 May 2019.
26. Nihar Nayak, "BBIN-MVA: Pushing Regional Integration through Sub-regional Cooperation," *IDSA Comment*, 19 June 2015. Online available at https://idsa.in/idsacomments/BBIN-MVAPushingRegionalIntegration_nnayak_190615. Accessed 10 September 2018.
27. Elizabeth Roche, "India to redraw BBIN connectivity project as Bhutan opts out," *The Mint*, 8 May 2017, Online available at https://www.livemint.com/Politics/ol0E49p8V9WqXpJUXBqFPL/India-to-redraw-BBIN-connectivity-project-as-Bhutan-opts-out.html. Accessed 10 September 2018.
28. See "Centre approves $1 billion Bangladesh-Bhutan-India-Nepal road connectivity project". *The News Minute*. 18 September 2016. Accessed 9 December 2017.
29. Dipanjan Roy Choudhuri, "India lines up projects to strengthen links with South, Southeast Asia," *The Economic Times*, 24 October 2017, Online available at https://economictimes.indiatimes.com/news/politics-and-nation/india-lines-up-projects-to-strengthen-links-with-south-southeast asia/articleshow/61191813.cms?utm_source= contentofinterest&utm_ medium= text&utm_campaign=cppst. Accessed 2 November 2017.
30. Ibid.
31. "PM Modi inaugurates Zojila project in Leh: All you need to know about India's longest tunnel," *The Indian Express*, 19 May 2018, Online available at https://indianexpress.com/article/india/j-k-pm-modi-inaugurates-zojila-tunnel-project-in-leh-all-you-need-to-know-about-indias-longest-tunnel-5182934/; "Modi inaugurates Zojila tunnel project," *The Hindu*, 19 May 2018, Online available at https://www.thehindu.com/news/national/modi-inaugurates-zojila-tunnel-project/article23937242.ece. Accessed 21 May 2018.
32. P. Stobdan, "Modi's Two Projects in Leh Can be an Answer to China's BRI," *The Quint*, 19 May 2018. Online available at https://www.thequint.com/news/india/prime-minister-narendra-modi-visit-to-leh. Accessed 2 June 2018.
33. Ibid.
34. See Ministry of Shipping Government of India Concept Note on Sagar Mala Project: Working Paper, 28th October 2014. Online available at https://www.academia.edu/16422932/Concept_on_Sagar_Mala_Project. Accessed 20 December 2018.
35. See http://www.ris.org.in/asean-india-maritime-connectivity-report. Accessed 20 December 2018.
36. "Sagarmala: Concept and implementation towards Blue Revolution," PMINDIA, 25 March 2015. Online available at www.pmindia.gov.in/en/news_updates/sagarmala-concept-and-implementation-towards-blue-revolution/ Accessed 3 September 2018.
37. See "Asia-Africa Growth Corridor Launched," *Times of India*, 25 May 2017, Online available at https://timesofindia.indiatimes.com/city/ahmedabad/asia-africa-growth-corridor launched/articleshow/58830900.cms. Accessed 10 July 2018.
38. See ASIA AFRICA GROWTH CORRIDOR, Partnership for Sustainable and Innovative Development: A Vision Document: African Development Bank Meeting, 22-26 May 2017, Ahmedabad, RIS, ERIA,IDE-JETRO, Online available at http://www.eria.org/Asia-Africa-Growth-Corridor-Document.pdf; Ruchira Beri, India's New Initiative in Africa: The Asia–Africa Growth Corridor, IDSA Comment, 13 June 2017, Online available at https://idsa.in/idsacomments/indias-new-initiative-in-africa-asia-africa-growth-corridor_rberi_130617and Asia Africa Growth Corridor: Towards a Shared Philosophy, *Africa Trends*, January-June 2017, available at https://idsa.in/africatrends/asia-africa-growth-corridor-rberi. Accessed 5 August

2018.

39. Ibid.
40. Avinash Nair, "To Counter OBOR, India & Japan propose Asia-Africa Sea Corridor," *Indian Express*, 31 May 2017, Online available at https://indianexpress.com/article/explained/to-counter-obor-india-and-japan-propose-asia-africa-sea-corridor-4681749/ Accessed 5 August 2018.
41. Dipanjan Roy Chaudhury, "India, Japan come up with AAGC to counter China's OBOR", *The Economic Times*, 26 May 2017, online available at https://economictimes.indiatimes.com/news/economy/policy/india-japan-come-up-with-aagc-to-counter-chinas-obor/articleshow/58846673.cms. *Accessed 28 May 2017.*
42. Ibid.
43. Dipanjan Roy Chaudhury, "Pushing back against China's One Belt One Road, India, Japan build Strategic 'Great Wall'," *The Economic Times*, 16 May 2017, online available at https://economictimes.indiatimes.com/news/economy/infrastructure/pushing-back-against-chinas-one-belt-one-road-india-japan-build-strategic-great-wall/articleshow/58689033.cms. Accessed 18 May 2017.
44. Dipanjan Roy Chaudhury, "India-Eurasia road almost ready, container dry run soon", *The Economic Times*, 3 April 2017, Online available at https://economictimes.indiatimes.com/industry/transportation/shipping-/-transport/india-eurasia-road-almost-ready-container-dry-run-soon/articleshow/57980716.cms; See Sandeep Dikshit, "Despite U.S. opposition, Iran to be transport hub for North-South Corridor", *The Hindu*, 31 May 2015, Online available at https://www.thehindu.com/news/national/despite-us-opposition-iran-to-be-transport-hub-for-northsouth-corridor/article3473943.ece; "Transport Corridor offers many opportunities for Indo-Russian trade", *Russia & India Report*, 29 November 2012. Online available at https://www.rbth.com/articles/2012/11/29/northsouth_transport_corridor_ offers_ many_ opportunities_ for_indo-ru_19421.html. Accessed 3 October 2018.
45. See Rohullah Osmani, "Chabahar Port: A Win for South Asia," *Foreign Policy*, 5 February 2016, Online available at https://foreignpolicy.com/2016/02/05/chabahar-port-a-win-for-south-asia/. Accessed 5 September 2018.

3

BRI: Elusive Mandarin Phraseology or Grand Geopolitical Strategy

Hemant Adlakha

Introduction

Ever since the idea of "One Belt, One Road" (一带一路, *yidaiyilu*, in short, OBOR) was introduced by Chinese President Xi Jinping, scholars around the world have pursued the idea with unprecedented interest and energy. The genesis of the concept can be traced back to Chinese President Xi Jinping's speech delivered at the University of Nazarbayev, Kazakhstan, in September 2013. In the speech titled "Promoting the Friendship for a Beautiful Future", he had mentioned the idea of a "Silk Road Economic Belt" (丝绸之路经济带, *Sichouzhilujingjidai*, SREB), the first component of the 'One Belt One Road', as a roadmap to enhance global connectivity. President Xi also outlined five objectives, viz., strengthening the policy communication, the road connectivity, the trade flow, the currency circulation and people-to-people interaction.[1] The second component "Maritime Silk Road" (海上丝绸之路, *Haishangsichouzhilu,* MSR) was mentioned with an objective to strengthen maritime cooperation and maritime partnership between China and ASEAN countries during a speech delivered in the Indonesian Parliament in October 2013.[2] Later, in April 2014, the Chinese Premier Li Keqiang highlighted these two concepts together at the Boao Forum, and since then the term 'One Belt One Road' has become a hot topic, both in China and the outside world.[3] Eventually, the concept has been officially defined as the Belt & Road Initiative (BRI).

This chapter reviews Chinese perspectives of the ideas of the Silk Road Economic Belt and the Maritime Silk Road that have proliferated in the last few years, now under the aegis of and visualized as the "Belt and Road Initiative" (一带一路倡议 *Yidaiyiluchangyi*). For this reason, this chapter makes an attempt to present a bird's eye view of how the concept of OBOR has evolved within China. As the title of the chapter spells out, the objective is to analyse the trajectory of Chinese discourse on the idea of OBOR in the immediate context of the prevailing COVID-19 crisis. This chapter also attempts to keep a balanced perspective by drawing from both the Chinese language as well from literature outside China.

The Chinese Narrative on BRI

In recent years, China has gained much attention around the world owing mainly to it assertively—some call it aggressively—pursuing a China-led global agenda. According to Xiang Debao, a professor at the Shanghai Institute for International Studies (SIIS), "By setting a China-led global agenda, China has ushered in a new way of interpreting the world through the Chinese framework and filled the world stage with Chinese content".[4] The above-mentioned objectives cannot be realized until there is a firm resolve among Chinese scholars to direct and redirect the narratives. The extensive debates inside China on concepts such as 'Peaceful Development', 'Harmonious World', 'China Model', 'Chinese Worldview', 'China Dream', etc., validate these claims. Following the inception of the OBOR and, as was expected, Chinese scholars have once again become pro-active in interpreting the Chinese government's perceptions of the BRI, which has presumably resulted in different narratives.

Echoing Professor Xiang Debao, in a preface for an edited volume published by the Communications University of China (CUC) in Beijing just before the Chinese Communist Party's Nineteenth National Congress was convened in November 2017, well-known Chinese scholar Professor Jin Xin wrote: "OBOR is China's gift to the world, its aim is to push the important initiative of a new model of globalization and regional integration. In establishing OBOR, it is extremely important to win popular support and build soft power. Policy communication, networking, smooth trade and easy financing, all are closely interlinked, and these features make the OBOR a complete and comprehensive package. *Popular consensus* forms indispensable latitude of the OBOR package and is of vital significance in ensuring its smooth, frictionless implementation as well its wider social acceptance. In building 'Belt and Road' soft power, it is of crucial import to ensure optimum utilization of the advantages of full participation from governments, political parties, social organizations and NGOs, think tanks, media, etc."[5]

Furthermore, following the concretization of the concept of 'One Belt One Road' into a proper grand plan called the 'Belt and Road Initiative', the PRC government has been spending huge resources and energy in spreading the idea both within the country and overseas. In December 2016, China National Reform Committee's leading group held a meeting to approve an important policy document, namely, "Guidelines to strengthen BRI soft power strategy". The core feature of the "Guidelines" was "soft power construction is the key tool in the implementation of the BRI strategy".[6] In a widely-read edited volume published by the Shanghai Social Science Academy Press, the author, Professor Liu Ma, claims that within China alone, since the inception of the concept in 2013, about 1,000 articles, analyses and commentaries specifically focussing on the OBOR or the BRI have been published. Almost all aspects and dimensions of the BRI have been included in the scholarly discourse. Some key areas extensively analysed include the economic significance and the political and security dimensions of the BRI, its implementation risks and challenges, how the concept is perceived abroad, responses and reactions towards the BRI from countries along the coastline, and so on. Some of the commentaries have also looked at the geopolitical dimensions of the BRI grand plan.[7] Broadly speaking, Chinese scholars have tried to analyse every aspect of the BRI.

Zhang Yongli and Hu Dandanin provide us with a good review of the Chinese domestic debates on OBOR strategy.[8] Scholars opine that the present research on the OBOR is very extensive but the formulation and planning of the concept is still in the exploratory stage and it needs further research. According to them, debate on the OBOR should involve a multidimensional approach comprising political, economic and social issues which is lacking in Chinese discourse.

Strategy or Initiative: The Debate Within and Without

There is a debate on whether the OBOR is a policy strategy aimed at challenging the international world order, or OBOR is just an initiative by China focused on internal or domestic economic development by aligning itself with the global economy. According to Benjamin Habib and Victor Faulknor, both from the La Trobe University, Australia, China's Belt and Road Initiative (BRI) is a multifaceted economic, diplomatic and geopolitical undertaking that has morphed through various iterations, from the "New Silk Road" to "One Belt, One Road". "The

BRI imagines a US$ 1.3 trillion Chinese-led investment programme creating a web of infrastructure including roads, railways, telecommunications, energy pipelines, and ports. This would serve to enhance economic interconnectivity and facilitate development across Eurasia, East Africa and more than 60 partner countries," the two scholars observed.[9] But underlining the ultimate Chinese goal of the BRI, Habib and Faulknor pointed out, is to spur a new round of globalization, however, in a changed international order in which China foresees for itself a vital role.[10]

Within China, the dominant view is by and large tilted in favour of the OBOR as an initiative in which many scholars in mainland China uphold the official view, which describes the OBOR as a major new element of Chinese foreign policy.[11] However, to some others, the OBOR initiative represents an ambitious spatial expansion of Chinese state capitalism, driven by an excess of industrial production capacity, as well as by emerging financial capital interests. There are also few and far between studies published recently by 'independent' professionals and the party-affiliated intellectuals, which claim the OBOR initiative, on the one hand, to be 'Chinese logic for global development' and the 'Rise of Chinese civilization' on the other.[12]

Many observers outside China have termed the OBOR initiative as China's 'Marshall Plan'. According to them, China's OBOR initiative and post-WW II reconstruction plan (Marshall Plan) led by the USA has many similarities. They argue that both the plans have meant boosting export, boosting currency export and fostering strategic division.[13] While, in sharp contrast, the Chinese discourse maintains that there is a fundamental difference between the OBOR and the Marshall Plan in terms of background, intention and the way of implementation.[14]

Zhang Junhua considers the OBOR as a product of Chinese *neomercantilist* thinking.[15] According to him, Chinese neo-mercantilism endorses global trade and its institutions while also pursuing a government-led globalization strategy to accumulate capital and wealth for the nation. The Chinese seem to convince the world that the OBOR will boost regional trade and economic development in Asia through inter-regional infrastructure improvement and industrial transfer. For this purpose, the Chinese government has come up with a plan '*Vision and Actions on Jointly Building the Silk Road Economic Belt and 21st Century Maritime Silk Road*' which demonstrates China's serious attempt to materialize its grand vision.[16] According to the Chinese view, OBOR initiatives will put China at the centre of geo-economics in the region and beyond, a position from which it hopes to strengthen its economic ties with other Asian countries.[17] This view is largely preoccupied with the economic gains that the OBOR promises to bring for China.

According to Shaun Breslin, a professor of politics and international studies at the University of Warwick, United Kingdom, China's proactive foreign policy has been influenced by an increasing sense of national pride, and the emergence of China as a global power and the world's second largest economy is reflected in the OBOR.[18] This grand strategy was also needed due to the rising regional interdependency in the era of globalization as the OBOR initiative will serve as an important tool for Beijing to flex its financial muscle to advance China's economic interests abroad. In Chinese discourse, scholars vehemently support this argument and maintain that the domestic economic situation is a major consideration for making and implementating OBOR initiatives.[19]

Then there are scholars who argue that China's OBOR is in response to the US 'Pivot to Asia'. One of the most talked about elements of the US 'Pivot to Asia' is the policy of geopolitical encirclement of China. On the other hand, in Chinese terms like 'Eurasian Pivot',[20] 'Pivot to the Middle East and Iran',[21] are increasingly becoming an important part of the emerging Chinese foreign policy discourse. Professor Lan Xinxiang, a noted mainland Chinese scholar and Head of the Centre for the Study of One Belt One Road at the Graduate Institute, Geneva, acknowledges the geo-economic element of the OBOR but also admits that the OBOR has a geostrategic dimension which aims at the reconfiguration of world politics. He explicitly agrees that the concept of "pivot to the West" underlies the OBOR but rejects the narrative of a counter-pivot strategy. He further observes that President Obama's strategy of the "pivot to Asia" was launched in 2011 while China's "pivot to the West" started much earlier.[22] China's "Pivot to the West" can be traced back to the transatlantic split over the Iraq war during the heated UN Security Council debates at that time.[23]

There is an impression outside China that the implications of the "One Belt One Road" are manifold and some scholars see the implication of this project beyond geopolitics. According to Chas W. Freeman, a senior fellow at Brown University's Watson Institute for International and Public Affairs, "A post-Bretton Woods global financial order is being born".[24] The new multilateral development bank, Asian Infrastructure Investment Bank (AIIB), which is devoted to the cause of the OBOR, is being viewed with scepticism by the USA and Japan, but it is being increasingly welcomed by many countries in Asia and Europe including India. Besides, there is a perception in the West that this could have a negative impact on the work of the World Bank and other institutions. Questions are also raised whether the AIIB, under China's "leadership", will meet international standards for granting loans to developing and emerging countries.[25]

The BRI concept, from the day it was first pronounced by the Chinese leadership, has been seen suspiciously and thus severely criticized by the USA and Japan. Experts in the USA have consistently maintained that the BRI is not only economically unviable but that it is a "debt-trap" for poor developing countries, especially in Africa. On the eve of the 2nd BRI World Forum, the *Financial Times* had published a feature article, in order to put pressure on the authorities in Beijing, by observing that several smaller countries have announced leaving BRI as they have been under mounting economic debt.[26] A week later, a similar scathing attack targeting BRI was carried in the *Wall Street Journal*, accusing Beijing of adopting unfair means in winning friends and favours in the recipient countries.[27] China, on the other hand, launched a counter-campaign both in the Chinese language and the English medium Chinese media agencies, defending the "win-win" goal for all as the ultimate goal of the BRI. On the same day as the *Financial Times* carried a frontal attack on the BRI, the Chinese ambassador to the USA, Mr. Cui Tiankai, denounced claims that the BRI was debt trap. "Some people have errantly characterized the BRI as a potential debt trap," Cui wrote in an article published on the *Fortune* magazine's website. "But countries who have participated in and benefited from the BRI have debunked such assertions", he emphasised.[28]

Chen Xiang and Wei Hong analyse the ramifications of the OBOR on local diplomacy.[29] According to them, the BRI has provided opportunities for China's local diplomacy but at the same time, China's local diplomacy is facing multiple problems due to the promotion of the BRI. They opine that there is a game and competition between the central government and the local government. They also admit that despite the fact that the OBOR strategy is destined to help the government's effort for strategic decentralization, there is a lack of professional qualities and innovative working mechanism to deal with the emerging political dynamics arising due to the OBOR. This article is more focused on the domestic administrative aspects in China; thus it helps in understanding the internal issues and their implication on the OBOR.

Liu Weidong first analyses the general background of the Belt and Road Initiative against economic globalization and the changing configurations of the world, and then discusses the Initiative's spatial connotation by revealing its regional and national characteristics.[30] This article points out that the Belt and Road Initiative is a national strategy, rather than a regional strategy, as it seeks to coordinate the all-around opening of China to the world and promotes further integration of the country with the global economy.

Yang Baojun, Chen Yixing, Lu Xiaobei and Zhu Yuyu attempt to study the 'internal structural adjusting' following the inception of the OBOR strategy and review the current strategies of national spatial development.[31] They argue that along with the implementation of the OBOR strategy, China's overall spatial development policies would be transformed from a one-way opening to a full opening, from fragmented land and ocean-oriented development to integrated development. They also examine the historical policy adjustments made by China and compare them with the present OBOR strategy.

On the other hand, from among the overseas scholars engaged in analysing the BRI, Michael D. Swaine discusses the relevance of the OBOR to Chinese policies and processes.[32] Swaine has used the English language writings published in Chinese newspapers and Chinese official websites to draw a map of Chinese perceptions about the OBOR. He opines that relatively few Chinese sources address the issue of the challenges and problems confronting the OBOR.

India vis-à-vis BRI

Historically, both India and China were connected with each other through the ancient Silk Route and both had prospered and shared their advancement and knowledge with the rest of the world. In the current scenario, India's geographical location in South Asia is very significant as it could be a link between 'SREB' and 'MSR' and of course a crucial juncture for China to realize its overall strategy of increasing its presence in the oceanic region. One can see the importance attached to India in the process of constructing the "One Belt One Road" (OBOR) initiative by and large due to the geopolitical significance India holds in the South Asian Region. Some observers have conceded that in the geographical regions encompassed by the OBOR Initiative, India was the only big country that has expressed hesitation in accepting the invitation from China. According to Chen Fei, China has been trying to align its national development strategy with the development strategies of other countries. But if one analyses the trajectory of the discourse in China, it is apparently clear that very little attention has been paid to the issue of India's concern regarding the China-Pakistan Economic Corridor (CPEC).

However, with India's consistent refusal to become a signatory to the OBOR Initiative, some Chinese scholars have been advocating 'ignore India' tactics. Moreover, they argue China need not pay undue attention to Indian participation in the Chinese road to globalization and instead pursue its own strategic implementation cautiously and carefully. Professor Xiao He, a senior researcher at the World Economics and Politics Research Centre of the China Social Science Academy, Beijing, has observed in an article in Chinese that "India is waiting for China to commit a mistake in realizing the OBOR strategy. Therefore, China much rather concentrate on its own efforts instead of counting on the Indian participation."[33] In other words, what professor Xiao He is advocating may be viewed as a significant shift in China's earlier position that Indian participation is crucial in the successful implementation of the OBOR strategy. The change in the Chinese stance on India's participation in the OBOR, therefore, renders India's joining or not joining a mere theoretical exercise. Does it mean China's "hardening" approach vis-à-vis India, as also the "rigidity" in the Indian position vis-à-vis China in the past year or so are the direct fallout of China's failure to win over India's support on the OBOR issue?

As there are widespread and extensive deliberations in China on India's OBOR participation, it would be interesting for Indian policy experts to see how China would convince India to join the OBOR Initiative. The narratives created in China on India's participation would certainly affect India's future role in the OBOR. Furthermore, despite there being differences in language, both Indian and Chinese discourses directly or indirectly make an impact on each other. Besides, the perceptions of both the countries also get modified due to the influence of non-Chinese and non-Indian discourse. Chinese understanding with regard to India's participation in many China-led initiatives, such as the SCO, the NDB, the AIIB, etc., despite the Indian indecisiveness on OBOR, could rightly be perceived as India's unaffordability to sideline China. In sharp contrast, however, in India, the same could be gauged as a policy dilemma. Narratives cannot remain unaffected from outside discourse. Thus, the objective examination of discourses developed in two different linguist realms for the same subject will have a great significance for coherent understanding.

Attempts have been made to consider India's 'Project Mausam' which promotes cooperation around the Indian Ocean region as a countermeasure to the OBOR initiative.[34] Comparisons are also drawn between China's OBOR and India's 'Project Mausam' both within and outside China. For example, some scholars in China see 'Project Mausam' as a roadblock for the successful implementation of OBOR. Feng Chuanlu even compares 'Project Mausam' with the 'Munroe Doctrine' and suggests that the restrictiveness of India's 'Project Mausam' severely limits space for Sino-Indian cooperation in linking the two initiatives.[35] Hence, strategic connectivity between the 'Belt and Road Initiative' and India's 'Project

Mausam' does not represent a viable policy option. But contrary to that, some scholars have advocated cohesion between these two projects and argued that through conceptual connectivity, functional connectivity, and cultural connectivity, China and India can avoid conflict, build consensus, and expand cooperation. The cooperation between the two Asian giants is not only beneficial to the progress of the OBOR initiative but will also promote regional economic cooperation.[36]

Yang Siling explores why India is hesitant in joining the OBOR Initiative.[37] According to Yang, India's ambiguity in joining the OBOR should not be seen as a roadblock to the success of the OBOR. He says that this kind of perception undermines rational thinking and is not beneficial for the healthy development of the China-India relationship. He protests against associating India's non-reciprocal act with non-cooperation. He gives insights into how Chinese scholars subjectively perceive that India's position is a manifestation of the Indian desire to become a world power and see China as a competitor.

Lin Minwang tries to study how the OBOR is perceived in Indian discourse and whether India should join the Initiative.[38] Lin also discusses the other aspect of the issues like the CPEC and Project Mausam and gives an idea of Chinese perception about India's position. It also gives a detailed analysis of the policy choices for China in the case of non-participation by India.

In Indian discourse also there is divergence in views on the question of joining the OBOR. The understanding of the OBOR in the Indian discourse has largely been revolving around the legitimacy and sovereignty issues regarding the China-Pakistan Economic Corridor (CPEC). As can be observed, in India, the majority of articles have mentioned the CPEC which runs across Pakistan-occupied-Kashmir as the primary issue for arguing the Indian opposition to joining the OBOR. Those who advocate for India joining the OBOR have mainly argued that this is a once-in-history opportunity to harness China's economic muscle for India's development. By joining the OBOR, India could invite Chinese investment in the Indian infrastructure development and India can use the connectivity which is created by the OBOR to increase trade and investment with other South Asian countries and, of course, with China.[39] An article in the *Economic and Political Weekly* even argues that India's opposition to the CPEC is flawed and geopolitics rather than geo-economics predominates India's thinking on the possibilities offered by the revival of the old Silk Road by the Chinese.[40] Alka Acharya, then director of the Institute of Chinese Studies (ICS), Delhi, noted in her keynote address delivered at the two-day international conference on "India, China and the New Silk Road Initiatives: Challenges and Opportunities" at the Mahatma Gandhi University, Kottayam, in Kerala, that "very low levels of mutual trust and confidence" between the two fastest developing countries are emerging as a big obstacle.[41]

Geethanjali Nataraj and Richa Sekhani argue for India's participation in the OBOR and claim that it will give a new start and a new bright spot in India-China cooperation as it will foster policy coordination, increase trade and investment and ensure people-to-people connections.[42] For India, MSR could prove to be a boon and help enhance its regional and bilateral cooperation. India does not have the same economic might that China has, but investing in neighbouring littoral countries will help in reducing China's sphere of influence to some extent.

Post COVID-19 World and BRI

The COVID-19 pandemic has added an altogether "novel" dimension to the discourse on the BRI both within and without China. While no one doubts the claim that COVID-19 is going to reshape the global order, opinion on its impact on the BRI seems to be varied or rather divided. Following China's claims of having contained the pandemic at home, the country is making all efforts to quickly restore its economic growth. In sharp contrast, world opinion is increasingly unanimous in proclaiming the 'death' of the BRI. Notwithstanding international opinion, the official media and scholars in China are emphatically advocating the view that the BRI will prove to be the driving engine for China's post-COVID-19 economic recovery. A well-researched paper released by the New York-based consultancy, Rhodium Group, predicts doom for China's most ambitious project yet. Based on reports that investment projects worth billions have been hit in Indonesia, Cambodia, Malaysia, Sri Lanka and Pakistan, Agatha Kratz, Rhodium Group report's author, has claimed that Beijing's global ambitions could be further hurt by domestic economic troubles being stirred by the pandemic, which are likely to limit the ability of Chinese financial institutions to splurge on overseas projects as they weigh between spending on domestic health and economic recovery and making loans abroad.[43] However, given China's past record of huge investments in overseas projects at the cost of economic inefficiency and economic non-sustainability, it cannot be ruled out that Beijing will continue to play the role of a saviour, especially when the USA seems to be ceding that role on President Trump's watch, said the report. "As the pandemic takes a toll on global economies and desperation sets in, Beijing could achieve the same or greater political goodwill even by spending less than in the past," claims the Rhodium Report. A joint blog written for the Council on Foreign Relations (CFR) also claims that "as the corona virus disease 2019 (COVID-19) pandemic spreads worldwide, the public health crisis and response will lay bare China's leadership aspirations as a great power. It is too soon to say precisely how the pandemic will change the broad contours of Chinese foreign policy, but it has already highlighted some of the frailties of the 'Belt' (BRI)—Xi Jinping's signature foreign policy agenda—to build traditional and digital infrastructure around the world."[44]

The Chinese, however, have refuted these claims and sound extremely firm and exude confidence that the BRI will lead China's post-COVID-19 economic recovery. Early in the deadly pandemic in mid-February, the Chinese foreign ministry spokesperson had ruled out any adverse impact on the goals and missions of the BRI. As Geng Shuang, spokesperson of China's Ministry of Foreign Affairs, puts it, "The outbreak has indeed posed a challenge to China's economy and foreign exchange. But it is only temporary. The Chinese economy has great resilience, potential and vitality. We appreciate and laud the political and material assistance from BRI partners after the pandemic broke out. We will continue to work with them for high-quality BRI cooperation."[45] More recently, Wang Linggui, senior research fellow and deputy director of the Institute of Intelligence and Information Research at the Chinese Academy of Social Science, Beijing, has noted, "the strong vigour of BRI construction has helped increase confidence and has provided direction and practical options for its partners during the global novel corona virus pandemic."[46]

Convinced that there is no way the Chinese economy or the BRI will not be affected by the prevailing pandemic as well as after the passing of COVID-19, an article in *The Diplomat* has commented, "Worse still, all the economies along BRI routes will find themselves in tatters in the wake of the outbreak. There will be an ever-growing demand for infrastructure in Eurasia and Africa, but already-limited available resources in recipient countries may evaporate altogether."[47] This article also casts doubts on the prospect of China getting its money back from BRI investments.[48] Citing lack of travel facilities for thousands of Chinese workers during the pandemic, writing in an Indian business newspaper, Dipanjan Roy Choudhury too expresses scepticism on the prospects of the BRI in the months ahead. Besides the problems faced by the Chinese workers stranded abroad or at home, "COVID-19 has also hampered China's manufacturing supply chains, and it is no secret that BRI projects are primarily reliant on Chinese, rather than local material and supplies".[49]

Critics of the BRI also point out that the project always made poor economic sense even before the global economy was hit by the COVID-19 pandemic. "This pandemic originating from China and leading to global recession may have spelt the death knell to the BRI."[50] One major problem for the Chinese government in the wake of the economic disaster following COVID-19 is that several beneficiary countries of the BRI project have now openly started criticising it. Countries such as Iran, Italy and Sri Lanka have accused the BRI projects in their countries for their devastated economies under the current circumstances. Even Pakistan, China's "all-weather friend" has started calling for a freeze of BRI projects in the country. Although the Pakistan government has repeatedly affirmed the country's full support to "friend" China in this hour of the COVID-19 crisis, there is a regular flow of reports which claim opposition to the ongoing CPEC is spiking in Pakistan. On 23 March 2020, a news report filed by the news agency ANI from Gilgit in Pakistan has claimed, "Political leaders from Gilgit Baltistan have called for an immediate end to China's One Belt One Road (OBOR) Initiative which they termed as the road on which the COVID-19 virus travelled to destroy not only Gilgit but large parts of the world."[51] Political activists in the region have also been demanding the closing of the border between China and Gilgit Baltistan as the number of corona virus infected patients with positive test reports has been on the rise.[52]

On the other hand, Italy, the only country in Europe to step aside from the rest of Europe and embrace the BRI most generously has now started critiquing BRI projects with its Prime Minister saying, "The Chinese initiative must...develop in an open and inclusive way, respecting the standards and principles enshrined in the EU strategy."[53] To the embarrassment of China, similar reports have been pouring in from all over from quite a few 'friendly' countries from Africa to South Asia to Brazil and other parts of the world. "For the past few years, what trended was One Belt, One Road (OBOR), the ambitious Chinese catchphrase to rope in 78 countries in its dream connectivity project for the economic domination of the world. Circa 2020, and two more words are added to that—one virus. Suddenly, Italy, Iran and others are realising that it is 'One Belt, One Road, and One Virus'."[54]

Since the outbreak of the pandemic, several Chinese commentators and scholars have supported the government outlook on the importance of the BRI's role in providing the much-needed impetus for China's quick economic recovery. These scholars reckon as the deadly pandemic has put the global economy as well as many individual countries to a severe test, China's performance in both overcoming the pandemic at home and in restoring its manufacturing has surprised the world. In addition, China's proactive measures in supplying medicines, medical equipment, and trained medical staff to several countries still reeling under the impact of the pandemic have earned China tremendous goodwill and positive acknowledgement. Some Chinese experts have even argued that these positive steps and goodwill will facilitate and further enhance China to reap the rich dividends it was enjoying from the previous BRI achievements, especially from the recipient countries. Though observers and China watchers have reacted with surprise, but there is definitely a large degree of resonance in the comments made by Professor Lan Shunzheng of the prestigious Charhar Institute in Beijing—considered close to the authorities. He has displayed remarkable optimism for the BRI by saying the New Health Silk Road would help China to emerge stronger out of the COVID-19 crisis. "It is true due to COVID-19 there will be some degree of a temporary setback to carry forward the BRI plan. It is also true that, for example, cross-border travel and commerce are facing multiple hindrances, several smaller or poorer countries along the Belt and Road are feeling the tightening of nerves due to mounting debt and shrinking finances, and China too is finding it difficult to mobilize financial resources for the BRI projects, but quite a few countries who are themselves in the midst of the pandemic have not only noticed but also appreciated China's sincerity and goodwill gestures. These countries have become hopeful and are expecting China to help them out. Therefore, these countries will also in return be willing to throw away whatever apprehensions they harbour and will not hesitate in coming forward and cooperate with China in carrying out China's BRI obligations smoothly."[55]

Besides, Professor Da Wei, a well-respected US specialist and Dean of International Studies at Beijing's elite University for International Relations (UIR), in an ICS webinar on 29 April 2020 said, "With the passage of time, the world will realize more and more the need for cooperation between and among nations to jointly fight the pandemic. This is so because there are no winners in this crisis. This is the first-ever global crisis in the genuine sense of the term."[56] Professor Da Wei underlined the unique dimension of the currently ongoing health crisis. He called the pandemic unique as, unlike in the past, this is for the first time that a pandemic has hit almost the entire world's population. The element of uniqueness also must be acknowledged because the world facing a global crisis had never been as closely interconnected and interdependent as in present times, he said. Viewing the BRI in this unique context, Professor Da Wei emphasized that since the world can emerge victorious from the current crisis only by cooperating with each other, therefore, as the world economy searches for a cooperation template, it will be well served by the BRI.[57]

To sum up, while foreign analysts have been consistently pointing out several inherent weaknesses—such as lack of transparency, economic non-sustainability, no accountability and, above all, no safety mechanisms to bail out mounting debt on the part of the recipient countries—in the manner in which the strategy was conceptualized, the biggest challenge facing China's most ambitious project is how to carry on with the extravagant projects under COVID-19 hit conditions. The critical voices at home questioning doling out money to economically weak countries are only making it worse for the authorities in Beijing. "The fact remains that the virus originated in China and the pandemic spread got initial boost due to China's poor handling, which has put the global economy on ventilator, thereby further jeopardising large extravagant BRI projects. To borrow from current medical jargon, there were pre-existing conditions and morbidities in the BRI. COVID-19 has just come at an inopportune time. In that sense, this virus may have just drained the water from the swimming pool revealing that many were simply swimming naked!"[58]

NOTES

1. Xi Jinping. "弘扬人民友谊共创美好未来" (Promoting the friendship for a better future), http://news.xinhuanet.com/world/2013-09/08/c_117273079_2.htm
2. Xi Jinping. "携手建设中国－东盟命运共同体" *Renshoujianshezhongguo-dongmengmingyungongtongti* (Come together to build a China-ASEAN community of common destiny) http://news.xinhuanet.com/world/2013-10/03/c_117591652_3.htm
3. Li Keqiang. "共同开创亚洲发展新未来" *Gongtongkaichuanyazhoufazhanxinweilai* (Jointly Open up New Vistas for Asia's Development) http://politics.people.com.cn/n/2014/0411/c1024-24876627.html
4. Xiang Debao. "One Belt, One Road: China's reconstruction for global communication and international discourse power", *The Newsletter (*International Institute for Asian Studies), 74, Summer 2016.
5. 金鑫 Jin Xin, "序 1" *Xu 1* (Preface One) in《融合与创新："一带一路" 软力量建设研究》*Rongheyuchuangxin : "yidaiyilu"ruanliliangjiansheyanjiu* (Integration and Innovation: A Study of Chinese Soft Power in the Belt and Road Initiative, 主编：周停王润珏 edited by Zhou Ting and Wang Runjue, 中国传媒大学出版社 Communication University of China Press, Beijing, June 2017.
6. Ibid., Preface 1.
7. 刘码 Liu Ma,《中国国际关系与外交理论前沿：探索与发展》*Zhongguoguojiguanxiyuwai-jiaolilunqianyan : tansuoyufazhan* (China's IR and Diplomacy Theoretical Front: Scope and Development) 上海社会科学文献院 Shanghai Social Science Documents Press, Shanghai, 2016.
8. Zhang Yongli and Hu Dandan, "一带一路": 国内文献综述——基于实践的角度" (Domestic Literature Review on "One Belt And One Road"-Based on a Practical Perspective), 财经理论研究., *Journal of Finance and Economics Theory*, 2016, 年 05 期, pp. 38-45.
9. Habib, Benjamin and Faulknor, Victor, "The Belt and Road Initiative: China's Vision for Globalization, Beijing Style," *In Conversation*, May 2017, https://theconversation.com/the-belt-and-road-initiative-chinas-vision-for-globalisation-beijing-style-77705, viewed in April 2020.
10. Ibid. To further understand how Europe will be benefitted from the BRI strategy, see Frans-Paul van der Putten, John Seaman, Mikko Huotari, Alice Ekman and Miguel otero-Lglesias (eds.) "Europe and China's New Silk Roads," December 2016, https://www.clingendael.org/sites/default/files/pdfs/Europe_and_Chinas_New_Silk_Roads_0.pdf, viewed in April 2020;

Georgiana Boboc, "The Belt and Road Initiative: China's Soft Power Strategy," in *China Daily*, June 2017, https://www.chinadaily.com.cn/opinion/2017beltandroad/2017-06/05/content_29618551.htm, viewed in April 2020.

11. 张缊岭 Zhang Yunling, 如何认识"一带一路"的大战略设计 *Ruherenshi "yidaiyilu" de da zhanluesheji* (Understanding the grand strategic design of 'One Belt One Road') in 《中国周边安全形势评估》 *Zhongguozhoubiananquanxingshepinggu* (*China's Regional Security Environment Review*, edited by 张洁 Zhang Jie, Beijing Social Science Documentation Press, p. 31. Viewed in January 2015.
12. 温铁军 Wen Tiejun: 用"一带一路"把过剩的产能转移出去 *Yong "yidaiyilu"baguoyu de channengzhuanyichuqu* ("OBOR" to Drive China's Excessive Production into the Outside World) January 24, 2017, https://v.qq.com/x/page/x0369wzfe8o.html, viewed in January 2017; Also see 冯并 Feng Bing, 《"一带一路"：全球发展的中国逻辑》 *"Yidaiyilu": Quanqiufazhan de zhongguoluoji* (One Belt and One Road: The Chinese Logic for Global Development), 中国民主法制出版社 Beijing, China Democracy Press 2015; 赵磊 Zhao Lei, 《"一带一路": 中国文明的崛起 *"Yidaiyilu": Zhongguowenming de jueqi* (One Belt One Road: China's Civilizational Rise), 中信出版社 China Trust Press ,Beijing, 2016, p. 283.
13. Simon Shen, "OBOR and the Marshall Plan" *China Policy Institute Analysis* https://cpianalysis.org/2016/10/11/obor-and-the-marshall-plan/
14. 王义桅 Wang Yiwei, "一带一路"绝非中国版"马歇尔计划" *"Yidaiyilu" juefeizhongguo ban "mashaerjihua"* (One Belt One Road is by no means A Chinese Version of Marshall Plan), *Qiushi*. 16.06.2015, http://world.people.com.cn/n/2015/0616/c1002-27163312.html, viewed in June 2017.
15. Junhua Zhang, What's driving China's One Belt, One Road initiative?', *East Asia Forum*, September 2, 2016, http://www.eastasiaforum.org, viewed in December 2019.
16. Lucio Blanco Pitlo III. "China's 'One Belt One Road' to where?" *The Diplomat*, 17 February 2015, http://thediplomat.com/2015/02/chinas-one-belt-one-road-to-where/
17. Hong Yu. "Motivation behind China's 'One Belt, One Road' Initiatives and Establishment of the Asian Infrastructure Investment Bank", *Journal of Contemporary China*, Published online: 1 November 2016. http://www.tandfonline.com/doi/full/10.1080/10670564.2016.1245894?src=recsys
18. Shaun Breslin, 'China and the global order: signalling threat or friendship?' *International Affairs* 89 (3), 2013, pp. 615–634.
19. Hong Yu. "Motivation behind China's 'One Belt, One Road' Initiatives and Establishment of the Asian Infrastructure Investment Bank", *Journal of Contemporary China*, Published online: 1 November 2016, http://www.tandfonline.com/doi/full/10.1080/10670564.2016.1245894?src=recsys
20. Michael Clarke. "Understanding China's Eurasian Pivot", *The Diplomat*, September 10, 2015. http://thediplomat.com/2015/09/understanding-chinas-eurasian-pivot/
21. Debalina Ghoshal. "China Pivots to the Middle East and Iran Thursday", *Yale Global Online*, July 7, 2016, http://yaleglobal.yale.edu/content/china-pivots-middle-east-and-iran
22. Lan Xinxiang. "The New Silk Road: Spinning A New and Ambitious Narrative" *Montrose Journal*. Winter 15 http://www.montroseassociates.biz/article.asp?aid=103
23. Ibid.
24. Chas W. Freeman. "China and the Economic Integration of Europe and Asia", Remarks at the Summer Roundtable of the Pacific Pension Institute at San Francisco, California. http://www.mepc.org/articles-commentary/speeches/china-and-economic-integration-europe-and-asia
25. Patrick Bessler, "China's AIIB: Competition for Bretton Woods or an opportunity for Asia?"

EU-ASIA Economic Governance Forum, http://www.kas.de/wf/doc/kas_43917-1522-2-30.pdf?160401025345

26. Hornby, Lucy and Zhang, Archie, “Belt and Road debt trap accusations hound Beijing as it hosts forum,” April 24, 2019 https://www.ft.com/content/3e9a0266-6500-11e9-9adc-98bf1d35a056, viewed in April 2020. Also see Deborah Bautigram, “Is China the World’s loan Shark,” *New York Times*, April 26, 2019 https://www.nytimes.com/2019/04/26/opinion/china-belt-road-initiative.html, viewed in April 2020.
27. Taplin, Nathaniel, “One Belt, One Road, and a lot of debt,” 2 May 2019, https://www.wsj.com/articles/one-belt-one-road-and-a-lot-of-debt-11556789446, viewed in April 2020. Also see Wezhen Tan, “China’s loans to other countries are causing hidden debt. That maybe a problem,” June 11, 2019, https://www.cnbc.com/2019/06/12/chinas-loans-causing-hidden-debt-risk-to-economies.html, viewed in April 2020.
28. “Chinese ambassador to U.S. denounces claims BRI is debt trap,” *Xinhua News*, April 24, 2019, http://www.xinhuanet.com/english/2019-04/24/c_138004514.htm, viewed in April 2020. Also see Ranaraja, Yasiru and Majueran, Maya, “Is the ‘Health Silk Road’ a ‘debt-trap’ of China’s BRI for Sri Lanka,” *China Global Television Network,* April 25, 2020, https://news.cgtn.com/news/2020-04-25/Is-the-Health-Silk-Road-a-debt-trap-of-China-s-BRI-for-Sri-Lanka—PXqPCPd7Ta/index.html, viewed in April 2020; Yingqun, Chen, “BRI not ‘debt trap’ but a boost for world trade,” *China Daily,* June 12, 2019 http://www.chinadaily.com.cn/a/201906/12/WS5d005e6fa310176577230b4e.html, viewed in April 2020.
29. Chen Xiang and Wei Hong, “一带一路”建设视野下的中国地方外交” (China’s Local Diplomacy under the Perspective of the “Belt and Road” Initiative), 国际观察 [*International Review*, 2016 Issue No. 6, pp. 31-43.
30. Liu Weidong, ““一带一路”战略的科学内涵与科学问题” (Scientific understanding of the Belt and Road Initiative of China and related research themes), 地理科学进展, *Progress in Geography*, 2015, Issue No. 5, pp. 538-544.
31. Yang Baojun, Chen Yixing, Lu Xiaobei and Zhu Yuyu, “一带一路”战略的空间响应” (Spatial Response to the “One Belt and One Road” Strategy), 城市规划学刊 Urban Planning Forum, 2015, Issue No. 2, pp. 6-23.
32. Michael D. Swaine, “Chinese Views and Commentary on the “One Belt, One Road” Initiative”, https://www.hoover.org/sites/default/files/research/docs/clm47ms.pdf
33. Xiao He. 印度坐等中国犯错，“一带一路”在南亚成功的关键是中国自己 (India Awaits China to Commit an Error: The Key to OBOR Success in South Asia is None Other Than China Itself), April 16, 2015 http://www.thepaper.cn/newsDetail_forward_1320397
34. Chen Fei. “‘一带一路’ 与印度 “季风计划” 的战略对接研究” (On Strategic Connectivity between the OBOR Initiative and India’s Mausam Project), *Global Review*, 2015, Vol. 6, p. 16.
35. Feng Chuanlu. “一带一路”与“季风计划”战略对接:有效政策选项抑或伪命题” (Strategic Connectivity between Belt & Road Initiative and Project Mausam :Viable Policy Option or Untenable Proposition?), *South Asian Studies*, 2016, p. 55.
36. Yang Hong, “‘一带一路’ 和印度 ‘季风计划’应有效对接” (“One Belt One Road” and the Indian “Project Mausam” should be effective docking), *China Economic Review,* 6.8.2016.
37. Yang Siling, “印度如何看待一带一路下的中印关系” (On How India Views Sino-Indian Relations under the “One Belt One Road” Initiative), *学术前沿,, Frontiers,* 2015, Issue No. 9, pp. 37-50.
38. Lin Minwang, “印度对 ‘一带一路’的认知及中国的政策选择” (Indian perceptions of ‘One Belt, One Road’ and China’s Policy Choices), *世界经济与政治, World Economics and Politics,* 2015, Issue No. 5, pp. 42-57.

39. Premshankar Jha. "Why India Must Embrace China's One Belt One Road Plan", *The Wire*, 13.8.2016, https://thewire.in/58810/india-must-embrace-chinas-one-belt-one-road-plan/
40. Atul Bhardwaj. "India's Opposition to China–Pakistan Economic Corridor Is Flawed", *Economic and Political Weekly*, 2017, Vol. 52, Issue No. 4, p. 10.
41. Alka Acharya, "Mutual Trust Low Between India, China", *The Hindu* (Kottayam) November 12, 2016, http://www.thehindu.com/news/national/kerala/%E2%80%98Mutual-trust-low-between-India-China%E2%80%99/article16443237.ece
42. Geethanjali Nataraj and Richa Sekhani, "China's One Belt One Road-An Indian Perspective", *Economic and Political Weekly*, Vol. 50, Issue No. 49, 5 December, 2015.
43. Kartz, Agatha, "Corona virus could force China to rein in Belt and Road Ambitions," April 17, 2020, see https://www.dw.com/en/coronavirus-could-force-china-to-rein-in-belt-and-road-ambitions/a-53159033, viewed in April 2020.
44. Lancaster Kirk, Rubin Michael and Rapp-Hooper Mira, "What the COVID-19 Pandemic May Mean for China's Belt and Road Initiative," March 17, 2020, https://www.cfr.org/blog/what-covid-19-pandemic-may-mean-chinas-belt-and-road-initiative, viewed in April 2020.
45. People's Daily online, "COVID-19 Myth Busters: Will the epidemic affect China's trade, cooperation projects, and cultural exchanges with BRI countries?" February 19, 2020 http://en.people.cn/n3/2020/0219/c90000-9659402.html, viewed in April 2020.
46. Xinhua News Agency, "Belt and Road extends amid mutual support, solidarity of co-builders," April 25, 2020, http://en.people.cn/n3/2020/0425/c90000-9683857.html, viewed in April 2020.
47. Tonchev, Plamen, "The Belt and Road after COVID-19," April 7, 2020, https://thediplomat.com/2020/04/the-belt-and-road-after-covid-19/, viewed in April 2020.
48. Ibid.
49. Roy Chaudhury, Dipanjan, "COVID-19 pandemic puts brakes on Chinese projects," April 6, 2020, https://economictimes.indiatimes.com/news/international/world-news/covid-19-pandemic-puts-brakes-on-chinese-projects/articleshow/75017723.cms?from=mdr, viewed in April 2020.
50. Gautam Pradeep Singh, "Can China's Belt-and-Road-Initiative Survive COVID-19?" April 21, 2020, https://www.news18.com/news/opinion/opinion-can-chinas-belt-and-road-initiative-survive-covid-19-2587113.html, viewed in April 2020.
51. "Gilgit and PoK leaders seek immediate end to China's OBOR," March 23, 2020, *ANI*, https://www.aninews.in/news/world/asia/covid-19-gilgit-and-pok-leaders-seek-immediate-end-to-chinas-obor20200323075941/, viewed in April 2020.
52. Ibid.
53. Ibid.
54. *Just Earth News*, "One Belt, One Road, One Virus: How Italy, Iran follow China's OBOR path to Perdition," March 23, 2020 https://www.justearthnews.com/economy-details/423/one-belt-one-road-one-virus-how-italy-iran-follow-china-s-obor-path-to-perdition.html, viewed in April 2020.
55. 兰顺正 Lan Shunzheng, 中国抗疫表现有利于“一带一路”的发展 (China's anti-epidemic performance will act as big incentive to future growth of BRI) April 28, 2020 http://www.ftchinese.com/story/001087444?adchannelID=&full=y, viewed in April 2020.
56. Da Wei, "COVID-19 and Sino-US Relations: The Sputnik Moment," ICS Webinar, April 29, 2020, https://soundcloud.com/user-728282248/covid-19-and-china-us-relations-is-it-the-sputnik-moment
57. Ibid.
58. Roy Chaudhury, Dhananjay, Ibid.

SECTION II

BRI in India's Neighbourhood

4

China's BRI Making Inroads as India Increased its Connectivity Corridors in South Asia

Sreeradha Datta

Introduction

Connectivity infrastructure has become the cornerstone of regional and global growth this decade. Nation-states have been engaged in building new infrastructure to create a cobweb of connections both within and outside their borders. Regional growth was spurred through connectivity and economic corridors. Three of the six largest economies in Asia today, China, Japan and India with varied political systems and different growth stories, are also deeply invested in the development of connectivity infrastructure regionally. The relatively new thrust on building connectivity corridors in Asia has been affected by notions of competition as against seeking a common platform for advancing similar goals of growth and development. While the connectivity corridor projects are being developed in similar geographical spaces, none of the planned corridors is dovetailing into each other's projects. It essentially points to the political environment being unsupportive of such endeavours. The rivalry gets more etched in South Asia, in the face of China's growing engagement with the region.

China's Belt and Road Initiative has projected in network of transport and economic corridors across the globe with a strong presence in South Asia too. The BRI is essentially an economic and transport corridor that proposes to link Asia with Africa and Europe through multimodal infrastructure including railways, ports and energy grids. Interestingly, a critical component of China's "New Silk Road" initiative is the China Pakistan Economic Corridor (CPEC) which passes through Gilgit-Baltistan in what is known as Pakistan occupied Kashmir (PoK). This, of course, has serious implications for India and how it views China's BRI.

China building roads and other infrastructural projects in South Asia is not a new phenomenon. Its engagement with the region has seen a focus on supporting such projects in several of the states of Bangladesh, Nepal, Sri Lanka, Pakistan and the Maldives. Much of China's sustained bilateral relationships in this region have centred on building and helping develop roads, bridges, ports and other physical infrastructure that these states required. The BRI now takes that a step forward by linking many of these projects and weaving them into a cross-border cobweb across South Asian borders. This chapter essentially argues that China's ambition in South Asia is not a recent phenomenon. The renewed attempt through the BRI is a reinforcement of those ties and establishing a deeper presence in the region. It also argues that India always harboured apprehensions about China's motives in the region and the completion of the CPEC was a reinforcement of how India viewed China and its BRI project. It also examines how China is able to offer several advantages in the South Asia region, and often India pales in comparison, even though India is also deeply engaged with building a cobweb of transport corridors in the region. This chapter will conclude with the understanding that while China has certainly greater wherewithal, given its economic strength and political system, India has many advantages in the neighbourhood. Regional growth was spurred through connectivity and economic corridors. But the one that has captured the attention and created a stir both within the South Asia region and every other region far and wide has been that of China's Belt and Road Initiative (BRI). The proposed BRI spreads across continents and regions, involving the largest number of states in the history of any such initiative. Undoubtedly, the reactions and response to this have been varied. It is essentially a unilateral initiative that is going to be executed bilaterally in the member-countries. As it appears, several of the states invited to be a part of this process have largely acquiesced, and states in South Asia too have been drawn into the grandiose plans. In this region, the BRI reflects the growing Sino-Indian competition.

BRI in South Asia

The Second Belt and Road Forum for International Cooperation titled 'Working together to deliver a Brighter Future for Belt and Road Cooperation", held in Beijing in April 2019, was attended by 36 heads of state and government, along with 5,000 other representatives from different countries and 90 members of international organisations. As has been pointed out, unlike the triumphalism that marked the first forum in 2017, this time there was a clear element of defensiveness in China's position. It was amply reflected in Xi Jinping's various speeches on the occasion where he came up with new promises to emphasise 'quality development', 'innovation', 'science', 'green', 'multi-culturalism' and 'sustainability'.[1]

China, over the years, has attempted to create trade and transport corridors with South Asia. Beginning with the Kunming Initiative through the south-western province of Yunnan connecting it with West Bengal through the route from Kunming, linking India, Myanmar and Bangladesh, it has attempted to revive the ancient Southern silk route. This renamed as the Kolkata to Kunming (K2K) initiative, largely being discussed at track one-and-a-half level without much positive movement forward, was subsequently subsumed under the larger connectivity corridor of Bangladesh, China, India and Myanmar (BCIM) discussions. Simultaneously, China has been engaging closely with the other South Asian neighbours and supporting many of the infrastructural developments, apart from defence and other aspects, in the region. This included Bangladesh, Sri Lanka, the Maldives and Nepal.

Sri Lanka

Certainly, China providing US$ 7 billion in loans, including for the construction of a Sri Lankan port in Hambantota has been one of the most talked-about projects, given that Colombo in 2017 was forced to hand over the lease of the underused port to a Chinese company for 99 years. Despite that, China has also been working on the land reclamation project for the Colombo port city and, as is known, China has extended the largest loans securing contracts to build roads, railways and ports. China is also engaged in defence cooperation with Sri Lanka too. In June 2019, China donated security equipment worth 187,000 USD to the Sri Lankan parliament. In July 2019, China donated a frigate "P625" to the Sri Lankan Navy. It is noteworthy in this context that India had also given Sri Lanka advanced offshore patrol vessels (AOPVs) SLNS *Sayurala* (P623) and SLNS *Sindurala* (P624) in 2017 and 2018, respectively. This AOPV built in the Goa shipyard is one of the most advanced ships in the Sri Lankan Navy fleet.

The Maldives

The Maldives, a middle-income country, with tourism and fisheries sectors contributing largely to its economy, has in the past few years been faced with a huge debt crisis with its current account deficit in the range of 16.1 per cent. Male was made to agree to interest rates on concessional loans between 1.5 and 2 per cent, and around 6 to 7 per cent for those loans under sovereign guarantee from China in lieu of the large infrastructural developments planned for the Maldives. These projects included the four-lane Sinamale Bridge linking Male to Hulhule Island, and a massive housing project on Hulhumale for which China gave an invoice for US$ 3.2 billion. Indeed, as per a recent IMF report, managing the rising public debt would be Male's main challenge in the days to come.

As has been brought out by its President, Ibrahim Mohamed Solih, former president Abdulla Yameen's ambitious plan allowed for China to portray its Maldivian projects as an example of how the BRI can be successfully implemented in smaller states.[2] While Solih has been trying to renegotiate many of these projects, it is clear that China has become a key player in this island nation.

Bangladesh

In Bangladesh, as part of the BRI, China has founded 81 education establishments and 35 cultural centres and spent around USD 39.3 million on Silk Road scholarships in the first half of 2018.[3] Under the BRI projects, Bangladesh will receive USD 26 billion for BRI projects and USD 14 billion for joint venture projects, together totalling to a USD 40 billion package[4] and specifically for Bangladesh beyond creating large scale infrastructure for the transport and energy sectors, the BRI also provides opportunities for further engagements with governments, private sector and civil society entities as well as think tanks and academia.[5] Development of the Confucius Institute at Dhaka University and the Tier-4 National Data Centre in Gazipur's Kaliakoir were some of the projects decided under the BRI. Chinese portfolio investment in the Bangladesh stock market and Bangladesh's opportunity to access China's equity (globally the second largest) and bond markets (globally the third largest) through this initiative hold great promise as many see it.[6] Most of the Chinese investments in Bangladesh come through soft Chinese loans, with interest rates of 2 per cent and repayment periods of 20 years.[7] The Chinese investments stand at 85.94 million dollars and 380 million in terms of stock in 2018 with engineering contracts signed between Bangladesh and Chinese companies reaching $ 10.4 billion.[8] While Bangladesh's external debt now stands at about $ 25 billion with a debt-to-GDP ratio of about 27 per cent, Bangladeshis presently seem sanguine about the BRI project. Experts have also argued that although 'Bangladesh carries about USD 8 billion in Chinese debt and has a close military relationship, purchasing many of its latest weapons systems from China,' it will be an unlikely source of anxiety.[9] But a note of caution is introduced about connectivity facilitating the greater movement of goods from China to Bangladesh, invariably aggravating the existing trade imbalance.[10]

Myanmar

For Myanmar, China will be the most important player in its economy and trade, and the recent developments in the Rakhine region have buttressed not only China's influence in Myanmar, but has also led the international community to censure Myanmar. On a recent visit by President Xi to Myanmar, the two sides signed 33 agreements shoring up key projects within the BRI.[11] Myanmar is involved in two out of six BRI corridors unveiled by China. Its initiative in Myanmar also runs through the land corridor of Bangladesh-China-India-Myanmar, and the maritime China-Indo-China Peninsula corridor. Aung San Suu Kyi, Myanmar's State Counsellor's statement that "Myanmar welcomes China's Belt and Road Initiative and the move to establish the Bangladesh-China-India-Myanmar Economic Corridor[12] clearly indicated the leadership's eagerness to join the project. The inevitability of the process was clear when others including economist U Zaw Pe Win agreed that Myanmar could not avoid joining the BRI but urged caution to negotiate deals that will be to the country's benefit saying these 'are good proposals if they are implemented well.'[13] This agreement, without a doubt, deepens the bilateral engagement. In the words of Zhu Zhenming, a professor at the Yunnan Academy of Social Sciences, this has entailed Myanmar fully embracing China's help 'to deal with its domestic economic challenges and rising global pressure.'[14]

Given the spate of joint projects, China's plans and ambitions in Myanmar are unlikely to face any opposition. On the contrary, while the leadership may be happy to sign up with China at a popular level, there are several issues surrounding the nature of China's engagement in Myanmar.

Nepal

Nepal also has been drawn into the BRI. Indeed, President Xi visit to Nepal in 2019, a first by any Chinese president after 1996, resulted in 18 memorandums of understanding and two letters of exchange. The most important MoU was on conducting a feasibility study of the China-Nepal cross-border railway project that connects Kathmandu to Jilong, a border town of the Tibet autonomous region of China.[15] Earlier, during his visit to Nepal, Shu Ya, founder of the One Belt One Road (OBOR) International Trade and Investment Platform, identified such areas of cooperation for investment purposes in Nepal as infrastructure development, commercial farming, energy, tourism, international trade and investment sectors. The Chinese have opened a commercial counsellor's office in Kathmandu to facilitate the work on Chinese-funded projects in Nepal.[16]

Pakistan

As mentioned earlier, the China Pakistan Economic Corridor is an essential component of the BRI project. As is well known, the China-Pakistan Economic Corridor has been touted as a "game-changer" for Pakistan's economy. Four years since launching, its implementation faces serious challenges, and the future course remains uncertain.[17]

Many of the above reflect the Chinese ambition in South Asia. While there are some apprehensions in Sri Lanka and the Maldives, elsewhere in Myanmar, Nepal and Bangladesh the prospects of BRI have been well received. Chinese engagement is distinct and likely to find greater depth in the region. Indeed, as a study reveals, China is greatly invested in the region:

> In the past decade, China has invested or committed more than $ 150 billion in the economies of Bangladesh, the Maldives, Myanmar, Pakistan, Nepal and Sri Lanka. China is now the largest overseas investor in the Maldives, Myanmar, Pakistan and Sri Lanka. Chinese penetration is the highest in the two economies that flank India—Myanmar and Pakistan—where Chinese money is bolstering governments that face international isolation due to human rights violations and terrorism, respectively. Bangladesh, the most vibrant economy in India's neighbourhood, is least dependent on China. China's playbook is clear: It first enters as a military supplier, then cultivates and partners with local elites, provides a modern infrastructure with deferred payments, and entrenches itself. Chinese investment is concentrated in hard infrastructure—power, roads, railways, bridges, ports and airports. In most cases, the contractors building these projects are Chinese. In many cases, the only capital available to fund these projects is also Chinese. Beyond hard infrastructure, China is thinking geo-economics. It is investing in the financial systems of these countries. Beijing has taken stakes in the Dhaka and Karachi stock exchanges and cultivated a Yuan trade between China and Pakistan. It is establishing China-based courts for arbitration of BRI disputes. Clearly, Beijing seeks to create new rules, governing business and financial systems in the region—changes that could cement its dominance in India's neighbourhood.[18]

While China's BRI proposals see greater visibility in the region, India has not lagged behind. There may be a difference in the size and expanse, but unlike the Chinese model, Indian projects have no debt issue inherent in it for the neighbours. India has been building many of these cross-border projects through grants and concessional loans which do not load its neighbours with undue debt.

India's Position on BRI

Drawing closer to the grand event of a conference on One Belt One Road in Beijing in 2016, there were several media reports about China and Pakistan encouraging India to join the OBOR meeting, more specifically the CPEC initiative, leaving aside "politics". There is clarity in their positions, and naturally so. But what about the Indian position and its options? Should it join or be isolated from Asia's grandest project? A certain section in India suggested that not joining the largest economic corridor that brings the world to your doorstep is hardly an option. Apparently, having missed out many such opportunities in the region and elsewhere has not been without a significant price for India. Political differences have not come in the way of China becoming India's largest trade partner so why stay out of OBOR, is a typical argument doing the rounds, since it appears to be a win-win situation for all partners. India preferred to stay out. The reasons were clear.

But apart from the CPEC, it is useful to briefly examine the ground realities. Despite the recent low record of growth, India has been on an economic and political high, especially with the re-election of PM Modi. An annual growth rate of 7 per cent, implementations of 'Make in India' proposals, domestic reforms galore, alongside an unprecedented foreign policy outreach undertaken by Prime Minister Narendra Modi himself, has given India a new standing in the global order.

And all this despite any of the proposed regional economic corridors taking off the ground from their drawing or discussion boards. The BCIM, BIMSTEC and TAPI are just some of the few connectivity projects that India is engaged in, both in the South Asian region and outside. Certainly, all these initiatives will, at some point, come together along with Asian Highway projects to form the largest web of roads, rail and waterways that the world would have witnessed. Of course, the one with some immediate potential was the Bangladesh-Bhutan-India-Nepal (BBIN) Motor Vehicle Act that was to facilitate free movement of goods and services sub-regionally, but that ran into obstacles from environmentally sensitive Bhutan due to its ecological implications.

So, while the BRI is a substantial project, it is not the only economic corridor traversing the region that India can hope to benefit from. More importantly, it's a plan drawn up by China who now wishes to sell it to all its friends and well-wishers. How does India see itself in that group? The bilateral economic cooperation between the two Asian powers was supposed to lead the way to resolve some of their outstanding political differences. But far from being resolved, political differences are, in fact, increasing over the CPEC, Dalai Lama, and other issues of strategic import to India.

The BRI was imagined, planned and designed to be executed completely by China. Thus, in its present conceptualisation, this proposal had very little appeal for India. As seen from India, China's apparent unilateral top-down impositional approach with very little transparency or clarity in the entire initiative is insupportable.

India's Planned Connectivity Projects

From Look East to Act East

This apart, India has also initiated several connectivity projects in the neighbourhood of both South Asia and Southeast Asia. Most of this began with India's Look East Policy, launched in the early 1990s, deepening its ties with South-East Asia, especially ASEAN. However, it was argued that while India has been able to engage deeply with the Southeast Asia region, its physical connectivity has been tenuous. The same was equally true for South Asia. For long in this region, borders were viewed more as barriers than windows of opportunity and possibility and have long remained stagnant. With the maturing of the economies, it was reasoned that 'these economies need to remove border barriers to realise the full impact of integration.'[19] As also highlighted in a World Bank study, for South Asia to be a leading sub-region in global trade, it is essential for it to reduce the cost of doing business. The issue is the cost of transport—and time is a major component of that cost. Over the last few years, bilateral agreements on cross-border connectivity have taken place but have not extended to multilateral levels.

Although India's Look East policy was initiated in the 1990s, it has found greater significance in recent times and coincided perhaps with the suggestions of US secretary of state Hillary Clinton to India "not just to Look East, but to engage East and act East".[20] India's focus towards its east has been the precursor to many of its connectivity projects.

Connectivity with Bangladesh

India was also able to improve its bilateral ties with Bangladesh drastically post 2009 and reinforce its engagement with Myanmar in the same period. Thus, India's engagement with its eastern neighbours also opened the scope of increasing physical connectivity linkages.

India's land connectivity with Myanmar or Southeast Asia was only possible through its Northeast region. Thus, the issue of South-Southeast land border connectivity is directly linked to India's Northeast states with common borders with Myanmar and Bangladesh. Indeed, several of the connectivity projects of the region will also connect with the Asian Highway and the various Asian Development Bank projects that are underway.

It was with the return of democracy and the Sheikh Hasina-led Awami League to Dhaka that India and Bangladesh were able to take their engagements to unprecedented heights. Thus, the visit of Bangladeshi Prime Minister Sheikh Hasina to India in January 2010 opened up a panorama of cooperation. The joint communiqué that was signed during this visit was clearly a leap of faith taken together by the two neighbours. The Framework Agreement on Cooperation often cited as a 'game-changer'[21] indeed set the tone for the years ahead. Apart from many other bilateral issues covered, a cross-section of transport facilities, roadways, railways and ports leading to a web of transport connectivity was agreed upon. In the past, there were several cross-border road links, but the facilitation of road and railway transport systems would now be initiated through these agreements. The bilateral initiatives would, as envisaged, also lead to growing into a regional transport corridor. Some of the cross-border connectivity and trade agreements are listed below:

- Ashuganj in Bangladesh and Silghat (Assam) in India were going to be ports of call.
- India can use Mongla and Chittagong seaports for movement of goods to and from India through road and rail. Bangladesh would allow Nepal and Bhutan access to Mongla and Chittagong ports.
- India will assist in financing the construction of the proposed Akhaura–Agartala railway link, 14-km line. If this can be combined with road transit rights to India, the distance between Kolkata and Agartala will be shortened by 550 km.
- Bangladesh can now use the Rohanpur–Singabad broad gauge railway link for transit to Nepal. Bangladesh also planned to convert the Radhikapur–Birol railway line to broad gauge.
- India will fully support the Bangladesh government with its project of dredging rivers for better flood control, navigation and access to ports.
- The land customs station in Muhurighat under Belonia subdivision in Tripura connecting with Feni Land Port in Bangladesh was inaugurated. Cement is a prime commodity of trade at this borderland port.
- Trucks from Bhutan and Nepal would be able to enter about 200 metres into Zero Point at Banglabandh at the Banglabandh-Phulbari land customs station.

- Land customs stations at Sabroom (India)-Ramgarh (Bangladesh) and Demagiri (India)-Thegamukh (Bangladesh) were also going to be operationalised soon.
- More border *haats* would be set up at selected areas.

In keeping with the spirit of creating greater transport connectivity, Bangladesh had earlier agreed to India using its waterways to Ashuganj river port for carrying food grains from Kolkata to Tripura. To recall, in one of the first agreements, Bangladesh had allowed the use of Ashuganj for a one-time transfer of Over Dimensional Cargo movement of its goods and other materials to the energy project at Palatana, Tripura. Earlier, in June 2015, India and Bangladesh signed the Coastal Agreement which allows goods to move by sea from Kolkata in West Bengal to Chittagong Port in Bangladesh, and renewed the Protocol on Inland Water Transit and Trade (PIWTT) indefinitely with additional ports of call and routes. [22]

Similarly, India has urged Bangladesh to use Kolkata and Haldia ports for transhipment of cargo. The initiative can make coastal shipping more cost-effective for bilateral trade, thereby shifting cargo from the costly land route, and create an opportunity for Bangladeshi garment exporters to reach European and American markets avoiding congestion at Chittagong port.[23]

Connectivity with Myanmar

India had also begun to work closely with Myanmar, with a visible thrust through greater engagement and provision of infrastructure support and other fiscal measures.

Beginning with the joint counter-insurgency Operation 'Golden Bird' launched by India and Myanmar conducted along the India-Myanmar border in the Northeastern state of Mizoram during 10–21 May 1995, India has travelled a long distance with Myanmar which also underwent dramatic domestic changes from being a tightly controlled military-led regime to initiating a façade of democratic norms. Indeed, India's ties with Myanmar improved substantially after Gen. Maung Aye's visit to New Delhi in 2000, the landmark visit by President U Thein Sein in October 2011 and the return visit by Prime Minister Manmohan Singh to Naypyitaw in May 2012, the first such visit in 25 years. These exchanges have fundamentally changed the context.[24] There were several projects that India planned with Myanmar, the Kaladan project being the largest and more significant than any other India has initiated at that time in its neighbourhood. The bulk of the assistance is grant-funded. That apart, it had also proposed the Trilateral

Highway Project, which is an East-West corridor connecting the Northeast with Myanmar and Thailand; the Rhi-Tiddim road.[25]

It was in 2008 that the Indian cabinet had approved the Kaladan Multi-Modal Transit Transport Project at an estimated cost of Rs. 535.91 crore. It would comprise the waterways component comprising Port and Inland Waterways Terminal (IWT) in April 2003 and the road component too. This delayed project seems moving towards completion soon. In the past (2001), India has built the 160-km Moreh-Tamu-Kalemyo-Kalewa (TKK) Friendship Road in Myanmar.

The trilateral highway connecting India, Myanmar and Thailand will connect with the Kaladan Multi-modal transit project that would link Kolkata port with landlocked Mizoram via Myanmar into economic highways with special economic zones. The main artery of the 2,800-km K (Kolkata)-2-K (Kunming) corridor is nearly ready. A stretch of less than 200 km from Kalewa to Monywa in Myanmar needs to be upgraded to an all-weather road apart from a short segment in India's Northeast region that also needs upgrading.

India, in the meantime, has decided to improve the 57 km of the old WW II Stilwell road from Lekhapani in Assam to Pangsu Pass on the Indo-Myanmar border, although the roads on the Myanmar side too would need to be restored to make them operational.

BBIN and BIMSTEC

Bilateral connectivity corridors aside, India has pursued two regional initiatives in its neighbourhood. The sub-grouping of Bangladesh, Bhutan, India and Nepal (BBIN) will introduce seamless cross-border trade and transportation by the signing of the Motor Vehicles Agreement, although Bhutan has held back for the time being because of environmental concerns, but the three other states are going ahead and will start operations shortly. The other regional organisation on which the Modi government has expended considerable focus is BIMSTEC (The Bay of Bengal Initiative for Multi-Sectoral Technical and Economic Cooperation). Dormant for over two decades, it has now been infused with a fresh lease of life. BIMSTEC comprises five South Asian states—Bangladesh, Bhutan, India, Nepal and Sri Lanka—and two Southeast Asian neighbours, Myanmar and Thailand. Clearly, India is keen to make this organisation effective as it is suitably poised to complement Indian efforts to increase its physical linkages with Southeast Asia.

India will be able to establish greater linkages with ASEAN and South Asia through these initiatives along with trade integration through ASEAN + India FTA and bilateral FTAs such as India-Singapore, India-Malaysia, including the service sector and eventually the agricultural sector. India has been keen to establish trade linkages and connectivity between the regions through land borders, maritime routes and air connections. But there has been some laggardness in the efforts as well. Interestingly, India took the initiative for connecting Raxaul-Kathmandu by railway only after Nepal made an agreement with China for its construction. In fact, India rushed its railway construction in Nepal according priority to the construction of the Raxaul-Kathmandu railway line which is estimated to cover a distance of 113 km.[26] It is clear that with these various connectivity projects and other bilateral agreements in the neighbourhood, India wants to ensure its close engagement with its neighbours.

While many of the projects are underway and some have been successfully completed, India has been able to extend its connectivity projects in the immediate neighbourhood. Although many have been beset with delays, but once they are completed in a few years from now, the network will be functional and prove very beneficial to all the parties concerned. While implementation has always been a problem with India, China's engagement in the neighbourhood, barring Bangladesh, has felt the sting of debt crises. On the other hand, Indian projects have not faced any debt related problems.

Concerns over Debt Crises

The question of debt has been a growing concern within Myanmar, the Maldives and Sri Lanka and each state in its own way has been trying to balance their partnership with China. This apart, the lack of transparency and keeping the public in the dark about project details have created local fears in many of these countries. Apparently, there are no publicly available official documents on China-financed projects in these countries. And most of these states are not aware of many of the project details before they sign such agreements. Also, the creation of employment opportunities for many of the BRI projects is also ambiguous. It has been pointed out that many of these China-backed projects employ Chinese citizens in management positions, and that locals are used only for labour-intensive work.[27] In fact, the machinery and hardware employed for these projects are often of Chinese origin having instructions and manuals available in the Chinese language only, and therefore can only be used by Chinese personnel.

Another cautionary note was sounded about the usage of Chinese standards that are usually adopted for such projects. This, in fact, would ensure China's position as the sole exporter of infrastructural goods in Belt and Road countries, leaving no scope for regional and global competitors.[28]

Interestingly, the problem is more deep-rooted than the immediate one surrounding the BRI project only. As was pointed out by a former ambassador, 'Pakistan is now worried about falling into a debt trap. For its part, China fears it has heavily invested in the country 'with little prospect of return, both strategic and economic.'[29] Similarly for Myanmar, according to a former diplomat,

> Even without BRI, there are linkages with China's economy, especially in northern Myanmar. Chinese goods are pouring in, but consumers prefer Japanese and even Thai brands. The barriers to Myanmar agricultural commodities exported to China are also an impediment. There are also hitches in the payment of transit royalties from the oil and gas pipeline, and transhipment is reported to have been stopped for some time. It's obvious that the linkages with China are asymmetrical, and this will bring problems. The Chinese are poor at public relations; they don't even know where to start.[30]

Similar 'mixed feelings' have been expressed by Khin Khin Kyaw Kyee, lead researcher at the Institute for Strategy and Policy, Myanmar, about the China Myanmar Economic Corridor (CMEC). While Myanmar 'welcomes investment in infrastructure' there are also valid concerns about 'the negative consequences of massive development projects,' especially given the 'poor record' of China's previous investments in Myanmar.[31] This example is equally true for many of the other South Asian neighbours. While India has always voiced its apprehensions about China's presence in South Asia, it appears that India may, if it is not careful, fall in a similar crevice too.

Indeed, it has been pointed out in the latest study that 'Over the last five years, China has quietly created a significant place for itself in India in the technology domain. Unable to persuade India to sign on to its Belt and Road Initiative, China has entered the Indian market through venture investments in start-ups and penetrated the online ecosystem with its popular smartphones and their apps. As per this study, Chinese tech investors have put an estimated $ 4 billion into Indian start-ups.'[32] This, of course, opens up a Pandora's Box. India will find it difficult to also design its growth and progress without Chinese content. Clearly, there are no easy solutions ahead. India will also be alongside others in the region to maintain a balance of political distancing while engaging economically.

Conclusion

Undeniably, China has been able to support and develop large infrastructure development within South Asia. Under the BRI banner, this initiative has only been strengthened. There is no doubt about the growing Chinese presence in the region. Given that most of South Asia does not share borders with China nor has any political ideology to follow, its engagement with China has been without much issues. However, as it is unfolding, the threat of falling into a debt trap alongside many unfair Chinese practices, have been seen with scepticism in the region.

While India has time and again failed to implement projects on time, and its reputation has suffered, it is not seen as one that would lead the neighbours into a debt hole. Also, the close social and cultural linkages with India have lent it with a traditional comfort and easier access with its neighbours. China is able to play upon the soft vulnerabilities of India and many of the neighbours enjoy having India and China balance each other, given the nature of the sub-continent's geography where the Indian position is enviable. While each neighbour is happy to work with China, India still remains a key partner for them. History and geography have determined that it remains to be seen if 'neighbourhood first' can actually bring dividends for the bilateral and regional ties India shares with its neighbours. India needs to use its skills and position to offer a greater opportunity to its South Asian neighbours and ensure that it becomes a win-win proposition for them to engage with India. Engagement with China will remain in the South Asian neighbourhood, but for all the neighbours, India will always be the first direct contact. India ought to, by greater outreach, and greater fulfilment of its promises and policies, manage its neighbourhood ties more effectively. India can address the gaps and make itself a more wanted partner in the region.

NOTES

1. Teshu Singh, The Second Belt and Road Forum for International Cooperation: An Assessment, at https://www.vifindia.org/2019/may/13/the-second-belt-and-road-forum-for-international-cooperation-an-assessment
2. Simon Mundy and Kathrin Hille, The Maldives Cut the Cost of its Debts to China, February 11, 2019, *Financial Times*, at https://www.ft.com/content/c8da1c8a-2a19-11e9-88a4-c32129756dd8
3. ANM Muniruzzaman,' Belt and Road Initiative: The hurdles along the way', *The Daily Star*, 13 December 2018, at https://www.thedailystar.net/opinion/global-affairs/news/the-hurdles-along-the-way-1672738
4. Belt and Road Initiative: Perspective from Bangladesh, 7 August 2019, at https://www.thedailystar.net/round-tables/news/belt-and-road-initiative-perspective-bangladesh-1782928
5. Author's interview with Prof. Munir Khusru.
6. Author's interview with Prof. Munir Khusru.
7. Serajul Quadir, 'China to develop Bangladesh industrial zone as part of South Asia push', Reuters, 4 April 2018, available at https://www.reuters.com/article/us-bagnladesh-china/china-to-develop-bangladesh-industrial-zone-as-part-of-south-asia-push-idUSKCN1HB1M2

8. 'Chinese ambassador proposes belt and road mechanism for Bangladesh', Bdnews24.com, 11 September 2018, at https://bdnews24.com/neighbours/2018/09/11/chinese-ambassador-proposesbelt-and-roadmechanismfor-bangladesh
9. 'China's 'debt trap' economics will likely result in it gaining greater access to nations around India: US think-tank', *Financial Express,* May 18, 2018, at https://www.financialexpress.com/economy/chinas-debt-trap-economics-will-likely-result-in-it-gaining-greater-access-to-nations-around-india-us-think-tank/1172743/(statement by Richard D. Fisher, Senior fellow at International Assessment and Strategy Centre).
10. Author's interview with Amb Shamsher Chaudhury of Bangladesh, 20 December 2019.
11. Myanmar, China ink deals to accelerate BRI as Xi courts an isolated Suu Kyi, January 18, 2020, available at https://www.business-standard.com/article/international/myanmar-china-ink-deals-to-accelerate-bri-as-xi-courts-an-isolated-suu-kyi-120011800385_1.html
12. Han Mya Htwe, 'Belt and Road Project Set to Usher in New Economic Dawn for Myanmar, Report HKTDC, 6 March 2017 at http://economists-pick-research.hktdc.com/business-news/article/International-Market-News/Belt-and-Road-Project-Set-to-Usher-In-New-Economic-Dawn-for-Myanmar/imn/en/1/1X000000/1X0A9954.htm
13. Chan Myan Hywe, 'China Proposals New Infrastructure in Myanmar', *Myanmar Times* 12 June 2018, at www.mmtimes.com/news/china-proposals-new-infrastructure-projects-myanmar.html
14. Wang Cong, 'Economic corridor can help Myanmar build closer ties with China: analysts', *Global Times,* 13 September 2018, Visit at https://eng.yidaiyilu.gov.cn/home/rolling/66123.htm
15. Nanda Lal Tiwari, Xi's visit ushers in new era of Nepal-China relations accessed at https://www.chinadaily.com.cn/a/201910/15/WS5da53ab6a310cf3e355708dc.html
16. Hari Bansh Jha, Chinese Investments in Nepal in the Context of BRI', 11 October 2019, *VIF Commentary,* at https://www.vifindia.org/article/2019/october/11/chinese-investments-in-nepal-in-the-context-of-bri
17. Shamil Shams, Has China-Pakistan Economic Corridor lived up to the hype? 30 September 2019. *DW,* at https://www.dw.com/en/has-china-pakistan-economic-corridor-lived-up-to-the-hype/a-50644617
18. Amit Bhandari and Chandni Jindal. 'Chinese Investments in India's Neighbourhood, 12 March 2018, *Gateway House,* visit at https://www.gatewayhouse.in/chinese-investments-in-indias-neighbourhood/
19. B.N. Bhattacharya, 'Prospects and Challenges of Integrating South and South East Asia', *International Journal of Development and Conflict,* 4 (2014), pp. 40–66 at http://www.ijdc.org.in/uploads/1/7/5/7/17570463/article_3.pdf
20. Sreeradha Datta, India—the bridge linking South and Southeast Asia, *ORF Commentary,* 10 February, 2017, at https://www.orfonline.org/research/india-the-bridge-linking-south-and-southeast-asia/
21. Sreeradha Datta, 'Indo-Bangladesh Relations: An Enduring Partnership? *IDSA Issue Brief,* January 6, 2010, at https://idsa.in/issuebrief/IndoBangladeshRelations_sdatta_060110
22. World Bank Project Information Document, Concept Stage Report No. PIDC24070, p. 1, 14 January 2016, at http://documents.worldbank.org/curated/en/794651468211152911/pdf/PID-Print-P154511-01-14-2016-1452768829641.pdf
23. Bose, Pratim Ranjan, "India asks Bangladesh to use Kolkata, Haldia as transhipment ports," *Businessline,* 11 October 2018, visit at https://www.thehindubusinessline.com/economy/logistics/india-asks-bangladesh-to-use-kolkata-haldia-as-transhipment-ports/article25194654.ece
24. P. Stobdan, 'Things that Modi should do in Myanmar,' *IDSA Comment,* November 10, 2014, at https://idsa.in/idsacomments/ThingsthatModishoulddoinMyanmar_pstobdan_101114

25. India-Myanmar Bilateral Relations, January 2019, at https://mea.gov.in/Portal/ForeignRelation/India_Myanmar_Bilateral_Brief_Website_jan_2019.pdf
26. Hari Bansh Jha, 'Chinese-Investments in Nepal in the Context of BRI', 11 October 2019, *VIF Commentary* https://www.vifindia.org/article/2019/october/11/chinese-investments-in-nepal-in-the-context-of-bri
27. Myat Myat Mon, Maximising Benefit and reducing Risk in the China Myanmar economic Corridor, *Global Asian*, at https://lkyspp.nus.edu.sg/gia/article/maximizing-benefit-and-reducing-risk-in-the-china-myanmar-economic-corridor
28. Myat Myat Mon, 'Maximising Benefit and reducing Risk in the China Myanmar economic Corridor', *Global Asian,* at https://lkyspp.nus.edu.sg/gia/article/maximizing-benefit-and-reducing-risk-in-the-china-myanmar-economic-corridor
29. Stephanie Findlay and Farhan Bokhari, Pakistan revives Belt-and-Road projects under Chinese pressure, *Financial Times*, 11 December. 2019, at https://www.ft.com/content/ab809f2c-1101-11ea-a7e6-62bf4f9e548a
30. Author's interview with Amb Khin Saw Win on 30 December 2020.
31. Sudha Ramachandran, 'China-Myanmar Economic Corridor Ambitions Meet Hard Reality', Jamestown Foundation, *China Brief*, Volume 18, Issue: 15, September 19, 2018, at https://jamestown.org/program/china-myanmar-economic-corridor-ambitions-meet-hard-reality/
32. Amit Bhandari and Aashna Agarwal, 'India in the virtual Belt and Road,' 27 February, 2020, Gateway House at https://www.gatewayhouse.in/india-virtual-belt-road/

5

Developing Connectivity or Rethinking Sovereignty: India's Considerations on China's BRI Project

Anu Sharma

Introduction

China's Belt and Road Initiative (BRI), previously referred to as One Belt, One Road (OBOR), is often publicised as China's most prestigious regional and global economic programme. While more than 60 countries are associated with this enormous project, India has emerged as one of the countries that have serious reservations against China's BRI plans in its neighbourhood. India does not see the BRI as a purely economic initiative but considers it as a security and strategic agenda by Beijing which is ingeniously camouflaged as an economic partnership engagement. Through CPEC, China is trying to create a set of interdependent institutions in the BRI partner-countries that will push China-centric security and economic aims. So, Beijing aims to create a supportive Pakistani army and a favourable civilian government in Islamabad. It has also indicated the assumption of China's probable leadership of the world. Proposed in 2013, the projected aim of the BRI is to strengthen China's connectivity with the world. The BRI is expected to develop an economic corridor, enhancing connectivity from China to Eurasia and Africa, both through land and sea involving various land, ports, and sea routes. At the Belt and Road Forum (BRF) held in May 2017, Chinese President Xi Jinping stated that "In pursuing the Belt and Road Initiative, we should focus on the fundamental issue of development, release the growth potential of various countries and achieve economic integration and interconnected development and deliver benefits to all".[1] Aside from the economic underpinnings of the Belt and Road, President Xi, in the BRF held in 2017, took the opportunity to reiterate the Chinese vision for regional and global peace and security, which according to him, was a prerequisite for the success of the BRI. It is necessary to mention here that the BRI is an umbrella initiative that covers a multitude of infrastructure and investment projects designed to promote the flow of goods, investment, and people to and from China. At the same time, there are chances that the new connections fostered through the BRI could reconfigure relationships, alliances, reroute economic activity and shift the power balance within and between states.[2]

In 2013, President Xi announced the launch of both the Silk Road Economic Belt and the 21st Century Maritime Silk Road, infrastructure development and investment initiatives that would stretch from East Asia to Europe. The Belt and Road, or *yidaiyilu*, is a "21st-century silk road", made up of a "belt" of land corridors and a maritime "road" of shipping lanes. Currently, the BRI involves almost 90 countries and international organisations. According to Chinese Foreign Minister Wang Yi, under the BRI, 75 economic cooperation zones have been set up in the participating countries.[3] In due recognition like the old silk road, BRI emerged as the network of old caravan trade routes that was immortalised by the term 'silk road' because Chinese silk was a much sought-after trading commodity. The term was coined in 1877 by Prussian geographer Ferdinand von Richthofen through the trade routes which go back 2000 years.[4] Two of the six routes connect China and Europe: one through Central Asia and Russia; the other via the South China Sea and the Indian Ocean. A third road connects China to West Asia via Central Asia, while a fourth takes in China, Southeast Asia, South Asia, and the Indian Ocean. The fifth route branches out from China through the South China Sea and into the South Pacific. Undoubtedly, there are geopolitical and geo-economic benefits accruing to China from its new silk roads.[5] According to Darshana M. Baruah, "...the BRI has garnered much attention, positive and negative, since its inception in 2013. It is one of the world's biggest initiatives for promoting connectivity and providing funds to finance infrastructure development. In South Asia, the BRI underscores the growing Sino-Indian competition in the subcontinent and the Indian Ocean region".[6] However, it should be noted that India is the second-largest contributor to the Asian Infrastructure Investment Bank (AIIB), which has allocated $ 100 billion for the BRI and also funds the Bangladesh-China-India-Myanmar Economic Corridor. India has over 8 per cent voting rights at the AIIB, and remains rightly concerned about the larger strategic issues of the BRI.[7]

India's Concerns Related to BRI

Indian perceptions of the BRI have to be understood in the context of the broader realm of India-China relations. According to Gulshan Sachdeva, "...one of the biggest challenges for Indian policymakers is managing its relations with China...and there remains a huge asymmetry between the two economies".[8] India-China relations have continued to remain an issue related to an underlying security dilemma. Since the 1960s, the security dilemma has manifested itself along three dimensions. Firstly, it is related to mutual mistrust and apprehensions between two countries—China's mistrust related to India's Tibet policy and Indian apprehensions centred on China's role on Indo-Pak issues. Secondly, it is related to China's quest to curtail and counter India's emerging power status in the South Asian region. And thirdly, it is India's growing role in the East Asian region.[9] To explain, the security dilemma, John W. Garver maintains that the security dilemma arises out of the anarchic nature of the state system. Without a superior power to protect it, each state bears ultimate responsibility for its own security and survival as a member of the state system. When confronted with this responsibility, states attempt to expand their power so as to defend themselves better in case the need arises. However, by augmenting their own power, states tend to make the neighbouring states insecure. This clearly explains the situation between India and China.[10] In this regard, the statement issued by Mike Pompeo, the US Secretary of State, in June 2019 during his visit to India endorsed India's apprehensions regarding the BRI. According to him, "...connectivity projects around the world have an element of "national security" and are less of an economic offer for host countries".[11] Furthermore, he added, "They (Chinese) are moving into the South China Sea; it is not because they want the freedom of navigation. Their efforts to build ports around the world are not because they want to be good shipbuilders and stewards of waterways, but rather they have a state national security element to each and every one of them".[12] However, on the apprehensions raised by India, the USA, and many other countries regarding the debt trap, Chinese Foreign Minister Wang Yi refuted the criticism stating that the BRI is driving smaller countries into debt traps. The BRI is not a "debt trap" that some countries may fall into but an "economic pie" that benefits the local population."[13]

In fact, various issues related to China's BRI plans involving Pakistan, including border disputes with India, plausible assistance to Pakistan's nuclear programme, and China's increasing penetration in the internal and international politics of South Asian nations, raises the issues of a 'security dilemma' as discussed by Robert Jervis. According to Jervis, international anarchy and the resulting security dilemma (i.e., policies that increase one state's security tends to decrease that of others) make it difficult for states to realise their common interests.[14] When viewed from this perspective, in the case of India and China, a security dilemma has emerged as an effect of various events that occurred in the past, including the 1962 Sino-India war and China's recurrent armed intrusions into the eastern borders of India. Consequently, these factors have led to a quest to secure borders, develop missile capabilities, and enter strategic and economic alliances (especially the alliance between China and Pakistan), which have pushed the rivalry beyond their borders.[15] This security dilemma, in turn, feeds into certain regional political dynamics, which are evident in China's unique and strategic relationship with countries in South Asia, specifically with India's neighbours such as Nepal, Myanmar, Sri Lanka, and Pakistan.

After two BRI forums (one in 2017 and the other in 2019), India's stand on China's BRI plans has become more vindicated. In fact, the concerns articulated in New Delhi's statement in May 2018 on the lack of transparency and financial sustainability in the mega project are being reflected in so many other quarters now. More recently, in January 2020, Allis Wells, the U.S. principal deputy assistant secretary of state for South and Central Asia, highlighted the lack of transparency in the existing deals and financial conditions imposed by China, which has increased Pakistan's overall debt.[16] This has again highlighted the issue of a "debt trap" in China's various infrastructure and developmental projects under the BRI. As a backgrounder, the multimillion-dollar China-Pakistan Economic Corridor (CPEC), which is being prescribed as a "game-changer" for Pakistan with an ailing economy, has raised apprehensions in Indian policy-making circles. It is pertinent to mention here that India chose not to attend both the BRI Forums that have happened so far.[17] India's decision to stay away from the BRI Forums stems from its long-known and repeatedly-expressed objection to an important component of the BRI—the CPEC Corridor—which passes through what India calls Pakistan-occupied Kashmir (PoK). India asserts that China's plan to build a major infrastructure project in what it considers to be Indian territory is an infringement of its sovereignty.

India's Concerns over CPEC

Envisaged in 2013, China launched the CPEC in April 2015, with a set of projects under the BRI umbrella. The CPEC, which comprises loans, investments, and grants that could grow to around $ 60 billion, travels a 2,700-km route. It starts from the Gwadar port in Pakistan, in Balochistan province, moving along the Karakoram highway through the Khunjerab pass in Gilgit-Baltistan, before crossing into the Kashgar region of China's Xinjiang province (Figure 1).

Figure 1: China-Pakistan Economic Corridor

Source: https://idsa.in/policybrief/ATaleofTwoDisputesChinasIrrationalityandIndias Stakes_rdahiya_290615. Accessed June 14, 2019.

As part of the CPEC, the economic and development projects prioritise the transport, infrastructure, industrial development, and energy security along with the development and modernisation of the strategically located Gwadar port. Additionally, agricultural modernisation and production also form another critical component of the CPEC.[18] The projected aim of the CPEC is cited as enhancement of geographical linkages with the improved road, rail and air transportation system with frequent and free exchanges of growth and people-to-people contacts, enhancing understanding through academic, cultural and regional knowledge and culture, the activity of higher volume of flow of trade and businesses, in order to have more optimal businesses and enhancement of co-operation by a win-win model which will eventually result in a well-connected, integrated region of shared harmony and development. Furthermore, it is often mentioned that the CPEC aims to be a journey towards economic regionalisation in the globalised world. China prophesies it as a win-win model for all the neighbouring countries with the purpose of supporting peace, development, and growth of the economy in the South Asian region.[19]

The ambitious CPEC programme has two main components. As mentioned above, one component plans to develop a new trade and transport route from Kashgar in China to the Gwadar Port. The other envisages developing special economic zones along the route, including power projects. In the first phase, projects will receive almost $ 45.69 billion in concessionary and commercial loans, for which financial facilitation to Chinese companies is being arranged by the Silk Road Fund.[20] Just three projects of the CPEC Corridor—all on the eastern route—received 90 per cent of the total Chinese financing of $ 1.8 billion in the fiscal year, i.e., 2017-2018.[21] Financial inflows into Chinese-funded projects indicate that there is hardly any meaningful progress on the western route that passes through Pakistan's hinterlands and on Gwadar schemes. In total, seven infrastructure projects received loans of $ 1.8 billion, and four of them were related to the CPEC. The three projects that received $ 1.6 billion were the Sukkur-Multan motorway, Thakot-Havelian motorway, and Orange Line Metro project, Lahore. The fourth CPEC project that received Chinese assistance was the Cross-Border Optical Fibre that got $ 16.5 million in 2017-2018.[22]

Pakistan and CPEC: Symbolism or Cooperation

The friendship between China and Pakistan has been growing for many decades. In fact, this friendship between China and Pakistan is often referred to as an "all-weather friendship" between the two. The most recent manifestation of this resolve is the CPEC. Since the inception of the CPEC, being proposed as a framework for regional connectivity and socio-economic development, Pakistan has appeared enthusiastic for a *de-facto* shift in its foreign policy. The CPEC can be visualised as an extension of the friendship and support that has existed between China and Pakistan for almost seven decades. According to *Xinhua* reports, CPEC will help provide Pakistan with progress through its "plentiful economic benefits and opportunities".[23] Furthermore, a *Xinhua* news report also mentioned that the 21 energy projects planned under the CPEC would double Pakistan's current capacity of electricity production by producing 16,400 megawatts of electricity after their completion along with changing the economic and business landscape through infrastructure and transportation development, establishing special economic zones, promoting tourism, and increasing trade and commerce.[24] Here it is necessary to mention that Pakistan has heavily relied on foreign remittances and foreign aid to support and augment its struggling economy. In these circumstances, Pakistan's joining China's 'big dream' through the CPEC is being seen as a blessing for Pakistan. As mentioned earlier, many analysts are referring to this project as a solution to Pakistan's economic woes and even termed it a game-changer, capable of producing millions of jobs and solving the country's unemployment problem.[25] However, in the present circumstances, it is still a promise that is far from being fulfilled. In addition, there is an estimated expectation that with investments in various road, railways, and ports, this Corridor offers enormous potential for Pakistan to boost its economy, reduce poverty, spread benefits widely, and eventually help those likely to be affected by the new trade route.[26]

Another important sector that might get a boost is tourism, which forms the insubstantial part of the earnings of the Baltistan region's economy. The CPEC, some believe, will also boost tourism in the 73,000 square km region of Gilgit-Baltistan. The region is considered a mountaineer's paradise since it is home to five of the 'eight-thousands' (peaks above 8,000 metres), as well as more than 50 mountains over 7,000 metres. It is also home to the world's second-highest peak, K2, and the Nanda Parbat.[27]

One of the vulnerable spots highlighted by the Pakistan government regarding the CPEC is that the educational, health, drinking water, and vocational training facilities might not become available to communities living outside this district's industrial zones. There are chances that this can result in resentment amongst the people that may not accrue the benefits of this massive project for Pakistan. These apprehensions have been growing in Pakistan and can create a hurdle for Pakistan's development path associated with the CPEC.[28]

It is important to mention here that the Balochistan region is important for China's CPEC project to be successful. However, the Baloch nationalists have been sceptical and up in arms against Beijing's plans in the region. A number of attacks in early 2019 against Chinese assets in Balochistan, which is also home to the Gwadar port, have roiled Beijing. Baloch nationalists, led by the Baloch Liberation Army (BLA), have alleged that China is a so-called 'partner in crime' with Pakistan's national government in "looting Balochistan's natural resources," said an expert who tracks Pakistan's internal affairs. Baloch rebels believe that China is militarily supporting the Pakistan Army in its efforts to crush the Baloch insurgency.[29] However, the Pakistani authorities have been continuously denying these apprehensions as being misplaced, at the same time suggesting that in order to realise these opportunities and mitigate the risks, the Pakistani government has to take several policy and institutional reforms along with easing bureaucratic hurdles. There are chances that in the absence of these measures, the benefits for Pakistan may have a lower turnout and elevate risks against what has been calculated.[30]

The question arises as to why the Balochs are targeting the Chinese. Lately, heavy-handed repression in China's Muslim majority region of Xinjiang is also stirring up anti-China sentiments in Pakistan. These factors, among others, have driven religious extremists to act against Chinese citizens in Pakistan. Baloch nationalists have long been opposed to the Chinese presence and investment projects in Balochistan. They are apprehensive about CPEC developments in their province as many Balochs fear the wave of investment will bring about demographic changes, turning them into a minority group in their own province.[31]

The recent resurrection of debate related to the CPEC suggests that the current government of Pakistan under the leadership of Imran Khan is trying to bring transparency related to the CPEC considering the raised concerns about the secrecy shrouding it in Pakistan. The new debate on the CPEC only brings China's "debt-trap diplomacy" to the forefront highlighting Pakistan's dilemma to choose between dragon and dollar.[32] This is hinted at by the visit of Chinese Foreign Minister Wang Yi to Pakistan just after US Secretary of State Mike Pompeo visited Pakistan.[33] In this context, there is a clear element of power competition between the USA and China over Pakistan. This also ranges from China's positioning itself as a defender of globalisation in the face of America's inward-looking policies under US President Donald Trump to the fact that BRI projects in many countries are also accompanied by a robust military relationship that the Chinese have promoted in the form of equipment sales and delegation visits. For example, this includes the actual operationalisation of a Chinese 'support base' at Djibouti in 2016 besides the whiff of dual-use that surrounds such Chinese-controlled ports as Gwadar in Pakistan and Hambantota in Sri Lanka.[34] At the same time, CPEC projects are likely to escalate the conflict between the Balochs and the state, as these two forces mistrust each other from the very beginning. Pakistan has already announced that it will provide a 10,000-strong security force to protect the CPEC, while Baloch separatists have carried out attacks on workers along the route.[35] In late 2019, after a few months of silence, the debate related to CPEC projects in the Baloch region and discontentment amongst the Balochi population has re-surfaced regarding Chinese plans under the CPEC. As a result of the increasing intensity of Baloch resistance to the CPEC, the Pakistan government has tightened the security apparatus to curb increasing instances of Baloch attacks on Chinese establishments in the region.[36]

However, the rising criticism on corruption, eventually led Beijing to rethink some projects that were part of the CPEC. Also, mounting criticism against the then Pakistani government and the growing public resentment amongst the Pakistani public led them as well as Beijing to rethink and formulate new guidelines related to a number of projects under the CPEC. These corruption charges have come to a halt for two reasons. One, China's increased arm twisting related to stopping the funding for road projects like the Karakoram Highway, after continuous reports of slips. Second, the media's hush-hush actions in Pakistan eventually brought the earlier courageous reporting to a standstill.[37]

India's Position on BRI and Issues Regarding CPEC

However, there exist significant areas of dissonance between India and China on the BRI. This is in addition to India's objections originating from the sovereignty concerns vis-à-vis the CPEC. As reiterated a number of times, the BRI is a Chinese initiative meant to utilise its surplus industrial and economic capacity for regional connectivity projects and seek ways to pump energy into its already decelerating economy. One of the concerns raised by India is that the BRI has a strategic and political agenda that remains impervious to the rights of the partner countries. India's concern also relates to the Chinese strategic ambitions that underpin the BRI. The geostrategic essence of BRI has been very appropriately described by Shyam Saran, India's former foreign secretary, "...as a conceptual application of precepts advocated by Mackinder, Mahan, and Sun Tzu". Further, he argues that the Belt, designed to secure Eurasia, indicates the influence of Mackinder; and the Road, which straddles the oceans, enabling maritime ascendancy, is indispensable in the pursuit of Mahan's hegemonic concept. Also, the relation between harmony and hierarchy in the concept of the BRI echoes the ideals of Sun Tzu.[38] India has also signalled apprehensions about the lack of transparency and financial viability of mega infrastructure projects envisaged under the BRI, along with the resultant risks of financial instability that might affect the region.

The Indian government's stand on the CPEC and the BRI bears no change and still declares that "CPEC violates India's sovereignty and territorial integrity. No country can accept a project that ignores its core concerns on sovereignty and territorial integrity. Additionally, the Indian government believes that connectivity initiatives must be based on universally recognised international norms, good governance, the rule of law, openness, transparency and equality, and must be pursued in a manner that respects the sovereignty and territorial integrity".[39] The inclusion of the CPEC, which passes through parts of the Indian state of Jammu & Kashmir under Pakistan's illegal occupation, as a flagship project of the BRI reflects a lack of appreciation of India's concerns on the issue of sovereignty and territorial integrity. The government has conveyed to the Chinese side, including at the highest level, its concerns about their activities in Pakistan occupied Kashmir (PoK) and asked them innumerable times to cease these activities.[40]

For India, the CPEC has become an issue of doubtful advantage—appalling economic logic on one side and sovereignty on the other. Of late, the idea to prioritise economic relation/cooperation/connectivity over territorial sovereignty appears to be gaining momentum among a section of policy-making circles. However, amidst the hype surrounding the CPEC, it cannot be ignored that Pakistan's increased connectivity with China need not necessarily turn out to be a boon for Pakistan.

Adding to the woes of the uneasy bilateral relations, China's opposition to India's entry to the Nuclear Suppliers' Group (NSG) and China's strategy in obstructing Jaish-e-Mohammed's chief Masood Azhar's proscription at the United Nations remains a disturbing trend. At the same time, it adds to India's trust deficit related to China. As mentioned earlier, the MEA statement[40] clearly emphasises that the BRI, rendered as a Chinese vision, comes with a price tag known only to Beijing. The issue of trust deficit also extends to India's assessments to regard the CPEC as a 'disguised political disturbance' with a high level 'strategic content', set to challenge India. One of the options suggested in this regard remains that India needs to muster efforts to ensure that its territorial position is not diluted further in order to avoid past situations such as Tibet and Aksai Chin.[41]

Some voices in Indian academic and policy-making circles maintain that the BRI sans its CPEC position should not be acceptable to India. The reason for it remains that India needs to concentrate on implementing its own connectivity and infrastructure projects to give itself space for manoeuvring and strengthen its bargaining position vis-à-vis the BRI. In this context, if India joins the BRI project, it would limit India's regional power status in the region. On the issue of sovereignty, it is evident that China does not recognise Indian sovereignty over Kashmir. The CPEC is nothing but a manifestation of this fact. It cannot be ignored that China's own economic interests and the concerns of its all-weather friend, Pakistan, shall be determining factors in shaping its Kashmir policy. As against all the arguments mentioned above, there is a school of thought emerging in China that believes that if India joins the BRI, then it has the possibility of strengthening India-China ties.

In the most recent scenario, with the world reeling under the dangerous pandemic, COVID-19, various projects under the BRI and the CPEC were affected due to this. Many CPEC projects were delayed due to lockdown and non-availability of local labour for these projects. Furthermore, the travel restrictions imposed by the Pakistani government has also hindered the accessibility of the Chinese workforce from travelling. Added to this, Beijing's push to its 'Health Silk Road' will help consolidate its position in the countries that have projects under the BRI, including the CPEC. However, both China and Pakistan have been continuously saying that this pandemic outbreak will not hinder CPEC projects.

Conclusion

Definitely, China's BRI plans challenge India's foreign policy objectives, strategies, and structures. It is necessary that India develops its future policies related to China, based on national interests rather than getting swayed by the pressures of external powers such as the USA. At the same time, it cannot be ignored that the dynamics of international relations fluctuate in a volatile manner. In these circumstances, the emerging geopolitical landscape in the region requires deft handling by New Delhi.

It is also important to understand that it is China that is expanding its monetary assets at considerable risk to itself to build up infrastructure in countries that have not received adequate attention from the developed West or from international development agencies. China's BRI, therefore, becomes a powerful alternative that democracies like the USA, the EU, or India, have little alternative to offer against it, given their own record in infrastructure development in the Third World.

It can be said that India's concerns about China's encirclement are real to a certain extent. China is trying to empower Pakistan as well as raise competition for influence among small states in the region against India. China's maritime understanding with Sri Lanka, its decision to sell eight submarines to Pakistan and enhance the facilities at Gwadar port, circle the Indian Ocean with its submarines as well as build a base in Djibouti in Africa have incensed New Delhi to look for options for itself. Also, in building up Pakistan's infrastructure, economy, and connectivity, as well as increasing its own strategic importance, China will be supporting Pakistan against India. On the other hand, for Pakistan, the threat from India has been the main incentive for grooming militants against India. With Gwadar port being leased to China for 40 years with the prospect of it turning into a deep-sea naval outpost for Beijing, it threatens India's energy and economic security, as more than two-thirds of India's petroleum imports pass through the area.

It can be said that China has tried to minimise India's apprehension about the CPEC by offering New Delhi to join the CPEC and maintaining its current status on Kashmir. However, the delays in the CPEC projects due to COVID-19 might work in India's favour. The delay in the projects comes as another major blow for China. With it already being at the receiving end of many nations worldwide as being the origin point of the pandemic affecting the world, the delays and disruptions in its ambitious CPEC project add more to Beijing's worries. However, still, Chinese ambitions will need a major reassessment as the anti-China rhetoric gains momentum due to the COVID-19 pandemic.

At the same time, the Chinese ideals of building a common destiny and a shared future remain a vague perspective for outside actors, especially India and the USA, who consider the BRI a threat to regional and global order. As one of South Asia's dominant powers, India has the resources to manage China's increasing presence in the region, whether by deterrence, compulsion or balancing. However, the flexibility in the respective stand of the two nations would be crucial. The dynamics of intentions will not be clear until increased interactions lead to more mutual learning and understanding. But various events such as the Doklam and LAC stand-off at Galwan valley in Ladakh between India and China will increase the mistrust over the CPEC, thereby making it difficult for India, China, and Pakistan to converge on the issues of mutual benefits. Given the current dispositions, there is not much scope, at least in the short run, for substantial economic ties between India and Pakistan, and there exists no real incentive for India to be a part of the CPEC. India needs to look for business opportunities that can be fruitfully exploited. One of the options can be that it can also adopt a more constructive attitude and engage Beijing in a discussion over the objectives of the BRI schemes in areas of its own interests. However, a big 'if' remains. Only if China agrees to negotiate on removing the CPEC from PoK, is there a chance that India can agree to have a more constructive dialogue with China related to the BRI. However, in the current scenario, it seems unlikely!

NOTES

1. Speech by Chinese President Xi Jinping at the opening ceremony of The Belt and Road Forum for International Cooperation, May 14, 2017, "Work Together to Build the Silk Road Economic Belt and The 21st Century Maritime Silk Road", available at http://www.xinhuanet.com/english/2017-05/14/c_136282982.htm, Accessed March 14, 2019.
2. "How will the Belt and Road Initiative advance China's Interests?" *China Power*, May 8, 2017, Online available at https://chinapower.csis.org/china-belt-and-road-initiative/, accessed March 15, 2019.
3. Speech by Chinese Foreign Minister Wang Yi, "Stronger Legal Cooperation for Sound and Steady Development of the Belt and Road Initiative", July 3, 2018, available at https://

www.fmprc.gov.cn/mfa_eng/zxxx_662805/t1573636.shtml, accessed March 22, 2019.

4. Rosita Dellios, "Silk Roads of the Twenty first Century: The Cultural Dimension," March 24, 2017, available at https://onlinelibrary.wiley.com/doi/full/10.1002/app5.172, accessed March 22, 2019.
5. Ibid. Speech by Chinese Foreign Minister Wang Yi, "Stronger Legal Cooperation for Sound and Steady Development of the Belt and Road Initiative", July 3, 2018, available at https://www.fmprc.gov.cn/mfa_eng/zxxx_662805/t1573636.shtml, accessed March 22, 2019.
6. Darshana M. Baruah, "India's Answer to the Belt and Road: A Road Map for South Asia", *Carnegie Endowment for International Peace*, Working Paper, August 2018, available at https://carnegieendowment.org/files/WP_Darshana_Baruah_Belt_Road_FINAL.pdf, accessed March 24, 2019.
7. Srikanth Kondapalli, "Why India is not part of Belt and Road Initiative Summit", *The Indian Express*, May 15, 2017, available at https://indianexpress.com/article/opinion/why-india-is-not-part-of-the-belt-and-road-initiative-summit-4656150/, accessed June 2, 2019.
8. Gulshan Sachdeva, "Indian Perceptions of Chinese Belt and Road Initiatives", *International Studies*, Issue 55, Number 4, December 2018, pp. 285–296, DOI: 10.1177/0020881718807359, available at http://journals.sagepub.com/home/isq, accessed on April 15, 2019.
9. John W. Garver, "The Security Dilemma in Sino Indian Relations", *India Review*, Issue 1, Number 4, October 2002, pp. 1-38, available at https://www.tandfonline.com/doi/abs/10.1080/14736480208404640, accessed April 15, 2019.
10. Ibid. p. 1.
11. PTI Washington, "BRI has the national security element: Pompeo", *The Hindu Business Line*, March 29, 2019, available at https://www.thehindubusinessline.com/news/world/bri-has-a-national-security-element-pompeo/article26673918.ece, accessed June 2, 2019.
12. Ibid.
13. Ibid.
14. Robert Jervis, "Cooperation under the security dilemma", *World Politics*, Vol. 30, No. 2, 1978, pp. 167–214, available at http://www.sfu.ca/~kawasaki/Jervis%20Cooperation.pdf, accessed June 14, 2019.
15. Radhika Chhabra, "The new phase of Sino-Indian cooperation under the security dilemma", *Young Voices* (ORF), February 14, 2019, available at https://www.orfonline.org/expert-speak/the-new-phase-of-sino-indian-cooperation-under-the-security-dilemma-48196/, accessed June 14, 2019.
16. Umair Jamal, "CPEC and Beyond: China and the US Fight for Influence in Pakistan", *The Diplomat*, January 24, 2020, online available at https://thediplomat.com/2020/01/cpec-and-beyond-china-and-the-us-fight-for-influence-in-pakistan/, accessed January 27, 2020.
17. Sachin Parashar, "For the Second Time, India Declines China's Invite for BRI Forum", *The Times of India*, April 8, 2019, available at https://timesofindia.indiatimes.com/india/for-the-second-time-india-declines-chinas-invite-for-bri-forum/articleshow/68769033.cms,accessed April 15, 2019.
18. "China-Pakistan Economic Corridor: Opportunities and Risks", *Crisis Group*, June 29, 2018, available at https://www.crisisgroup.org/asia/south-asia/pakistan/297-china-pakistan-economic-corridor-opportunities-and-risks, accessed March 31, 2019.
19. "China-Pakistan Economic Corridor", online available at http://cpec.gov.pk/introduction/1, accessed on March 31, 2019.
20. Engr Hussain Ahmad Siddiqui, "CPEC Projects: Status, Costs and Benefits", *The Dawn*, July 13, 2015, available at https://www.dawn.com/news/1194014, accessed on April 5, 2019.
21. Shahbaz Rana, "Bulk of Chinese Financing goes to Three CPEC Projects", *The Express Tribune*,

July 24, 2018, available at https://tribune.com.pk/story/1765050/2-bulk-chinese-financing-goes-3-cpec-projects/, accessed on April 5, 2019.

22. Ibid.
23. "China-Pakistan Economic Corridor brings Economic Benefits to Pakistan: Report", *Xinhua*, March 2, 2018, available at http://www.xinhuanet.com/english/2018-03/02/c_137009278.htm, accessed April 14, 2019.
24. "China-Pakistan Economic Corridor brings Economic Benefits to Pakistan: Report", *Xinhua*, March 2, 2018, available at http://www.xinhuanet.com/english/2018-03/02/c_137009278.htm, accessed April 14, 2019.
25. Adnan Aamir, "Just Who Will the China-Pakistan Economic Corridor Really Benefit?" *South China Morning Post*, September 13, 2017, available at https://www.scmp.com/comment/insight-opinion/article/2110802/just-who-will-china-pakistan-economic-corridor-really, accessed April 14, 2019.
26. This information was part of the report published by the Asian Development Bank (ADB), the United Kingdom's Department for International Development, the Japan International Cooperation Agency (JICA), and the World Bank titled "The Web of Transport Corridors in South Asia", CPEC offers enormous potential to Boost Pakistan Economy", *World Bank Report-Press Release no. SAR 2018*, available at https://www.worldbank.org/en/news/press-release/2018/03/22/cpec-offers-enormous-potential-boost-pakistan-economy, accessed April 14, 2019.
27. — "How will CPEC Boost Pakistan's Economy?" available at https://www2.deloitte.com/content/dam/Deloitte/pk/Documents/risk/pak-china-eco-corridor-deloittepk-noexp.pdf, accessed April 15, 2019.
28. Ishrat Hussein, Shahid Rashid and Yasir Arrfat (eds.), "CPEC and Pakistani Economy: An Appraisal", *Centre of Excellence for CPEC*, pp. 1-40, available at http://cpec.gov.pk/brain/public/uploads/documents/CPEC-and-Pakistani-Economy_An-Appraisal.pdf, accessed April 14, 2019.
29. Dipanjan Roy Choudhury, "Balochistan: China's Achilles Heel", *The Economic Times*, February 26, 2019, available at https://economictimes.indiatimes.com/news/defence/balochistan-chinas-achilles-hill/articleshow/68163847.cms?from=mdr, accessed June 15, 2019.
30. Ibid.
31. Muhammad Akbar Notezai, "Why Balochs are Targeting China", *The Diplomat*, November 26, 2018, online available at https://thediplomat.com/2018/11/why-balochs-are-targeting-china/, accessed June 15, 2019.
32. Zaineb Akhter, "Pakistan and the Politics Of CPEC: A Rethink on the Anvil?" *South Asian Voices*, October 21, 2018, available at https://southasianvoices.org/pakistan-and-the-politics-of-cpec-a-rethink-on-the-anvil/, accessed April 14, 2019.
33. Shafqat Ali, "China a big Shield for Pakistan if US persists on "Do More", *The Nation*, August 30, 2018, available at https://nation.com.pk/30-Aug-2018/china-a-big-shield-for-pakistan-if-us-persists-on-do-more, accessed April 15, 2019.
34. Jabin T. Jacob, "China's Belt and Road Initiative and its implications for India" February 19, 2019, available at https //in.boell.org/2019/02/25/chinas-belt-and-road-initiative-and-its-implications-india, accessed June 2, 2019.
35. Note 30.
36. Philip Kowalski, "Balochistan: From the Periphery to the Centre of Attention", October 21, 2019, online available at https://www.mei.edu/publications/balochistan-periphery-center-attention, accessed January 27, 2020.
37. Tara Kartha, "CPEC is China-Pakistan Corruption Corridor. This Challenges Indian Security in New Ways", *The Print*, June 8, 2020, available at https://theprint.in/opinion/cpec-is-china-pakistan-corruption-corridor-this-challenges-indian-security-in-new-ways/437329/, accessed August 2, 2020.

38. Abhay Kumar Singh, "Emerging Contours of Maritime Security Architecture under the Belt and Road Initiative", *Journal of Defence Studies*, Vol. 12, No. 4, October-December 2018, pp. 35-55, online available at https://idsa.in/system/files/jds/jds-12-4-2018-emerging-contours-of-maritime-security-architecture-aksingh.pdf, accessed April 8, 2019.
39. "Official Spokesperson's response to a query on media reports regarding possible cooperation with China on OBOR/BRI", *Ministry of External Affairs*, April 5, 2018, online available at https://www.mea.gov.in/media-briefings.htm?dtl/29768/Official+ Spokespersons+ response+ to+a+query+on+media+reports+regarding+possible+cooperation+with+China+on+OBORBRI, accessed May 29, 2019.
40. Ibid.
41. Priyanka Singh, "India's Participation in CPEC: The Ifs and Buts," *Issue Brief IDSA*, February 17, 2017, online available at https://idsa.in/system/files/issuebrief/ib_india-in-cpec_psingh_170217.pdf, accessed June 1, 2019.

6

CPEC in PoK: Prospects and Challenges

Sanchita Bhattacharya

Introduction

The Belt and Road Initiative (BRI) carries topographical focus on the "Belt" referring broadly to China's historical trade partners in the Eurasian mainland within China's latitude and the "Road" to coastal developing countries in South East Asia and across the Indian Ocean Rim.[1] During a visit to Kazakhstan in late 2013, China's President Xi Jinping first raised the idea of the new Silk Road Economic Belt (SREB) leading from China to Europe, via Central Asia, to rebuild one that had existed 2,000 years ago. Within a year, the idea transformed into a major foreign policy and economic strategy initiative that was first called the One Belt One Road (OBOR) and later, the BRI, by incorporating a maritime component called the 21st Century Maritime Silk Road (MSR).

The rudimentary purpose of the BRI is to amplify regional connectivity through roads, pipeline and maritime connections. The BRI consists of six major projects: China-Mongolia-Russia Economic Corridor; China-Central Asia-West Asia Economic Corridor; New Eurasia Land Bridge Economic Corridor; Bangladesh-China-India-Myanmar Economic Corridor; China-Pakistan Economic Corridor and China-Indochina Peninsula Economic Corridor. Therefore, these corridors are expected to link China with more than 150 countries through a network of roads, railways and sea routes. The Chinese have staunchly argued that the outreaching benefits of these economic corridors would enable people to get out of poverty and improve their wellbeing.[2] According to the

Austrian Chamber of Commerce in Vienna, the BRI covers around 70 per cent of the world's population, and the countries en route account for about 29 per cent of the global economic output. Accordingly, the implementation of this initiative is correspondingly time-consuming. In total, the estimated amount of the BRI projects could be up to USD 1.3 trillion, which would be about seven times as extensive as the Marshall Plan. And that is the biggest investment in human history.[3]

CPEC: An Important Constituent of BRI

The China-Pakistan Economic Corridor (CPEC) is the flagship project of the BRI, connecting Kashgar in China's Xinjiang province with Gwadar port in Balochistan province of Pakistan. There are four types of projects under the CPEC related to energy, infrastructure, Gwadar port and industrial cooperation. It has been estimated that besides creating two million new employment opportunities, the CPEC would benefit Pakistan with at least two per cent increase in its GDP per annum, and develop wider regional connectivity.[4] On the other hand, there is anticipation that the CPEC will give a much-needed fillip to China's economy and stature by putting to use the previously idle infrastructure technology capabilities of its State-owned Enterprises (SoEs), huge unemployed labour, and the unutilised fiscal reserves accessible with its banks, in revenue-generating ventures abroad. This, in turn, will further enable China in its quest to outspread economic influence and military power well beyond its borders to dominate the region.[5]

The Chinese and Pakistani top leaderships planned an overall new dimension in bilateral relations, and the presidential level interaction in 2006 and 2008 resulted in the formulation of what in 2015 was termed as the CPEC that was placed under China's broader economic vision of the BRI.[6] Since its inception as the OBOR in the early days and later as the BRI (though its Chinese name has remained unchanged), the grand Chinese initiative has been the new buzzword at government, transport, logistics and business events throughout Eurasia, since Xi Jinping brought it forward in late 2013. As its flagship, the CPEC is a project of USD 56 billion which encompasses a massive network of numerous development projects including motorways, hydropower and thermal power stations, railways, and industrial corridors to booster Pakistan in the upcoming years.[7]

For Pakistan, this Corridor is viewed as a representation of the resolute relationship it shares with China. The bilateral relationship between both the states is characterised by a high degree of mutual cooperation and convergence of strategic interests. Yet, at the same time, Pakistan's geographical proximity to

Afghanistan and constant hostilities with India require a geopolitical assessment of the Corridor's expected consequences for Pakistan and the rest of South Asia. On the other hand, for China, the CPEC is an integral component of its 21st-century initiative promoting economic expansion and regional connectivity while strengthening its status as a global player in international affairs. The CPEC's motivations can be explicated through the prism of realist and liberal internationalist theories of geopolitics, as there are elements of both competition and cooperation driving state behaviour.[8]

The CPEC project encompasses political, economic, and strategic dimensions. Nevertheless, it is important to note that the success of the project lies on several factors. Since 1947, Pakistan has been facing a number of internal constraints that range from domestic politics, ethnic conflict, energy deficiency and strained foreign relations within its region. These factors would greatly affect the viability of the CPEC project, considering that a noteworthy amount of investments is being made in Pakistani territory. China also faces constraints within its own borders. Xinjiang province would be a vital geographical point for the CPEC. This means that the peace and stability of the region would play an imperative role in maximising the CPEC. Like Pakistan, China has been observing ethnic unrest in the province due to the conflict between its Muslim Uighur population and the Han Chinese. These issues serve as an overall challenge for the expansion of the CPEC.[9]

CPEC in the Region of PoK

It is also anticipated that CPEC-related projects will turn the disputed territory of Pakistan occupied Kashmir (PoK) into Pakistan's economic engine. Under the CPEC, nine SEZs are slated to be established across Pakistan, including one in PoK's Mirpur. Also, an expressway is planned to connect Mirpur and Muzaffarabad with Mansehra, further connecting them with the main CPEC route; a few other hydropower projects are also in the pipeline in the region. But the core route of the CPEC goes over the Gilgit-Baltistan area of PoK, connecting Khunjerab, Gilgit and Raikot with Sazin in Khyber Pakhtunkhwa. Since Pakistan connects with China in this region of Gilgit-Baltistan, it is naturally the gateway of the CPEC to Pakistan.

Gilgit-Baltistan is one of the most obscure areas of this planet. Since the 1990s, it has come into the limelight due to the interest of international travellers in the Hunza Valley of the region. The pristine environment and the allure of Hunza water bring tourists from all over the world to this particular region. However, since the initiation of China's BRI, the territory of Gilgit-Baltistan has gained importance as it determines an essential part of the CPEC, which is heralded as a 'game-changer' for Pakistan and the whole region.

Since the end of British colonial rule over the Indian subcontinent in 1947 and the ensuing restructuring of the political map of the region, and the transfer of power to the successor states, the former princely state of Jammu & Kashmir (J&K) turned into a major crisis zone in South Asia. Despite the fact that the then ruler of J&K declared its accession to India, Pakistan not only illegally holds large parts of the territory but also questions India's legitimate claims over the said territory and tries to systematically destabilise parts of J&K. Today, the erstwhile princely state of J&K is divided into several territorial entities administered by three countries, namely China (Aksai Chin and Shaksgam Valley), Pakistan (PoK and Gilgit-Baltistan),[10] and India (Union Territories of Ladakh and J&K).

The most significant geographical unit within the PoK, which is, in a way a deciding factor in the entire projected success story of CPEC is the area of Gilgit-Baltistan. In India, PoK is most often referred to as forming part of the CPEC route, but one must keep in mind that the CPEC actually connects China with the Pakistan mainland as it passes through the region of Gilgit-Baltistan. Thus, keeping in mind this fact, we shall discuss the CPEC projects in PoK with special focus on the Gilgit-Baltistan region and have a comprehensive discussion regarding the various basic characteristic of the region.

Reportedly, China's presence in Gilgit-Baltistan is an extension of its ambitions of reconstructing the ancient Silk Road. The construction of the CPEC is an important pawn in this New Great Game. The origins of this Corridor can be traced to the Border Agreement of 1963, in which Pakistan ceded more than 5,000 sq miles of illegally occupied Jammu & Kashmir to China. Part of this 3,000-km-long network of railways, roads and pipelines, will pass through Gilgit-Baltistan, which does not fall within the jurisdiction of the Constitution of the Islamic Republic of Pakistan. Since 1947, the region has been treated as a disputed territory which was earlier known as the Northern Areas of Pakistan; it is the northernmost administrative territory in Pakistan.[11]

Gilgit-Baltistan is loosely defined as a centrally-administered, partially-empowered and economically-dependent part of Pakistan. With all its natural resources of gemstones, and mineral and water resources, the area is one of the best tourist destinations in the world.[12] For about 50 years, the common people of Gilgit-Baltistan were deprived of basic political rights. It was only in the 1970s that discussion on the region started and later, Benazir Bhutto's government tried to bring the territory within mainstream Pakistan and provide the people with a few basic democratic rights. However, even Benazir could not succeed due to the military's dominance. Eventually, the Legislative Assembly was instituted in Gilgit-Baltistan. The Pakistani Parliament also instituted the Gilgit-Baltistan Council. Gilgit-Baltistan, like the Gwadar port in Balochistan, is fundamental for the successful implementation of the CPEC in the short run as well as for smooth functioning in the long run. More importantly, Gilgit-Baltistan is the only land connection between Pakistan and China and all the roads and pipelines and most of the communication networks must run through this mountainous area.[13]

In the past six decades, China has aggressively increased its geographical presence vis-à-vis India through military campaigns along the China-India border in J&K, as well as by making investments and undertaking infrastructure development activities in PoK. The selection of PoK for developing the strategically significant CPEC yields multi-dimensional advantages that go beyond the noticeable economic benefits. The CPEC will give China access to the Arabian Sea and develop an alternate route for its critical energy imports and other resources and acquire yet another gateway to Afghanistan.[14] In this light, the CPEC appears central to the hegemonic pursuits of China in South Asia.

Projects Envisaged Under CPEC in PoK

The range of infrastructure projects China has undertaken in the PoK region in the recent past highlights its importance to China. The area provides China with a strategic edge both in the economic and security realms. China has invested a massive amount of money and manpower in improving and expanding the Karakoram Highway. In September 2015, Pakistan's then Prime Minister Nawaz Sharif inaugurated seven km of five tunnels, which are part of the 24-km-long portion of the Highway. These tunnels are known as the Pakistan-China Friendship Tunnels, constructed by China over Attabad Lake in Gilgit-Baltistan's Hunza valley.[15] At least 440 km of the Karakoram Highway, the lifeline of the CPEC, passes through Gilgit-Baltistan. This mega project has further magnified the geo-strategic and geo-economic significance of Gilgit-Baltistan. The following are some of the other major projects being planned in this region.

Special Economic Zone in Maqpoondass Area: In May 2019, Pakistan's Board of Investments (BoI) permitted the fast-track development of nine SEZs, including Moqpoondass, about 40 km from the city of Gilgit. While 250 acres have been acquired for Moqpoondass SEZ and a feasibility study has been submitted by the Gilgit-Baltistan industries department, the National Assembly was informed that a "formal application for declaration of SEZ as per provisions of the SEZ Act 2012 is still awaited".[16]

Kohala Hydel Project: The Kohala Hydro Project is located by the Jhelum river near Muzaffarabad district. The dam site is proposed just upstream of Domel, 174 km from Islamabad and will have an installed capacity of 1,100 MW. The average annual energy generation of the main power station will be 5.079 billion kWh. The project is part of the CPEC. The Kohala Hydro Company (Pvt.) Limited was incorporated in 2015 and is responsible for executing the Kohala Hydropower Project. It is expected to be completed by December 2025, with a projected total cost of USD 2,364.05 million.[17] The Kohala Hydro Company is a subsidiary of China Three Gorges Corporation (CTGC). However, as reported in February 2020, the project has hit a snag after the Chinese firm refused to accept a dispute resolution plan approved by the government.

Special Economic Zone at Mirpur: As reported in June 2019, throwing light on the CPEC projects in PoK, Sardar Masood Khan, President of PoK, said that special incentives have been offered by the PoK government for investment in Mirpur economic zone. These incentives include tax-free import of machinery and other equipment, construction of infrastructure, and permission to prospective investors to generate their own electricity to run industries at the local level.[18]

Mansehra-Mirpur Expressway: This China-funded road project would connect the entire PoK to the CPEC's central route stretching across 200 km. On completion, it will be the shortest route from Central Punjab to the CPEC, shortening the existing route by 50 km and saving around four to six hours of travel time. It is at the preparatory stage with an estimated cost of USD 2.5 billion.[19]

Phandar Hydropower Project: The project area is located between Phandar Lake and Chhashi Gol in Ghizar district of Gilgit-Baltistan. Phandar lake is located about 168 km north-west of Gilgit town and 772 km north of Islamabad.[20] The project has an installed capacity of 80 MW and is under review of the experts from both sides.[21]

Azad Pattan Hydropower Project: In 2019, Pakistan and China agreed to include 700 megawatts of Azad Pattan hydropower project in the CPEC framework. This project would be financed through Chinese currency. The Azad Pattan hydropower project is a run-of-the-river pondage scheme on the Jhelum river in the PoK with the capability of four hours of daily peaking. The project would be located near the Azad Pattan bridge upstream of the 720 MW Karot hydropower project and downstream of the 640 MW Mahal hydropower project and would be part of the Jhelum river hydel cascade.[22]

China-Pakistan Optical Fibre Project: In May 2016, construction began on the $ 44 million Fibre Optic Project, a cross-border optical fibre cable that will enhance telecommunications and the ICT industry in the Gilgit-Baltistan, Khyber Pakhtunkhwa and Punjab regions, while offering Pakistan a fifth route by which to transmit telecommunication traffic. The 840-km project will connect Karimabad, Gilgit, Babusar, Naran, Mansehra, and Jarkyas to Rawalpindi/ Islamabad. It has been suggested that the territory of Gilgit will benefit from it, for out of the 840-km-long optic fibre cable line, 466 km will pass through areas of Gilgit-Baltistan. It will, apart from providing secure voice traffic, also generate employment opportunities in the Gilgit-Baltistan region.[23]

KIU Hydropower Project: The hydropower project was approved under the B2B model in the CPEC.[24] With an installed capacity of 100 MW, the project is under review from experts of both sides.

Chitral CPEC Link Road from Gilgit, Shandor, and Chitral to Chakdara: This CPEC project is in the planning and development phase. It will connect Chakdara in Khyber Pakhtunkhwa to Gilgit in Gilgit-Baltistan via Chitral and Shandora. In September 2017, the project was officially included in the CPEC. A detailed design and feasibility study were completed in October 2017, and planning was underway in November 2017.[25]

CPEC's Effect on PoK

It is affirmed that PoK is contributing less than two per cent to the total GDP of Pakistan and its population is 1.95 per cent of the country's total population. The poor performance of the PoK economy is not due to scarcity of economic potential but due to the underutilisation of natural and human resources. Predominant lack of infrastructure development, deficient industrial structures and underutilisation of hydropower potential are the central causes of underdevelopment of the PoK region. This area has a mountainous topography with enchanting natural beauty, rivers, waterfalls, streams and lakes. The area is also known for its natural as well as mineral reserves such as coal, gold, potassium and rubies. But these precious resources have never been explored due to financial constraints and the low intent of the government. Consequently, PoK has a huge probability of establishing an industry of precious stones and other minerals.

Through the CPEC, natural resources can be explored, and the mining and coal industry could be established to acquire value-added contribution.[26] The CPEC is considered by many as a supplement and not a substitute to the PoK economy.

Furthermore, the demographic policies of Pakistan have also contributed to the underdevelopment of this region. Over the years, the Pakistan government settled outsiders, mostly Punjabis, in the region by allowing them to invest in manufacturing units. It preferred the non-Kashmiris, mostly Punjabis, over the locals to accord preferential treatment, so that in due course Pakistani nationals came to control all the banks in PoK. As a result, Pakistani banks restricted all foreign exchange earnings from remittances sent by the Kashmiri Diaspora settled in the UK, further contributing to the backwardness of the region.[27]

The area of Gilgit-Baltistan is already facing grave environmental problems because of climate change and water and air pollution, inadequate waste disposal, natural resources depletion, loss of biodiversity, deforestation and glacier melting. Geologists have noted that erosion and weathering processes, seismic activity, steep terrain, rainfall and irrigation for agriculture, snow melting and sediment carried by glacial melt into rivers have been the key triggers of the landslide in 2010, which created the Attabad Lake in Hunza area in Gilgit-Baltistan.[28] Moreover, around 36 glacial lakes of Gilgit-Baltistan have been declared endangered due to the CPEC project. Clearing of forests, cutting of mountains and increase in heavy vehicular movement is harming the area. Most CPEC projects lack adequate cost-benefit calculations and Environmental Impact Assessments (EIAs). Also, many of the executing companies do not recognise the need for environmental awareness. As a consequence, the local population suffers immensely from environmental degradation. Traditional livelihoods are also affected, as it appears that there is a causal link between negative environmental impacts on biodiversity, destruction of traditional livelihoods, and subsequent modern forms of slavery. The situation faced by the common people has become even worse due to the increasing economic distortion inflicted by Islamabad.[29]

The local communities have claimed that the Pakistani government awards licences secretly to ghost companies either operating on behalf of the Pakistani Army or the Chinese. Pakistan has illegally awarded more than 2,000 leases in Gilgit-Baltistan for the mining of gold, uranium, copper and molybdenum to China. Far more grave is the creation of 'no-go' zones constructed by the Chinese, who stop local people from accessing these areas. This is prominent in some areas in upper Hunza, like Chapursan Valley, where the Chinese have done both tunnel building and mineral exploration.[30]

Also, Pakistan is seizing forest and agricultural lands to transfer them to Chinese companies for large-scale infrastructure projects. In addition to ex-army officers and Sunni extremist clerics, Pakistani Sunni settlers are also being brought in as workers for various Chinese projects. Wahhabi Sunni settlers have displaced the Shia population from villages along the Karakoram Highway to secure the CPEC. Moreover, hundreds of Chinese nationals have permanently settled in Gilgit-Baltistan to establish businesses, consequently abusing local natural resources. China plans to build roads, dams, and industrial zones in the region without taking into account the impact on an ecologically sensitive region.[31]

The dominant economic concern was that once the CPEC project is completed, with rail tracks and motorways laid, the existing economic trade activities of the people of Gilgit-Baltistan with China will halt. As cargo trains will leave from China to the proposed dry port in Havalian in Khyber Pakhtunkhwa directly, the existing Sost dry port will become useless. Also, Gilgit-Baltistan will be used to tread rails and trucks, the goods of which will be uploaded in China and reach Havalian, detouring the region.[32] It is reported that in the context of the CPEC's implementation, local citizens were forcibly evicted and their land allocated to state authorities to be used for Corridor projects. Those affected claim that they did not get adequate compensation for their land and property—or any offer for relocation.[33]

Also, prolonged delay in the execution of the projects sanctioned for the PoK under CPEC will result in a hike of the estimated costs and will provide opportunities to certain vested groups to politicise these projects. This has been underlined in a special report titled "CPEC in J&K: a gateway to regional connectivity and beyond". Authored by Sabur Ali Sayyed and published by the Islamabad based Centre for Peace, Development and Reforms (CPDR), the report provides a comprehensive critique of the CPEC projects in the region.[34]

Less than one-third of the announced CPEC projects have been completed, totalling about USD 19 billion. The Pakistan government bears much of the fault. It has frequently missed construction targets as it ran out of money; it got a USD 6 billion bailout from the International Monetary Fund in 2017, the country's 13th since the late 1980s. Two successive prime ministers have also been jailed on corruption charges.[35]

The third interim report of the Special Committee of Senate on China-Pakistan Economic Corridor revealed that while around USD 36 billion of the CPEC was targeted towards electricity generation in Pakistan, power generation in Gilgit-Baltistan remains without any funding whatsoever. The CPEC offers the potential of hydroelectric power generation through various energy projects but these demand greater planning and consultation with the people and policymakers in Gilgit-Baltistan. Any advancement in this direction of consultation and consensus-building remains dark, to say the least.[36]

A major challenge for Pakistan in the context of the CPEC is to negotiate better terms with the Chinese companies to get a good profit in the investment sector. The primary concern for the Pakistani leadership is how to implement the CPEC program so that structural imbalances are removed, and the economy attains sustainable progress. The region of PoK with dubious legislative participation is definitely in the high-risk zone of financial fraud, which is unfortunately commonplace in Pakistan.

The popular mandate also needs to be taken care of with respect to various CPEC projects in PoK. People of this area, especially in Gilgit-Baltistan, have been protesting against the step-motherly treatment meted out to their region by Pakistan since the late 1940s. Regardless of Pakistani claims to the opposite, the government's record of investment in the area's economy is meagre and irregular.

In the context of Gilgit-Baltistan, the local leaders welcomed the CPEC, but over a period of time, they are of the opinion that the concerns and interests of the area and its people have not been taken into account. They wish for more direct participation in steering the project.

Conclusion

China says that the BRI is the project of the century, a Chinese-built infrastructure plan that is remaking South Asia and Pakistan is at the heart of it. With the initiation of CPEC projects in the region, the development of PoK—an otherwise disputed and neglected area—is now 'dependent' on China, as is well projected and publicised by the Pakistani administration. Pakistan's move to allow road construction, SEZs and other CPEC projects in PoK changed the fundamentals of the actual Kashmir issue and cemented China's stake in this political squabble. In a way, China has taken a calculated risk with regard to its investment in the project and to establish its own clout in the region with an all-pervasive road that is expected to connect PoK with other extreme regions of Pakistan. There is no doubt that the actions of Pakistan totally refute the interests of the people of PoK and their future.

Also, the CPEC is not helping to reduce tensions in PoK by improving the living conditions of the people. On the contrary, the project is further embedding the existing ill-fated trajectories. Consequently, it comes as no surprise that the local people of the region perceive the CPEC as a device to continue the exploitation of their natural resources. China and Pakistan conceive that the CPEC initiative has the possibility to have a substantial impact in establishing China's credentials as a subtle and generous partner to its neighbours and contributing to the much-needed renovation of Pakistan's economy. Nevertheless, from the common man's point of view, the Pakistan economy still follows the age-old feudal system and corruption along with financial bungling are the core of it, not to forget the influence of the military in the economic field. If the interests of domestic constituencies, the army and the feudal system supersede the broad goals of 'development', then the glitches in the PoK, as in other parts of the country, will definitely get worse.

NOTES

1. Johnston, Lauren A., 'The Belt and Road Initiative: What is in it for China?' *Asia Pacific Policy Studies*, 2019, pp. 1-19.
2. Sabir, Sameena, 'CPEC and Azad Kashmir: Prospects and Potential', *Daily Times*, February 14, 2020, at https://dailytimes.com.pk/557512/cpec-and-azad-kashmir-prospects-and-potential/
3. Reiff, George, 'One Belt, One Road (OBOR)', 2018, at https://www.academia.edu/37694544/China_-_ONE_BELT_ONE_ROAD_OBOR_BRI_
4. Sharma, Rakesh, 'China-Pakistan Economic Corridor (CPEC) In Pak Occupied Jammu And Kashmir (POJK)', *CLAWS*, December 4, 2019, at https://www.claws.in/china-pakistan-economic-corridor-cpec-in-pak-occupied-jammu-and-kashmir-pojk/
5. Ranade, Jayadeva, 'Does the China-Pakistan Economic Corridor Really Help Pakistan?' *Liberal Studies Journal*, 2(1), 2017, pp. 33-41.
6. Hassan, S. Kanwal, 'A Pakistani Overview of Pakistan-China Relations: From Geopolitical Compulsions to a Strengthening Co-operation', 2017, at https://centreasia.hypotheses.org/files/2018/03/19-KanwallHassan-ChinePakistan_Juil2017.pdf.
7. Muneer, Sania, Ammara Rabbani and Asif Iftikhar, 'CPEC: Crafting a Rational Way towards Kashmir Dispute', *Journal of the Punjab University Historical Society*, 31(1), 2018, pp. 189-198.
8. Rifaat, Hamzah, and Tridivesh Singh Maini, 'The China-Pakistan Economic Corridor Strategic Rationales, External Perspectives, and Challenges to Effective Implementation', *Stimson Working Paper*, 2016, at https://www.stimson.org/wp-content/files/file-attachments/The%20China-Pakistan%20Economic%20Corridor%20-%20Final.pdf.
9. Gill, Don McLain, 'The Geopolitics of the China-Pakistan Economic Corridor (CPEC) and its Security Implications for India', *The Korean Journal of International Studies*, 17 (3), 2019, pp. 337-354.
10. Wolf, Siegfried O., 'The myth of Pakistan acting as 'protector' of the Kashmiri people', *SADF Focus*, Issue No. 47, 2019, pp. 1-12.
11. EFSAS, 'China Pakistan Economic Corridor and Jammu & Kashmir', Amsterdam, 2017.
12. Hussain, Amir, 'Development challenges in Gilgit-Baltistan', *The News*, March 23, 2018, at https://www.thenews.com.pk/print/295630-development-challenges-in-gilgit-baltistan
13. Ramachandran, Sudha, 'Unrest in Gilgit-Baltistan and the China-Pakistan economic corridor', September 29, 2016, at https://www.cacianalyst.org/publications/analytical-articles/item/

13396-unrest-in-gilgitbaltistan-and-the-china-pakistan-economic-corridor.html.

14. Bhatt, Prajanya, 'Revisiting China's Kashmir Policy', *ORF Issue Brief,* Number 326, 2019, pp. 1-16.
15. Sharma, Surinder Kumar, Yaqoob ul Hassan and Ashok Behuria, *Pakistan Occupied Kashmir Politics, Parties and Personalities*, New Delhi, Pentagon Press, 2019.
16. Wasim, Amir, 'Technical hitches hinder work on economic zones', *Dawn,* August 14, 2019, at https://www.dawn.com/news/1499413
17. Belt and Road Initiative, 'Kohala Hydro Project', at https://www.beltroad-initiative.com/kohala-hydro-project/
18. Qureshi, Arif, 'Special Economic Zones will be established in Mirpur under CPEC: President AJK says', *The Fortress*, June 19, 2019, at https://thefortress.com.pk/special-economic-zones-will-be-established-in-mirpur-under-cpec-president-ajk-says/
19. Centre for Strategic and International Studies, 'Mirpur-Muzaffarabad-Mansehra Road (Construction)', at https://reconnectingasia.csis.org/database/projects/mirpur-muzaffarabad-mansehra-road-construction/d2c7ad2e-1398-45ac-809e-607864499278/
20. Pakistan Water and Power Development Authority, 'Hydro Potential in Pakistan', October, 2012, at http://climateinfo.pk/frontend/web/attachments/datatype/WAPDA%20(2012)%20Hydro%20Potential%20in%20Pakistan.pdf
21. UNDP, 'Sustainable Energy for All Investment Prospectus', December 19, 2019, at https://www.undp.org/content/dam/pakistan/docs/Environment%20&%20Climate%20Change/Investment%20Prospectus%20copy.pdf
22. 'CPEC includes Kashmir hydropower project', *The News*, November 18, 2019, at https://www.thenews.com.pk/print/552274-cpec-includes-kashmir-hydropower-project
23. Shafique, Muhammad, and Gohar Ali Iftikhar, 'Regional Dynamics of China Pakistan Economic Corridor (CPEC): The Case of Gilgit Baltistan', *Journal of Historical Studies*, 3 (II), 2017, pp. 15-29.
24. Khan, Zulfikar Ali, 'Gilgit-Baltistan at the Crossroad of CPEC: Part-II', *Pamir Times*, July 5, 2019, at https://pamirtimes.net/2019/07/05/gilgit-baltistan-at-the-crossroad-of-cpec-part-ii/
25. Centre for Strategic and International Studies, 'Chakdara-Chitral-Shandora-Gilgit Road (Construction)', at https://reconnectingasia.csis.org/database/projects/chakdara-chitral-shandora-gilgit-road-construction/7817ba5f-3f94-4def-b672-76845a5690ab/
26. 'CPEC is imperative to Azad Kashmir's development', *China Pakistan Institute*, February 12, 2020, http://cpecinfo.com/cpec-is-imperative-to-azad-kashmirs-development/
27. Pandya, Abhinav, 'Focus 50–China and Pakistan: Original Sinners of Gilgit-Baltistan and the 'Azad Jammu and Kashmir': A tale of genocide, covert demographic engineering, slavery, and suppression', *SADF*, April 16, 2020, at https://www.sadf.eu/focus-50-china-and-pakistan-original-sinners-of-gilgit-baltistan-and-the-azad-jammu-and-kashmir-a-tale-of-genocide-covert-demographic-engineering-slavery-and-suppressi/
28. EFSAS, op. cit., pp. 2 and 3.
29. Wolf, op. cit., p. 9.
30. Sharma, op. cit.
31. Pandya, op. cit.
32. Sial, Safdar and Peer Muhammad, 'Silk route monitor A review of developments on China-Pakistan, Economic Corridor', 2018, pp. 161-199, at https://www.pakpips.com/web/wp-content/uploads/2018/03/CPEC-1.pdf
33. OHCHR, 'Report on the Situation of Human Rights in Kashmir: Developments in the Indian State of Jammu and Kashmir from June 2016 to April 2018, and General Human Rights Concerns in Azad Jammu and Kashmir and Gilgit-Baltistan' *Office of the United Nations High Commissioner for Human Rights*, June 14, 2018, at https://www.ohchr.org/Documents/

Countries/PK/DevelopmentsInKashmirJune2016ToApril2018.pdf.
34. 'AJK CPEC projects in a doldrums', *The Nation*, October 8, 2020, at https://nation.com.pk/08-Oct-2019/ajk-cpec-projects-in-a-doldrums
35. Prasso, Sheridan, 'CPEC–China's most ambitious project in Pakistan has become a corridor to nowhere', *The Print*, March 3, 2020, at https://theprint.in/world/cpec-chinas-most-ambitious-project-in-pakistan-has-become-a-corridor-to-nowhere/374430/
36. Shafqat, Saeed, and Saba Shaid, *China Pakistan Economic Corridor: Demands, Dividends and Directions*, Lahore, Centre for Public Policy and Governance, 2018.

7

The China-Pakistan Economic Corridor in Balochistan and India's Concerns

Aditya Mani

The China Pakistan Economic Corridor (CPEC), proposed in May 2013 by Chinese Premier Li Keqiang during his visit to Pakistan, is a $ 62 billion connectivity project running from Kashgar in Xinjiang Uyghur Autonomous Region in northwest China to Gwadar in the Pakistani province of Balochistan covering a distance of around 3,000 km. It is a "flagship project" of the Belt and Road Initiative (BRI), a grand connectivity project launched by China to revive the ancient silk route connecting Asia with Europe and Africa via land and sea. The BRI is considered to be an outcome of several factors such as globalisation of China's manufacturing industry, middle easternisation of China's oil imports, the industrial over-capacity crisis at home, slowing down of economic growth, domestic security concerns and not to mention the extension of China's global diplomatic influence among others.[1] Economic prosperity remains an official objective of the BRI according to the White Paper "Vision and Actions on Jointly Building Silk Road Economic Belt and Twenty-first Century Maritime Silk Road" released by the National Development and Reform Commission, Ministry of Foreign Affairs, and Ministry of Commerce of People's Republic of China in 2015.

The BRI has land and maritime components that intend to develop the vital infrastructure for trade and commerce for which economic corridors become crucial, and the CPEC is one such Corridor. Of all the proposed corridors, the

CPEC stands out to be the most notable and ambitious, pegged at around 62 billion dollars.[2] Divided broadly into three routes, western, central, and eastern, the CPEC constitutes a network of roads, railway lines, oil and gas pipelines, Special Economic Zones (SEZs), and the most important, the development of the Gwadar port that will provide China easy and quick access to West Asia, the Arabian Sea, and the Indian Ocean Region.

The CPEC was formally launched in April 2015 by President Xi Jinping during his visit to Islamabad. With the unveiling of 51 MoUs, initially, Chinese investments were pegged at $ 46 billion, which later rose to $ 62 billion. The CPEC has four key focus areas, namely, the development of Gwadar port, energy, transport infrastructure, and industrial cooperation.[3] The broader objective of the CPEC is to build and modernise the undeveloped infrastructure that includes a web of railways, highways, oil and gas pipelines, optical fibre networks, bridges, dams, and so on stretching from Kashgar to Gwadar. The projects are to be completed in three phases wherein the short-term projects will be completed by 2020, medium-term projects by 2025, and the long-term projects by 2030. A large chunk of investments, around 75 per cent, is for energy projects, while the rest are for transportation and other projects.[4] Of the initial $ 46 billion investment, $ 34 billion was allocated for power projects.[5] It is in line with Pakistan's much-needed overhaul of the energy sector. For long, Pakistan has been reeling under an energy crisis with a shortfall of electricity ranging from 4000 MW to 7000 MW. Close to 140 million Pakistanis have either no access to electricity or suffer around 12 hours of load shedding.[6] The blackouts cost Pakistan's economy $ 18 billion in 2015.[7] As a country with a severe energy crisis and feeble transport infrastructure, the CPEC offers Pakistan an easy and fast solution to these issues.

Besides energy, investments in the transportation sector are expected to boost economic activity not only in the domestic market, but the enhanced connectivity will also help integrate Pakistan's economy with its neighbours. According to the Economic Survey 2017-18, the efficient transportation system will have a positive impact on stimulating trade, the expansion of markets, mobility of products, employment opportunities, education, and social welfare.[8] As per the report entitled "The Benefits of the Modern Economic Silk Road; The China–Pakistan Economic Corridor (CPEC)" published by the Association of Chartered Certificate Accountants (ACCA) and the Pakistan-China Institute (PCI) in 2017, the estimated job creation will hover between 700,000 and 800,000 by 2030.[9] The CPEC is also credited for being behind the increase in Pakistan's GDP to 5.3 per cent in 2017, the highest in a decade. The report came in the context of widespread criticism of the CPEC over the 'debt trap' and unfavourable negotiations on projects. It is this promise of socio-economic development that, despite facing considerable criticism, the CPEC is being regarded as a much-needed lifeline or 'game-changer.'[10]

Through the CPEC, the government is also hoping to contain the political instability at home that has turned out to be a challenge for the execution of the CPEC, especially in the restive province of Balochistan where the flagship Gwadar project is located. The Baloch insurgency has exacerbated concerns about the security and viability of the CPEC projects. The government's non-inclusive policies, widespread exploitation of natural resources, and rising unemployment due to little or no infrastructure, among others, have made Balochistan restive. Despite being rich in natural resources and contributing close to 40 per cent of the country's energy requirements, Balochistan itself is deprived of the benefits. It can be gauged from the fact that only 14 towns of 34 districts of Balochistan get gas supply despite being the second-largest producer of gas after Sindh.[11] Adding to its woes is the lack of access to clean water, sanitation, electricity, and dismal state of agriculture. The policymakers believe that the CPEC will address these issues by establishing the necessary infrastructure and facilitate economic development by connecting the province to other commercial hubs. It is also claimed that several energy projects in other provinces will lessen the burden on Balochistan and reduce the exploitation of resources. In all, the government expects that the CPEC has the potential to stabilise the restive province of Balochistan by bringing economic growth and development and generating employment opportunities.[12]

Despite the pleasant and favourable picture put forward, scepticism persists about the uneven distribution and execution of the projects, not to mention the viability of the CPEC. Provinces like Balochistan and Khyber Pakhtunkhwa have expressed their unease about the discriminatory treatment in the allocation of CPEC projects.[13] Corruption has been another key concern in the execution of projects. For instance, a committee formed by Prime Minister Imran Khan to examine the high electricity cost unveiled corruption of about 100 billion Pakistani rupees.[14] Nevertheless, contrary to all the fuss about the CPEC, in November 2019, Pakistan's Foreign Minister, Shah Mahmood Qureshi, while addressing a conference on the BRI in Islamabad, declared that Pakistan's top priority is to complete the CPEC.[15] Before that, Army Chief Qamar Javed Bajwa travelled to China in 2018 to reassure China of Pakistan's commitment to the CPEC against all odds.[16]

On the other side of the border in India, however, the CPEC, which is being promoted as a game-changer not only for Pakistan but for the entire South Asia, has not gained much traction. Ever since the CPEC was announced, India has vehemently protested against it on the grounds of infringement of its territorial sovereignty since the CPEC passes through the Gilgit-Baltistan region of Pakistan occupied Kashmir (PoK). Consequently, India has not joined the CPEC and the BRI as a whole. Concerning India's cooperation on the CPEC or the BRI, the official spokesperson of India's Ministry of External Affairs, on 5 April 2018, stated that India's position is clear that the CPEC violates its sovereignty and territorial integrity. Hence, India does not accept participation in such a project. Furthermore, India has cited other concerns such as lack of transparency, debt concerns, equality, and disregard for universally recognised international norms.[17] Not only is the CPEC traversing through PoK, India's concerns have been exacerbated by the CPEC projects in Pakistan's Balochistan province. According to the CPEC portal, Balochistan has a share of close to 20 projects. This includes road connectivity, port development, energy infrastructure projects, and others. Amongst these, the development of Gwadar port has drawn significant attention from India due to its strategic location and its potential to undermine India's interests. It is against this backdrop that this chapter attempts to understand how and up to what extent the development of Gwadar port and other projects in Balochistan impact India's economic, political and strategic interests.

CPEC in Balochistan

The CPEC has brought opportunities as well as raised concerns in Balochistan, the largest province of Pakistan, covering around 43 per cent of the total area with a long coastline. However, it is sparsely populated with approximately 12 million people and is most impoverished with a Human Development Index of 0.477, second from the bottom, despite being a resource-rich province.[18] Sitting on mineral wealth of around $ 1 trillion, neglect and political instability have resulted in minimal socio-economic development of the province.[19] According to the World Bank, Balochistan's poverty rate in 2015 stood at 42.5 per cent, the highest in Pakistan.[20] Multi-dimensional poverty is the highest in Balochistan, with access to health facilities standing at 17.3 per cent and school attendance at 10.5 per cent.[21] It is this underdevelopment in the province that the CPEC pledges to address by delivering economic prosperity. Despite being in such a wretched state of affairs, Balochistan, bordering Afghanistan and Iran, becomes strategically and economically crucial for Pakistan and is vital for the success of the CPEC as its flagship project that is Gwadar port lies in Balochistan. Gwadar is also home to almost half the CPEC projects in the province.[22]

The CPEC is supposed to connect Balochistan with Pakistan's economic hubs to bring much needed economic development and political stability. The proponents of the CPEC claim that the resource-rich province will benefit hugely from Chinese investments and technology. With estimated investments worth $ 7.1 billion in Balochistan, the province can serve as a focal point of economic activity in the region. The Pakistan government has planned 29 industrial parks and 21 mineral processing zones, many of them in Balochistan. Of all the projects, Gwadar port is the most significant as it will be a centre of economic and commercial activities. Provided the projects are executed as planned, several factors go in favour of Gwadar, such as its location, natural seawater port, quick turnaround, and the presence of a free zone for manufacturing, warehousing, and other purposes.[23] Despite the discontent that Balochistan has been discriminated against in the allocation of the projects, as stated earlier, it has got some key CPEC projects such as Gwadar port with substantial strategic significance. Along with the development of the Gwadar port, there are other projects concerning energy and transport infrastructure.

Table 1: CPEC Projects in Balochistan

S. No.	*Name of Project*	*Estimated Cost in PKR/USD*
1	Khuzdar-Basima Road N-30 (110 km)	19.19 billion PKR
2	Khuzdar-Quetta-Chaman Section (N-25) (421 km)	NA
3	Upgradation of D.I. Khan (Yarik)–Zhob (N-50) (210 km)	Rs.76,486 million
4	Zhob-Quetta (N-50) (331 km)	NA
5	Surab-Hoshab (N-85) (449 km)	Rs. 17.97 billion
6	Gwadar–Turbat–Hoshab (M-8) (193 km)	Rs. 13 billion
7	Gwadar East-Bay Expressway (Approx 19 km)	$ 168 million
8	Naukundi-Mashkhel-Panjgur Road Project connecting with M-8 & N-85	NA
9	HUBCO Coal Power Project, Hub Balochistan	$ 1,912.2 million
10	300MW Imported Coal Based Power Project, Gwadar	$ 542.32 million
11	New Gwadar International Airport	$ 230 million
12	Gwadar Smart Port City Master Plan	$ 4 million
13	Necessary Facilities of Fresh Water Treatment, Water Supply and Distribution,	$ 130 million
14	China-Pakistan Faqeer Primary School Project	$ 0.4 million
15	Pak-China Friendship Hospital	$ 100 million
16	Pak-China Technical and Vocational Institute at Gwadar	$ 10 million
17	Development of Free Zone, Gwadar	$ 32 million
18	CPEC Emergency Medical Centre in Gwadar	$ 1.6 million
19	Construction of Breakwaters	$ 123 million
20	Dredging of Berthing Areas & Channels	$ 27 million
21	Quetta Mass Transit	$ 1,626 million
22	Quetta Water Supply Scheme from Pat Feeder Canal, Balochistan	NA

Source: http://cpec.gov.pk/

Gwadar port, the flagship project of the CPEC, has seen speedy progress. The projects at Gwadar have been allocated around $ 770 million. These include Eastbay Expressway, Gwadar International Airport, construction of breakwaters, dredging of berthing areas and channels, infrastructure for Free Zone and EPZ-port-related industries, necessary facilities for fresh-water treatment and supply, hospital, and technical and vocational institute.[24] Since Gwadar has been a dusty and neglected town, these projects aim to make Gwadar more habitable and equipped to serve as serviceable trade and transit points. It is to be noted that Gwadar port is not entirely a new enterprise that appeared with the CPEC. The idea first gained currency in January 2000 when Pakistan President Pervez Musharraf visited Beijing and floated the idea of constructing Gwadar with China's assistance. Initially, the Gwadar project appeared insignificant to China with little or no value. Nevertheless, in May 2001, the Chinese Prime Minister, during his visit to Pakistan, declared China's interest in constructing the Gwadar port.[25]

During phase one of the Gwadar port development, China invested $ 198 million along with another $ 200 million in building the Karachi-Gwadar Highway. China had also provided technical expertise and a workforce for Gwadar. There can be several motivations behind China's interest in Gwadar. Contrary to earlier scepticism about Gwadar, China now looks at Gwadar from a strategic point of view. Besides providing an overland route to its western provinces, Gwadar may serve as a naval facility along the lines of China's Djibouti naval base.[26] The announcement of the CPEC made Gwadar the epicentre of this multibillion-dollar project. However, solely developing the Gwadar port is not sufficient since Pakistan's transport infrastructure is pretty undeveloped. Hence, the development of a corridor with rail and road networks, including other facilities, becomes imperative if China and Pakistan aspire to capitalise on the CPEC.

In this regard, the projects mentioned on the CPEC portal that can bridge this gap are the motorway and highway projects connecting Gwadar, Khuzdar, Quetta, Hoshab, Turbat, Zhob, Basima and Chaman, among others. Upon materialisation, this will help connect Gwadar not only to the rest of Balochistan but to other towns and cities in Pakistan and further to Afghanistan and Central Asia. There are rail and road projects in other provinces that will work as an add-on to the CPEC transport infrastructure. For instance, the roads linking Dera Ismail Khan-Angor Ada-Ghulam Khan, Peshawar-Torkham, and Jalalabad-Torkham connect Pakistan with the Paktika and Khost provinces of Afghanistan. When integrated with CPEC projects in Balochistan, this network of roads and railways can serve as a bridge not only for Pakistan and China but also for Afghanistan and the Central Asian Republics, providing suitable infrastructure to carry out trade and commerce through Gwadar port.[27]

Challenges to CPEC in Balochistan

Ever since the multibillion-dollar project was announced, differing voices on the CPEC have gained currency in Balochistan. Despite repeated assurances from the government that the CPEC will transform the impoverished province of Balochistan, there exists scepticism that the CPEC bears no significant value to Balochistan and is more of a political project, especially in the case of Gwadar. There has been a growing concern that the CPEC will result in the arrival of the Chinese workforce that will turn the locals into a minority.[28] According to one estimate, around one million newcomers are expected to settle in Gwadar alone, presenting a demographic challenge to the Baloch people.[29] Along with issues of state-led land grab and fishermen being denied entry to the sea, there has been criticism about the non-transparent nature of the deals casting doubt about the government's intentions. In 2013, the China Overseas Port Holding Company was given the leasing rights of the Gwadar port with Beijing getting 91 per cent profits and Islamabad the remaining 9 per cent, depriving Balochistan of any revenue.[30]

It is also alleged that Balochistan has not got its due share in the CPEC. The accusations of neglecting Balochistan in the CPEC have been reinforced by news reports about the dismal progress of the projects. The project completion rate has been around 24 per cent in Balochistan, which is almost half that of Punjab and Sindh with 47 per cent and 45 per cent completion rates, respectively. The CPEC comprises three routes, western, central, and eastern, where the western route passes through Balochistan. As per the design, priority was to be given to the western route. However, news reports indicate that most projects on the western route have come up with misleading assurances. There has been a realisation that rather than focussing on the western route in Balochistan, the government has prioritised the eastern route passing through Punjab and Sindh that forms its political support base. These allegations seem to have some currency as several major projects which were completed quickly are in the Punjab province, the political bastion of then Prime Minister Nawaz Sharif.[31]

There were also accusations that the government has betrayed the people of Balochistan by coining the term 'western route' when no such route exists and that it was just a word to ease the pressure from Balochistan. For instance, in 2015, the then Prime Minister Nawaz Sharif, inaugurated what was to be called the western route in Zhob, Balochistan. However, later it was discovered that this had nothing to do with the CPEC, and that the Asian Development Bank had funded the project.[32] This gave impetus to the allegations of false promises on the CPEC to Balochistan.[33] The irritation was evident when, in 2018, the Chief

Minister of Balochistan refused to attend a CPEC coordination meeting in Beijing.[34] With the new dispensation in Islamabad, Balochistan expects to get its due share in the mega project. During his visit to Quetta in October 2018, Prime Minister Imran Khan affirmed that Balochistan would be paid more than its due share in the CPEC. However, contrary to the government assurances, Balochistan's share in the CPEC remains as low as 4.5 per cent. This works out to a mere 1 per cent if the Gwadar and Hubco projects are not considered.[35]

Moreover, as stated earlier, the insurgency in Balochistan has also posed a challenge to the CPEC. Baloch insurgent groups level the accusation that Islamabad, with China's assistance, is looting the natural resources of the province. Baloch insurgents are also apprehensive that Chinese presence is aimed at crushing the insurgency. This has resulted in attacks by Baloch armed groups on project sites and workers. In 2018, there was an attack on a bus carrying Chinese engineers followed by an attack on the Chinese consulate in Karachi the same year. In May 2019, BLA gunmen attacked the Pearl Continental Hotel in Gwadar. The security situation in Balochistan has posed a serious challenge to the execution of CPEC projects. To address the security situation, China has been trying to engage with Baloch political and tribal leaders while Pakistan is planning to raise a special force to protect the CPEC. For instance, in 2019, Beijing invited the governor, former chief minister of Balochistan, along with tribal leaders who were critical of CPEC projects in Balochistan. However, it may not yield the desired results as it is the Baloch insurgent groups that pose a serious challenge, and there was no representation from them.[36]

India's Concerns

The CPEC in Balochistan has sparked off a debate on likely implications for India. The most noteworthy point of the debate is Gwadar, which is widely believed to undermine India's economic, security and strategic interests in the immediate neighbourhood and beyond. Gwadar is located close to the international sea lanes for shipping of oil and strives to become a transit hub providing China easy and fast access to West Asia and Africa along with serving as a gateway to landlocked Afghanistan and further to the Central Asian Republics. Since the very beginning, there has been a contest on the potential use of Gwadar port. While China and Pakistan have maintained that India's apprehensions are uncorroborated and that Gwadar is essentially an economic enterprise to serve as a transit hub, India is apprehensive that Gwadar may turn out to be a potential naval base for the Chinese military.

This argument may warrant some merit since Pakistan had earlier expressed its desire to make Gwadar a naval base. In 2011, during his visit to China, the Pakistani Prime Minister invited China to build a naval base at Gwadar. Gwadar port has all the prerequisites to serve as a naval base due to its ability to accommodate submarines and aircraft carriers.[37] India's concerns vis-à-vis Gwadar were further exacerbated with China taking over Hambantota port in Sri Lanka, which only added to the fears of China's military plans in the region. Moreover, if it materialises as expected, Chinese investments in Gwadar and other projects in Balochistan are likely to improve the transport infrastructure, which may attract more trade and commerce from Afghanistan and the Central Asian Republics. This will invariably be an economic blow to India's interests in Chabahar in Iran and Afghanistan.

Strategic Concerns

Apart from the CPEC passing through Pakistan occupied Kashmir (PoK), the primary concern regarding the CPEC, as mentioned above, is the development of the strategically located Gwadar port in Balochistan. Notwithstanding the Chinese and Pakistani stance on Gwadar being just a port for trade and commerce, India has repeatedly expressed its concerns about Gwadar. India's concerns come in the light of China's rising geopolitical clout and influence in the region, perhaps aimed to fill the vacuum created by waning US influence and its imminent withdrawal from Afghanistan.

Moreover, in the wake of rising tensions between the USA and China over several issues, especially China's assertive behaviour in the South China Sea, if at all there is any blockade, Gwadar can be of considerable use to China. Although Gwadar can drastically cut the distance from the Arabian Sea to Xinjiang, the sheer feasibility of Gwadar dramatically transforming the energy import scenario for China remains doubtful. For instance, there has been a proposal to build a gas pipeline from Gwadar to Kashgar with an estimated capacity of 1 billion barrels per day.[38] However, the harsh geographic conditions, challenging terrain, and harsh climatic conditions with frequent landslides can raise the cost of the infrastructure manifold, raising the cost of transportation. It is also doubtful whether Gwadar alone can transport enough for China's growing energy appetite. Such ambiguities give further impetus to India's concerns regarding the development of Gwadar.

India's foremost concern with Gwadar is that it can be used as a naval base by China, threatening India's security and energy interests in the region. India imports two-thirds of the oil and half of the LNG via the Strait of Hormuz and Chinese military presence at Gwadar will undoubtedly be of concern to India.[39] Even though there are no visible signs of Chinese naval presence at Gwadar as of now, India's concerns may not be unfounded. This stems from the fact that China Overseas Ports Holding Company gets a 91 per cent share in the revenue from Gwadar Port for 40 years. That points towards the extent of influence that China can exercise on Gwadar.[40] Moreover, the takeover of Hambantota port in Sri Lanka has also augmented India's concerns that Gwadar may repeat Hambantota, further consolidating the Chinese presence. Also, China's track record of adopting a belligerent attitude in the South China Sea adds to the fear. Chinese acquisition and infrastructural projects in the Indian Ocean Region such as in Kyaukpyu in Myanmar, Hambantota in Sri Lanka, and islands in the Maldives have opened the debate that China is seeking to establish and strengthen its presence in the Indian Ocean Region.[41]

Gwadar has also risen as a challenge to India's strategic outreach attempt in the context of Chabahar port. Chabahar is around 100 km from Gwadar and is being developed by India, giving it access to Afghanistan and Central Asia. However, the developments in the last few years have attracted Iranian resentment on India's commitment and conviction, paving the way for China to play a more significant role in the region, which is already invested in Gwadar. Unlike China, India reduced the import of Iranian oil to a large extent due to US sanctions. Iranian Ambassador to India Ali Chegeni remarked on the development that India's decision has been different from Russia, Turkey, and China, who have retained their energy engagements with Iran. The envoy also discussed Chabahar port and stated that India's progress has been relatively slow despite the waivers in the sanctions. This allows China to play a more significant role in Iran. It sounds possible as China is already present at Gwadar and is seeking to expand its foothold. The CPEC has also attracted Iran, which looks forward to building a pipeline from Iran to China along the CPEC. According to the Iranian envoy, this is the result of India's lost interests in LNG imports from Iran.[42]

In the absence of India's firm conviction about the projects in Iran due to various constraints, the CPEC, especially in Balochistan, has come as a viable alternative for Iran to develop and integrate its South Eastern region with it. In this regard, Iranian Foreign Minister Javad Zarif, during his visit to Pakistan in March 2018, invited Pakistan and China to participate in the Chabahar project.[43] Iran's efforts yielded results, when in August 2019, during Javad Zarif's visit to Beijing, China pledged to invest about $ 400 billion in the oil and gas sectors along with transportation and manufacturing sectors over the next 25 years along with the stationing of 5,000 Chinese security personnel to protect the investments.[44] Since India has invested in Chabahar, Iran's offer to Pakistan and China does not bode well for India. China's involvement at Chabahar can be a strategic blow to India, but for China, it serves as hedging with multiple openings rather than solely relying on Gwadar.[45] Also, in the wake of rising tensions between the USA and Iran, there are chances of increased US presence in the region. The USA is leading the International Maritime Security Construct (IMSC) that patrols the shipping lanes. In such a scenario, there is a probability that China will have a military presence to protect its interests if any conflict arises. Therefore, China's presence at Gwadar and Chabahar can be detrimental to India's strategic outreach attempts in the region.[46]

Economic Concerns

Besides the threat to India's strategic and security interests, the CPEC can impair India's economic interests too. The flagship project of the CPEC, Gwadar, can be an economic impediment for India in the light of the Chabahar port being developed by India, which may lose much of its business to Gwadar that became operational in November 2016. Chabahar port gives India access to Afghanistan and the Central Asian Republics bypassing Pakistan. In 2016, a trilateral agreement, also called the Chabahar Agreement on the Establishment of International Transport and Transit Corridor, was signed by India and Afghanistan to develop Chabahar port.[47] Consequently, India issued $ 150 million in credit for the project. In October 2017, the first Afghanistan-bound wheat shipment left India, marking a new strategic window to Afghanistan.[48] The port was formally inaugurated in December 2017 by Iranian President Hassan Rouhani.[49] In January 2019, Chabahar port commenced operations. In February 2019, Afghanistan exported the first shipment to India via Chabahar containing textiles, carpets—more than 500 tons of dried fruits and other items.[50] Since its inauguration, around 4,500 containers with about half a million tonnes of cargo from India have moved through Chabahar.[51] However, there is a possibility that in the near future, India's efforts at Chabahar may be dwarfed by Gwadar port, which has pulled far superior investments than Chabahar.

Gwadar's development, including other rail and road projects, has placed some critical economic challenges before India, especially when it comes to India's Chabahar venture. This includes the better rail and road connectivity of Gwadar to various towns and cities within Pakistan, consequently improving Gwadar's connectivity with the rest of Pakistan and further to Afghanistan and Central Asia. While crippling US sanctions on Iran already exist, due to the recent escalation of tensions between the USA and Iran in the wake of the killing of General Qassim

Soleimani the situation has become more complex. The USA has indicated that more sanctions will follow, putting further constraints on India's Chabahar venture, further crippling India's efforts. Such a situation can undermine the economic viability of Chabahar and give an edge to Gwadar.

After Chabahar became operational, Afghanistan shifted much of its cargo from Pakistan's ports to Chabahar, as reflected in 2017 when Afghanistan's Chief Executive, Abdullah, stated that Afghanistan is no more dependent on Pakistan.[52] This was undoubtedly a welcoming statement for India, but Chabahar comes with its own challenges that can tilt the Afghan businesses towards Gwadar. Despite India getting a waiver to develop Chabahar port, Afghan businesses and banks are hesitant in employing Iranian facilities due to USA-Iran tensions, and USA-imposed sanctions.[53] Companies doing business have been facing issues in transferring funds since there remains ample ambiguity about how the exemptions will work for the businesses in the port's free zone.[54] On the other hand, Gwadar does not face the wrath of US sanctions and hence comes with greater financial flexibility and feasibility.

Compared to Gwadar, where the progress seems relatively fast, India's conviction at Chabahar and other associated rail and road projects has displeased Iran. This is reflected in India's decision to decrease the funds for Chabahar, which came down to INR 45 crore in 2019 from INR 150 crore. India was to build a railway line from Chabahar to Zahedan and further to Zaranj in Afghanistan and further to be extended to Sarakhs on the Turkmenistan border. This will boost India's trade with Afghanistan and Central Asia. However, in July 2020, unconfirmed media reports stated that India has been dropped from the Chabahar rail project citing India's reluctance due to US sanctions and that Iran would build it by itself. However, Iran denied any such move and India's Ministry of External Affairs also ruled out the media reports.[55]

Moreover, other projects under the CPEC in Balochistan are likely to boost the transportation apparatus in the region. During the China-Afghanistan-Pakistan Foreign Ministers' dialogue in September 2019, China expressed its support to construct refrigeration storages, clinic centres, immigration reception centres and supply water along the Afghanistan-Pakistan border to facilitate trade and commerce.[56] This will strengthen CPEC infrastructure and is likely to attract more trading activities to Gwadar from Afghanistan and Central Asia than Chabahar. In such a scenario, less traffic at Chabahar will make it economically less viable while turning Gwadar, the jewel of the CPEC, into a relatively better alternative. At a time when India wishes to utilise the economic potential of Afghanistan and Central Asia by making Chabahar the fulcrum of its Central

Asia policy, Gwadar, with relatively better facilities and robust infrastructure, can turn out to be an economic blow to India.[57]

Conclusion

The CPEC, which India has been vehemently opposed to ever since it was announced, is there to stay, as indicated by the Chinese and Pakistani leadership. Despite facing considerable challenges in Balochistan, several CPEC projects have been completed, or work is being done at a rapid pace. One such project is the Gwadar port in Balochistan. Being the fulcrum of the CPEC, it contributes to India's concerns immensely since it has the potential to undermine India's security, strategic and economic interests in the region. Besides the fear that Gwadar may become a Chinese naval base in the future, India's concerns vis-à-vis Gwadar also arise in the context of Chabahar port, where deep-pocketed China dwarfs India's efforts. Therefore, it becomes imperative for India to play a proactive role in both Iran and Afghanistan on whom depend the viability and success of Chabahar. Also, India needs to effectively capitalise on the exemptions by the USA on Chabahar port to speedily and effectively complete the infrastructure projects in the region in a time-bound manner to create backward and forward linkages for smooth movement of cargo. Moreover, it cannot be denied that there exists a possibility of some sort of cooperation with China and Pakistan to fill the infrastructure gap in the neighbourhood and safeguard its interests at the same time. This, perhaps, is the most daunting challenge at hand for India.

NOTES

1. Zou, Lei (2018). *The Political Economy Of China's Belt And Road Initiative*. Vol. 1. World Scientific.
2. Aneja, Atul (2016). "Emphasis on Gwadar-Kashgar Corridor." *The Hindu*. August 30. Visit at https://www.thehindu.com/news/international/emphasis-on-gwadarkashgar-corridor/article7126901.ece.
3. Manish and Prashant Kaushik (2019). "CPEC, Afghanistan and India's Concerns". *India Quarterly: A Journal of International Affairs* 75 (2): 253–61. DOI: https://doi.org/10.1177%2F0974928419841790.
4. Roy, Nalanda (2019). 'China-Pakistan Economic Corridor–Is It the Road to the Future?' *Asian Affairs* 50 (02). DOI: https://doi.org/10.1080/03068374.2019.1614767.
5. Markey, Daniel (2020). *China's Western Horizon: Beijing and the New Geopolitics of Eurasia*. Oxford University Press.
6. '7 Facts about Pakistan's Energy Crisis %and How You Can Help End It'. 2016. *Dawn*. August 5. Visit at http://www.dawn.com/news/1275116
7. https://blogs.worldbank.org/endpovertyinsouthasia/what-s-keeping-pakistan-dark
8. Ali, Kalbe (2018). 'CPEC Dominates Transport Sector'. *Dawn*. April 27. Visit at https://www.dawn.com/news/1404159
9. 'The Benefits of the Modern Economic Silk Road; The China–Pakistan Economic Corridor

(CPEC)'. 2017. Association of Chartered Certified Accountants and Pakistan-China Institute (PCI). Visit at https://www.accaglobal.com/ca/en/professional-insights/global-economics/the-economic-benefits-of-the-modern-silk-road.html

10. Andersen, Lars Erslev and Yang Jiang (2018). 'Pakistan and the Belt and Road Initiative'. Danish Institute for International Studies. https://www.jstor.org/stable/resrep21436.8
11. Jan Shohaz, Sher (2020). 'Balochistan Gas'. *Dawn.* January 16. https://www.dawn.com/news/1457876.
12. Saleem, Ali Haider (2017). 'CPEC and Balochistan: Prospects of Socio-Political Stability'. *Strategic Studies* 37 (4). Institute of Strategic Studies, Islamabad: 118–32. doi:10.2307/48537575
13. Wolf, Siegfried O. (2020). *The China-Pakistan Economic Corridor of the Belt and Road Initiative: Concept, Context and Assessment.* Springer.
14. Haqqani, Hussain (2020). 'Pakistan Discovers the High Cost of Chinese Investment'. *The Diplomat.* Accessed May 19. https://thediplomat.com/2020/05/pakistan-discovers-the-high-cost-of-chinese-investment/
15. 'Completion of CPEC Pakistan's Top Priority: Mahmood Qureshi'. 2020. *AAJ News.* Accessed May 19. https://www.aaj.tv/english/national/completion-of-cpec-pakistans-top-priority-shah-mahmood-qureshi/
16. Markey, Daniel (2020). *China's Western Horizon: Beijing and the New Geopolitics of Eurasia.* Oxford University Press.
17. https://bit.ly/2LSJWCo
18. Hillman, Jonathan E. and Maesea McCalpin (2020). "The China-Pakistan Economic Corridor at Five." Centre for Strategic and International Studies (CSIS). Visit at https://www.csis.org/analysis/china-pakistan-economic-corridor-five
19. Siddiqui, Ehtesham (2010). 'Untapped Mineral Deposits in Balochistan'. *Dawn.com.* June 18. Visit at http://beta.dawn.com/news/861369/untapped-mineral-deposits-in-balochistan
20. Redaelli, Silvia (2019). 'Pakistan at 100/ : From Poverty to Equity'. 135319. The World Bank. Visit at http://documents.worldbank.org/curated/en/868741552632296526/Pakistan-at-Hundred-From-Poverty-to-Equity
21. https://www.pk.undp.org/content/pakistan/en/home/library/development_policy/dap-sp-issue-balochistan.html
22. Hillman, Jonathan E. and Maesea McCalpin (2020). "The China-Pakistan Economic Corridor at Five." Centre for Strategic and International Studies (CSIS).
23. Khetran, Mir Sher Baz and Muhammad Anjum Saeed (2017). "The CPEC and China-Pakistan Relations: A Case Study on Balochistan." *China Quarterly of International Strategic Studies* 03 (03): 447–61. doi:10.1142/s2377740017500191
24. Khetran, Mir Sher Baz and Muhammad Anjum Saeed (2017). "The CPEC and China-Pakistan Relations: A Case Study on Balochistan." *China Quarterly of International Strategic Studies* 03 (03): 447–61. doi:10.1142/s2377740017500191
25. Markey, Daniel (2020). *China's Western Horizon: Beijing and the New Geopolitics of Eurasia.* Oxford University Press.
26. Ibid.
27. Chandran, Anurag Ram (2017). "Why Afghanistan Should Join CPEC." *The Diplomat.* May 5. Visit at https://thediplomat.com/2017/05/why-afghanistan-should-join-cpec/
28. Khan, Sattar (2020). 'Gwadar–Pakistan2 s Impoverished Colony or an Economic Hub?' *Deutsche Welle.* Accessed April 10. Visit at https://www.dw.com/en/gwadar-pakistans-impoverished-colony-or-an-economic-hub/a-19185999
29. Wolf, Siegfried O. (2020). *The China-Pakistan Economic Corridor of the Belt and Road Initiative: Concept, Context and Assessment.* Springer.

30. https://www.crisisgroup.org/asia/north-east-asia/china/national-ambitions-meet-local-opposition-along-china-pakistan-economic-corridor
31. Rafiq, Arif (2019). 'The China-Pakistan Economic Corridor: The Lure of Easy Financing and the Perils of Poor Planning'. *Asian Affairs* 50 (2): 236–48. doi:10.1080/03068374.2019.1602384
32. Aamir, Adnan (2019). 'The Myth of CPEC's Western Route'. *The Friday Times*. November 8. https://www.thefridaytimes.com/the-myth-of-cpecs-western-route/
33. In a briefing provided to the Balochistan cabinet by the CPEC Cell, it was revealed that except Gwadar, there has not been any noticeable progress in any of the projects. Of the allocated amount of around $ 5.5 billion, less than $ 1 billion has been spent. View: https://www.dawn.com/news/1450773
34. Markey, Daniel (2020). *China's Western Horizon: Beijing and the New Geopolitics of Eurasia*. Oxford University Press.
35. Akbar, Malik Siraj (2019). 'Eight Months in, How Is Balochistan Faring?' *Dawn.com*. April 4. https://www.dawn.com/news/1473862
36. Aamir, Adnan (2019). 'China's Efforts to Speed up Belt and Road in Pakistan Falters'. *Nikkei Asian Review*. September. Visit at https://asia.nikkei.com/Spotlight/Belt-and-Road/China-s-efforts-to-speed-up-Belt-and-Road-in-Pakistan-falters
37. Bokhari, Farhan and Kathrin Hille (2011). 'Pakistan Turns to China for Naval Base'. *Financial Times*. May 23. https://www.ft.com/content/3914bd36-8467-11e0-afcb-00144feabdc0
38. See, https://bit.ly/2tufPHR
39. Chaudhury, Dipanjan Roy (2020). 'India Engages with Iran to Keep Strait of Hormuz Safe'. *The Economic Times*. Accessed May 19. See, https://economictimes.indiatimes.com/news/politics-and-nation/india-engages-with-iran-to-keep-strait-of-hormuz-safe/articleshow/73197846.cms
40. Aamir, Adnan (2017). 'Will Gwadar Go the Way of Hambantota? Why Chinese Loans to Pakistan Are Sparking Takeover Fears along the Economic Corridor'. *South China Morning Post*. December 27. See https://www.scmp.com/comment/insight-opinion/article/2125783/will-gwadar-go-way-hambantota-why-chinese-loans-pakistan-are
41. Iwanek, Krzysztof (2019). 'No, Pakistan's Gwadar Port Is Not a Chinese Naval Base (Just Yet)'. *The Diplomat*. November 19. See, https://thediplomat.com/2019/11/no-pakistans-gwadar-port-is-not-a-chinese-naval-base-just-yet/
42. Haidar, Suhasini (2019). 'India Should Not Have Joined U.S. Ban, Says Iran'. *The Hindu*, September 10. See https://www.thehindu.com/news/national/india-should-not-have-joined-us-ban-says-iran/article29386180.ece
43. Syed, Baqir Sajjad (2018). 'Iran Invites Pakistan to Participate in Chahbahar Project'. *Dawn.com*. March 13. See https://www.dawn.com/news/1394938
44. 'China "Pledges $400bn" to Develop Iran's Energy, Transport and Manufacturing Sectors'. 2019. *Global Construction Review*. September 6. See, http://www.globalconstructionreview.com/news/china-de5velop-arctic-silk-road/
45. Mohan, C. Raja (2014). 'Afghanistan: The Great Game Folio'. *The Indian Express*. December 12. See https://indianexpress.com/article/opinion/columns/the-great-game-folio-36/
46. Fazl-e-Haide, Syed (2019). 'Shifting Alliances in the Gulf a Boon to China'. *The Lowy Institute*. November 18. See, https://www.lowyinstitute.org/the-interpreter/shifting-alliances-gulf-boon-china.
47. See https://pib.gov.in/newsite/printrelease.aspx?relid=151240
48. See https://www.thehindubusinessline.com/economy/logistics/india-sends-first-wheat-shipment-to-afghanistan-via-chabahar-port/article9929741.ece
49. Pant, Harsh V. and Ketan Mehta (2018). 'India in Chabahar: A Regional Imperative'. *Asian*

Survey 58 (4). University of California Press: 660–78. doi:10.1525/as.2018.58.4.660

50. See, https://www.rferl.org/a/afghanistan-first-exports-india-chabahar-iran/29787862.html
51. See, https://www.thehindubusinessline.com/economy/logistics/india-looks-to-leverage-chabahar-port-to-boost-trade-with-central-asia/article30462511.ece
52. Manish and Prashant Kaushik (2019). "CPEC, Afghanistan and India's Concerns". *India Quarterly: A Journal of International Affairs* 75 (2): 253–61. doi: https://doi.org/10.1177%2F0974928419841790
53. Haidar, Suhasini (2019). 'U.S. Curbs, Chabahar Downgrade Choke Indo-Afghan Trade'. *The Hindu*, July 8. See https://www.thehindu.com/news/national/us-curbs-chabahar-downgrade-choke-indo-afghan-trade/article28313199.ece
54. Kapoor, Sanjay (2019). 'The Chabahar Angle to Iran Sanctions'. *The Hindu Business Line.* July 9. See https://www.thehindubusinessline.com/opinion/the-chabahar-angle-to-iran-sanctions/article28334469.ece
55. Sandhu, Kamaljit Kaur (2020), 'Chabahar-Zahedan Railway Line: MEA Says India Not Dropped from Key Project, Puts Ball in Iran's Court'. *India Today.* Accessed July 30. See https://www.indiatoday.in/india/story/chabahar-zahedan-railway-line-mea-says-india-not-dropped-from-key-project-puts-ball-in-iran-s-court-1701322-2020-07-16
56. See https://www.mfa.gov.af/statements/1272-joint-statement-of-the-3rd-china-afghanistan-pakistan-foreign-ministers-dialogue.html
57. Kapoor, Sanjay (2020). 'The Chabahar Angle to Iran Sanctions'. *The Hindu Business Line.* Accessed May 19, https://www.thehindubusinessline.com/opinion/the-chabahar-angle-to-iran-sanctions/article28334469.ece

8

BRI and Nepal-China Relations

Sanjay K. Jha

Introduction

Nepal's relationship with China and India has been conditioned by geographical, historical and cultural factors, and domestic political imperatives. Since Nepal is a landlocked country, its geographical position makes it a buffer state between these two rising powers, with a history of chequered relationship. This geopolitical rivalry has been witnessed in two broad trends that are visible in Nepal's foreign policy. The first is related to a gradual increase in China's presence and influence in Nepal's polity, and the second is the periodic ups and downs in Nepal's relations with India. However, it would be premature at this juncture to make a definite assessment as to whether these trends represent a permanent shift in the relationship of Nepal with India and China.

Since the initiation of the BRI by China, the relationship between these two countries also represent the emerging realignment of power politics at the regional and global levels. In this context, Nepal's decision to join the BRI needs to be viewed not only through the prism of domestic developmental imperatives in Nepal but also from the perspective of the unfolding geopolitics of the region. The pertinent question that merits examination in this context is the timing of Nepal's decision to join the BRI. It joined the BRI in 2017 when there was growing anxiety and apprehensions in many countries about many aspects of the BRI, particularly in terms of financing, possibilities of a debt trap, institutional capacity of recipient states to execute mega projects and strategic entrenchment of China in participating countries of the BRI.

Infrastructure and Connectivity under BRI in Nepal

Infrastructure and connectivity have emerged as a central focus of China's engagement with Nepal under the BRI banner. These projects intend to connect both countries through an elaborate network of connectivity projects, strengthen related institutional and policy architecture with an objective to facilitate smooth economic transactions and enhanced people-to-people contact. These initiatives will benefit areas like agriculture, tourism, education, health, and culture. Reports of the Nepal government on infrastructure projects suggest that the railway network, hydropower projects, trans-border transmission lines, optical fibre connectivity and so on, are marked as priority areas.[1] These projects aim at enhancing Nepal's connectivity with China and the outside world via railways, highways, optical fibre networks, transmission lines, and gas pipelines.[2] In this context, it would be worth mentioning that the cross-border optical fibre network established between Nepal and China for the first time would connect Nepal with global telecom and Internet services, significantly reducing Nepal's dependence on India.[3] These infrastructure and connectivity projects have been

Map 1: Road Connectivity Projects in Nepal under the BRI

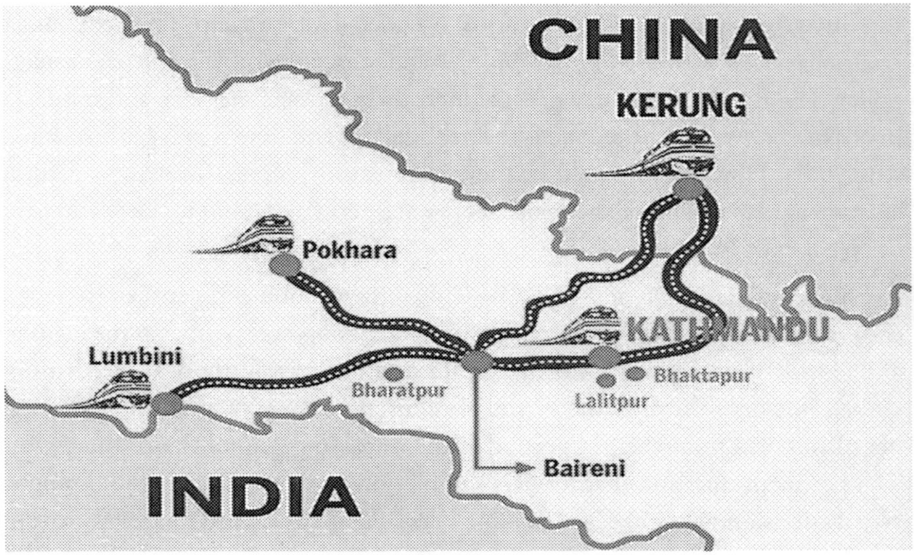

Source: Abhilasha Pokhrel, "BRI for socio-economic development, not for political objective', January 31, 2020, Accessed at https://nepal24hours.com/bri-for-socio-economic-development-not-for-political-objective/

able to get substantial public support because of hardships that they had to endure during the 'informal' economic blockade in 2015 in the aftermath of the promulgation of a new constitution in Nepal.

Under the BRI, Nepal agreed to work on a US$ 2.75 billion Trans-Himalayan Multi-dimensional Connectivity Network for the construction of a tunnel along the road from Jilong/Kerung to Kathmandu and also for conducting a feasibility study for the construction of a railway line.[4] For China, the trans-Himalayan railway has been projected as a game-changer for Nepal with the potential of unlimited possibilities for further development.[5] The Qinghai-Tibet railway line, which runs through the world's highest plateau, was expected to touch the Nepal-China border point of Kerung by 2020.[6] Further, the proposed 550-km-long railway would connect China's western Tibet region to Nepal's capital, Kathmandu, and carry goods and passengers.

During discussions between the two countries, many other connectivity projects with far-reaching implications have been identified. Some of them include the Kimathanka-Leguwaghat section of the Koshi Highway, development of three North-South corridors in Nepal: the Koshi Economic Corridor, Gandaki Economic Corridor, and Karnali Economic Corridor. A joint communique between the two countries also proposed the establishment of a multi-disciplinary Madan Bhandari University for Science and Technology in Nepal with Chinese

Map 2: Proposed Trans-Himalayan Rail Network in Nepal

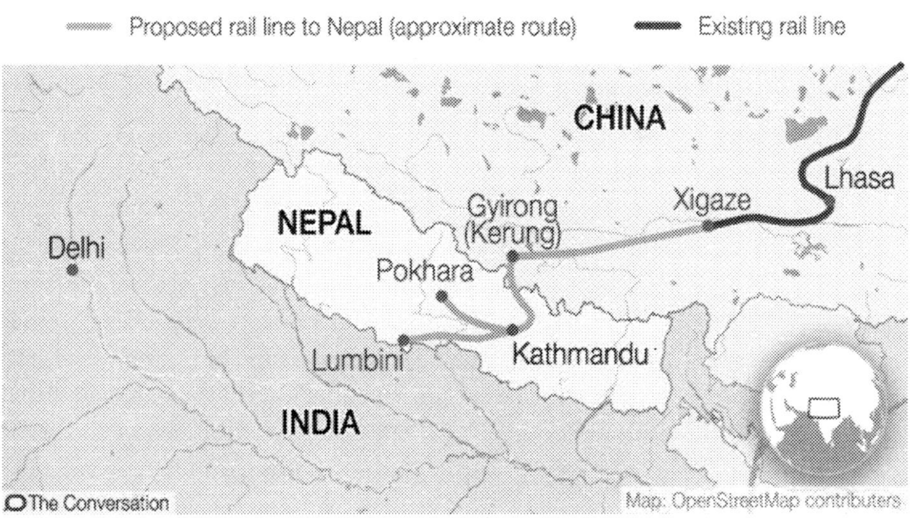

Source: Ramesh Bhushan, "Nepal-China railway project: fantasy or reality?" *The Third Pole*, June 18, 2019, accessed at https://www.thethirdpole.net/2019/06/18/nepal-china-railway/

support. Investment worth $ 500 million has been pledged in different projects. The Chinese also agreed to provide 100 Confucius Institute scholarships to the Nepalese.[7] Many of these projects are aimed at creating favourable public opinion for China in Nepal.

Nepal's Journey to BRI

Though Nepal's leadership showed considerable interest in the BRI, progress between 2013 (when the BRI, then OBOR, was formally announced) and 2017 (when Nepal formally joined the BRI) was relatively slow. There was no clear roadmap, articulation of interest, and systematic thinking on the BRI. In 2014, the government, led by Sushil Koirala, while welcoming the BRI expressed the desire, "to work in close cooperation with China towards enhancing more connectivity and integration between nations and boost their infrastructure, trade, energy sector and tourism, which would ultimately contribute to regional harmony, peace and development".[8]

With the emerging geostrategic environment concerning the ambitions of China, Nepal's estranged relationship with India, and the pro-China tilt of the ruling CPN, Nepal expressed its readiness to actively participate in the BRI to push 'Nepal-China all-round cooperation to a new and higher level'.[9] During K.P. Sharma Oli's first tenure as Prime Minister, Nepal signed the "Trade and Transit Agreement" with China in March 2016. The agreement, in many ways, opened the door of BRI projects for Nepal. The signing of a transit and transportation protocol between the two countries intended to give Nepal access to Chinese sea and land ports.[10] This was seen as an important step towards reducing its traditional trade dependence on India.

During Sher Bahadur Deuba's government, around 22 different development projects were identified to be taken up under the BRI. They covered areas such as Physical Infrastructural, Transportation, Culture, and Tourism, Civil Aviation, Water Supply, Sanitation, Irrigation, and Hydro-energy sectors. However, due to inadequate progress in negotiations, both the countries finally identified nine projects to be taken up on priority. Of these, four projects were related to road construction, two hydropower projects, one on transmission lines, and a feasibility study for a Kerung-Kathmandu railroad construction. One of the stated objectives of these connectivity projects was to facilitate connectivity between India and China through Nepal.[11] However, despite greater coordination between the two countries, actual progress on these projects remained slow.

The Pushpa Kamal Dahal-led government, in the final months of its tenure, agreed to formally join the BRI with the signing of an MoU with China in May

2017. It is worth mentioning here that the MoU was signed just two days ahead of a summit on the BRI Forum for International Cooperation in Beijing. The major thrust of the MoU was to promote mutually beneficial cooperation between Nepal and China on infrastructure and trade connectivity, financial integration, and movement of people. The 2017 MoU was expected to bring tremendous opportunities creating a win-win situation for both China and Nepal.[12] Major areas identified under the MoU were the connectivity infrastructure related to railways, roads, civil aviation, power grid, information, and communication.[13] It was expected that the focus on infrastructure would bring investment to different parts of Nepal and will help develop local industries. Nepal's government and media hailed the MoU as a new chapter in the area of foreign investment and cooperation. It was expected that Nepal would reap the benefit from major Chinese projects in different parts of the world, including those in Europe and Africa.[14]

Another major push to Nepal's journey to the BRI came during the visit of Prime Minister Oli to China in June 2018. During his meeting with his Chinese counterpart, Li Keqiang, at the Great Hall of the People in Beijing on 21 June 2018, Prime Minister Oli presented a list of 35 projects to be funded under the BRI. Both the governments agreed to intensify the implementation of the MoU on the BRI, particularly on connectivity projects such as ports, roads, railways, aviation, and communications as part of the trans-Himalayan Multi-Dimensional Connectivity Network. Major components of these projects were the reopening of Zhangmu/Khasa port; improving the operation of the Jilong/Kerung port; ensuring proper operation of Araniko Highway; and carrying out the repair, maintenance, and improvement of the Syaphrubesi-Rasuwagadhi Highway and push forward the construction of a bridge over the Karnali River at Hilsa of Pulan/Yari port at an early date.[15] The Oli government presented the BRI as a significant achievement of Nepal's development endeavour with prospects for opening up a new door with multiple opportunities for infrastructure development and economic growth.

During President Xi Jinping's visit to Nepal in October 2019, the first by a Chinese President in 23 years, both the countries signed 20 agreements. China also committed to extend aid for rebuilding the road between Kathmandu and Rasuwandhi (Nepal)/Kerung (Tibet) border point in the next four to five years. This route has been projected as more significant compared to the existing Kathmandu-Tatopani-Lhasa route built in the 1960s as it could reduce the transportation time between the two places from almost six hours to two hours. Two sister-city agreements were also signed between Kathmandu and Nanjing, and Butwal Xi'an. There was also an agreement for setting up Confucius Institutes at Tribhuvan University in Kathmandu. China also committed Rs. 56 billion as economic assistance for the period 2020-2022.[16] As per reports, President Xi asserted during the visit that Nepal and China are strategic partners. This assertion was interpreted by many commentators as an attempt by China to 'secure the space that India occupied in Nepal'.[17]

There was a high level of Nepali participation in the second edition of the BRI Forum for International Cooperation held in Beijing in the last week of April 2019. President Bidya Devi Bhandari, Foreign Minister Pradeep Gyawali, other ministers, and top leaders of the ruling Nepal Communist Party attended the event. This participation sought to demonstrate Nepal's commitment to the BRI despite significant delays in conceptualisation and execution of different projects due to reasons such as political instability within Nepal and lack of clarity on the modality of Chinese funding and the BRI's risk potential.[18] After attending the Forum meeting, visiting Nepalese President Bidhya Devi Bhandari said in Beijing that the BRI offers new opportunities for Nepal. She hoped that Chinese investors and enterprises can invest more in Nepal.[19]

The deepening of relationship between the two countries in political, economic and strategic areas becomes evident when we examine the dimensions of the growing economic profile of China in Nepal. Over the years, Chinese investments in Nepal have been growing steadily, particularly after 2015 in areas of trade, investment, and regional connectivity. Currently, China is Nepal's largest source of foreign direct investment and its second-largest trading partner. Trade between the two countries in 2018 was US$ 1.29 billion.[20] China is Nepal's biggest foreign investor, accounting for more than 58 per cent of foreign direct investment in 2018-19, at $ 79.26 million, that is twice that of India's $ 36.63 million.[21] Chinese investors committed to spend over $ 8.3 billion in Nepal during the Nepal Investment Summit concluded in Kathmandu in March 2017. In terms of Foreign Direct Investment (FDI), China remains at the top in 2015-16, 2016-17, and in 2017-18. Areas such as hydropower, cement, herbal medicine, and tourism have attracted significant investment from China in recent years.[22] Infrastructure and hydropower are two areas in which China has committed substantial investment.[23] In the infrastructure sector, Chinese investment increased from $ 8 million in 2008 to $ 42 million in 2017-18, contributing 42 per cent of Nepal's total FDI.[24] In the hydropower sector also, Chinese companies have made great strides in the last few years.[25]

Developments during the Oli regime suggest that the BRI acquired greater momentum in Nepal. The bilateral relationship during this period was marked with visible warmth, high-profile visits, and the signing of a number of agreements.

On the other hand, Nepal's relationship with India during the same period was marked with bitterness, growing suspicion, an increase in anti-India rhetoric, and mounting tensions on a number of issues. Domestic political factors were major drivers behind developments with regard to the relationship with India and China and Nepal's decision to join the BRI. Domestic public opinion, particularly among the elite and a section of the media, has always been a factor in the Nepal-India relationship. A section of public opinion, political leadership, bureaucracy, and media has always believed that Nepal is too dependent on India to chart an independent foreign policy course. There has always been an emotional element in Nepal's public opinion, which has viewed India's policies as one with a lack of sensitivity towards Nepal's legitimate concerns and interference in domestic politics. Moreover, this has always been a rallying point used by successive governments to balance their relationship with India and explain its pro-China stance. This perception was reinforced further after protests by Madheshi groups after the promulgation of Nepal's Constitution and the resultant disruption of economic activities, which was also seen as an informal economic blockade by India in 2015.

Challenges and Concerns over BRI Projects

Since the initiation of BRI projects in Nepal, certain concerns have been expressed particularly related to lack of adequate planning and groundwork resulting in delays, and failure in many cases to meet deadlines. This was visible in the undue haste shown by the government in many cases where lots of preparatory work was required. Lack of clarity has also been visible in many aspects of funding and the likely benefit in terms of economic development and return on investment, particularly in view of the massive resources required for major connectivity and infrastructure projects. Many experts have also argued about the need to learn from the experiences of other participating countries and from the evolving post-COVID international geo-economic and geostrategic environment that are likely to impinge on the trajectory of the BRI in Nepal. If we examine the conceptualisation and progress on many BRI projects in Nepal in the light of stated objectives behind connectivity projects, which clearly outlines economic development in partner countries, growth of local enterprises, skill and capacity enhancement of human resources and institutions and dominant local stakes and ownerships; it clearly emerges that a holistic view of challenges and opportunities has not been undertaken. The question of proper alignment of BRI projects with short and long-term national priorities has also been raised with regard to many projects, particularly those related to trans-Himalayan connectivities.

Concerns over Delayed Projects

Though the Nepal government appeared very ambitious and optimistic about most of the projects conceived under the BRI, a closer examination of progress made on various projects reveal that implementation has been slow, and the expected progress has not been achieved in most cases. Available evidence suggests that many of the projects, particularly those related to connectivity and infrastructure did not move further. As a result, the government had to review many projects. As stated earlier, Prime Minister Oli, during his visit to China in June 2018, presented a list of 35 projects to be taken up and funded under the BRI. However, after negotiations, the government prepared a list of nine projects to be funded under the BRI.[26] They include:

(i) Kerung-Kathmandu rail
(ii) Kimathanka-Hile road construction
(iii) Rasuwagadhi-Kathmandu road upgradation
(iv) Galchhi-Rasuwagadhi-Kerung 400 KV transmission line
(v) Construction of road from Dipayal to the southern Chinese border
(vi) Tokha-Bidur road
(vii) 426 MW Phukot-Karnali hydroelectric project
(viii) 762 MW Tamor hydroelectricity project
(ix) The Madan Bhandari Technical Institute.

These projects are related to the infrastructure, connectivity, and hydropower sectors. Except for completing the feasibility study of the Kerung-Kathmandu railway, no significant progress has been made in any of the projects. According to Nepali media reports, even initial work such as preparation of a Detailed Project Report (DPR) or financing modalities have not been worked out for many of the projects under discussion.[27] The feasibility study of the Kerung-Kathmandu railway has been completed and the long-awaited rail link was listed as part of the Second International Belt and Road Initiative in Beijing, under the Nepal-China Trans-Himalayan Multi-Dimensional Connectivity Network.[28] With the objective to boost tourism, the construction of this railway line through the Himalayas will link the Tibetan border town of Kerung with Kathmandu, Pokhara, and Lumbini. It is estimated that more than 2.5 million Chinese tourists will visit Nepal every year.[29] Progress on all the other projects has been very slow.

Government officials and analysts have highlighted internal political dynamics, emerging geopolitics in the region and lack of proper homework on various aspects of the BRI for lack of desired progress. Media reports quoted Foreign Minister Pradeep Gyawali's concerns over lack of institutional wherewithal in dealing with complexities associated with BRI projects. In one of the media reports, he was quoted as saying, "when we signed the agreements with China, there was political instability, and the government's focus was on holding elections. Then we came to power and renewed our commitment, and trimmed down the number of projects from 35 to nine.... But our institutional capacity is weak. We do not even have cost estimates or detailed project reports. We just focus on preparing a wish-list without doing adequate homework". Lack of coordination among state agencies in Nepal is also a factor impeding progress on many of the BRI projects.[30]

Opinion among the political spectrum in Nepal suggests that the country could reap benefits from the BRI if a cost-benefit analysis of each project is done based on domestic needs, available resources, institutional capacity, and long-term planning to generate resources for the projects and repayments of debts. There is also a need for evolving consensus through consultation among stakeholders such as the private sector, political parties, civil society, and experts to ensure that the opportunities and risks that the BRI presents are properly analysed.

Concerns over Funding

One of the areas that have been frequently debated concerning BRI projects is the financial implications for recipient countries, funding pattern, repayment mechanism, and apprehensions of a debt trap. Though the estimates of the cost of BRI projects in Nepal vary, most assessments agree that it will be difficult for Nepal to execute these projects on the existing and proposed financial terms under the BRI. Therefore, most experts have cautioned Nepal on this count. They have been suggesting that the government maintain caution while dealing with projects under BRI. The enormous amount required to operationalise these projects have raised several questions about the funding patterns and benefits that Nepal is likely to get out of these projects. Available reports suggest that the two countries are yet to arrive at an understanding of the mode of funding for BRI projects. Reports in June 2020 suggested that many projects have not made any headway on infrastructure negotiations in these years on the question whether they should be taken forward on loans or grants or interest-free loans/concessional loans.[31] The country has not even prepared a blueprint for agreements worth US$ 2.4 billion that PM K.P. Sharma Oli signed with China in areas including infrastructure, energy, and post-disaster reconstruction efforts.[32] Pro-Chinese publications, while admitting lack of adequate progress on this count, attribute it to international pressure and a lack of willpower on the part of the government on evolving a framework for a financing pattern for BRI projects.

A closer examination of debates over the construction of a railway line through the Himalayas, linking the Tibetan border town of Kerung with Kathmandu, Pokhara, and Lumbini would highlight several issues relating to the financial aspects of the project. The rail link has been presented as a very ambitious project with enormous benefits to Nepal.[33] It was estimated that more than 2.5 million Chinese tourists will visit Nepal every year.[34] However, apart from a funding pattern, other aspects such as geographical and environmental issues have not been examined properly. Though a pre-feasibility report was issued, the same has not been adopted for implementation as yet. According to available reports, a pre-feasibility study of this rail link of 72.25-km track from Kerung to Kathmandu is estimated to cost around US$ 2.25 billion. There is no official confirmation on the financing of this huge amount. The key question being asked in this regard relates to the financial feasibility of this project, given the current economic condition of Nepal. Under the existing framework of BRI projects, China provides loans at commercial rates, often with hidden motives—to serve its own geostrategic interests. The issue of loans to fund BRI projects remains an area of concern for Nepal. In one of the media reports, the former Vice Chairman of the National Planning Commission, Dr. Shankar Sharma, was quoted as saying, "First we should be clear whether Nepal will get grant or loan under BRI.... We need to thoroughly access the cost and its financial modality of the projects under BRI".[35] If these projects are proposed to be implemented through loans, there are genuine possibilities of delayed repayment and a looming debt trap for Nepal. These apprehensions reinforce the existing perception that the rail link will facilitate increased Chinese influence on Nepal for its own strategic objectives at the cost of Nepal's dependence and possible subjugation to Chinese strategic interests.

Therefore, one of the key factors has been fears over a loan that Nepal will not pay back. Many experts see this as an imminent threat that could end up leaving Nepal with unsustainable debts. Concerns over the debt trap were raised overtly by a senior US State Department official in Kathmandu in May 2019. Apart from the USA, some other Western countries have also suggested that Nepal remains cautious while dealing with projects under the BRI. However, the then Foreign Minister, Gyawali, rejected the notion of a 'debt trap', calling it 'imported psychology'.[36] According to Hari Bansh Jha, Executive Director of the Centre for Economic and Technical Studies in Nepal, it is still unclear how a developing country like Nepal could repay Chinese loans, especially with China's own fiscal and monetary limitations.[37] Due to its geographical location, size, slow and uneven economic growth and internal resource base and skill, Nepal has not yet arrived at a stage where it could compete with China in terms of trade in goods and services. Therefore, the possibility of economic gain would be less than what China would be able to extract from BRI projects. Report published by the US-based Centre for Global Development estimated that BRI investments have caused debt-related crises in countries like Laos, Mongolia, Montenegro, the Maldives, Djibouti, Pakistan, Tajikistan, and Kyrgyzstan. For example, Laos is in a difficult situation with a loan liability of US$ 6 billion for the rail line being built by China, with its debt reaching 68 per cent of its GDP. The Maldives also faces a looming debt trap of US$ 92 million in annual payments. In South Asia, countries like Sri Lanka and Pakistan are struggling to deal with the financial aspects of the BRI. For example, in Sri Lanka, the infrastructure projects built by China have not yielded the desired economic gains for the country, but China was able to entrench itself deeply by creating strategic assets. Currently, Sri Lanka is finding it difficult to pay back the loan amounting to US$ 8 billion. Therefore, the possibilities of a 'debt-trap'-like situation are real for Nepal and the experiences of other countries that were put in a similar situation could help Nepal evolve a viable financing framework for BRI projects. According to foreign policy analyst, Pramod Jaiswal, China does not offer grants for BRI projects. He said one of the reasons why Nepal has not prepared any projects for immediate funding is because it favours grants, which is not possible under the BRI framework. Nepal did not agree to put money in large projects and also did not want to take risks as Pakistan did with the China-Pakistan Economic Corridor".[38] There are hiccups in Chinese-funded hydropower projects like West Seti, Budhi Gandaki, etc. So far, Nepal has not been able to ensure the feasibility of these projects. The Chinese really do not want to invest here.[39]

If a situation leading to a debt trap is to be avoided, Nepal needs to conceptualise BRI projects keeping in view its requirement, economic resource base, institutional resilience and a long-term perspective to implement projects. The prudent approach would require negotiating favourable terms of financing BRI projects. Suggestions in this regard have been to avoid projects that require massive economic investment and instead plan medium and small projects like hydropower and roads. Such projects with a careful risk analysis would bring economic benefits to the people.[40] For example, focus on hydropower projects may help create jobs and generate revenue from selling electricity. Road construction and better connectivity in the countryside will facilitate faster economic growth compared to road connectivity with China and building railway infrastructure in the northern region.

With the current level of economic development and an insufficient domestic resource base, Nepal would require substantial international support and FDI to fund its requirements. Support from international institutions such as the World Bank, the European Investment Bank, and the European Bank for Reconstruction and Development could help finance many of the projects and avoid a situation leading to substantial dependence on China. With FDI remaining at a sub-optimal level, Nepal needs to make efforts through institutional reforms. Also, based on its internal strength, priority areas need to be identified to realise untapped potential in areas such as hydropower, tourism, medicinal herbs, forest produce, etc. International cooperation needs to be complemented with augmenting internal capacity, institutional reforms, enhancing production capacity and building infrastructure and connectivity around these areas.

Debates within Nepal on BRI projects also suggest the need for a multi-stakeholder approach and a greater internal consultation process and careful risk analysis before committing to them. Nepal's former secretary, Gyan Chandra Acharya, was quoted in one of the media reports as saying, "There are good and bad examples of BRI in many countries. There is a need for undertaking cost-benefit analysis, and investment should be transparent, and projects should be selected as per our priority and national interest".[41]

Geopolitical Implications

The Nepal-China relationship and developments with regard to BRI projects have been viewed with considerable interest and concern in India. China's growing engagement with Nepal, particularly economic assistance and connectivity projects, have been interpreted as China's strategic moves to counter India's deep multi-layered engagements in Nepal. In this context, the projected impact of the BRI as an alternative gateway for Nepal to reduce its dependence on India merits attention. As a landlocked country surrounded by India from three sides, Nepal is dependent on India for most of its essential items. Given the current trajectory of the BRI and associated challenges, it would be premature to consider China as an alternative. Nepal's economic dependence on India is around 76 per cent, with substantial dependence on supply of essential goods. India is Nepal's largest trading partner, with Nepalese exports accounting for $ 447 million and imports of $ 7.7 billion.[42] Dr. Posh Raj Pandey, a member of Nepal's National Planning Commission, was quoted by the media as saying that Nepal's imports from India account for two-thirds, whereas that of China is only 14 per cent.[43] He added that as far as exports are concerned, India receives 60 per cent of Nepal's exports, whereas China receives only two per cent. Open border with restriction-free movement of people, deep historical and cultural ties and people-to-people contacts make this relationship special for both the countries. The same level of ease and comfort in interaction is not there with China. Geography, terrain, and cultural affinity make Nepal more accessible to India, both in terms of ease in an economic transaction, trade facilitation, and people-to-people contacts. There is no significant Chinese community to influence decisions, and Nepal has a small market for Chinese goods.

India's Prime Minister, Narendra Modi's, visit to Nepal in 2014 successfully highlighted the deep historical, cultural ties and mutual respect between the two countries. He emphasised the cultural ties that bind the two nations go beyond strategic and economic factors. He declared Nepal to be the centrepiece of his government's 'neighbourhood first' policy. However, the relationship between the two countries suffered seriously in the wake of the making of Nepal's constitution in 2015, when India attempted to persuade the Nepal government to address the grievances of the Madheshi, Janajati and other underprivileged sections of Nepalese society.[44] The agitation that followed the promulgation of the Constitution severely impacted Nepal's economy as supplies from India were blocked. This temporary disruption in economic transactions, also termed as the 'unofficial blockade of 2015' triggered a wave of anti-India sentiment in the country. The 'Neighbourhood First' policy adopted under Prime Minister Modi's leadership suffered a setback in Nepal. The six-month-long agitation by Madheshi groups during K. P. Sharma Oli's premiership from September 2015 to February 2016, in which more than 50 people were killed, became a turning point in the recent India-Nepal relationship. The Oli regime, with a visible pro-China tilt, exploited this anti-India sentiment, and his election victory was interpreted as a result of his standing up to Indian hegemony. It is, therefore, not surprising to note the linkages between the post-2015 development in the India-Nepal relationship, the Oli-led regime and the strengthening of the Nepal-China relationship. Major developments with regard to BRI projects in Nepal are linked to this phase of the India-Nepal relationship.

The India-Nepal bilateral relationship came under severe strain again in May 2020, after India's Defence Minister, Rajnath Singh, inaugurated an 80-km-long strategically crucial road going up to the Lipulekh Pass. Nepal reacted sharply to the inauguration of the road claiming that it passed through Nepalese territory. India held that the road lies entirely in Indian territory. Nepal updated the constitution to upgrade the national emblem by incorporating in the existing map Lipulekh, Kalapani, and Limpiyadhura in India's Uttarakhand. India's External Affairs Ministry said, "This artificial enlargement of claim is not based on historical facts or evidence and is not tenable. It is also violative of our current understanding to hold talks on outstanding boundary issues".[45] A number of incidents during this period contributed to further deterioration of ties with India. These developments have also been viewed as decisions taken at Chinese behest to create a wider rift between two neighbours tied with deep historical bonds. Noted Nepalese scholar Hari Bansh Jha views these developments as attempts by Nepal to maintain a distance with India. He maintains that examples such as Nepal's stand on abrogation of Article 370 and 35A, attempts to generate favourable public opinion in favour of China's membership of SAARC, views of certain NCP leaders on Indo-Pacific strategy, etc., have suggested that Nepal is trying to maintain a distance with India.[46]

The centrepiece of Nepal's foreign policy has been to maintain a balance between its relationship with China and India and leverage this to further its interests. Over tilt towards China could have far-reaching implications for Nepal also. There are geopolitical concerns over increased Chinese engagement in Nepal. Chinese interests in Nepal are strategic in nature. Against the backdrop of Chinese strategic ambitions in the region, it would be difficult for Nepal to protect its interests, particularly the benefits expected from BRI projects.

Nepal also needs to be sensitive to the region's emerging geopolitics, particularly in the post-COVID international order. Even though Nepal and China share a long border and history, having a blanket dependency on China in the prevailing international geopolitical landscape may not be in Nepal's long-term interests. Nepal cannot remain insulated from growing concern over Chinese expansionism, mounting border tension between India and China, USA-China Cold War, and emerging post-COVID international order where many countries are reviewing their economic engagement with China. Nepal should be looking at a diverse source of economic engagements. Echoing the sentiment, visiting Japanese Foreign Minister Taro Kano said in Kathmandu in January 2019 that financial support from developed countries should be concessional, and such support should be transparent.[47] Many experts have warned that over-dependence on China would not be wise at the cost of deep engagement with India. The role of the USA also needs to be factored in. The US administrations, on a number of occasions in the past, have emphasised the importance of its engagement with Nepal. Apart from the USA, some other Western countries have also suggested that Nepal remains cautious while dealing with BRI projects.

Given its strategic location, it would be important for Nepal to manage its relationship with its neighbours in the wake of growing tension between India and China. If Nepal can manage its relationships with India and China and their engagement on the issue of trade and connectivity continues, the BRI could open a window of opportunity for India also. Through connectivity and skilful management of sensitive and fragile geopolitics, Nepal can be a gateway to South Asia for China and a gateway to China for India. Many of the BRI projects in Nepal have been conceptualised on the assumption that India would be on board as an active participant and, sooner or later, India would find BRI lucrative for its economic development.

Through careful management of its relationship with India and China, the BRI has the potential to provide Nepal with an opportunity for diversification of cross-border trade and connectivity with China. The enhanced connectivity could benefit areas like infrastructure connectivity, tourism, hydroelectricity and technology that are essential for the economic progress of Nepal.[48]

Conclusion

Though India has always remained an important factor in Nepal's relationship with China, the developments associated with BRI projects in Nepal have largely been conditioned by Nepal's internal political dynamics and gradual increase in Chinese interest in Nepal in recent years. The Oli-led government facilitated an accelerated pace of negotiations on many BRI projects in which the post-2015 relationship with India provided a context. A careful examination of different aspects of infrastructure projects reveal lack of proper conceptualisation and careful risk assessment on the feasibility of many of the projects. Political factors overweighed sustainability, financial viability and long-term economic benefits of these projects. Fragile domestic politics and the capacity of institutions to conceptualise and negotiate complex mega projects also provided a window for China to further entrench its strategic presence in Nepal.

The current political instability with growing factionalism within the ruling dispensation will also have far-reaching implications for the trajectory of BRI projects in Nepal. The recent political crisis resulting from the dissolution of the lower house of parliament by Prime Minister K.P. Sharma Oli has unearthed deep-seated differences among political factions and the role and perception of an elite section of Nepalese society. The political disposition of top Nepal's leadership toward China and India defines a great extent of Nepal's political trajectory. The BRI, in this context, is a test case for Nepal's approach to its two larger neighbours.

NOTES

1. "Nepal in talks with China to build $ 8 billion cross-border rail link - finance ministry official", Reuters, May 13, 2017, at https://in.reuters.com/article/uk-china-silkroad-nepal/nepal-in-talks-with-china-to-build-8-billion-cross-border-rail-link-finance-ministry-official-

idUKKBN18A05U

2. "Only qualified BRI projects will meet Nepal's long-term interests: Dr. Xu Wenhong", https://therisingnepal.org.np/news/30409
3. "Nepal-China cross-border fiber network to come into operation in June", *Xinhua*, 27 May 2017, at http://www.xinhuanet.com/english/2017-05/27/c_136321051.htm
4. Kallol Bhattacharjee, "Nepal, China ink road connectivity deal", *Hindu*, 13 October 2019, at https://www.thehindu.com/news/international/nepal-china-ink-road-connectivity-deal/article29674718.ece
5. "Only qualified BRI projects will meet Nepal's long-term interests: Dr. Xu Wenhong", https://therisingnepal.org.np/news/30409
6. Akhilesh Upadhyay, "Nepal PM Oli's visit to Delhi signals a new equilibrium", *The Indian Express*, April 2018, at https://indianexpress.com/article/opinion/nepal-pm-kp-sharma-oli-visit-to-delhi-signals-a-new-equilibrium/#:~:text=The%20Qinghai%2D Tibet%20railway%20line, Gyirong%20or%20Kyirong)%20by%202020.
7. Ministry of Foreign Affairs Nepal, "Joint Statement Between Nepal and the People's Republic of China", 13 October 2019, at https://mofa.gov.np/joint-statement-between-nepal-and-the-peoples-republic-of-china-2/
8. Dinesh Bhattarai, "Understanding the Belt and Road Initiative", 29 September 2020, at https://www.nepjol.info/index.php/JAPFCSC/article/view/26750
9. Ministry of Foreign Affairs Nepal, "Joint Statement between Nepal and the People's Republic of China", 21 June 2018, at https://mofa.gov.np/joint-statement-between-nepal-and-the-peoples-republic-of-china/
10. "Nepal gains access to China ports", *Nepali Times*, 21 March 2016, at http://archive.nepalitimes.com/blogs/thebrief/2016/03/21/nepal-gains-access-to-ports/
11. Lila Nyaichyai , "The Consequences of China's Belt and Road Initiative in Nepal", at https://www.eleventhcolumn.com/2020/07/26/the-consequences-of-chinas-belt-and-road-initiative-in-nepal/
12. "Belt and Road Initiative to boost socio-economic development in Nepal: experts" Belt and Road Initiative to boost socio-economic development in Nepal: experts - Xinhua | English.news.cn (xinhuanet.com).
13. Xiang Bo, "Belt and Road Initiative can open door of development for Nepal: experts", 12 February 2018, accessed at http://www.xinhuanet.com/english/2018-02/12/c_136970232.htm
14. Rashtriya Samachar Samiti, "Nepal signs MoU on OBOR with China", 12 May 2017, accessed at https://thehimalayantimes.com/kathmandu/nepal-signs-mou-related-obor-china
15. "Joint Statement between Nepal and the People's Republic of China", https://mofa.gov.np/joint-statement-between-nepal-and-the-peoples-republic-of-china/
16. "Nepal and China sign and exchange 20 agreements", *The Kathmandu Post*, 13 October 2019, at https://kathmandupost.com/national/2019/10/13/nepal-and-china-sign-and-exchange-20-agreements
17. Hari Bansh Jha, "Xi Jinping's visit to Nepal: A diplomatic victory for China?", at https://www.orfonline.org/expert-speak/xi-ping-visit-nepal-diplomatic-victory-for-china-56932/
18. Kamal Dev Bhattarai, "Nepal's Delicate Dance with China on BRI", 3 May 2019, at https://southasianvoices.org/nepals-delicate-dance-with-china-on-bri/
19. "China shores up projects in Nepal, Myanmar under Belt and Road", https://www.hindustantimes.com/world-news/china-shores-up-bilateral-projects-in-nepal-myanmar-under-bri/story-T5qSfhQHADeWVa2ao32GyN.html
20. "List of Deliverables of the Second Belt and Road Forum for International Cooperation", *China Daily*, 28 April 2019, at http://www.chinadaily.com.cn/newsrepublic/2019-04/28/content_37463762.htm

21. Harsh V. Pant, "India's Nepal Challenge Intensifies", 30 June 2018. https://thediplomat.com/2018/07/indias-nepal-challenge-intensifies/
22. Nepal-China Relations, at https://mofa.gov.np/nepal-china-relations/#:~:text=With%20the%20signing%20of%20the,areas%20are%20expected%20to%20open, accessed on 27 September 2020.
23. "Nepal's delicate balancing act between China and India", https://www.dw.com/en/nepals-delicate-balancing-act-between-china-and-india/a-52693835
24. Amar Bhushan, "Let us Deal with Nepal Normally", https://www.newindianexpress.com/magazine/voices/2020/jun/28/let-us-deal-with-nepal-normally-2161417.html
25. Harsh V Pant, "India's Nepal Challenge Intensifies", https://thediplomat.com/2018/07/indias-nepal-challenge-intensifies/
26. Anil Giri, "Nepal trims projects under BRI from 35 to 9 at Chinese call", https://kathmandupost.com/national/2019/01/18/nepal-trims-projects-under-bri-from-35-to-9-at-chinese-call
27. "With just 10 months left in BRI pact, not a single project has made any real progress", *Kathmandu Post*, 17 July 2019, at https://kathmandupost.com/national/2019/07/17/with-just-10-months-left-in-bri-pact-not-a-single-project-has-made-any-real-progress
28. Anil Giri, "With just 10 months left in BRI pact, not a single project has made any real progress", https://kathmandupost.com/national/2019/07/17/with-just-10-months-left-in-bri-pact-not-a-single-project-has-made-any-real-progress.
29. Amrit Raj Kaphle, "Nepal makes no headway on BRI projects", 8 June 2020., https://english.khabarhub.com/2020/08/100408/
30. https://kathmandupost.com/national/2019/07/17/with-just-10-months-left-in-bri-pact-not-a-single-project-has-made-any-real-progress
31. Ibid.
32. Ibid.
33. Kamal Dev Bhattarai, "Nepal needs to speed up the selection of BRI projects to improve local quality of life", *Global Times*,23 July 2019, at https://www.globaltimes.cn/content/1158906.shtml
34. Amrit Raj Kaphle, "Nepal makes no headway on BRI projects", 8 June 2020., https://english.khabarhub.com/2020/08/100408/
35. Ibid.
36. *Kathmandu Post*, 17 July 2019.
37. Quoted in Natasha Fernando and Vijay Prasad Jayshwal, "From landlocked land-linked: OBOR in Nepal" https://www.oboreurope.com/en/obor-in-nepal/
38. "With just 10 months left in BRI pact, not a single project has made any real progress", *Kathmandu Post*, 17 July 2019, at https://kathmandupost.com/national/2019/07/17/with-just-10-months-left-in-bri-pact-not-a-single-project-has-made-any-real-progress
39. Ibid.
40. Kamal Dev Bhattarai, "Nepal needs to speed up selection of BRI projects to improve local quality of life", *Global Times*, 23 July 2019, at https://www.globaltimes.cn/content/1158906.shtml
41. Ibid.
42. Amar Bhushan, "Let us Deal with Nepal Normally", https://www.newindianexpress.com/magazine/voices/2020/jun/28/let-us-deal-with-nepal-normally-2161417.html
43. Nepal-India ties shouldn't deteriorate; China no substitute to India: Senior Nepali economist, https://economictimes.indiatimes.com/news/politics-and-nation/nepal-india-ties-shouldnt-deteriorate-china-no-substitute-to-india-senior-nepali-economist/articleshow/76383133.cms?utm_source=contentofinterest&utm_medium=text&utm_campaign=cppst

44. Hari Bansh Jha, "Nepal Distancing itself from India", Observer Research Foundation, 14 October 2019, at https://www.orfonline.org/expert-speak/nepal-distancing-itself-from-india-56612/
45. Nepal-India ties shouldn't deteriorate; China no substitute to India: Senior Nepali economist, https://economictimes.indiatimes.com/news/politics-and-nation/nepal-india-ties-shouldnt-deteriorate-china-no-substitute-to-india-senior-nepali-economist/articleshow/76383133.cms?utm_source=contentofinterest&utm_medium=text&utm_campaign=cppst
46. Hari Bansh Jha, "Nepal Distancing itself from India", https://www.orfonline.org/expert-speak/nepal-distancing-itself-from-india-56612/
47. "With just 10 months left in BRI pact, not a single project has made any real progress", *Kathmandu Post*, 17 July 2019, at https://kathmandupost.com/national/2019/07/17/with-just-10-months-left-in-bri-pact-not-a-single-project-has-made-any-real-progress
48. Sumitra Karki, "China's Belt and Road Initiative (BRI): Opportunities and Challenges for Nepal", November 07 2019, NIICE Commentary 3153, at https://niice.org.np/archives/3153

9

Revitalising BCIM for Integrating South Asia vis-à-vis BRI: Politico-Economic Implications for India

Oindrilla Dattagupta

The idea of sub-regionalism has been acting as a major tool for India's foreign policy to advance its national interests through the cooperative mechanism. In this context, the prominence of sub-regionalism is not merely because of geographical proximity but also due to the sharing of cultural space that needs to be nurtured and sustained. Intensification of sub-regional co-operation has helped to deepen the bilateral engagements within the region where India can act as a developmental agent (Hook and Kearns 1999). The efforts for sub-regionalism in South Asia, such as Bangladesh-Bhutan-India-Nepal (BBIN) and Bangladesh-China-India-Myanmar (BCIM) have been commenced to boost regional connectivity through economic and transport corridors for intra-regional trade (Pattanaik 2017). Bangladesh-China-India-Myanmar, has been an important sub-regional project of India's integration with the regional and global market vis-à-vis its strategic space. The 'Neighbourhood First' policy of India under the present NDA government also seeks to ensure the active role India will play to intensify co-operation at the regional and sub-regional levels. India's foreign policy at the regional level has shown a mixed bag of pragmatism by the strengthening of economic as well as military bases, and managing its borders to ensure a greater role in South Asia. This chapter discusses the BCIM as a foreign policy tool of India to build a well-integrated South Asia. It is divided into three major sections: the first section looks at the economic corridors in the international political economy as well as the foreign policy strategy playing a multi-dimensional role in regional integration. In this context, it will draw reference to the BCIM and the BRI to understand greater links with the neighbourhood. The second section deals with the BCIM and the BRI vis-a-vis South Asia analysing India's leadership role in the region for promoting regional integration vis-a-vis China's BRI. The third section delves into the geo-political and geo-economic impact of the BCIM and the implications it will have on Northeastern India as well as India's neighbourhood policy.

Role of Economic Corridors in Regional Integration: Locating BRI and BCIM in the Grid

The regional integrative framework acts as a road to promote economic co-operation along with political goodwill within a region keeping in mind the geo-political and geo-economic circumstances. Considering the ambitious goals of China to expand its outreach within the South Asian region and the Indian Ocean, the regional groupings must be taken seriously by India to build collaborations and strengthen cultural affinities among the neighbours. China's history of regional integration has been much more successful and rigorous compared to that of India which has not managed to take off well in regional and sub-regional ventures because of regional politics and economic instability. From the perspective of Asia, regional co-operation has been defined in terms of complex interdependence, multilateralism, co-operation and collaboration that could promote economic growth and institutionalism at the systemic levels. Sub-regionalism at the local levels has emerged as a means to exploit the geographical contiguity and to speed up the developmental process in the micro-region. A good example in this context is the BCIM that includes Bangladesh, China, India and Myanmar—a quadrangle that aims to integrate the two Asian giants and the developing countries from South and South East Asia by reaping socio-economic benefits (Thomas and Das, 2018).

Corridors, which cut across a geographical space, generate economic agglomeration, thus making transportation costs and time critical factors for ensuring their success. Corridor-based development further promotes economic growth and regional development of an area by reducing the time and cost of the transaction and also contributes to poverty reduction. Conceptually, an economic corridor is understood as a route for easy movement of goods, services, and people for stimulating economic growth. The model of the economic corridor, as an approach for economic development, gained popularity in the 1990s with the inception of the Greater Mekong sub-region in South East Asia through the Asian Development Bank for improving the infrastructure, economic activity, labour mobility, investment in transport, energy, and telecommunications along with cultural relations. Economic corridors can be national (Delhi-Mumbai Economic Corridor); regional (Greater Mekong Corridor) and international (China-Pakistan Economic Corridor). Corridors stimulate competitiveness, industrial development, and infrastructural expansion within a region leading to increased production, decreased transport costs to attract export-oriented manufacturing units and investments, along with cultural and social exchanges (Kumar, 2015). An economic corridor presents a holistic strategy to improve connectivity and investment in transport and energy, which escalates economic growth and regional development (ADB, 2008) with trade facilitation being the main catalyst. A corridor helps strengthen industrial (or services) agglomeration over time through the establishment of industrial zones (or SEZs) and facilitates cluster-type development of enterprises. In terms of economic integration, to cite a case, East Asia has been successful with fewer hindrances to trade and investment and acting as a link to the South East Asian countries whereas South Asia remains one of the least economically integrated regions in the world. Economic corridors become crucial for Asia for network expansion for generating trade advantages at a high magnitude (Blanchard, 2017). Realising the salience of regional connectivity, India has been striving for better connectivity through sub-regional initiatives such as the Bay of Bengal Initiative for Multi-Sectoral Technical and Economic Cooperation (BIMSTEC) or Mekong-Ganga Cooperation (MCG) reaching out to South East Asia, and the India-Myanmar-Thailand Trilateral Highway and the Kaladan Multi-Modal Transit Transport Project linking South Asia with the Mekong sub-region through various connectivity projects (Pant and Yhome, 2020).

BRI and BCIM: Connecting Cities through Economic Corridors

The BRI of China has evolved as a development strategy to construct a network between China and Mongolia, Russia, Eurasian countries, Central and West Asian countries as well as Indochina and the Indian subcontinent. As the Asian Development Bank Report of 2017 states, the Silk Road Economic Belt and the 21st Century Maritime Silk Road could provide a boost to regional co-operation by building infrastructural strength and creating new markets for investment.

The BRI acts as a modern version of the ancient Silk Road of the Han Dynasty to expand the trade network system throughout Afghanistan, Central Asia, and all the way to Europe and Africa and to make the Chinese Yuan a truly international currency. The BRI is best summarised by President Xi, "China will actively promote international co-operation through the Belt and Road Initiative. In doing so, we hope to achieve policy, infrastructure, trade, financial, and people-to-people connectivity and thus build a new platform for international co-operation to create new drivers of shared development" (Xi, J., 2017b: 61). It goes without saying that the BRI also aids in making China the nucleus of economic, political and cultural power in Asia. The World Bank Report (2017) has estimated that the BRI has a trade potential between 1.7 and 6.2 per cent, and the implementation of related reforms will help to reduce border delays and ease trade restrictions.

While the BRI could be a mega project for China to exert its power, the BCIM emerges as a concept for sub-regionalism and a part of its statecraft involving its south-western region, eastern India, Myanmar and Bangladesh. The BCIM sub-regional zone (initiative launched in 1999 in China's Yunnan province) is taken as the meeting point between South Asia and South-East Asia that will help to connect the markets of China and India as well as proper utilisation of the resources to bring this region out of underdevelopment and poverty. As the sub-regional zone connects the markets within Asia, it also integrates the region with the global market. It thereby assists in socio-economic development, and technological and tourism co-operation, thereby helping to curb the menace of drug trafficking rampant in the region. The idea harps on 3Ts and 1E—transport, tourism, trade and energy—that look into the livelihoods and the aspirations of those living in the borderlands. The BCIM has been initiated as an economic approach and is "moving towards people-centric, inclusive approach mindful of local social realities" (Uberoi, 2013) keeping in mind the geo-strategic implications of promoting the link between the remote parts of the region to the global. The idea of multimodal transportation has added to BCIM connectivity for promotion of port development and coastal shipping to improve trade ties (Uberoi, 2016 in Thomas *et al.*, 2016). Both the BCIM and the BRI help in intra-regional and inter-regional connectivity through cities such Guwahati, Nagaon, Jorhat, Dibrugarh, Tinsukia, Dhubri, Imphal, Gangtok, Itanagar, Shillong and Aizwal which act as emerging economic nodes. These are examples of the cities acting as manufacturing, management, research and education hubs and sites for investment along the Corridor. The cities play a crucial role in infrastructural development within six economic corridors—New Eurasia rail route to Europe via Kazakhstan,

Russia, Belarus, Poland; a land bridge linking China, Mongolia, Russia Economic Corridor; China, Central Asia, West Asia Economic Corridor linking Kazakhstan, Kyrgyzstan, Tajikistan, Uzbekistan, Turkmenistan, Iran, and Turkey; Indochina Peninsula Economic Corridor linking Vietnam, Thailand, Lao People's Democratic Republic, Cambodia, Myanmar, and Malaysia; China, Pakistan Economic Corridor linking Kashgar city in Xinjiang Province with Gwadar port in Pakistan and China, Bangladesh, India and Myanmar Economic Corridor. In China, there are seven cities like Baotou, Zhengzhou, Xi'an, Lanzhou, Urumqi, Kunming and Qujing which are more important within the BRI networks and would become critical to how China engages with BRI countries. These cities, along with other cities located en route each corridor is well placed to benefit significantly from improvements made in the trade networks. Urban centres such as Novosibirsk, Irkutsk Yekaterinburg, and Krasnodar (Russia), Almaty and Astana (Kazakhstan), Tehran (Iran), Istanbul (Turkey), Kabul (Afghanistan), Yangon (Myanmar), Kuala Lumpur (Malaysia), Bangkok (Thailand), Hanoi (Vietnam), Singapore (Singapore), Rawalpindi, Bahawalpur, Islamabad and Karachi (Pakistan), Dhaka (Bangladesh), Kolkata (India), Baotau, Zhengzhou, Xian, Lanzhou, Urumqi, Kunming and Quijing are central to the economic corridors, thereby, showing the vitality of cities in the context of promotion of regional corridors and network (Derudder 2018).

BCIM and South Asia: India's Leadership Role in the Region

As a foreign policy initiative under Prime Minister Modi, India's Act East Policy looks forward to India playing a greater role in the region in a multi-dimensional and action-oriented manner. The BCIM EC (Economic Corridor) has the potential to link South Asia and South East Asia along with China making the Act East Policy assertive and pragmatic (Muni and Mishra, 2019). The BCIM can be taken as a 'cooperative zone' (Che, in Uberoi, 2016) expanding from south-west China to the Himalayas and the Bay of Bengal covering important countries and sitting at the conjunction of three markets—South Asia, South East Asia and China—which could pave the way for smooth trade between India and China and wider regional integration by conjoining BIMSTEC, SAARC, and ASEAN.

BRI without BCIM: Geo-Economic and Geo-Political Potentialities

The 21st-century Maritime Silk Route that connects the South China Sea with the Indian Ocean has given rise to new ports, trade routes and investment prospects. Taking the BCIM as a part of the BRI allows significant sub-regional co-operation

Figure 1: The BCIM EC Marked as 4—Extending from Kunming to Kolkata

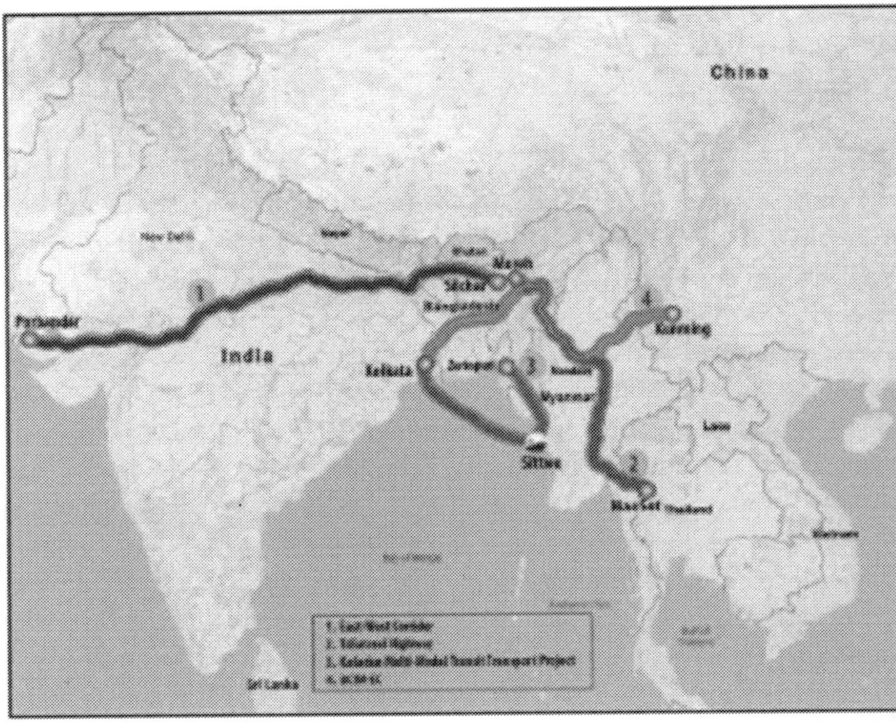

Source: Research and Information System for Developing Countries, RIS, 2018, p. 52.

through commerce, connectivity and cultural linkages. The BCIM region helps in energising the old silk route that connects China, Myanmar, Bangladesh and Northeast India. It has been successful historically, and in contemporary times, it should be used for reopening borders. The Northeast region which is vital for the BCIM provides an international market for finished cloth, handicrafts, etc., that can not only harness the economic linkages but also benefit the indigenous groups by making a market community (Sharma and Chowdhury, 2018).

The most important part of the BCIM EC is that it can be utilised to materialise the Act East Policy and revisit the historical mercantile activities through India's Northeast to Myanmar and China. This was the case during colonial times when trade was carried out through this route in commodities such as jade and teak from Burma, muslin from Dhaka and silk and tea from China. It goes without saying that the revitalisation of the BCIM can help in boosting the local economies of India's Northeast.

Table 1: International Trade of Northeastern States

(in km)

State	Bangladesh	Bhutan	China	Mvanmal	Nepal	Total
Arunachal Pradesh	-	217	1080	520	-	1817
Assam	263	267	-	-	-	530
Manipur	-	-	-	398	-	398
Meghalaya	443	-	-	-	-	443
Mizoram	318	-	-	510	-	828
Nagaland	-	-	-	215	-	215
Sikkim	-	32	220	-	98	350
Tripura	856	-	-	-	-	856
Total	1880	516	1300	1643	96	-

Source: Ministry of Development of NER, GoI, 2018 cited in De at al 2018.

India's trade with Bangladesh was in the range of $ 9 billion in 2017-18. Indian exports included cotton, vehicles and cereals, and imports from Bangladesh were textiles and apparel. India's trade with Myanmar touched $ 1.5 billion in 2018. Pharmaceuticals have been the most exported item from India, while beans and cereals were imported from Myanmar. India, however, accounts for less than one per cent of Myanmar's land-based trade, whereas China, Thailand and Bangladesh are ahead of India (De *et al.*, RIS Report, 2018). Various trade statistics of Myanmar (given below) provide an idea about India's economic engagement with Myanmar.

Table 2: Economic Corridors and the Connected Indian States and Other Countries

Sl.No.	Corridor	Connecting Indian States and Countries	
		Indian States	*Neighbouring Countries*
1	Kaladan corridor	Arunachal Pradesh, Assam, Manipur, Meghalaya, Mizoram, Nagaland, Odisha, Sikkim, Tripura, West Bengal	Myanmar
2.	Trilateral Highway	Arunachal Pradesh, Assam, Bihar, Jharkhand, Manipur, Meghalaya, Mizoram, Nagaland, Odisha, Sikkim, Tripura, West Bengal	Bangladesh, Thailand, Myanmar
3	BCIM-EC	Arunachal Pradesh, Assam, Bihar, Jharkhand, Manipur. Meghalaya, Mizoram, Nagaland, Odisha, Sikkim, Tripura, West Bengal	Bangladesh, Myanmar, China
4	East-West corridor	Assam, Bihar, Gujarat, Madhya Pradesh, Rajasthan, Uttar Pradesh, West Bengal	Not applicable

Source: RIS 2018.

Figure 2: India's Trade with Myanmar

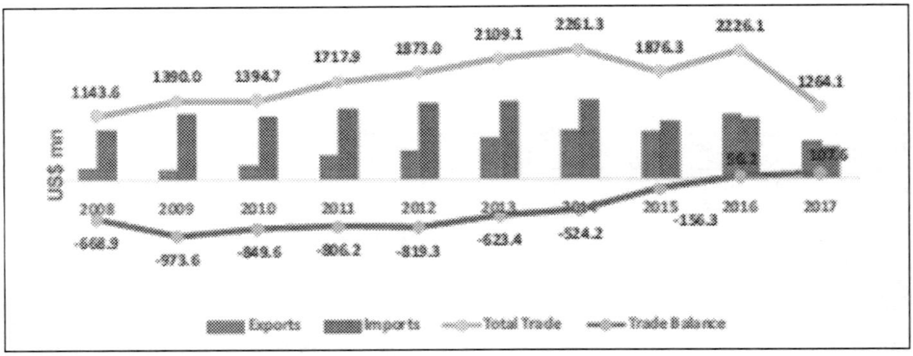

Source: UN COMTRADE 2018.

Table 3: Major Exporters of Myanmar

Exporters	*2010*		*2017*		*CAGR (2010-17, %)*
	Value (US$ mn)	*% Share*	*Value (US$ mn)*	*% Share*	
China	6.789.1	25.6	15.202.7	32.9	12.2
India	3.016.6	11.4	5,807.1	12.6	9.8
Singapore	1,7033	6.4	2,882.9	6.2	7.8
Japan	1023.0	3.9	1,741.0	3.8	7.9
Brazil	538.0	2.0	1,600 1	3.5	16.8
Indonesia	1,018.6	3.8	1,596.6	3.5	6.6
Malaysia	1,259.3	4.8	1,516.6	3.3	2.7
Hong Kong	831.1	3.1	1,509.1	3.3	8.9
USA	575.7	2.2	1.,464.6	3.2	14.3
South Korea	1.5543	5.9	1278.0	2.8	2.8

Source: ITC Trade Map, derived from UN COMTRADE, 2018.

Table 4: Major Importers of Myanmar

Importers	*2010*		*2017*		*CAGR (2010-17, %)*
	Value (US$ mn)	*% Share*	*Value (US$ mn)*	*% Share*	
China	476.3	6.2	4,766.7	40.8	39.0
Thailand	3.177.2	41.7	2,241.5	19.2	-4.9
India	958.1	12.6	1,038.1	8.9	1.2
Singapore	276.3	3.6	890.8	7.6	18.2
Japan	215.2	2.8	663.4	5.7	17.5
South Korea	125.4	1.6	334.8	2.9	15.1
Hong Kong	1,611.8	21.1	192.6	1.7	26.2
Germany	-	-	172.4	1.5	-
USA	1.7	-	1503	1.3	89.8
Malaysia	162.8	2.1	144.4	1.2	-1.7

Nate: - not available/negligible

Source: ITC Trade Map, derived from UN COMTRADE, 2018.

Figures 2 and 3 show that India has a fairly good position in import and export exchanges with Myanmar. However, compared to the China-Myanmar trade, India-Myanmar trade lags, and it can be improved if the BCIM gets materialised. No doubt that the BCIM borders are also space for smuggling of arms and drug trafficking. However, a formal trade route through the BCIM can reduce illegal trade across borders (Bose, 2018). This can be made possible if the northeastern region of India is utilised for border trading and if there is an increase in import-export with Bangladesh, Myanmar, Bhutan and China.

Analysing Indo-Bangladesh trade relations, it can be observed that India is the largest trade partner of Bangladesh and the trade relations have been comparatively steady.

Figure 3: India's Trade with Bangladesh in 2008-2017

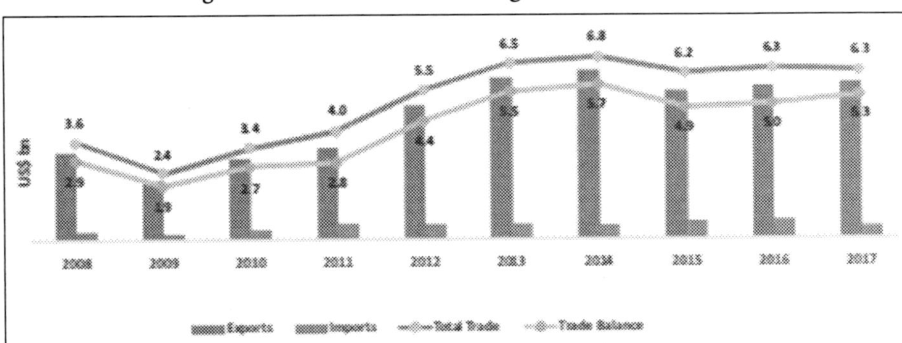

Source: UN COMTRADE, 2018.

The BCIM can enable the region for export-led growth in India as has been by the ASEAN through efficient economic integration of a region demonstrating that economies at different levels of development can benefit reciprocally (Kundra, 2018). The BCIM, in the long run, can allow the Northeastern region of India to emerge out of the periphery and establish linkages with legalised trade routes preventing illegal trade across borders. Chattogram and Mongla ports in Bangladesh can provide access to open sea trade routes to India's Northeast so that products such as food grains, fruits, organic products, tea, fish, jute, etc., could be transported easily.

The top five ports showing imports and exports to Bangladesh in 2016-17 are Petrapole (land), Tuticorin (sea), Ghojadanga (land), and Nhava Sheva (sea). Over 75 per cent of India's total imports from Bangladesh are routed through these ports.

Tables 5, 6, 7, 8 and 9 show that export and import from Bangladesh and Myanmar to India are through seaports showing that trade continues between the border countries through waterways. Ensuring smooth transportation and

Table 5: Top 10 Ports showing Exports to Bangladesh

Ports	*2012-13*		*2016-17*		*CAGR (2012-13 to 2016-17 %)*
	Value (US$ mn)	*% Share*	*Value (US$ mn)*	*% Share*	
Petapole (Land)	1,793.0	34.8	2,340.4	34.3	6.9
Nhava Sheva (Sea)	576.8	11.2	830.3	12.2	9.5
Mundra	215.8	4,2	439.7	6.4	19.5
Ghajadanga	157.7	3.1	280.6	4.1	15.5
Chennai (Sea)	271.4	5.3	204.2	3.0	-6.9
Tuticorin (Sea)	152.9	3.0	152.8	2.2	-0.002
Ranaghat	67.2	1.3	146.7	2.2	21.6
Kolkata (Sea)	24.9	0.5	139.7	2.0	53.9
Hili (West)	149.5	2.9	118.6	1.7	-5.6
ICD Sabarmati	35.8	0.7	107.6	1.6	31.7
Top 10 Ports Exports to Bangladesh	3,444.8	67.0	4.760.7	69.8	8.4
Total Exports to Bangladesh	5.145.0	100.0	6,820.1	100.0	7.3

Source: Directorate General of Commercial Intelligence and Statistics (DGOI&S), Ministry of Commerce and Industry (MOCI), Government of India (GOI), 2018.

Table 6: Top 10 Ports showing Imports from Bangladesh

Port	*2012-13*		*2016-17*		*CAGR (2012-13 to 2016-17, %)*
	Value (US$ mn)	*% Share*	*Value (US$ mn)*	*% Share*	
Petrapole (Land)	408.4	63.9	4072	58.0	-0.1
Tuticorin (Sea)	0.4	0.1	37.9	5.4	212.0
Ghajadanga	4.7	0.7	28.9	4.1	57.5
Kotwaligate (Mohedipur)	8.0	1.3	28.7	4.1	37.6
Nhava Shevd (Sea)	35.4	5.5	26.4	3.8	-7.1
Agartala	'40.8	6.4	20.9	3.0	-15.4
Mumbai (Sea)	-	-	18.5	2.6	771.5
Chengrabandha Rly. Station	103	1.6	18.5	2.6	15.8
Delhi (ICD)	1.1	0 2	16.5	2.4	97.8
Chennai (Sea)	11.2	1.8	14.3	2.0	6.2
Top 10 Ports Imports from Bangladesh	520.2	81.4	617.8	88.0	4.4
Total Imports from Bangladesh	639.3	100.0	701.7	100.0	2.4

Note: - not available/negligible

Source: DGCI&S, MOCI, GOI, 2018.

Table 7: Total Exports to Myanmar

Port	*2012-13*		*2016-17*		*CAGR (2012-13 to 2016-17, %)*
	Value (US$ mn)	*% Share*	*Value (US$ mn)*	*% Share*	
Nhava Sheva (Sea)	1912	35.1	213.7	19.3	2.8
Kolkata (Sea)	87.9	16.1	175.4	15.8	18.9
Mundra	73	1.3	116.5	10.5	199.1
Chennai (Sea)	43.0	7.9	53.4	4.8	5.5
Delhi (ICD)	19.4	3.6	33.3	3.0	14.4
Mumbai (Air)	31.6	5.8	32.8	3.0	0.9
Tuticorin (Sea)	9.4	1.7	*28.9*	2.6	32.4
Delhi (Air)	*72*	1.3	*27.7*	2.5	39.8
Kolkata (Air)	3.0	0.6	26.3	2.4	71.4
Hyderabad Airport	2.6	*0.5*	22.1	2.0	70.3
Top Ten Ports of Exports to Myanmar	402.7	73.9	730.0	65.9	16 0
Total Exports to Myanmar	544.7	100.0	1107.9	100.0	19.4

Source: DGCI&S. MOD, GOI, 2018.

Table 8: Top 10 Ports in India showing Imports from Myanmar

Port	*2012-13*		*2016-17*		*CAGR (2012-13 to 2016-17, %)*
	Value (US$ mn)	*% Share*	*Value (US$ mn)*	*% Share*	
Chennai (Sea)	365.3	25.9	532.1	49.9	9.9
Nhava Sheva (Sea)	308.0	21.8	264.2	24.8	-3.8
GMK Hyd. Aviation Ltd. SEZ	-	-	50.7	4.8	-
Kolkata (Sea)	167.4	11.8	48.6	*4.6*	-26.6
Cochin (Sea)	46.7	3.3	43.9	4.1	-1.5
Mundra	0.8	0.1	25.7	2.4	135.9
Moreh	3.4	*0.2*	17.7	1.7	27.2
Delhi (ICD)	4.4	0.3	11.4	1.1	27.2
New Mangalore (Sea)	149.8	10.6	8.5	0.8	-51.2
Tuticorin (Sea)	137.8	9.8	8.2	0.8	-50.6
Top 10 Ports of Imports from Myanmar	1183.7	83.8	1011.2	94.7	-3.9
Total Imports from Myanmar	1412.7	100.0	1067.3	100.0	-6.8

Note: - not available/negligible.
Source: Ministry of Commerce and Industry, GOI, 2018.

Table 9: Imports from and Exports of Myanmar to India

Year	*Myanmar's Exports to India*	*Myanmar's Imports from India*	*Total Trade*	*Balance of Trade*
2011-12	8.9	6.5	15.4	2.3
2012-13	8.9	3.2	12.0	5.7
2013 14	28.0	17.2	45.1	10.8
2014-15	42.6	18.1	60..7	24.5
2015-16	*53.0*	18.6	71.6	34.4
2016-17	63.5	24.7	88.2 :	38.7

Source: Ministry of Commerce, Myanmar, 2018.

development of logistics hubs across the northeastern region in a Public-Private Partnership framework can enhance trade through roadways and waterways. Upgradation of integrated check posts with warehousing facilities and land customsfacilities with manufacturers will be crucial for export and flourishing markets between Northeast India and Myanmar and Bangladesh. At the 13th meeting of BCIM Regional Cooperation that was held from 10 to 11 June 2019 at Fuxian Lake, Yuxi, in China, the emphasis was on cooperative mechanisms for fostering opportunities between the neighbouring countries. The BCIM, which was mentioned as part of the BRI in 2013, did not make it to the list of 35 corridors mentioned during the 2nd Belt and Road Forum (BRF) that was held in 2019.

The 2,800-km-long BCIM corridor linking Kunming with Kolkata through Mandalay and Dhaka could provide new business opportunities in the changing geo-economic setting. The BCIM can be employed as a foreign policy mechanism to connect the region through air, water and railways, thereby filling the gap between the coastal and land border regions. The improvement in border relations can also help in cultural interaction between the ethnic groups settled across the borders of the four countries based on language and cultural ties (Yhome, 2017).

Conclusion

As an inter-regional integration mechanism, the BCIM brings together South-East Asia, East Asia and South Asia within its cooperative circuit where it not only connects the adjacent countries but also conjoins the urban centres as nodal points of economic, political and cultural interaction. Due to the strategic location of India's Northeastern region, which shares borders with Bangladesh, China and Myanmar, the BCIM could help in facilitating the north-south corridor to enhance trade linkages. As it acts like a gateway to South East Asia, it can help in strengthening India's neighbourhood policy by energising transport connectivity, especially the waterways. The geo-political advantages of India marketing the BCIM vis-a-vis the BRI will open up markets for various goods that can prevent the dumping of Chinese products and can also act as a counter to the encircling policy undertaken by China through the BRI. Economic corridors, as a part of a neo-liberal agenda, best serve as trade facilitators and help in restricting illicit imports that have been taking place across the Northeastern states of India bordering Bangladesh and Myanmar. The development of sub-regionalism can help local entrepreneurs to participate in foreign trade and build a market for their products. The interconnectedness ensuring multilateral trade and greater market accessibility also benefits port services and opens the landlocked Northeastern region to build an integrated regional trade network with Bangladesh and Myanmar, thereby allowing the BCIM to be a successful sub-regional endeavour.

REFERENCES

Asian Development Bank (2006). *Regional Co-operation and Integration Strategy*. Manila.

'BCIM economic corridor beneficial for North-East economy', 25 November 2014 available at https://www.deccanchronicle.com/141125/nation-current-affairs/article/%E2%80%98bcim-economic-corridor-beneficial-north-eastern-regions, accessed 25 June 2019.

Blanchard, Jean-Marc F. (ed.) (2017), "China's Twenty-First Century Maritime Silk Road Initiative and South Asia: Political and Economic Contours, Challenges, and Conundrums" in *China's Maritime Silk Road Initiative and South Asia: A Political Economic Analysis of its Purposes, Perils, and Promise*, California: Palgrave.

Das, G. C. and J. Thomas (eds) (2019), *BCIM Economic Cooperation: Interplay of Geo-economics and Geo-politics*, New York: Routledge.

De, P. (2014), "Economic Corridors and Regional Economic Integration", in Prabir De and Kavita Iyenger (eds) *Developing Economic Corridors in South Asia,* Asian Development Bank (ADB), Manila.

De, P. *et al.* (2018), "Assessing Economic Impacts of Connectivity Corridors: An Empirical Investigation," *Research and Information System for Developing Countries*, pp. 1-96.

Derruder, et al.(2018), *Connectivity Along Overland Corridors of Belt and Road Initiative,* avaliable at http://worldbank.org/curated/en/264651538637972468/pdf/Connectivity-Along-Overland-Corridors-of-the-Belt-and-Road-Initiative.pdf accessed on 23 June 2019

Gong, X and Adriono, A. (2018) *Securing the Belt and Road Initiative Risk Assessment, Private Security and Special Insurances along the new wave of Chinese Outbound Investments*, Singapore: Palgrave.

Hook, G. and Ian Kearns (1999), "Introduction: the Political Economy of Sub-regionalism and World Order" in *Subregionalism and World Order*, Berlin: Springer Publications.

Kumar, A. (2015), Book review of Prabir De and Kavita Iyengar (eds), *Developing Economic Corridors in South Asia,* Asian Development Bank, *South Asia Economic Journal,* New Delhi: Sage Publications.

Ministry of Commerce, Government of India (2018), available at http:// https://commerce.gov.in/ accessed on 25 April 2019.

Ministry of Commerce, Department of Trade, Import and Export Office, Myanmar (2018), available at http:// https://www.dica.gov.mm/en/investment/ministry-commerce-department-trade-export-import-office accessed on 15 May 2020.

Pant, H. and K. Yhome (2020), "India's Sub regional Connectivity Initiatives: Re-imagining the Neighbourhood," *India Review*, 19(1):33-51.

Pattanaik, S. (2016), "Sub-regionalism as New Regionalism in South Asia: India's Role," *Strategic Analysis*, 40(3): 210-217.

Sarker, P. (2019), "One Belt One Road Project is a Driving Force for Holistic Development of Eurasian Region: Challenges to Bangladesh," in Islam, Nazrul, I. (ed) (2019), *Silk Road to Belt Road: Reinventing the Past and Shaping the Future*, Singapore: Springer.

Sharma, A. and Chowdhury, S. (2018), "Mainstreaming the Northeast in India's Look and Act East Policy", New Delhi: Palgrave.

UN COMTRADE (2018), available at http://comtrade.un.org accessed on 24 March 2019.

Yhome, K. (2017), *The BCIM Economic Corridor: Prospects and Challenges,* Observer Research Foundation, available at https://www.orfonline.org/research/the-bcim-economic-corridor-prospects-and-challenges/ accessed 24 March 2019

10

South Asia, India and BRI: Chinese Perspectives

Prashant Kaushik

Introduction

India shares a very 'special' relationship with China; it is close yet intricate, perhaps as intricate as it could become, marked by ever-increasing dialogue, cooperation and competition as well as confrontation.[1] They are each other's strategic partners and yet share thousands of miles of unresolved borders. Perhaps no other bilateral relationship could compare with the intricacies decipherable in the India-China relationship. They are seen standing together on many platforms and yet spare no chance to point bickering fingers at each other. In the course of its emergence from nowhere to become the world's second-largest economy and a potential future number one, China's promotion of the Belt and Road Initiative has created no less ripples in the world of ideas and projects than in the power corridors of various countries; India undoubtedly is no exception. While there exists a certain understanding of India's position on the BRI, attempts need to be made to comprehend how China sees India's position on the BRI. This chapter attempts to understand China's perceptions of India's position on the BRI by reading Chinese writings by some of China's renowned international relations scholars and India watchers.

Gleaned from Chinese writings, one, South Asia figures prominently in China's foreign policy deliberations as one of its most important neighbourhoods now where it is keen to extend the BRI. Two, given India's overarching presence in South Asia, and its open refusal to join the BRI, India also remains a major challenge for China in South Asia. Three, while there is a line of thinking in China that India's stance of opposing the BRI originates from a host of misperceptions and that there is a need for China to work for bringing India onboard by making efforts to change these misperceptions; there also exists a line of thinking which argues that India's participation is not essential for the BRI's overall success or for its success even in South Asia, for that matter. To put it in other words, India is not indispensable for the success of the BRI. Four, Chinese writings betray a consensus that China must not make wooing India a policy and let India take its time on the issue; such a consensus is also discernible in the stance taken by the Chinese government in not addressing India's concerns emanating from the BRI which range from violation of sovereignty to lack of mutual consultation.

South Asia, India and BRI

As we see from Chinese writings, China attaches great importance to South Asia in the context of the BRI, given its geostrategic position and proximity to China. Given the priority attached to neighbourhood diplomacy in China's overall diplomacy, emphasis on the social development of its western regions through various domestic policies, the need to safeguard sea-lanes passing through the Indian Ocean and multi-pronged implementation of the BRI, South Asia has emerged as an extremely significant strategic region in contemporary China's geostrategic perspective where China feels the need to thoroughly co-ordinate between geopolitics and geo-economics. Moreover, South Asia has also emerged as a region where China is actively seeking certain breakthroughs, and there can be no doubt that in the medium to long term China's strategic attention to South Asia is bound to grow (Lin, 2015; Ye, 2016; Feng, 2017).

The Chinese acknowledge that there is hardly any direct connection between the BRI routes traversing through Eurasia and South Asia, hence, the region is essentially seen as an independent variable affecting the development of the BRI. The BRI being an important part of China's neighbourhood strategy, and the logical starting point of it being China's neighbourhood, China is keen to see major South Asian countries with relatively stable development join the BRI. Given the geo-economic and geo-strategic salience of South Asia, China believes that the region may also create a new paradigm for China's peripheral strategy (Zhao, 2015). This was amply visible during Chinese premier Li Keqiang's visit to India and Pakistan in May 2013, where he formally announced China's intention to push forward the construction of the Bangladesh-China-India-Myanmar Economic Corridor and the China-Pakistan Economic Corridor.

With regard to India's role in South Asia, there is a broad convergence of opinion in Chinese writings that no matter whether South Asia becomes the core of China's push for the BRI, India is the most important factor that any Chinese policy in the region must face (Ye, 2016). China tends to see India as the "core power" or the "centre of gravity" "力量中心" located in the centre of the subcontinent incomparable to any other country in South Asia and the entire Indian Ocean region and a "dual status country" (双重身份国家) from the perspective of the BRI as both the Belt and the Road can pass through it (Lin, 2015; Feng, 2017; Yang & Wang, 2019). India is also the largest economy in the region as well as a huge market of billion-plus customers. India's special geographical position creates a unique geopolitical pattern in South Asia where all South Asian countries share borders with India but not with each other. Hence, the Chinese acknowledge that India is an important hub country along the BRI whose influence cannot be matched by any other country, at least not in South Asia (Jin, 2017).

Chinese scholars are in agreement that as one of China's most important neighbours in the southwest frontier, how India deals with the Silk Road strategy is of great significance for China. More so, since India also shares the longest land border with China, and the two also intersect in the Indian Ocean (Zhao, 2015). It has also been argued in Chinese writings that being at the centre of the "centre-periphery" regional structure in South Asia, India can have a strong influence and control in South Asia, something which India can use to challenge the BRI in the short term. On the other hand, as an important economy with a large size and huge population, India's attitude is of great significance for the smooth implementation of the BRI (Luo Huijun and Liu Peidong, 2018).

Hence, Chinese scholars believe that China is promoting the BRI in South Asia in a complex situation where its relationship with India is marked by competition and cooperation, coordination and conflict. The nature and extent of India's role clearly need to be carefully assessed by China, which involves two aspects. One is India's attitude towards "One Belt and One Road". Second, the impact of India's policies on the participation of other South Asian countries in "One Belt and One Road" (Ye, 2016,14).

Why so? Because as per the Chinese, South Asia is the region where India is most likely to exert influence on the BRI, no matter what India's attitude towards the BRI remains. Whether measured by the intensity of high-level diplomacy or the amount of resources invested, India's diplomacy remains dominated and prioritised by South Asia. India has historically resorted to various means to stop other smaller countries in the region to move away from its influence and prevent any outside power to enter the region (Tao, 2015, 98). South Asia is also the region where India can best demonstrate its power and make its strategy work. The Chinese believe that India has a considerable free hand in South Asia; it can apply its will to other countries and achieve the results that it wants. India enjoys the power to take the strategic initiative in South Asia that the rest of the region is incapable of stopping, and there is no strong hindrance to such an initiative from outside the region as well.

With China increasing its focus on South Asia through a multi-pronged approach including the BRI, and given India's denial to join the BRI, and its geographical location and strategic position, India also appears as a concern in Chinese literature, as Zhu Cuiping, Executive Deputy Director of the Research Institute for Indian Ocean Economies, Yunnan University of Finance and Economics and Deputy Secretary-General of the Chinese Association for South Asian Studies, puts it, "India remains one of the biggest hurdles in the path of BRI in South Asia". In the current BRI radiation zone, India is the only major country that is "sceptical" or even "hesitant" to China's invitation and has taken preventive and countermeasures to some extent (Zhu, 2017).

India's Position on BRI: A Case of Misperceiving China?

Chinese IR literature has sought to understand India's position on the BRI through several paradigms such as hedging strategy (Liu Hongliang, 2019; Tu Bo, Zhang Yuan & Zong Wei, 2018), prospect theory (Xu Juan and Wei Ling, 2014), "odd man out" theory (Tu Bo, Kim Tae Wan & Zhang Yua, 2017), issue-by-issue diplomacy (Ye Hailin, 2017), perceptions and misperceptions (Yang Shenglan & Zhu Xinguang, 2017; Luo Huijun & Liu Peidong, 2018), game theory (Wen Yaqin, Du Jun & Yan Bo, 2018) and so on. However, the reference to India's misperception of China remains a recurring theme in Chinese literature as Zhu Cuiping puts it, "the obstacles to cooperation between China and India are more rooted in the traditional geopolitical thinking of India and the deep-rooted perception and cognition of the threat of China under the circumstance of 'information asymmetry" (Zhu, 2015).

Therefore, it becomes pertinent to take a look at how Chinese look at India's position on the BRI through the framework of perception and misperception. Chinese scholars have taken a cue from Robert Jervis's theoretical framework of perception and misperception in international politics (Jervis, 1976, 2017) to understand India's position and argue that Indian views of the BRI are biased and suffer from misperception (Yang & Zhu, 2017; Luo & Liu, 2018).

According to Jervis, three elements which affect perceptions are 'cognitive consistency', 'evoked set' and 'historical experience'. In terms of cognitive consistency 认知相符, Yang and Zhu argue that India's perception originates from the China-India boundary dispute, the failure to make Tibet a buffer zone between India and China, and the perceived threat arising out of the 'String of Pearls' strategy. Hence, compared with the differences existing in bilateral relations between China and India, the principle of jointly building, sharing and win-win cooperation advocated by the BRI is inconsistent with India's previous perception of China. Besides, Indian policymakers are more willing to believe that the BRI is China's version of the "Marshall Plan" and take extra precautions (Yang & Zhu, 2017; Luo & Liu, 2018).

In terms of evoked set 诱发定势 , India's failure to positively respond to the BRI in the initial phase has a lot to do with its concerns about the 'String of Pearls strategy'. India sees the 'String of Pearls' strategy as a strategic containment of India and thus it has been paying a lot more attention to it than the BRI. Moreover, the Chinese argue that some Indian scholars tend to perceive the BRI as an "upgraded version" "升级版" of the 'String of Pearls' strategy or its "another version" "翻版". Hence, based on previous memories of the 1962 conflict, India's impression of the BRI has always been that of a strategic stratagem or even worse (Yang & Zhu, 2017, 57; Luo & Liu, 2018, 88; Zhu, 2015, 5). Instead of seeing the BRI as an economic project, India tends to see it from the perspective of strategy (Ye, 2016a).

In terms of historical experience 历史经验, it has been argued in Chinese writings that the deterioration in India's image of China can be traced back to the 1962 border dispute, after which India saw China as an "enemy from the north" "北方敌人" and an "aggressor" "侵略者"against whom India must never lower its guard. After the end of the Cold War, India regarded China as mainly "neither enemy nor friend" "非敌非友". It cooperated with China pragmatically in areas where cooperation was possible and remained alert to China in areas of disagreement. Based on historical cognition, India's relatively indifferent attitude towards China's BRI is closely related to this chequered history of the bilateral relationship between China and India (Yang & Zhu, 2017, 57). Hence, the Chinese argue that to a great extent, India's pessimistic perception of the BRI is largely derived from the "reference to historical experience", including the "misplaced reference" to the 1962 Sino-Indian conflict and the idea of "strategic independence" guided by India's great power aspirations (Luo & Liu, 2018, 88).

Some Chinese scholars also argue that India overestimates its influence and the extent to which it is affected by the BRI, thus resulting in major misperceptions. Since India's independence, especially after the introduction of the "Indira Doctrine", known as "India's version of the Monroe Doctrine", the deep-rooted thought in India has been that the "Indian Ocean is India's Indian Ocean" and "South Asia is India's South Asia", and hence India is sensitive to external forces entering South Asia and the Indian Ocean. India's larger-than-life economic, geographical, political and strategic presence in South Asia has led to the misperception among its decision-makers that India is fully capable of achieving exclusiveness of the South Asia and lead region's development. Hence Chinese writings mention that based on the blind assessment of its power, India dares to have a negative attitude towards the BRI and also proposes 'Project Mausam', the 'Cotton Road', the 'Blue Economy Cooperation Plan', 'Sagarmala Project' and so on in order to offset China's influence in South Asia by co-opting and suppressing countries in the region. Though it is undeniable that India can cause difficulties to the BRI in the short term by exerting its own influence, at the same time India lacks the ability to fill the economic void left by the loss of Chinese capital, thus rendering its various policy initiatives ineffective in the long term in South Asia (Luo & Liu, 2018, 89).

Changing India's Misperception Towards BRI

Quite notably, there are also Chinese writings which argue that China should make efforts for bringing India on board the BRI; more so, in the face of the lack of strategic mutual trust between China and India and the huge influence India exerts on Nepal, Bhutan and other countries, China should actively communicate and co-ordinate through peaceful diplomacy so as not to let the relationship derail, lead to confrontation or get out of control (Zhou, 2019). A section of Chinese scholarship seems to recognise the need for China to make efforts to change India's misperception about the BRI to diffuse Sino-Indian strategic distrust and ensure that India has tangible economic benefits to gain from the BRI (Lin, 2015). They suggest that first of all there is a need, without expecting a miracle in the short-term, to view and handle China-India relations from a strategic vantage point, taking the peaceful rise of China and India as the starting point, and prudently handling the existing differences between the two countries. The two should enhance dialogue, timely communication and mutual understanding (Jin, 2017).

Second, there is a need for China to look for an opportunity to link the OBOR with two of India's most significant connectivity projects, namely, 'Project

Mausam' and 'Spice Route' (Lin, 2015). Cooperation between Project Mausam and the 21st-Century Maritime Silk Road is conceivable through recognition of each other's plans and their smooth implementation by China and India. China needs to exhibit that the OBOR is a transparent project by making the details of its implementation public and try to dispel India's doubts or at least make India understand the huge economic benefits that OBOR may bring (Tao, 2015). Moreover, China and India must translate their respective cooperation needs into tangible cooperation projects by promoting the building of the BCIM and signing of the FTA, linking of the OBOR with Project Mausam and carrying out communication and coordination on sensitive issues (Jin, 2017). In fact, the template for such cooperation already exists between Russia and China with regard to cooperation between the BRI and the Eurasian Economic Union (EAEU) which can be borrowed by China and India (Lin, 2015).

Third, it has been suggested that in order to remove various suspicions and doubts, China can build an informal multilateral consultation mechanism with India and other South Asian countries. Since most of India's worries concerning the BRI are about the distant future scenario related with its security, such a mechanism could go a long way in resolving its various doubts by providing a voice to India (Lin, 2015). China may ensure the openness of regional cooperation on the Maritime Silk Road by discussing its implementation plan with India (Xu & Wei, 2014). Moreover, a template for such a mechanism already exists in the form of the AIIB and BRICS.

Fourth, China must be careful to deal with any "spill over effect" of its strong steps taken to protect its sovereignty like in the South China Sea which might be adding to the narrative of a "China threat". It is immensely difficult for China to ensure a friendly neighbourhood when its every action is seen suspiciously by its neighbouring countries. Hence, there is a need for China to resolve the issue of trust deficit and enhance political and strategic trust with some of its ASEAN neighbours and India in the course of promoting OBOR (Lin, 2015).

Fifth, China needs to promote political and economic development and strengthen cooperation in key areas with India like the building of its ports, highways, railways airports and smart cities. There is also a need to strengthen cooperation in the financial sector, the opening of more financial services for each other, and strengthening of coordination between regulatory authorities and financial companies of the two countries. In addition, the two countries should leverage their unique strengths in practical cooperation and explore and advance cooperation in new energy, traditional medicine, aerospace and other fields (Jin, 2017).

Sixth, there is a need for China to rationally deal with the current trade deficit with India, which can be solved by promoting bilateral investment cooperation. The deepening of economic and trade cooperation with India is conducive to weakening of India's bias against BRI upgradation of a cooperative partnership with India (Jin, 2017). China must actively seek India's participation in the BRI through deepening of economic and trade cooperation because that could be the best way to help India come out of the security dilemma vis-à-vis China. Given India's heft in South Asia, China must try to bring India on board to expand the scope of the BRI. A convergence of Chinese and Indian economic interests ensures the security of various maritime energy routes passing through the Indian Ocean, and it creates a secure and reliable external environment for the implementation of the BRI (Jin, 2017). At present, China should give full play to its advantages in technology, management and capital and combine with India's advantages in finance, law, language and human resources to jointly promote the construction of demonstration projects and form investment experiences that can be copied and popularised as soon as possible. China must encourage its industry to take up contracts related to the Smart Cities Mission and the Digital India programme in India (Xu & Wei, 2014; Jin, 2017).

Seventh, China must enhance non-traditional security cooperation with India to fight piracy, terrorism, and natural disasters like tsunamis (Xu & Wei, 2014). China must work with India to enhance people-to-people exchanges and cooperation in arts, sports, conservation of cultural heritage, media, youth exchanges, tourism, science and technology and so on. China must further strengthen various dialogue mechanisms with India and lay out a policy to actively promote cooperation with India in the areas of biomedicine, agricultural sci-tech, IT, and environment protection. China must continue to mark "Year of China India Friendship", "International Yoga Day", and continue other cultural exchange programmes with India for enhancing mutual understanding and promoting bonding between the two peoples (Jin, 2017).

India's (in)dispensability for BRI?

Despite the suggestions offered for bringing India on board, the question of whether to actively seek India's participation in the BRI or not has become a point of debate in China. Lin Minwang argues that given the significance of South Asia for the OBOR, since both the Belt and the Road pass through this region, and the predominant position that India holds in this region, there is a need for China to ensure India's participation. Ensuring India's participation is important; first, given India's economic heft in South Asia, second, OBOR is being built by China as an open economic framework around its periphery, so it would be really a matter of regret if a giant market like India remains outside its pale and third, most of the governments in South Asia are pro-India, e.g., the Sheikh Hasina government in Bangladesh and the Sirisena government in Sri Lanka, Modi's Neighbourhood First policy is likely to influence their policy outlook; hence, for all these reasons, it becomes imperative for China to seek India's participation in the BRI (Lin, 2015).

Making a case for India on almost similar lines, Jin Ruiting, assistant researcher at the Institute for International Economic Research of the National Development and Reform Commission, argues that India enjoys a natural geographical advantage in South Asia since it has common borders with all other countries in this region, whereas no other country share border with each other. This has greatly enhanced India's strategic position in the subcontinent. At the same time, the Modi government has adopted the strategy of "neighbour first", through the Indian version of "connectivity" and measures such as expanding trade and investment have greatly reduced the "psychological distance" among all South Asian countries except Pakistan. Given the current state of affairs in South Asia, most countries are wary of anything India opposes. When India supports something, most countries choose to follow suit. It is in this context that China must deepen China-India economic and trade cooperation and strive for India's participation in the BRI as soon as possible. Moreover, India influences the world with its dominant position in the Indian Ocean. Under the current world trade pattern and energy layout, the "Malacca dilemma" may be difficult to break in the short term. Expanding the convergence of economic interests between China and India is conducive to ensuring the security of China's trade and energy channels, thus creating a safe and reliable external environment for the implementation of the BRI (Jin, 2017).

At the other end of the spectrum, a section of Chinese writings presents the counterview that India negatively influences other South Asian countries as far as the BRI is concerned. Ye Hailin, Deputy Director-General, National Institute of International Strategy, Chinese Academy of Social Sciences (CASS), argues that India's actions demonstrate that it can have a big impact on at least some South Asian countries' participation in the OBOR process if it wants to. The effect is also twofold. First, India's obstruction may, in fact, have inspired China's determination to push ahead with the OBOR more aggressively in South Asia, as evidenced by China's aid to Nepal and the resumption of cooperation with Sri Lanka. Second, the Indian factor could also become a reason for other South Asian countries to bargain with China over specific OBOR projects. China must guard against the formation of mentality in South Asian countries where they might depend on India for security and on China for economic well-being, a mentality which has formed among countries in South East Asia, where they depend on the USA for security and rely on China for economic prosperity. Third, China's promotion of the OBOR in South Asia should place more emphasis on the mutually beneficial nature of bilateral projects, reduce the promotion of slogans such as providing public goods, dilute the so-called security strategic appeal, and highlight the nature of economic cooperation (Ye, 2016, 14-5).

As regards the question of how China must respond to India in South Asia, Ye Hailin argues that first, China is unlikely to engage in a fierce and expensive struggle for partnership with India in the subcontinent, nor need it voluntarily slow down its engagement in South Asia's development in order to gain India's understanding. Second, China must remember that India can slow down Chinese projects by incurring a little cost, but it cannot fill the gap left by the withdrawal of Chinese capital and technology from South Asia. Hence, as long as China keeps its strategic patience, avoids a situation where South Asian countries start seeking advantage from an India-China confrontation and persists in "bottom-line thinking" while dealing with possible reversals, it can return OBOR to the nature of economic cooperation and avoid paying unnecessary costs (Ye, 2016, 14-5).

It is perhaps in this context that one gets to read Chinese opinions arguing that seeking India's participation in the BRI must not become a policy priority for China because India is not indispensable for the success of the BRI and, if at all, it should join it due to the sheer economic gains which are being offered by the BRI than for any other reason. Ye Hailin argues that ideally India must join the Maritime Silk Road project and benefit from the infusion of Chinese industry and capital in India, but such a need is a mutual one. India's joining will be beneficial to both India as well as China. If the Maritime Silk Road gains a foothold in the Indian Ocean, then India will have to join it sooner or later, but if it does not gain a foothold, then India's participation or non-participation will hardly make any difference. Ye mentions that in the long run, India's participation is important and perhaps indispensable as well, and for this reason seeking India's participation can become China's posture, stand or may be principle;, but no matter what, it should not become a policy and definitely not a condition for the success of the Maritime Silk Road. Seeking India's participation just for the sake of it is a bad policy which will unnecessarily enhance India's status (Ye, 2015b).

Ye Hailin further argues that when it comes to India's participation in the OBOR, China should adopt a practical and realistic attitude, considering the possible benefits of India's participation, and recognising India's suspicious and profit-seeking mentality on this issue. More emphasis should be placed on the openness and equality of the OBOR strategy and less on the special strategic value of India to the OBOR. This value might be existing, but China needs to see that the more China talks about this issue, the more India's 'precious goods' mentality will grow, and the less likely will it become to win India's support. China should clearly emphasise the nature of the economic cooperation of the OBOR and reject any proposal that combines political, security and territorial issues with the OBOR strategy. China, in other words, should seek India's participation in the OBOR by seeking the truth from the facts. Particularly, India's participation should not be taken as the criterion to measure the success or failure of OBOR strategy (Ye, 2015a, 13).[2]

Posturing against the proponents of alignment of the BRI with India's regional initiatives such as Project Mausam, Feng Chuanlu argues that docking of the BRI and India's Project Mausam does not represent a viable policy option. India's Project Mausam is restrictive in nature which limits space for Sino-Indian cooperation and reflects Monroe Doctrine-style thinking and works to erode mutual trust. Its strategic ambiguity further weakens practical motivation for China and India to dock the two initiatives. Prospects of strategic alignment between the two initiatives are further dimmed by the intent of India's "Look East Policy" to create a regional power balance. Moreover, India's larger strategic ambitions and policy calculations are not encouraging for the initiatives of the two countries to dock with each other (Feng, 2016).

Chinese Consensus on India's Position

As time has elapsed since the announcement of the BRI and owing to India's constant refusal to join it, Chinese IR literature has also begun to betray a broad consensus with regard to the complexity and duality of China-India relations and what principles China should adhere to when formulating its policy towards India. Zhao Gancheng, Director, Centre for Asia-Pacific Studies, Shanghai Institute of International Studies, argues that though India is unlikely to have a positive and helpful bearing in China's periphery in the foreseeable future, "China still needs to make stability-promoting yet hedging policies" vis-à-vis India. On the one hand, China must regard India as a potential partner and remain committed to promoting and shaping a strategic partnership of cooperation with India. On the other, it is necessary to guard against negative incidents arising from India's perception of China as a major competitor and curb potentially damaging trends leading the two countries towards confrontation (Zhao, 2014). According to Zhu

Cuiping, under the influence of factors at individual (Indian political leadership), state and system levels, India tends to misperceive China as a challenge to its rise and a threat to its national security, which leads to India's 'strategic dilemma' of either aligning with the USA to contain China or continue with non-alignment and an independent foreign policy; 'cooperation dilemma' arising out of India's perception of China as a threat but yet the need to promote economic relations and 'security dilemma' reflected in the choice between hedging strategy against China or enhancing cooperation through the BRI. Although the BRI offers a huge opportunity for India, nevertheless, under the impact of geopolitical factors, misperception and misinterpretation of China's strategic intent, India tends to see the BRI suspiciously (Zhu, 2015). In addition to seeing the CPEC-BRI as impinging on its sovereignty, India also believes that the BRI has a geopolitical agenda. It is afraid that if it completely supports the BRI, then a host of small South Asian countries will end up decisively leaning towards China, something which India does not want and hence it maintains its reservations on the issue (Lin, 2019). Hence, China's South Asia policy needs to respect regional realities carefully.

As regards India's participation in the BRI, it appears that India's participation is not seen as a necessary condition for its success. Although, India's significance for the BRI has been underscored time and again in Chinese writings, no concrete step has been taken by China to address India's concerns regarding its territorial integrity and sovereignty with regard to the passing of the China Pakistan Economic Corridor through Pakistan-occupied-Kashmir. What China seems to realise is that the key to the success or failure of BRI construction is whether China can carry out bilateral or minor multilateral cooperation with the host countries of specific projects such as Pakistan, Nepal, Sri Lanka, the Maldives and Bangladesh in South Asia (Lin, 2019).

It appears that China is ready to be patient as far as India's participation in the BRI is concerned due to several reasons. First, by opposing the CPEC on grounds of sovereignty and territorial integrity, it has become impossible for India to join a BRI which regards the CPEC as its flagship project. Second, India's economic growth is not dependent on China. The little alignment that exists between Indian and Chinese economies predates the BRI. Third, China has a burgeoning trade surplus with almost all the BRI participant countries, and China's trade surplus is already a very sensitive issue in India. Fourth, China recognises that there are hardly any chances of attaining a breakthrough in the short-term with India as regards the BRI since the China-India relationship remains mired in a persistent trust deficit and security dilemma (Ye, 2017; Zhu, 2017).

Nevertheless, Chinese scholars believe that India has already stepped over the threshold of the BRI by joining the AIIB and the BCIM. In the short term, India might refuse to join the BRI, but it will go against India's strategic interests and realistic demands of economic development if it remains adamant on maintaining the threshold status of standing out of the BRI alone in South Asia when other South Asian countries join it. However, in the long run, it is highly probable that with the resolving of the strategic anxiety between China and India and their myriad interests increasingly converging, the two would end up cooperating on the BRI (Jin, 2017).

Conclusion

China has long divided its diplomacy into three categories of major power diplomacy, neighbourhood diplomacy and diplomacy of the developing countries "大国是关键、周边是首要、发展中国家是基础". Among them, how to co-ordinate the interests, goals and strategies of major power diplomacy and neighbourhood diplomacy has always been a key challenge. The question of whether to prioritise the neighbourhood or the major power has never disappeared for China (Ye, 2018). It is in this context that India remains the quintessential "elephant in the room" for China, simply too big to be ignored in South Asia. In order to draw a contrast, it is also pertinent to mention the CPEC here and how the majority of Chinese IR writings tend to talk about the risks and challenges that the CPEC faces in Pakistan, besides, of course, its economic and strategic significance. The trend is different in the case of India and most of the Chinese writings tend to see India in the context of extension of the BRI in South Asia and India's significance thereof and per se. One may say that this is because since Pakistan has already joined the BRI, the Chinese tend to focus more on the risk and challenge aspect of the actual implementation of the BRI there, whereas with India not joining the BRI anytime soon, they tend to underscore India's significance only.

There is no doubt that in the ideal scheme of things, China would like to see India join the BRI; however, there is also reluctance on the part of China to walk the talk which it has done in the course of establishment of the Asian Infrastructure Investment Bank (AIIB), and BRICS New Development Bank, the two most significant templates of multilateral cooperation where India remains a steadfast partner and supporter of China. Given Chinese stubbornness to address India's concerns and lack of proper consultation mechanisms on the BRI, incorporating India in the BRI schema has proved next to impossible for China.

NOTES

1. Ye Hailin (2013), sees Sino-Indian relations in terms of 4 Cs, namely conflict, competition, coordination and cooperation.
2. Although the English translation of "一带一路" has been rendered as the "Belt and Road Initiative", but in Chinese language literature the term "战略" "strategy" is most often appended with "一带一路" ("一带一路" 战略), rather than "倡议" "initiative".

REFERENCES

Feng Chuanlu, (2016), 'Strategic Connectivity between Belt & Road Initiative and Project Mausam: Viable Policy Option or Untenable Proposition?' *South Asian Studies*, Issue 2, 2016, pp. 44-66. 冯传禄 (2016) '"一带一路"与"季风计划"战略对接: 有效政策选项抑或伪命题', 载《南亚研究》2016 年第 2 期, 第 44-66 页.

Feng Chuanlu (2017), 'Observations of the Geo-Political Context and Regional Order in South Asia: Perspectives from the Belt and Road Initiative', *South Asian Studies*, Issue 3, 2017, pp. 1-32. 冯传禄 (2017) '"一带一路"视野下南亚地缘政治格局及地区形势发展观察', 载《南亚研究》2017 年第 3 期, 第 1-32 页.

Jin Ruiting (2017), 'The Importance, Strategy and Policy Suggestions to Deepen Economic and Trade Cooperation Between China and India under the Background of "The Belt and Road"'. 金瑞庭 (2017) '"一带一路"背景下深化中印经贸合作重要性、策略构想与政策建议',《全球化》, 2017 年第 5 期, 90-103.

Lin Minwang (2015), 'Indian Perception of "One Belt One Road" and China's Policy Choices, *World Economics and Politics*', No. 5, 2015, pp. 42-57. 林民旺 , 2015 '印度对"一带一路"的认知及中国的政策选择', 《世界经济与政治》, 2015 年第 5 期, 第 42-57 页. ·

Lin Minwang (2019), 'India is incapable of stopping China, at best it can only express dissatisfaction', 13 February 2019. 林民旺 , (2019), '印度无力阻止中国, 最多就是表示很不满而已', 2019-02-13. Retrieved 12 July 2019 from https://www.guancha.cn/LinMingWang/2019_02_13_489920_s.shtml

Liu Hongliang (2019) "On the Resilience of India's China Strategy with respect to Hedging and Cooperation" *South Asian Studies*, Issue 1, 2019, pp. 1-28. 刘红良 , (2019) "论印度对华政策的对冲刚性与合作韧性" ,《南亚研究》, 2019 年第 1 期, 第 1-28 页.

Luo Huijun & Liu Peidong (2018), 'India's Perceptions of the Belt and Road Initiative and China's Response from Misperception Perspective', *Journal of Liaocheng University* (Social Science Edition), No. 6, 2018, pp. 84-91. 罗会钧, 刘培东 (2018) '错误知觉下 印度对"一带一路"的认知及我国的对策建议'《聊城大学学报（社会科学版）》, 2018 年第 6 期, 第 84-91 页.

Tao Liang (2015), '"Project Mausam", India's Maritime Strategy and the "21st Century Maritime Silk Road', *South Asian Studies*, Issue 3, 2015, pp. 95-110. 陶亮 (2015) '"季风计划"、印度海洋战略与"21 世纪海上丝绸之路',《南亚研究》, 2015 年第 3 期, 第 95-110 页..

Tu Bo, Kim Tae Wan & Zhang Yua (2017) "The Strategic Dilemma of Cooperation with India under China's Belt and Road Initiative", *Journal of Contemporary Asia-Pacific Studies*, No. 6, 2017, pp. 48-66. 涂波, 金泰完, 张元 (2017) "论印度在中国"一带一路" 区域合作倡议下的战略困境——以"边缘人"为理论基础" 《当代亚太》2017 年第 6 期 , 第 48-66 页.

Tu Bo, Zhang Yuan & Zong Wei (2018) "India's Hedging Strategy against the Belt and Road Initiative", *South Asian Studies Quarterly*, No. 2, 2018, Sum No. 173, pp. 84-93. 涂波, 张元, 涂波, 张元, 宗蔚 (2018) ""印度对"一带一路"倡议的对冲战略发展变化"《南亚研究季刊》2018 年 02 期, 总第 173 期, 第 84-93 页。思瑞坎: 《印度对华对冲战略分析》, 载《当代亚太》2013 年第 4 期, 第 25 页.

Wen Yaqin, Du Jun & Yan Bo (2018) "A Solution to the Prisoner's Dilemma in the Context of the 21st Century Maritime Silk Road: A Game Theory Perspective Based on China-India Relations", *Contemporary Economics*, No. 3, February 2018, pp. 16-19. 温亚琴 , 杜军 , 鄢波 (2018) "21 世

纪海上丝绸之路背景下"囚 徒困境"之破解——基于中印关系的博弈论视角"《当代经济》 2018 年2 月刊第 3 期，第 16-19 页.

Xu Juan &Wei Ling (2014) 'India's Perception of 21st Century Maritime Silk Road', *South Asian Studies Quarterly*, Sum No. 158, No. 3, 2014, pp. 1-6. 许娟, 卫灵(2014),'印度对 21 世纪"海上丝绸之路"倡议的认知',《南亚研究季刊》，总第 158 期，2014 年第 3 期，第 1-6 页.

Yang Shenglan & Zhu Xinguang (2017), 'U.S. and India's Perceptions and Misperceptions of the "One Belt One Road" Initiative and China's Response', *Academic Exploration*, No. 8, 2017, August 2017, pp. 53-59. 杨胜兰，朱新光 (2017),'美国、印度对 "一带一路" 的知觉与错误知觉及中国的应对策略',《学术探索》, 2017 年 8 月, 第 53-59 页.

Yang Shu & Wang Shusen (2019), 'The Unique Role of Dual Status Countries in the Building of BRI', 7 January 2019. 杨恕, 王术森 (2019),'"双重身份"国家在"一带一路"建设中的独特作用', 7 January 2019. Retrieved 10 January 2019 from https://www.yidaiyilu.gov.cn/ghsl/gnzjgd/76609.htm

Ye Hailin (2013), "Cooperation, Coordination, Competition and Conflict Coexist in the 21st Century Sino-Indian Relations", *National Humanity History*, Issue 20, 2013, p. 41. 叶海林 (2013) "合作、协调、竞争与冲突并存 21 世纪的中印关系",《国家人文历史》，2013 年第 20 期，第 41 页.

Ye Hailin (2015a), 'India's China Policy under the Strong Government Leadership', *Indian Ocean Economic and Political Review,* No. 3, 2015, pp. 4-15. 叶海林 (2015a) '"强势政府"心态下的印度对华政策'，《印度洋经济体研究》2015 年第 3 期，第 4-15 页.

Ye Hailin (2015b), 'Must China seek India's participation in 21st Century Maritime Silk Road?' 19 January 2015. 叶海林 (2015b) '中国必须争取印度参加"21 世纪海上丝绸之路"吗？', 2015-01-19. Retrieved 13 June 2019 fromhttps://www.thepaper.cn/newsDetail_forward_1295387

Ye Hailin (2016), 'India's South Asian Policy and its Impact on China's BRI', *Indian Ocean Economic and Political Review,* No. 2, 2016, pp. 4-15. 叶海林 (2016) '印度南亚政策及对中国推进一带一路的影响'.【印度洋经济体研究】2016 年第 2 期，第 4-15 页.

Ye Hailin (2017), "The Modi Administration's "Issue by Issue Diplomacy" Strategy towards China, and Related Attitude towards the Belt and Road Initiative", *Journal of Contemporary Asia-Pacific Studies,* No. 6, 2017, pp. 24-47. 叶海林 (2017), "莫迪政府对华 "问题外交" 策略研究——兼论该视角下印度对 "一带一路" 倡议的态度"《当代亚太》2017 年第 6 期，第 24-47 页.

Ye Hailin (2018), 'The Prospects of "Indo-Pacific" Concept and China's Countermeasures', *Indian Ocean Economic and Political Review,* No. 2, 2018, pp. 1-14. 叶海林 (2018) '"印太"概念的前景与中国的应对策略',《印度洋经济体研究》2018 年第 2 期，第 1-14 页.

Zhao Gancheng (2014), 'The India Factor in China's Peripheral Strategy', *Global Review*, Vol. 6, No. 2, March/April 2014, pp. 34-46. 赵干城 (2014) '中国周边战略中的印度因素',《国际展望》, 2014 年第 2 期，第 34-46 页..

Zhao Gancheng (2015), 'One Belt One Road" in South Asia and India's Choices', *Contemporary World,* No. 6, 2015, pp. 19-22. 赵干城 (2015) '"一带一路"战略的南亚方向与印度的选择',《当代世界》,2015 年第 6 期，第 19-22 页.

Zhou Wentong (2019), 'The Evolution of the International Strategic Pattern in the New Era and the Future Development of Sino-Indian Relation', *The Theoretical Platform of Tibetan Development,* No. 2, 2019, pp. 31-36. 周文桐 (2019) '新时代国际战略格局的演变与中印关系未来发展的展望',《西藏发展论坛》2019.02,第 31-36 页.

Zhu Cuiping (2015) "Dilemmas and Strategic Options vis-à-vis India's China Policy under the Modi Administration" *South Asian Studies,* Issue 3, 2015, pp.1-15. 朱翠萍 (2015) "印度莫迪政府对华政策的困境与战略选择"，《南亚研究》2015 年第 3 期，第 1-15 页.

Zhu Cuiping (2017), 'Strategic Directions for the Belt and Road Initiative in South Asia: Geo-politics, the Question of India and Possible Paths for Progress', *South Asian Studies*, Issue 2, 2017, pp. 1-28. 朱翠萍 (2017),'"一带一路"倡议的南亚方向:地缘政治格局、印度难点与突破路径',《南亚研究》,2017 年第 2 期,第 1-28 页.

SECTION III

BRI in India's Extended Neighbourhood

11

China's Belt and Road Initiative in Central Asia: Challenges and Policy Options for India

Ramakrushna Pradhan and Atanu Mohapatra

The chapter deals exclusively with China's Belt and Road Initiative (BRI) in Central Asia. The centrality of Central Asia in the geopolitics of India and China, and the unprecedented rise of China pose serious challenges for India; indeed, it hampers New Delhi's strategic and economic efforts in the most vital heartland. The effort, therefore, in this chapter is to analyse China's grand strategy in Central Asia largely through a geopolitical lens. This chapter argues that Beijing is asserting itself to gain political leverage over its neighbours, especially the energy-rich Central Asia, and establish hegemony in the region as part of its strategic calculation to achieve global supremacy.

Conceptualizing the BRI

The Belt and Road Initiative (BRI), also known as One Belt, One Road (OBOR) Initiative, is one of the most ambitious foreign and economic policies in recent times put forward by any country. Given the sheer scale and objectives various scholars have drawn parallels between the BRI and the Marshall Plan. This project is close to President Xi Jinping's heart and aims to strengthen Beijing's economic leadership through a vast program of infrastructure building throughout China's neighbouring regions. The project has been touted as the transcontinental multi-mode connectivity network that aims to foster economic cooperation and has also been well supported by several analysts as New Silk Road Economic diplomacy of China to carry out trade and transportation across the globe.

The BRI is an umbrella project initiated by Chinese President Xi Jinping at the end of 2013. Etymologically, the term 'BRI' has been derived from the Chinese "*yi dai yi lu*", which means 'One Belt One Road' (Magiri, 2017; Escobar 2017). It is a commitment to easing bottlenecks to Eurasian trade by improving and building networks of connectivity across Central, Western, and Southern Asia and reaching out to the West Asia , East and North Africa. Through collective and collaborative efforts, it aims to build a network of roads and high-speed rail connectivity, pipelines, ports, fibre optic cables, and state-of-the-art telecom links, which will link China to the rest of the world. The BRI is arguably one of the largest development projects in modern history. China is using it to assert its regional leadership through a vast program of economic integration. Apart from aiming to erect a network of infrastructure projects, the BRI aims at promoting cooperation in trade, investment and bolster cultural as well as people-to-people contacts. More than 60 countries are participating in the BRI (*The Economic Times,* 2017; Pantucci, 2017). According to China, the BRI is a flexible alignment which may be adjusted and expanded as required, based on agreements and understandings with partner countries. As mentioned above, the initiative has two components, the first is Belt and the second is Road:

- Belt–The "Belt" refers to the land-based "Silk Road Economic Belt". Here, Beijing aims to connect China's underdeveloped western hinterland to Europe through Central Asia.
- Road–The "Road" refers to the ocean-going "Maritime Silk Road". It aims to connect the fast-growing South-East Asian region with China's southern provinces through ports and railways. The plan is also to connect the Pacific Ocean and the Indian Ocean.

Three financial institutions have been specially created to support this initiative, namely, the Asia Infrastructure Investment Bank (AIIB), the Silk Road Fund, and the New Development Bank (Lee, 2015). The creation of these institutions have met with some resistance from the West given that they provide alternatives to the World Bank, International Monetary Fund (IMF) and Asian Development Bank (ADB). The BRI encompasses a population of 4.4 billion people with a collective GDP of $ 21 trillion (one-third of the world's wealth) and links the emerging markets having strong growth potential with China. China already has close connections with the countries along the proposed BRI route, but it further hopes to strengthen the transportation infrastructure and create new regional hubs and clusters of massive industrial parks (Rolland, 2015).

Figure 1: One Belt, One Road (OBOR) Project

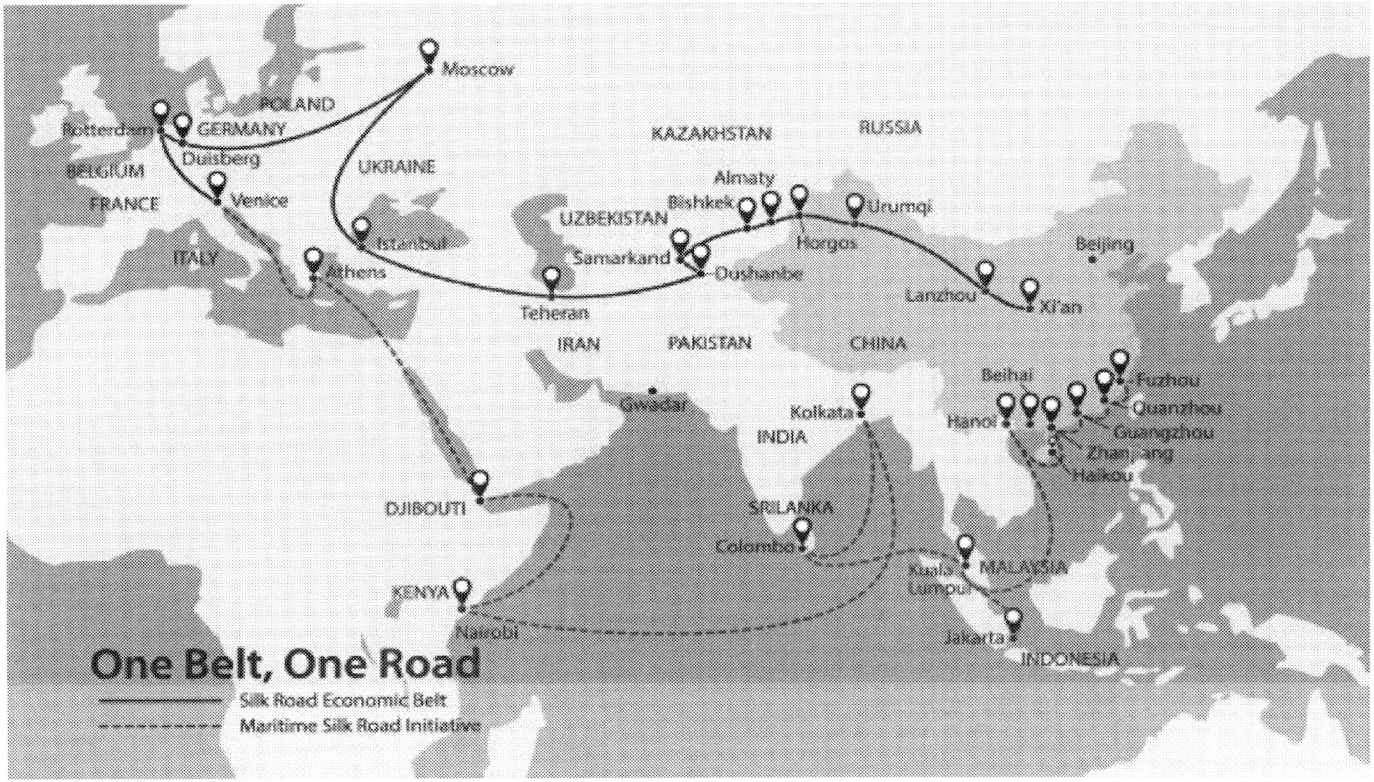

Source: (Escobar, 2017. Online available at http://www.atimes.com/article/xis-road-map-chinese-dream/)

Table 1: List of BRI Countries

Region-wise	*Countries*
East Asia	China, Mongolia
Southeast Asia	Brunei, Cambodia, Indonesia, Laos, Malaysia, Myanmar, The Philippines, Singapore, Thailand, Timor-Leste, Vietnam.
Central Asia	Kazakhstan, Kyrgyzstan, Tajikistan, Turkmenistan, Uzbekistan
The Middle East and North Africa	Bahrain, Egypt, Iran, Iraq, Israel, Jordan, Kuwait, Lebanon, Oman, Qatar, Saudi Arabia, Palestine, Syria, United Arab Emirates, Yemen.
South Asia	Afghanistan, Bangladesh, Bhutan, India, The Maldives, Nepal, Pakistan, Sri Lanka.
Europe	Albania, Armenia, Azerbaijan, Belarus, Bosnia and Herzegovina, Bulgaria, Croatia, Czech Republic, Estonia, Georgia, Hungary, Latvia, Lithuania, Macedonia, Moldova, Montenegro, Poland, Romania, Russia, Serbia, Slovakia, Slovenia, Turkey, Ukraine.

Source: (Chin. Helen & He. Winnie, 2016. Online available at https://www.fbicgroup.com/sites/defult/files/B%26R_Initiative_65_Countries_and_Beyond.pdf)

Chinese Narrative of the BRI

Although China proposes the BRI as a connectivity initiative, there can be no doubt that it is Beijing's strategic game-changer and diplomatic master card to expand and maintain its influence not just in Asia but also in Africa and Europe and to create an alternative to America in world politics. Evidently, the BRI is highly ambitious having a set of interesting and overwhelming objectives which may be summed up as follows:

- To play a bigger role in world affairs and expand circle of China's friends across the continents.
- To serve diplomatic, strategic, and economic purposes of China in a multi-pronged manner.
- To address China's domestic needs in economic transformation, enabling an increase in industrial output and revitalizing its economy.
- To create a Sino-centric regional, economic and strategic order in Asia.
- To (re)build China's soft power through demonstrative projects.
- To counter US propaganda of China Threat by offering an economic solution to global problems through a win-win proposal for all.
- To facilitate China's access to ports around the globe, enabling China to establish maritime superiority.

Advancing the Chinese perspective on the BRI, Li Zigou identifies three main motivations. First, Li emphasizes the importance of the OBOR in fostering the development of China's less-developed western provinces by connecting them with China's wealthy eastern provinces. Li suggests that the OBOR "will turn the western interior into the frontier in opening up to the world, (create) development opportunities in the central and western regions (which) will increase, and new growth points will emerge" (Claudio, 2016, 35). Second, "OBOR seeks to enhance Asia's status in the industrial world by promoting economic development among the Asian developing countries that are lagging behind Europe (Ibid., 35-36)." Third, "through the OBOR initiative, China would promote a 'community of destiny' based on mutual growth and win-win cooperation with its bordering countries" (Ibid., 35-36).

During the Boao Forum in 2015, Chinese President Xi Jinping emphasised that "China will follow the principle of wide consultation, joint contribution, and shared benefits. The programs of development will be open and inclusive, not exclusive. They will be a real chorus comprising all countries along the routes, not a solo for China itself. To develop the Belt and Road is not replacing existing mechanisms or initiatives for regional cooperation. Much to the contrary, we will build on the existing basis to help countries align their development strategies and form complementarity" (Jinping, 2015). Similarly, Chinese foreign minister Wang Yi holds that "China seeks equal-footed consultation and grants no interference in other countries' decision-making." While maintaining that the initiative is based on transparency and openness, and it complements the existing regional cooperation mechanisms (Yi, 2015). However, notwithstanding the Chinese claims, the strategic impact of the BRI is ostensibly evident on many fronts.

Central Asia: The Silk Road Region

The concept of the Silk Road is not new with regards to Central Asia. Central Asia witnessed the opening and thriving of the ancient silk road first-hand when almost two millennia ago products from Asia, particularly silk, reached the Roman Empire. As an economic and political concept, the BRI is as romantic as its old version and can develop a social construction of economic development based on a historical narrative. It also allows China to take a cue from the ancient Silk Road to advance its strategic design to (re)connect Europe with Asia and Africa with the use of modern transportation, to boost trade, investments, and economic development, as well as to improve diplomatic relations, scientific progress and cultural exchange with all countries and regions across the Eurasian continent. No wonder that Central Asia figures prominently in the BRI, both in terms of its historical connections and modern significance.

Central Asia, strictly speaking in geographical terms, consists of five 'stans':

Kazakhstan, Kyrgyzstan, Tajikistan, Turkmenistan and Uzbekistan. As a single geopolitical entity, the region is situated at the crossroads of Russia, China and the Islamic world. It covers a vast area of approximately 4 million square kilometres, i.e., almost one-sixth the size of the former Soviet Union (Kaushik, 1970). It stretches from the shores of the Caspian Sea and the Volga River in the west to China in the east and Russia in the north to Afghanistan, Iran and India in the south. Central Asia enjoys unique geographical location, and hence played a significant role in redefining the world, both literally and figurately, since the disintegration of the erstwhile Soviet Union.

Geopolitically, Central Asia is the geographic hub of Asia and is located at the heart of Eurasia. Positioned literally in the middle of the ancient Silk Route and modern Silk Road Economic Belt, the region is strategically vital not just for Russia and China but also the USA, Europe, and other countries in Asia and outside. Central Asia shares a long 6,200 km border with Russia in the north, a 3,500 km border with China in the east, approximately a border of more than 3,500 km to the west with the Caspian Sea, and a huge length of the inland border with Iran and Afghanistan in the south-west and the south (Akiner, 1994).

Central Asia's geopolitical importance cannot be explained without taking recourse to Halford Mackinder's view of 'he who controls the heartland controls the world' (Mackinder, 1904). Central Asia's vast untapped energy reserves and promising potential on the hydro- and nuclear energy fronts underpins its position as the heartland, a la Mackinder. Energy resources are among the most abundant and valuable natural resources of the countries of Central Asia. The region offers opportunities for discovery, production, transportation, and refining of enormous quantities of oil, gas, and other energy resources. While Kazakhstan is especially known for its large oil and coal reserves and some significant amount of uranium deposits, Turkmenistan and Uzbekistan are noted for their gas reserves. Kyrgyzstan produces a significant amount of hydroelectricity. With proven oil reserves estimated to range from 9 to 40 billion barrels and natural gas reserves possibly exceeding 131 trillion cubic feet (tcf) (Patnaik, 2016; BP, 2018), Central Asia is poised to become a major world supplier of energy. With 23,000 tons of uranium, Kazakhstan is the world's largest producer and has the second largest reserves as of 2014. It is also home to minerals, including iron ore, coal, oil, gas, gold, lead, zinc, molybdenum, etc., in commercially viable quantities (Sajjanhar, 2016; Sachdeva, 2017). Uzbekistan has large reserves of gas, uranium, and gold. Turkmenistan is endowed with the world's fourth-largest reserves of natural gas. Tajikistan is blessed with huge hydroelectric potential. Kyrgyzstan is rich in gold and hydroelectric power. Since most of its reserves are undeveloped and promising, the Central Asian region excites international interests.

As far as China is concerned, Central Asia is both an embodiment of vast opportunities and unpredictable challenges. The rich energy resources of Central Asia provide immense opportunities for a net energy importer like China whereas the proximity of the Central Asian region with a violent and turbulent Afghanistan poses immense security challenge to Beijing, especially in a period of withdrawal of NATO forces from Afghanistan and given the upsurge in Islamic militancy and Uyghur nationalism in Xinjiang Uyghur Autonomous Region of China.

China's Strategy in Central Asia

Chinese President Xi Jinping laid down his vision of the Silk Road Economic Belt in Astana during his visit to Kazakhstan in September 2013 (MFA 2013). The core aim of the 'belt' concept is to initiate and strengthen bilateral trade and economic relations between China and the Eurasian region. In a significant addendum in May 2015, China and Russia agreed in Moscow to integrate the former's Silk Road Economic Belt with the latter's vision of a trade and infrastructure network across Eurasia. The Eurasian Economic Union was formally launched in January 2015 comprising the former Soviet Union States of Russia, Armenia, Belarus, Kazakhstan and Kyrgyzstan (Dijk and Martens, 2016). This reinforces Russia's own 'pivot to the East' and serves to dispel the perspective that Russia and China are natural adversaries. Furthermore, the Silk Road Economic Belt directly links China to the EU, strengthening economic ties and raising doubts that there is a new great game at play in Central Asia and the Caucasus involving Russia and China in an alliance against the West. China has certain critical interests in the Central Asian region as discussed below, and the strategies it has in place to secure those make China a powerful contender in the region having the tools and means to influence this region. The following discussion makes it amply clear as to why the Central Asian Region is of vital importance to China so much so that Beijing cannot afford to lose its grip or let others hold sway in the region.

China's Interests and Initiatives in Central Asia

Energy

China has a great interest in gaining access to the rich deposits of hydrocarbon resources in the Central Asian region. Presently, China is the second largest consumer of oil and gas globally and might be importing 50 per cent of the region's oil by 2020 (Hart, 2016). As the second biggest economy in the world and a country with 1.4 billion population, China, in all probability, is going to depend profoundly on Central Asia to satisfy its energy needs as a net energy importer. An energy rich Central Asia having proven oil and natural gas reserves running into trillions of barrels and cubic meters provide a natural destination for China to satisfy its energy needs. It makes economic sense for China to import hydrocarbon resources from its neighbourhood rather than depending on the West Asia and remain wary of the Malacca Dilemma. Hence, it is not surprising to see China enhancing its engagement in the region to tap and develop the vast untapped and underdeveloped hydrocarbon resources. China is already controlling 20 per cent of Kazakh oil production and has constructed the longest pipeline running about 2,300 kilometres from the Caspian Sea to Xinjiang province (Hart, 2016). Beijing has also been actively participating in exploring Alktyuinks and Mangyshlak oil deposits and building an oil pipeline in the Kazakhstan-Xinjiang region (Pradhan, 2010). China's national oil company, China National Petroleum Corporation (CNPC), owns a significant stake in the Kashagan oil field in the Caspian Sea, while several other Chinese companies own and have developed several key oil fields in the western city of Aktobe (Hart, 2016). With Turkmenistan —the major gas producer and exporter of the region—China has negotiated the transfer of gas through the Central Asia-China gas pipeline directly. One of the most ambitious projects signed by China includes a 5,730-kilometres gas pipeline project between Turkmenistan-Uzbekistan-Kazakhstan and China estimated at $ 11 billion (Pradhan, 2019). Chinese inroads into the Central Asian energy markets have decisively oriented the flow of oil and gas from Central Asia eastwards and have undoubtedly established a Chinese dominance in the region that until now was controlled by the West and Russia. The participation of majority of the Central Asian Countries in the two BRI forums held in 2017 and 2019 amply shows that Chinese hegemony is looming large over Central Asia.

Security Interests

Since the collapse of the Soviet Union, China and its Central Asian neighbours have developed a close relationship, initially economic but increasingly involving political and security spheres as well. Until recently, Chinese security engagement in the region remained modest, largely due to its military weakness, possible negative international perception, and fear of drawing into a zero-sum game with Russia. However, this has changed in the last few years. China is not just taking steps towards greater military cooperation with the countries of the region but also adopting a broader security interest and strategies in the region. The world's largest regional organisation in terms of geographical coverage and population—

the Shanghai Cooperation Organisation—was actually created as the Shanghai Five grouping on 26 April 1996 with the signing of the Treaty on Deepening Military Trust in Border Regions by China, Kazakhstan, Kyrgyzstan, Russia and Tajikistan.

Border Security

The peripheral security of China in Central Asia has two dimensions. First, the preservation of the stability, economic well-being, political order, and security of its western-most province, Xinjiang Uyghur Autonomous Region (XUAR), which shares a long and common border with Russia, Mongolia, and the three Central Asian states of Kazakhstan, Kyrgyzstan, and Tajikistan. Intricately linked to this goal is the second aim of creating a friendly and secure belt of states around the Xinjiang region. "A central aim of its regional security policy is to ensure that Central Asia remains free from the hegemonic control of powerful rivals such as the United States now that Russian power has considerably declined and partnership with Russia is seen to advance strategic goals". (Dutta, Sujit, 2003) The 3,000 kilometres of border that China shares with Central Asia was given priority by Beijing to resolve all disputes and stabilize the region critically linked to the security stability of its western border (Zhi, 2016). In this direction, the BRI has been a masterstroke by China to take full control of the region in the disguise of economic growth and infrastructure development.

Buffer Zone

Central Asia, sharing a 3,500 kilometres long border with China in its west, provides a safe and friendly buffer zone to China saving it from the direct onslaught of radical Islam and terrorism emanating from Afghanistan and beyond. The rapid rise of Taliban in Afghanistan posed serious challenges to China in its Xinjiang region. However, Central Asia, located centrally between China and Afghanistan, cushioned the impact and provided China room to handle the crisis. The most important threat China is now encountering is the eastward expansion of NATO beyond the Central Asian borders. Here again, Central Asia stands as a strong support base for China. The region is mostly pro-communist and provide an additional cushion to Chinese security concerns. That is why China rates the region high above everything else with regards to its security priorities.

Strategic Interests

Central Asia is not just a trade and investment hub for China but a strategic area as well. China's strategic interests rest upon four pillars in Central Asia, viz. countering terrorism and Islamic militancy backing the Uyghur independence, military cooperation with Central Asian countries, countering the influence of major powers in the region inimical to China, and strongly influencing Central Asia's multilateral security arrangements. China also seriously views Central Asia as a gateway to the vast regions of Eurasia, the energy centres of Central Asia, and as a landmass which could link China to Russia, West Asia, Europe and to the ports of Pakistan and the Gulf. Therefore, it is obvious on the part of China not to allow Central Asia to become a backyard of Russia and a chessboard for America. Hence, China has been cementing its position in Central Asia.

Economic Interests

China's interests in Central Asia are defined in terms of a reliable supply-demand relationship based on fair and reasonable oil and gas prices. This has further helped Beijing to propel gradual economic cooperation with Central Asian states. On the other hand, Central Asia has provided a huge and fertile market for cheap Chinese goods. Also, China is eyeing the Caspian Sea Region (CSR) for importing cheap oil and clean gas. Thus, it is no surprise that China treats economic relations with Central Asia as top priority. The increasing interests of China in the Central Asian economy can be seen in terms of the following points.

1. "The territory serves as a transit road for economic ties between China and Europe, South Asia and the West Asia.
2. Central Asia is rich in natural resources. Oil, gas, gold, uranium, cotton, etc., attract international forces and boosts its economic importance.
3. The newly independent states turned the region into a vacant and easily accessible market for Chinese goods and a source of cheap raw materials. Land transport communications offered more advantageous conditions for Chinese exports.
4. The sovereign Central Asian countries can now establish direct ties with the APR (Asia Pacific Region). Some of them (Japan and South Korea) have come to the fore. In these conditions, China, connected with Central Asia by a railway and highways, has become the most convenient and reliable link between Central Asia and the APR (Asia-Pacific Region), which earns it additional money.
5. The region needs Chinese consumer goods" (Khojaev, Ablat, 2007).

Therefore, it is not surprising to ascertain that after energy, the economic relationship with Central Asia remains China's topmost priority. The launch of China's Western Development Strategy and Central Asia's geostrategic location further propels China to use the region as a transportation hub to link up with West Asia and Europe. No wonder that Chinese President Xi Jinping chose to propose the building of the BRI in one of the Central Asian countries in September 2013.

Why is India Upset?

Central Asia constitutes India's extended neighbourhood. Given its historical roots, close friendship, and superb bonding since the ancient silk route days, India has long recognised the Central Asian region as an area of strategic importance. India's "Look North" policy in the 1990s is a standing example of this. During a visit to Turkmenistan in September 1995, Prime Minister P.V. Narasimha Rao made it amply clear that for India, Central Asia is an area "of high priority, where we aim to stay engaged far into the future" (Muni, 2003; Pradhan, 2015). The region was placed among high priority areas in the 'Gujral Doctrine' and during the Vajpayee government. The present government, led by Prime Minister Narendra Modi, treats the region as India's "Extended Neighbourhood" and has adopted various means to develop multifaceted connections with the region. Several reasons urge India's close engagement with Central Asia. The first is to give India a substantial footprint on the hydrocarbon map of the region. Second, because Pakistan pursues a strident Islamist agenda, India's security interests demand a check on the rise of radical Islam as a political force in Central Asia. Third, it is vital to keep a tab on drug trafficking and potential weapon proliferation in this geo-strategically important region. Fourth is to promote India's interests in the commercial arena. Finally, the Central Asian countries can provide support for India's emerging regional/global power status, India's permanent membership of the UN Security Council, counter Pakistan's anti-India rhetoric and, importantly, they can provide India with a grand stage alongside the USA, Russia, and China to play a greater role in Asian regional dynamics. However, New Delhi is concerned about Chinese moves in Central Asia. Strategically, the BRI effectively blocks India's entry into Central Asia and checkmates it through a massive cheque-book diplomacy. Economically, the BRI aims at creating vassal states around China thereby planning to contain and isolate India in its own neighbourhood.

China Factor in India's Central Asia Policy

Energy procurement and preservation on account of heavy domestic demand remains China's important agenda in the post-Cold War years. Hence, China can be seen going around the world scouting for energy resources. China's current involvement in Central Asia with which it shares a 3,500 kilometres long border has not been an isolated matter. China started investing heavily in the downstream sector, building oil refineries and pipelines across the region to satisfy its domestic demands in a planned manner. Kazakhstan is China's most important energy partner in Central Asia. Beijing controls approximately 20 per cent of Kazakhstan's oil production and has constructed the world's longest pipeline running 2,300 kilometres from the Caspian Sea to Xinjiang province (Pradhan, 2016). The Chinese National Petroleum Company (CNPC) owns a significant stake in the Kashagan oil field. It also owns several small oil fields in Kazakhstan. Besides, Kazakhstan serves as the transit route for Chinese oil transportation.

China also directly imports gas from Turkmenistan—the leading gas exporter of the region. Beijing has constructed the Central Asia-China gas pipeline. Uzbekistan also supplies gas to China through the upgraded pipeline network. China and Uzbekistan have inked a bilateral energy deal of $ 15 billion in 2013. China has also financed two refineries in Kyrgyzstan, in the towns of Kara-Balta and Tomak. The 2013 visit of Chinese President Xi Jinping resulted in the signing of an energy deal with Central Asia that envisages expenditure amounting to tens of billions of dollars. Given China's current energy engagement in Central Asia, the International Energy Agency (IEA) has estimated that China will be importing up to 50 per cent of the region's oil and gas by 2020, leading to a decisive shift in Central Asia's energy flow from the west to the east (Hart, 2016).

In the context of Central Asia-China relations, scenarios of both confrontation and cooperation will have consequences for India. Three out of five Central Asian countries share a boundary with China. This allows China to be a proximate player in the region. In certain quarters it is also believed that although Central Asia is a Russian hinterland, it is not Russia but China whose presence in the region worries the USA the most. The same is also true with India. Growing Chinese presence in Central Asia and its massive economic package, military aid, and political dominance in the region hamper India's strategic vision towards Central Asia. Both the Shanghai Cooperation Organization (SCO) and the BRI help China to push its agenda in Central Asia. Though India might appear alongside China on platforms like SCO, BRICS and AIIB, that does not translate into cooperation between India and China for joint-bidding of energy resources, certainly not in Central Asia.

Policy Options for India

So far, India has not achieved any success in winning any deals in the Central Asian oil sector. The reasons range from technical hurdles to high stake politics. Apart from the problem of inaccessibility, the issue of avoiding transit through Pakistan itself has become a fact of life for India. Hence, it becomes pertinent to deliberate on the possible options available to India in the present scenario.

First, India should look forward to capitalising its SCO membership. India could use the SCO mechanism to garner its interests in the region, or it could try to create a sub-regional framework involving China, Kyrgyzstan, Tajikistan, Kazakhstan, and Afghanistan while keeping itself at the core for ensuring long-term cooperation.

Second, New Delhi needs to seriously pursue the International North-South Transport Corridor (INSTC) as an alternative route to access Central Asia bypassing Pakistan and China. INSTC envisages a 7,200 km multimode network of ship, rail, and road routes for moving freight between India and Russia through Iran, Europe, and Central Asia. Though the concept is not new, it was proposed and initiated by India, Russia, and Iran in St. Petersburg in September 2000. The objectives of the corridor are to increase trade connectivity between major cities such as Mumbai, Moscow, Tehran, Baku, Bandar Abbas, Astrakhan, etc. The agreement was signed on 16 May 2002, and the first dry run of two routes was conducted successfully in 2014 (Chaudhury, 2017). The result was amazing as the cost of transportation was reduced by $ 2,500 per 15 tons of cargo (MEA, 2017). Since India is facing roadblocks in materialising the TAPI (Turkmenistan-Afghanistan-Pakistan-India) and IPI (Iran-Pakistan-India) pipeline projects due to their transit through Pakistan, INSTC offers India bounties of opportunities to side-line Islamabad by working out the INSTC option through the Bandar Abbas and Chabahar port of Iran to Mumbai through the Arabian Sea. Also, from the cost-benefit analysis point of view, this has been seen as cheaper than other available routes and, importantly, it is secure and safe.

Conclusion

The implicit objective of the BRI has been to rejuvenate ancient trade routes and further open up markets within and beyond the BRI routes, but the real intention has always been to expand China's influence. Hence, from an Indian perspective, it is apparent that the BRI will seriously hamper India's efforts both strategically and economically. India could not afford to remain a mute spectator to the global churning unleashed by the BRI, it needs to manoeuvre a host of multipronged strategies to establish its connectivity network with the countries of Asia, Africa, Europe, and Oceania and strengthen them accordingly to provide an Indian alternative to both its neighbourhood and the world at large. Given the String of Pearls and the precedent of the China-Pakistan-Economic Corridor (CPEC), India should not take China lightly or ignore its strategic designs put forth to contain India. New Delhi needs to be more cautious while dealing with China in its neighbourhood and must display its economic strength and political willpower to actualise its long-overdue interests in its neighbourhood, particularly in Central Asia.

REFERENCES

Akiner, Shirin, "Post-Soviet Central Asia: Past is Prologue", in Peter Ferdinand (ed), *The New Central Asia and Its Neighbors,* The Royal Institute of International Affairs, London: Pinter Publishers, 1994.

Amighini, Alessia, China's Belt and Road: A Game Changer? Milano: The Italian Institute for International Political Studies (ISPI), 2017.

BP, BP Statistical Review of World Energy. *British Petroleum,* March, available at www.bp.com, 2018.

Chaudhury, Dipanjan Roy, 'International North-South Transportation Corridor for better Indo-Russian Connectivity inches towards reality', *The Economic Times,* 10 April, 2017.

Claudio, Passalacqua, 'China's New Opening Up Policy: The One Belt, One Road Initiative', LUISS . Guido Carli University, Rome, Italy, 2016.

Dutta, Sujit (2003), "China's emerging ties with Central Asia," in Nirmala Joshi, ed., Central Asia: The Great Game Replayed, New Delhi: New Century Publishers.

Escobar, Pepe, 2017. "Xi road map to the Chinese Dream", *Asia Times.* 21 October 2017, Available at https://www.atimes.com/article/xis-road-map-chinese-dream/

Frankopan, P, *The Silk Roads: a New History of the World,* London: Bloomsbury, 2015.

Hart, Michael, 'Central Asia's Oil and Gas Now Flows to the East', *The Diplomat,* 18 August, 2016.

Jinping, Xi, Towards a Community of Common Destiny and A New Future of Asia, Boao Forum, March 2015.

Kaushik, Devendra, *Central Asia in Modern Times,* Moscow: Progress Publishers, 1970.

Khojaev, Ablat, China's Central Asian Policy, *Central Asia and the Caucasus,* No. 3 (45), 2007, https://www.ca-c.org/journal/2007-03-eng/03.shtml

Lee, Alexios, 'A brilliant plan—One Belt, One Road,' CLSA, 2015.

Mackinder, Halford, 'The Geographical Pivot of History', *The Geographical Journal,* Vol. 170, No. 4, December 1904.

Magiri, Palo, Introduction in Amighini, Alessia (ed). *China's Belt and Road: A Game Changer?* Milano: The Italian Institute for International Political Studies (ISPI), 2017.

MEA, International North-South Transport Corridor, *Ministry of External Affairs,* Government of India. New Delhi, 2017.

MFA, President Xi Jinping Delivers Important Speech and Proposes to Build a Silk Road Economic Belt with Central Asian Countries, Ministry of Foreign Affairs of the People's Republic of China, 7 September, 2013, available at
https://www.fmprc.gov.cn/mfa_eng/topics_665678/xjpfwzysiesgjtfhshzzfh_665686/t1076334.shtml

Muni, Sukhdeo, 'India and Central Asia: Towards a Cooperative Future', in Nirmala Joshi, (ed) *Central Asia–The Great Game Replayed: An Indian Perspective,* New Delhi: New Century, p. 110, 2003.

Pantucci, Raffaello, 'China: Understanding Beijing's Belt and Road Initiative', *RUSI.* 14 May, 2017.

Patnaik, Ajay, *Central Asia: Geopolitics, Security and Stability,* Routledge: New Delhi, 2016.

Pradhan, Ramakrushna, *Geopolitics of Central Asia: China-US Engagement.* VDM Verlag-Muller: Germany, 2010.

Pradhan, Ramakrushna, 'Mapping India's Look North Policy: Why Central Asia Matters?' *IUP Journal of International Relations,* Vol. IX, No. 4, October 2015.

Pradhan, Ramakrushna, 'Chinese Interests in Central Asia: Policies and Challenges', *Eurasian Report*, Vol. 3, No. 2, p. 39, 2016.

Pradhan, Ramakrushna, 'Petropolitics, and Pipeline Diplomacy in Central Asia: Can India afford to wait in the Wings?' *India Quarterly*, Vol. 75, No. 4, 2019.

Pradhan, Ramakrushna, 'The Rise of China in Central Asia: The New Silk Road Diplomacy,' *Fudan Journal of the Humanities and Social Sciences*, Vol. 11, No.1, 2018.

Rolland, Nadege, 'China's New Silk Road,' *The National Bureau of Asian Research,* 12 February 2015.

Sachdeva, Gulshan, Chaining Dynamics of India-Central Asia Ties, *Bishkek Project*, 5 April, 2017, available at https://www.bishkekproject.com/memos/24

Sajjanhar, Ashok, India-Central Asia Relations: Expanding Vistas of Partnership, 22 June, New Delhi: *Observer Research Foundation,* 2016.

The Economic Times, Multibillion-dollar CPEC to benefit China more than Pakistan: Report, *The Economic Times,* 29 October, 2017.

Yi, Wang, Foreign Minister Wang Yi's Press Meet, *The Third Session of the Twelfth National People's Congress,* 8 March, 2015.

Zhi, Wang, 'China's New Silk Road Strategy and Foreign Policy Towards Central Asia', *Southeast Review of Asian Studies,* 38: 69–77, 2016.

12

Iran and Saudi Arabia in China's BRI Plans

Anu Sharma

Introduction

Through the Belt and Road Initiative (BRI), China has been trying to increase its economic and diplomatic engagement with the West Asian region. Most of Beijing's investments in the region focus on energy, infrastructure construction, nuclear power, new energy sources, agriculture, and finance. These investments serve not only China's interests but also those of Middle Eastern countries hoping to boost their economies as a means of strengthening social stability. Of the six BRI corridors, the West Asian corridor is the most critical for Beijing as it acts as a gateway to Chinese connectivity with Europe and the Mediterranean. On the one hand, it means securing the much-needed energy security for China and on the other hand, it means expanding economic ties between China and various West Asian nations.

At the same time, China's policy toward West Asia is necessarily defined within a complex regional context that involves a multitude of local rivalries enmeshed with serious great power competition. In this context, this chapter will try to analyse and understand the placement of Iran and Saudi Arabia in China's BRI plans. The regional rivalry between Iran and Saudi Arabia has placed China in a tricky position to balance itself in the regional rivalries without interfering and taking sides despite both Iran and Saudi Arabia being critical pieces in China's BRI puzzle.

China's announcement of the BRI in 2015 changed the course of Chinese foreign policy. China is trying to appropriate the ancient civilisational and historical linkages to engage economically and strategically with the nations of Asia, Africa and Europe. Referred to as the enhancement of the 'ancient Silk Road', the BRI has become more of an initiative for the partner-countries and a strategy for China. This significant use of nomenclature—initiative versus strategy—by China indicates its desire for BRI plans to succeed. Furthermore, a strategy is typically understood as being against a third party, whereas an initiative is an inclusive mechanism. In this context, through BRI the Chinese leadership is trying to highlight it as a joint partnership. Along with it, the economic benefits are highlighted; however, issues related to hard power and military were conspicuously left out. The "Vision and actions on jointly building Silk Road Economic Belt and 21st-Century Maritime Silk Road," document on BRI mentions the five cooperation priorities initiated by China which include policy coordination, facilities connectivity, unimpeded trade, financial integration, and people-to-people connections. All these points indicate that through this, China wants to be politically neutral, highlighting the development and economic goals—clearly highlighting Beijing's consistent 'win-win' policy. In this context, the BRI is an extensive framework of trade and commercial ties between China and various world regions and is the flagship foreign policy of the President Xi Jinping's administration and its most significant diplomatic and economic activity of the 21st century. Moreover, it seeks to open up new markets and secure global supply chains to help generate sustained Chinese economic growth and thereby contribute to social stability at home. This chapter will assess how China is trying to balance in the West Asian region with two powerhouses being the important stakeholders in China's BRI plans. Through these, China aims to create a multinational network connecting China with Europe and Africa through West Asia.

Geopolitically, West Asia is one of the significant regions of the world. The strategic geographical positioning of this region has made it vulnerable to attacks and the centre of international politics among nations and empires since ancient times as they tried to control the trade route towards the East. This strategic positioning of West Asia at the crossroads of the three continents of Asia, Europe and Africa has made it susceptible to power plays. Geographically, this region extends from the Atlantic coast of North Africa to the western edges of Central Asia and lies between the southern littoral of the Mediterranean and the north-western shores of the Indian Ocean. Owing to this fact, the tri-continental location and its central position of this region has historically been the gateway for South and East Asia's approach to Europe and beyond. The presence of abundant oil and gas resources in this region has made it the centre of global power politics which lies in the complex inter-mixture of its geostrategic, geopolitical and geo-economic richness around these hydrocarbon resources. It also becomes strategic choke points in the region through which various sea lanes of communication traverse transporting vital energy resources to various parts of the world. All these aspects have considerably enhanced the significance of this region. Till the late twentieth century, the role of the USA in the region's monarchies was more pronounced. However, this changed after the terrorist attacks on the USA and the American war on terror against Afghanistan (2001) and war on Iraq (2003) which changed the course of regional politics somewhat diminishing the American influence in the region. As a spin-off to the American military (mis)adventures in the region, China has moved full throttle to increase its engagement and influence in the region, both militarily and strategically. However, it cannot be ignored that the region holds strategic significance for China due to its energy resources which are crucial to write China's success story through the BRI. In this respect, West Asia becomes the quest for increasing China's influence as well as counter the existing American hegemony in the region. The introduction of China's plans under the BRI comes across as a two-fold opportunity for many West Asian nations—one, it provides various West Asian countries to diversify and modernise their economies and two, initiate infrastructure plans. Additionally, China acts as a bigger market for the hydrocarbon resources of this region. In all these aspects lies the salience of this research. The sections below discuss in detail the role and impact of China's Belt and Road Initiative in West Asia, especially in countries such as Saudi Arabia and Iran.

China's Belt and Road Initiative in West Asia

As mentioned above, the BRI is a sprawling framework of trade and commercial ties that China wants to explore with other regions. This is the flagship foreign policy initiative of President Xi Jinping's administration and has emerged as the most significant diplomatic and strategic activity of the 21st century. It aims to diversify China's reach to global markets and secure global supply chains as well as generate sustained economic activity and growth, especially in China's western provinces. The BRI is progressing with six corridors, namely, the Eurasian Land-Bridge, the China-Central Asia-West Asia Corridor, China-Pakistan Economic Corridor, Bangladesh-China-Myanmar Corridor, China-Russia-Mongolia Corridor and China-Indochina Peninsula Corridor. All these corridors aim to boost the land and maritime connectivity of China with different regions such as Central Asia, West Asia, South Asia, Africa, etc. At the same time, they seek to improve the oil and gas supply chains emerging or ending in China. The maritime factors of the BRI are various sub-branches of the Maritime Silk Road (MSR) which includes ports and coastal developments which can improve China's strategic positioning in the world.

Expansive geostrategic benefits will accrue to China as it realises its Silk Road vision as well as also act as China's raw material appendage. The scope of the BRI is enormous and plays a significant role in China's strategy. It has been argued that China's BRI plans and MSR initiatives are an effort to forge 'win-win' projects all along the same routes of strategic choke points that open the way to major infusions of Chinese trade, aid and investment while enhancing its favourable image and military power projection capabilities throughout the West Asian region.[1]

However, China's BRI plans in this region are the least clearly articulated, though China issued a White Paper in 2016 which enumerated China's blueprint with the West Asian region. However, specifically, being an Arab policy paper, it ignored the non-Arab states of this region, i.e., Iran, Israel, etc. Still, it provided a clear outline of China's grand plans related to this region. As mentioned above, the West Asian region requires significant infrastructure; it is a critical energy source; a land bridge to Europe; and a major focal point for Chinese efforts to stabilise its broader neighbourhood and address threats from militancy. However, several ambiguities related to China's future and its broader strategy vis-à-vis West Asia also apply more forcefully to the BRI. Though the uncertainties related to the BRI in other regions are also increasing, yet the ramifications related to BRI plans in West Asia are prone to the political and strategic great game at play in this region. But in West Asia, one of China's foremost objectives has been to dissociate trade and economics from the complexities of the regional politics, whereas one of the BRI's defining characteristics has been the deployment of economic tools to serve strategic and political purposes. There are chances that China may seek to resolve these paradoxes by acknowledging the political choices in West Asia that it had previously avoided; through a realisation of the BRI that places "balance" over other political and economic objectives; utilising activities which were of least concern in other regions related to political neutrality.[2]

It cannot be ruled out that the significance of West Asia in the world economy is one of the foremost reasons for China becoming the largest investor in this region. China has surpassed the investments in the region as compared to the USA, with almost one-third of the total investments coming from China. It is also one of the major importers of West Asian oil and is the largest exporter to this region of its manufactured products. It has exceeded to the extent that China has emerged as one of the largest trading partners with various countries of this region, including Iran and Saudi Arabia.[3]

China claims that its interests in West Asia are largely economic. As a result, it has been trying to follow a balanced approach while dealing with other major actors in the region such as Iran and Israel, apart from Arab partners. As part of this, China has been investing in Israel's ports, railways, and high-tech sector. It is also Iran's primary trading partner, and this relationship has not ended with the re-imposition of sanctions on Iran by the USA after its withdrawal from the Iranian nuclear deal in late 2018.[4] Saudi Arabia has also been trying to develop strategic relations with China even though it does not fall directly in the line of the China-Central Asia-West Asia Corridor. China has been assisting Saudi Arabia by developing railway networks, infrastructure parks and developing electricity networks. In 2017, Saudi Arabia negotiated 65 billion dollars worth of bilateral agreements in oil, technological, petrochemical, space, and renewable energy sectors.

Iran-China's Dilemma in West Asia

China has detailed BRI plans for Iran—a nation in the West Asian region that is geographically situated at the crossroads of various important regions such as West Asia, Central Asia and Eurasia. Sino-Iranian cooperation goes way back before BRI plans were announced in which Iran figures prominently. In China's BRI plans, Iran appears to be the premium beneficiary. Geopolitics plays an important role in this growing bilateral relationship. There are several internal and external factors both at the mutual, global and regional levels that have a direct influence on Sino-Iranian relationships. Added to this, China's projection of the BRI as a geo-economic and connectivity initiative has forced penurious nations like Iran for its own benefit to look towards China and be a part of this multi-billion dollar initiative. Through the China-Central Asia-West Asia Corridor under the BRI, China plans to connect physically with the West Asian region. Based on the ancient Silk Road, historical, geographical and religious ties plan to bind the 'ancient silk road economies' together. In the whole paradigm developed for the BRI, West Asia holds a significant position. This region is of particular interest to China as it proposes developing roads, rail and ports in order to access emerging major markets for Chinese goods by creating transit access to the Eurasian region. Another factor influencing China's approach to this region in general and Iran in particular is for the uninterrupted supply of energy resources and various infrastructure projects that are of commercial and strategic importance to China in this region. Almost representing the pieces of an extensive geopolitical puzzle,

China is pursuing the constituents of its infrastructure network in West Asia. And in all this strategic planning, Iran is the locus of China's BRI plans in West Asia. It is for the same reason that Iran has welcomed China's initiatives under the BRI. However, even after asserting the ambitious goal under the BRI, what is awaited is the implementation of projects under it in a region with constrained resources and volatile geopolitics. Countries like Iran and Turkey in the West Asian region that require Chinese investments are preoccupied with other issues ailing this region such as sanctions, inter-state regional rivalries, sectarian violence and intra-state domestic turmoil. All these factors contribute to the hesitation in both the host nations looking forward to investment and China.

China and Iran established diplomatic relations in 1971. Despite modest initial interactions, it was a long time before China acquired substantial vested interests in the region and with Iran specifically. Also, at that time, China did not have the financial means or the diplomatic or political weightage to promote and protect its interests in this unstable region. The Iranian Revolution of 1979 changed the political leanings of various Western nations towards it and Iran's choices in choosing its allies were also changed. Then Iranian Supreme Leader Ayatollah Khomeini's "Neither East nor West" forced Iran to look for alliances cautiously. However, there are a number of factors that have influenced the Sino-Iranian relationship. Firstly, the mutual distrust of the USA; secondly, China's energy requirements for its growing economy which requires energy security, in turn, led it to look towards energy-rich Iran; thirdly, Iran's isolationism due to international sanctions also brought Iran and China together. At the same time, Iran's ability to play against the big powers in the region was visualised by China as making it a possible ally in the region; and fourthly, China's economic reforms and its emergence as a major power, both economically and strategically, made it look towards Iran not only as an energy supplier but also in the form of unexploited markets for Chinese products. All these factors, combined with the geographical positioning of Iran, led China to forge a strong relationship with this nation.

There are also reasons which have forced Iran to have closer relations with China. One of the biggest reasons is that Iran visualises China as a counter-weight to its long-time nemesis—the USA. Iran has been a vocal critic of the actions of the USA and its allies in the region. In all this, association with China can help Iran to go a long way.

China-Iran BRI Collaboration: An overseas investment in the energy sector has been the most significant aspect of the BRI. This also forms part of the strategic developments as part of China's energy security nexus. In this context, Iran plays an important role in China's energy security strategy. With China's aim to achieve energy security through the BRI, various Chinese oil companies to increase their engagement abroad and have increase their overseas equity production to almost three million barrels per day in 2016.[5] The predicted usage of oil and gas by China also indicates that its demand for coal might decline giving way to increasing demand for low-carbon fuel by 2040. This will also lead to an increase in demand for gas by China to about 400 billion cubic metres (bcm) or more up to 600 bcm in the same period.[6] This burgeoning need for oil and gas has forced China to utilise proactive strategies related to countries like Iran and Saudi Arabia, which have become the top energy suppliers to China. It has also resulted in a shift in the strategic priorities and calculus of strategic policy-making of China.[7] China has been the largest consumer of Iranian crude oil in 2018 amounting to almost one-third oil exports of Iran.[8]

Along with it, the withdrawal of the USA from the Iran nuclear deal has paralleled President Trump's escalation of trade and geopolitical tensions with China. This has made China look towards Iran with mutual interests against their common adversary, i.e., the USA. With China being the second-largest consumer of oil and gas in the world and the growing GDP of 8-10 per cent, there are chances that energy consumption in China will increase and the maximum share of this is fulfilled by Iran.

In the case of Iran, the infrastructure development and other strategic investments will help it to sustain itself during the difficult sanctions imposed on its economy. With Iran seeking to reduce its reliance on its key hydrocarbon resources, it gives way to industrial development. With the presence of huge oil and gas reserves in the region, Iran faces difficulty in the supply of these resources due to international sanctions. In such a scenario, relations based on 'oil for goods' with China can help Iran to sustain itself in the difficult sanctions regime.

Trade and connectivity are the primary requirements of China's BRI plans. This is indicated in the Chinese initiative to develop the Iranian railway infrastructure. It is a two-way beneficial initiative for both Iran and China. Therefore, in this lies the salience of a framework for improving Iranian interconnectivity by development and construction of roads, railroads, and harbours. The success of the BRI in Iran also largely depends on its participation and support to various geopolitical and logistical issues as proposed by China under its BRI plans. This Iranian infrastructure is seen as key for the often-referred Southern Corridor (China Central-West Asia Economic Corridor) of the BRI traversing through China, Central Asia, Iran, Turkey, and to the Balkans.

However, it should be noted that China has actively participated in Iranian construction projects even before the launch of the BRI. This is indicated in building the world's tallest dam in the Iranian province of Lorestan and parts of the Tehran metro system with support from China.[9] Furthermore, China is also taking the initiative to upgrade and electrify the Iranian railways also. The China Railway Engineering Corporation, a state-owned company, is building a high-speed rail line between Tehran and Isfahan via Qom and a railway between Kermanshah and Khosravi in western Iran. Another example is the construction and development of five metro lines in Tehran by Chinese companies. The rail cars are built by an Iranian-Chinese joint venture enterprise, the Tehran Wagon Manufacturing Company.[10]

A Chinese firm, Sinomach (aka China National Machinery Industry Corporation), has signed the $ 845 million worth of agreements with Iran for the development of 410 km of railway in western Iran. According to this contract, Sinomach is responsible for "the engineering, procurement and construction work for the railway that will link three of the country's major cities, i.e., Tehran, Hamedan and Sanandaj".[11] The Chinese government has extended a $ 10 billion loan to Chinese companies to build dams, power generators, and other infrastructure in Iran, such as the recent instalment of a rail link between Bayannur in China's Inner Mongolia region and Tehran. Other transportation projects include building or funding rail lines to the eastern city of Mashhad and the Persian Gulf port of Bushehr. The electrification process of the Tehran-Mashad rail line will enhance the rail link between Iran's two largest urban agglomerations. Studies for the project have been finalised, and construction of the same was set to begin in 2019.[12] A number of rail projects have been completed and are operational which demonstrate China's determination to connect with Central Asia and Eurasia through Iran. An example of this is the Samarkand-Mashad rail link.[13]

All things considered, the eventual success of the BRI in the West Asian region depends to a large extent on Iranian participation and support, especially related to geopolitical and logistical issues. Therefore, there are plausible chances that the Chinese will go a long way in order to please their Iranian counterparts and the Iranians will also do as much as possible to attract Chinese investors and benefit from Chinese BRI plans.

Saudi Vision 2030: Aligning with China's BRI Plans

The alignment of Saudi Arabia's "Vision 2030" with China's BRI plans indicates the growing significance and influence of China in the West Asian region. Even though Saudi Arabia does not fall directly in the path of the China-Central Asia-

West Asia Corridor, however, being one of the major regional players has made China and Saudi Arabia join hands under the BRI umbrella. For sure, oil trade is the pillar of this relationship between the two nations; however, the Kingdom's desire to upgrade its infrastructure has proved to be beneficial for Beijing. Saudi Arabia is China's largest trading partner in the region with burgeoning trade volume between the two countries. Through this improved trade relations and growing mutually beneficial relationship, the Kingdom anticipates improving its roads, airports, oil tankers, offshore engineering facilities and container ports. Furthermore, with the demographic advantage of Saudi Arabia's side adds to the advantage of having a favourable relation with China and forms part of Riyadh's "Look East" policy. Due to Saudi Arabia's dominance in the global oil market, China is increasingly focusing its attention on the Kingdom as a reliable energy partner; while Saudi Arabia visualises China as a nation with an enormous potential market and a possible strategic partner. Moreover, Saudi Arabia's accepting stance to China's appeasing policies towards Tehran clearly states the significance of Beijing's policies for Riyadh. Also, the shift in the global geopolitical landscape has resulted in Saudi Arabia accepting China as a crucial partner for realising its Vision 2030 plans. The relationship between China and Saudi Arabia is based on economic, strategic and military relations, which dominate China's contemporary relations with the Kingdom after the proclamation of the BRI in 2013.

Diplomatic relations between the two nations were established in 1990. Till the late 1980s, Saudi Arabia was the only Arab nation in the West Asian region that had not recognised the People's Republic of China even though Riyadh had diplomatic relations with Taiwan. By 1993, China had become the net importer of oil from Saudi Arabia. During the early 2000s, when Saudi ally and net security provider—the USA—was engaged in waging war against terror and Iraq, China gained the position to be a substitute partner of the Kingdom. Furthermore, China's large and dynamic economics along with the ideologically non-interfering foreign policy and the ability to provide the Kingdom with up-to-date military technology facilitated this relationship.

The growing partnership between China and Saudi Arabia in the last two decades indicates the changing dynamics in the international system and the growing implications of the influence that Beijing has over smaller states. At the same time, China's burgeoning relationships with strategically important countries such as Saudi Arabia which also specifies Beijing's geopolitical strategy is moving beyond energy security and developing into the political and strategic realms.[14] It can be said that China's association with Saudi Arabia is emerging as a collaborative and mutual development plan where both the associated parties mutually benefit.

At the same time, it raises questions related to the adjustment of Chinese policies in the volatile region such as West Asia—an issue which was also reflected in the 2018 BRI Forum. Furthermore, it also demonstrates the Kingdom's somewhat restlessness to reach out to non-regional global players beyond the USA in order to diversify their economies and move beyond single resource rentier incomes.[15]

According to Chinese Foreign Minister Wang Yi, "Saudi Arabia forms an important part of China's BRI plans in the West Asian region and interconnection between China and the Eurasian hinterland as well as an important hub connecting China with the extensive African market."[16] Furthermore, at various diplomatic meetings between the leaders of both the nations it has often been highlighted that the convergence of China's BRI plans and Saudi Vision 2030 reform plan will help in enhancing the military ties.[17] Chinese companies from the private sector and state-owned enterprises such as Sinochem Group and China Communications Construction have also diversified their operation strategies in Saudi Arabia and other markets in West Asia. These companies have, in a way, transformed from goods and equipment suppliers to full-fledged construction project providers and investors.[18] It clearly indicates that oil, infrastructure and technology are among the various industries that are set to benefit from this strong evolving partnership between Saudi Arabia and China.

As mentioned above, since 2016, the convergence between China and Saudi Arabia on their strategic vision plans such as Vision 2030 and the BRI form the basis of this burgeoning relationship. Riyadh and Beijing established a strategic partnership in 2008; and in 2013, China became Saudi Arabia's largest trading partner. In 2016, while visiting Saudi Arabia, Chinese President Xi Jinping extended this partnership and forged a comprehensive strategic partnership. In 2017, Saudi King Salman visited Beijing and supported and promoted China's BRI plans and, in return, China extended its support to Saudi Arabia's Vision 2030 as well as willingness to contribute to Saudi's diversified economy.[19]

Various Saudi scholars have analysed the convergence between the Saudi Vision 2030 and China's BRI plans to highlight the interconnected investment projects as the key feature of both. They have also indicated that signing contracts with China will improve Saudi's economic position, thereby contributing to the Kingdom's Vision 2030.[20] Vision 2030 offers Beijing various bilateral cooperative opportunities that fit well in its BRI plans from the Chinese perspective. Furthermore, this kind of bilateral cooperation will also enhance development in the region, which is in turmoil. The Chinese support to Vision 2030 is visible when both the nations signed the joint statement in 2017.[21]

Emerging Alignment between China and Saudi Arabia: As mandated under the BRI, China's major investments in Saudi Arabia are in energy, infrastructure and technological development. Saudi Arabia is China's topmost oil supplier. Since 2018, Saudi Arabia's oil exports to China has increased manifold. Since 2016, several agreements were signed between Saudi Arabia and China related to the oil trade. In March 2019, Saudi oil exports to China surpassed those of Russia.[22] China pays significant attention to comprehensive strategic development of its relations with Saudi Arabia focusing on Chinese investments in refineries in Saudi Arabia, Saudi investments in oil facilities in China and Chinese participation in geological surveys in Saudi Arabia. China and Saudi Arabia signed an agreement on a joint venture in 2012 with a total investment of 8.6 billion dollars, with 62.5 per cent of the equity interests owned by Saudi Aramco and 37.5 per cent by Sinopec, the Chinese company. The joint venture company, known as YASREF—Yanbu Aramco Sinopec Refining Company (YASREF)—started gaining profits from 2016 by producing 49.97 million tons of crude oil.[23] More recently, in September 2019, Saudi Arabia's biggest oil company, Aramco, signed an MoU with China's Zhejiang Free Trade Zone with an emphasis to incentivise Aramco's greater investment in Zhejiang's future downstream growth. Aramco acquired 9 per cent stakes in Zhejiang integrated refinery and petrochemical complex.[24] With soaring energy requirements in China, there are chances that China will become an important buyer and partner with Aramco in the next few years.[25] This will also help Saudi Arabia to strengthen its position in the wake of other crude supplying actors such as Russia and Iraq. In this regard, such investment and collaboration projects can work well for Saudi Arabia. China and Saudi Arabia's growing partnership is also increasing in the renewable energy sector. It is necessary to point out here that Saudi Vision 2030's main endeavour is its pivot towards cleaner sources of energy—renewable and nuclear—and the Kingdom is looking to invest billions of dollars in wind and solar energy. Because of this, Saudi Arabia has begun acquiring positions in Chinese publicly traded wind and solar companies, setting the pace for further partnerships in the renewable energy sector.[26] Two Chinese solar giants unveiled Saudi manufacturing plans in early 2019. These announcements clearly indicate that Chinese interests are well-positioned to benefit from the growth of the renewable energy sector in the Kingdom, which is predicted to develop 41 gigawatts of solar energy by 2032. In January 2019, Saudi Arabia announced a 1.5-gigawatt solar procurement round that is expected to be dominated by Chinese companies alongside Middle Eastern renewable heavyweights such as Acwa Power and Masdar.[27]

In 2019, Saudi Arabia issued a decree mandating the establishment of the

Authority for Data and Artificial Intelligence. It also ordered the creation of the National Centre for Artificial Intelligence and Data Management Office. For organising this, Saudi officials were provided 90 days to make preparations.[28] Furthermore, the goal is to develop performance efficiency through the applications of Artificial Intelligence (AI) and big data.[29] According to Minister of Communications and Information Technology of Saudi Arabia, Abdullah Alswaha, "the establishment of the centre was a clear indication of the Kingdom's determination to develop its digital capabilities and build a future based on AI and innovation. This would help enhance productivity, boost decision-making processes across all sectors, render services provided to Saudi citizens more innovative, and open new horizons to stimulate entrepreneurship and support young people."[30] The Kingdom is also planning on introducing smart devices to enhance the experience of Haj pilgrims. These measures are all direct reinforcements of the Kingdom's 2030 Vision.[31] Here it is pertinent to mention that almost 70 per cent of the 96 strategic goals under Saudi Vision 2030 reform plans are closely related to data and AI.

Infrastructure development is another important sector in which China plans to maximise its investments in Saudi Arabia. The China Railway Construction Corporation (CRCC) has proved to be beneficial in developing various projects within Saudi Arabia. Part of China's railway diplomacy, Chinese companies have been at the forefront of railway construction in the wider West Asian region as many companies boost their spending on creating new or upgrading existing rail infrastructure. This also lies at the heart of the BRI's connectivity plans. In this context, the Mecca Metro Project is one of the two railway links aimed at easing pilgrim traffic to Saudi Arabia's holy cities of Mecca and Medina. Another major development in this sector is when the Saudi Railway Company (SAR)—national railway agency of the Kingdom—and the Chinese technology firm, Huawei, signed an MoU for the joint development of a smart railway system.

Compared to its relations with the USA, Saudi Arabia's partnership with China can be considered relatively new. The US opposition is the largest immediate obstacle to China-Saudi Arabia economic cooperation. Another major factor complicating China's relationship with Saudi Arabia is the former's growing partnership with Iran. Being Saudi Arabia's arch-rival in the region, Iran presents a major hiccup in Sino-Saudi relations if Beijing does not tread carefully. The importance of China being an important strategic partner of Saudi Arabia is clearly visible when the Kingdom introduced Chinese as the third language in its schools. It is easier for China and Saudi Arabia to maintain a free-flowing economic partnership without either country claiming a moral high ground over the other–as as often been the case with the West.

Impact of COVID-19 on China's Plans in West Asia

As the ripple effect of the Corona virus pandemic is being felt by almost every nation across the world, there are chances that it will also affect China's Belt and Road Initiative both in the short term and in the long term. Despite the challenges posed by to this pandemic to manufacturing and supply chain activity, the momentum of digital BRI activity has increased along with the interest in Chinese tech companies and the general healthcare industry. West Asia is fast emerging as one of the worst-hit regions from this virus, and its effect is doubled due to the lack of healthcare services in this region's countries. While many West Asian countries have been caught off guard to handle this crisis; at the same time, the spread of the virus among the millions of people affected by wars and refugee crises in Iraq, Syria, Yemen, and elsewhere can be catastrophic not only to this region but also adjacent regions such as Central Asia and South Asia. The Corona virus has hit the West Asian region at a time when the region is already fraught with numerous problems related to a series of long-running conflicts, sectarian tension, economic crises, and widespread political unrest.[32] Consequently, due to this Corona virus, there emerges a question related to the transparency and equality of gains that were expressed as part of the BRI. With China being the epicentre of this pandemic's breakout, the trust factor is at an all-time low. The disruption in the supply chain in BRI projects in West Asia and other parts of the world has brought to light issues related to labour resourcing, equipment and machinery that were being sourced from China. With most countries imposing restrictions on entry, these interruptions have eventually led to delays in major projects. At the same time, there has been increased analysis related to the nature of these delays.

In the case of West Asia, the situation seems bleaker. The region is marred by various geopolitical and regional issues. Amidst all this, the chaos in the oil markets and retrenchment of the GDP will present an unyielding challenge for many years to come. One of the important effects of COVID-19 is its impact on oil prices and an eventual collapse of the same. Along with it, an overall drop in oil demand and the ensuing Russo-Saudi tensions related to oil prices have made the situation grimmer for a number of West Asian countries. In all of this, the USA's role as an imperfect guarantor of international financial stability will remain an important factor, especially in times witnessing the rise of other major players in international politics. Definitely, due to these two reasons, there might be an increase in intense American involvement in the region and an increased profile of China.[33]

After the outbreak of COVID-19, it has become crystal clear that oil is the globally traded commodity which is beyond the control and manipulations of major players like the USA. Global oil prices witnessed a major slump as soon as it was known that China is the epicentre of this outbreak. As the countries started shutting down, including the USA and Western Europe, the global Brent crude oil benchmark price collapsed. The incoherent response by major oil producers began almost immediately and lasted until early April. As prices continued to fall, no major producer wanted to be the first to cut its production and lose its market share to others. Even with bare minimum crude oil consumers in the line, oil producers continued with their production.[34] Considering the possibility in the near future, it seems that various emergency measures along with the need to restrain normal economic activity will probably aggravate the budget and currency issues for the countries of this region which are also vulnerable subjects. It will also, at least in the short term, increase the influence of the American sanctions, which are dependent on the significance of the dollar to global commerce.[35]

However, in order to counter the growing resentment against China for being the reason for the spread of this virus and pandemonium over the shortage of masks and ventilators mounted, Beijing started sending aid and donations to countries struck by COVID-19. When the pandemic reached West Asia, China swiftly activated a support system for the GCC countries to counter this catastrophe. In association with China's actions, Riyadh also finalised a $ 265 million deal with Beijing to combat the virus. This also enabled the launch of China's 'medical corridor' in which the West Asian region fits perfectly. As part of this policy, the GCC countries began policy co-ordination mechanisms such as the China-Arab Cooperation Forum and the Strategic Dialogue between China and various oil-rich nations of this region. Interestingly, China's 'Health Silk Road' is a mechanism that planned to work in tandem with the Digital Silk Road and was one more branch of the BRI. This was initiated in January 2017.[36] Using the logistics deployed along the BRI land and sea corridors, it was feasible theoretically; however, progress remained slow. The Health Silk Road has only been properly implemented since the pandemic.[37] In the light of China's global aspirations, its efforts to present itself as a global health leader should come as no surprise. In a situation where the USA has not done itself any favours with its own pandemic response, and its relative absence from global health leadership has left China plenty of room to manoeuvre, the world's road to pandemic recovery will be long and winding. But if China has its way, it will run through Beijing.

Conclusion

Definitely, BRI has emerged as a profitable opportunity for a number of West Asian countries, especially Iran and Saudi Arabia. Aspiring to diversify their economies and capitalise on the new wave of globalisation, these countries are the world's major energy suppliers. With energy being the pillar of their economics and commerce, these developments in their infrastructure and technology can help diversify their economies through the BRI. With this aim to lessen their dependence on the income generated from the energy trade, the promotion of their developing status as a financial, logistical and transportation and connectivity hub could help boost their economic and political status in the region. However, in the case of China, there exist a number of hiccups in case its involvement in the West Asian region increases. These relate to increasing Iran-Saudi Arabian rivalry in the region, increasing sectarian tensions and growing political unrest. All these factors add to China's woes in the region. At the same time, China must take adequate steps and measures to successfully implement BRI plans without any threat to its workers in this violent region and without hurting the cultural and religious sentiments of its partners in this religiously dynamic region. At the same time, it can be said that as protectionism rises in some parts of the world, China is offering the Gulf countries access to a new global marketplace. Still, there are chances that riding the BRI wave would be more beneficial than detrimental for countries like Iran and Saudi Arabia. One such emerging obstacle is the impact of COVID-19 on this relationship. With China being the harbinger of the spread of this deadly virus, there are chances that the trust factor of Tehran and Riyadh in Beijing could be hampered to a certain extent. Definitely, the aim of the BRI is economic with the objective to emerge as the strategically influential player in this geopolitically significant region. In all this, the China-Central Asia-West Asia Corridor indicates significant designs as to how the political components of Chinese strategies can be perceived by other nations in this region, thereby creating a more challenging geopolitical environment.

NOTES

1. Stephen Blank, Silk Road and Global Strategy: China's Quest" in James Reardon-Anderson (ed), *The Red Star and the Crescent: China and the Middle East*, (Oxford University Press: New York, 2018), pp. 171-187.
2. Andrew Small, "Choosing Not to Choose: The Belt and Road Initiative and the Middle East" in James Reardon-Anderson (ed), *The Red Star and the Crescent: China and the Middle East*, (Oxford University Press: New York, 2018), pp. 189-203.
3. Liana M. Petranek, "Paving a Concrete Path to Globalisation with China's Belt and Road Initiative Through Middle East" *Arab Studies Quarterly*, Vol. 41, No. 1, Winter 2019, pp. 7-32, online available athttps://www.jstor.org/stable/10.13169/arabstudquar.41.1.0007?seq=1

accessed 13 May 2020.
4. Ibid.
5. Frank Umbach, "China's Belt and Road Initiative and the Mediterranean Region: The Energy Dimension", *Mediterranean Dialogue Series*, No. 14, online available at https://www.kas.de/documents/252038/253252/7_dokument_dok_pdf_52761_1.pdf/8f5d7f3c-9e1c-3bd4-614b-9b6379ac4e27?version=1.0&t=1539647333202 accessed 23 May 2020.
6. Ibid.
7. Ibid.
8. Cathleen D. Cimino-Isaacs *et al.*, "Iran: Efforts to Preserve Economic Benefits of the Nuclear Deal," *US Congressional Research Service*, 26 February 2019, online available at https://fas.org/sgp/crs/nuke/IF10916.pdf accessed 24 May 2020.
9. J. Garlick & R. Havlová, "China's "Belt and Road" Economic Diplomacy in the Persian Gulf: Strategic Hedging amidst Saudi–Iranian Regional Rivalry", *Journal of Current Chinese Affairs,* 30 January 2020, https://journals.sagepub.com/doi/full/10.1177/1868102619898706#articleCitationDownloadContainer accessed 24 May 2020.
10. Alex Vatanka, "China's Great Game in Iran", *Foreign Policy*, September 5, 2019, online available at https://foreignpolicy.com/2019/09/05/chinas-great-game-in-iran/ accessed 24 May 2020.
11. Jonathan Dyble, "China's Sinomach to Construct 410 km railway in western Iran", *Global Construction*, 21 March 2018, online available at https://www.constructionglobal.com/infrastructure/chinas-sinomach-construct-410km-railway-western-iran accessed 23 May 2020.
12. Tristan Reed & Alexandr Trubetskoy, "Assessing the Value of Market Access from Belt and Road Projects", *Policy Research Working Paper 8815, World Bank Group*, April 2019, online available at http://documents.worldbank.org/curated/en/333001554988427234/pdf/Assessing-the-Value-of-Market-Access-from-Belt-and-Road-Projects.pdf accessed 24 May 2020.
13. Ibid., p. 51.
14. Iain Macgillivray, "Maturing Sino-Saudi Strategic Relations and Changing Dynamics in the Gulf", *Global Change, Peace and Security*, 8 May 2018, see, https://doi.org/10.1080/14781158.2018.1475350 accessed 26 May 2020.
15. Rentier Income—It is the income accruing to financial institutions and the holders of financial assets. All rentier income data are presented as shares of a nation's GDP.
16. Jonathan Fulton, "For China, Belt and Road Run Through the Middle East", *South China Morning Post*, 14 July 2018, online available at https://www.scmp.com/news/china/diplomacy-defence/article/2155258/china-belt-and-road-run-through-middle-east accessed 24 May 2020.
17. Ming Mei (ed), "China, Saudi Arabia Pledge to Strengthen Economic, Military Cooperation", *Xinhua*, 29 March 2019, online available at http://www.xinhuanet.com/english/2019-03/29/c_137934740.htm accessed 24 May 2020.
18. Yuan Shenggao, "China, Saudi Arabia Strengthen Economic Ties", *China Daily*, 26 April 2019, online available at http://www.chinadaily.com.cn/cndy/2019-04/26/content_37462645.htm accessed 25 May 2020.
19 — "Zhang Gaoli meets with Saudi King Salman and presides over China-Saudi bilateral cooperation mechanism meeting", *People's Net—People's Daily*, 26 August 2017, online available at http://cpc.people.com.cn/n1/2017/0826/c64094-29496065.html accessed 25 May 2020.
20. Chen Juan, Shu Meng &Wen Shaobiao, "Aligning China's Belt and Road Initiative with Saudi Arabia's Vision 2030: Opportunities and Challenges", *China Quarterly of International and Strategic Studies*, Vol 4, No. 3, pp. 363-379, online available at https://www.worldscientific.com/doi/pdf/10.1142/S2377740018500203 accessed 27 May 2020.
21. — "China, Saudi Arabia Agree to Boost All-round Strategic Partnership", *Xinhuanet*, 16 March 2017, online available at http://www.xinhuanet.com//english/2017-03/16/c_136134528.htm; "Xinhua: China, Saudi Arabia agree to deepen cooperation", *Embassy of People's Republic of China in Saudi Arabia*, 19 March 2017, online available at http://sa.china-embassy.org/eng/xwdt/t1446850.htm accessed 26 May 2020.

22 — "Saudi beats Russia to top spot among China crude oil suppliers in February—according to customs", *Gulf Business*, 25 March 2019, online available at https://gulfbusiness.com/saudi-beats-russia-top-spot-among-china-crude-oil-suppliers-february-according-customs/ accessed 26 May 2020.
23. — "Yanbu's Joint Venture Refinery Shines as Example for Beneficial China-Saudi Energy Cooperation", *Xinhua*, 9 July 2018, online available at http://www.xinhuanet.com/english/2018-07/09/c_137312287.htm; Mishaal al Gergawi, "China is eyeballing a major strategic investment in Saudi Arabia's oil", *Foreign Policy*, 26 October 2017, online available at https://foreignpolicy.com/2017/10/26/china-is-eyeballing-a-major-strategic-investment-in-saudi-arabias-oil/ accessed 27 May 2020.
24. — "Saudi Aramco Expands Downstream Investment in China Zhejiang Free Trade Zone", 5 September 2019, online available at https://www.saudiaramco.com/en/news-media/news/2019/aramco-expands-downstream-investment-in-china-zhejiang-free-trade-zone# accessed 28 May 28, 2020.
25. — "Saudi Aramco Boosts Ties with China", *The Economist*, 12 November 2019, online available at http://www.eiu.com/industry/article/1718678555/saudi-aramco-boosts-ties-with-china/2019-11-12 accessed 28 May 2020.
26. Robin Mills, Sarmad Ishfaq, Roa Ibrahim, & Aaron Reese, "China's Road to the Gulf: Opportunities for the GCC in the Belt and Road Initiative", October 2017, online available at https://emerge85.io/wp-content/uploads/2017/10/Chinas-Road-to-the-Gulf.pdf accessed 28 May 2020.
27. Jason Deign, "Saudi Arabia looks to China for Solar as Power Politics Shift", *Green Tech Media*, 5 February 2019, online available at https://www.greentechmedia.com/articles/read/saudi-looks-to-china-for-solar-as-power-politics-shift accessed 28 May 2020.
28 — "AI Centre Confirms Saudi Arabia's Drive towards Innovative Future", *Arab News*, 1 September 2019, online available at https://www.arabnews.com/node/1548051/saudi-arabia; —"Data & AI Authority Furthers Saudi Arabia's Drive Toward Innovative Future", *Ministry of Communications and Information Technology*, 30 August 2019, online available athttps://www.mcit.gov.sa/en/media-center/news/176239 accessed 29 May 2020.
29. Ibid.
30. — "AI Centre Confirms Saudi Arabia's Drive towards Innovative Future", *Arab News*, 1 September 2019, online available at https://www.arabnews.com/node/1548051/saudi-arabia accessed 30 May 2020.
31 — "Saudi Arabia Gears up for Innovation with New AI Centre", *MAGNiTT News*, 2 September 2019, online available at https://magnitt.com/news/50528/saudi-arabia-gears-innovation-new-ai-center accessed 30 May 2020.
32. Mordechai Chaziza, "The Impact of the Coronavirus Pandemic on China's Belt and Road Initiative in Middle East", *Middle East Initiative*, 28 April 2020, online available at https://www.mei.edu/publications/impact-coronavirus-pandemic-chinas-belt-and-road-initiative-middle-east accessed 13 May 2020.
33. — "Geo-economic Fallout of the COVID-19 for the Middle East", *Belt and Road News*, April 25, 2020, online available at https://www.beltandroad.news/2020/04/25/geo-economic-fallout-of-covid-19-for-the-middle-east/ accessed 20 May 2020.
34. Ibid.
35. Ibid.
36. Kirk Lancaster, Michael Rubin & Mira Rapp-Hooper, "Mapping China's Health Silk Road", *CFR*, 10 April 2020, online available at https://www.cfr.org/blog/mapping-chinas-health-silk-road accessed 23 May 2020.
37. — "Mapping China's Health Silk Road in the Middle East", *Belt and Road News*, 21 May 2020, online available at https://www.beltandroad.news/2020/05/20/covid-19-diplomacy-mapping-chinas-health-silk-road-in-the-middle-east/ accessed 23 May 2020.

SECTION IV

Maritime BRI

13

India and the Maritime Silk Road

G.V.C. Naidu

China's ascent from being one of the most backward countries to emerge as the second-largest economy and soon to become the largest, surpassing the USA in one generation is unprecedented. Beijing may not wield the same reach and power to influence financial developments across the world as the USA does, nor is its currency the Yuan anywhere near the American dollar, which remains the king of currencies, nor does it have the military wherewithal to project power and intervene in any part of the world; neither can China match the vast soft power the USA has at its disposal. Yet, there is no question that China has emerged as a key driver of the global economy—its share in the global GDP has gone up from 15 per cent in 2012 to nearly 19 per cent in 2018 and is predicted to reach 21 per cent by 2022; correspondingly the American share will decrease from 16 to 14 per cent during the same period (adjusted for purchasing power parity). From being an isolated country that was at war with itself and with most of its neighbours, China today is commanding enormous influence across the vast Indo-Pacific region. A major advantage that China enjoys is that it is in the midst of the world's fastest-growing Indo-Pacific region. Moreover, the Chinese economy is also in the midst of a fundamental change: moving from export-led growth to consumption-driven growth.

The saying goes, 'When the US sneezes, Asia catches a cold!' but now the situation is that if China sneezes, the world may catch a severe cold. It became starkly clear when Apple's CEO Tim Cook announced on 2 January 2019, that iPhone sales in China had slumped, and thus its revenues will primarily take a big hit. All major companies that had been heavily dependent on the mammoth Chinese market and this also includes the companies that have invested substantial sums in setting up manufacturing bases and are now dealt with a double whammy—the slowing down of the Chinese economy and the USA-China trade conflict; the December 2019 trade agreement between the two is a minor consolidation.

It's worth mentioning here that President Trump's 'America First' policy and the trade war has already done considerable damage to the global economy, and things are unlikely to be the same. As if the Chinese leadership was prescient about its future, it had embarked upon a massive infrastructure and connectivity project under the One Belt-One Road project, which has since been rechristened as the Belt and Road Initiative (BRI).

The twin problems of relatively sluggish economic growth and mounting pressure from Washington to reduce trade deficits and protect intellectual property rights over advanced technologies will fundamentally alter the way China will manage its economy, and it will have implications for the BRI and thus the Indo-Pacific region, which is the main focus of the Initiative. It can either result in China considerably scaling down its very ambitious BRI plans or it will pursue it even more vigorously to offset the domestic deceleration. As of now, there are no signs of any notable curtailment of BRI plans. In any case, China will continue to loom large in the Indo-Pacific expanse, and its engagement with this region will intensify, for this is economically the most vibrant zone in the world that accommodates the fastest and largest expanding markets, whereas the most developed economies of the Western countries and Japan are either stagnant or witnessing very low growth rates. If executed properly without being seen as extortionist and exploitative, the BRI can accrue huge benefits to China and also help in building badly needed infrastructure in most countries across the region that lack both resources and technical expertise. Even though it has come under criticism and greater scrutiny, BRI projects are taking place in many countries, with Beijing pouring hundreds of billions of dollars and millions of Chinese to work in those projects. Between the Belt and Road, the maritime component is obviously more important, given the trend that the centre of gravity is shifting from the continental focus to the maritime, and much of economic activity is in the vast Indo-Pacific maritime zone. Viewed from any perspective, developments in the maritime domain will influence the Indo-Pacific in general and India and China in particular for a long time to come. Hence this chapter examines China's Maritime Silk Road, its drivers and contours, and their implications for India.

Belt and Road Initiative

President Xi Jinping declared the BRI proposal in two speeches in Kazakhstan (2012) and Indonesia (2013), (along with another at the onset of the launch of the Asian Infrastructure Investment Bank (AIIB) in 2015. The Initiative came about against the backdrop of the world-wide recession in the early 2010s while the Chinese economy continued to grow at breakneck speed. Beijing was certainly looking at markets elsewhere along with potential investment opportunities as, by then, it had accumulated more than US$ 4 trillion foreign exchange reserves. Thus, economic factors appear to be more at the root of the BRI than a grand, well-thought-out geostrategic design. Apart from some commentaries, a document that provides some details about the BRI is the '*Vision and Actions on Jointly Building Silk Road Economic Belt and 21st Century Maritime Silk Road*' issued jointly by the National Development and Reform Commission, Ministry of Foreign Affairs, and Ministry of Commerce on 28 March 2015.[1] A close scrutiny of this indicates that China realised that it would have to undertake certain measures to ensure that its economic progress was not hampered by the developments, especially in the West, due to its heavy dependence and that it would have to take proactive steps to create a niche market for its products and explore investment opportunities. The *Vision and Actions* states: "In the 21st century, a new era marked by the theme of peace, development, cooperation and mutual benefit, it is all the more important for us to carry on the Silk Road Spirit in the face of the weak recovery of the global economy, and complex international and regional situations." Signs of a slowing economy and huge excess industrial capacity, especially in sectors such as steel and cement, the two most critical ingredients in infrastructure building, appeared to have a key role in Beijing coming up with the BRI proposal. Of course, as China spreads its economic influence, it will yield political dividends and also aid in recasting a new regional order.

The second dimension is the connectivity. Connectivity is critical for robust economic cooperation at the regional level, which can contribute to the region's overall economic development. As the largest and most dynamic economy and as the largest trading partner for most countries in the Belt and Road region (and now major investor too), China's prosperity, as a result, will largely depend on how prosperous and interdependent the rest of the regions around it would be. These factors have necessitated Beijing to take steps to build a solid infrastructure and improve connectivity greatly, which theoretically will not just contribute to the economic development of the rest of the region but would also benefit China. The *Vision and Actions* elucidates that the BRI "...is aimed at promoting orderly and free flow of economic factors, highly efficient allocation of resources and deep integration of markets; encouraging the countries along the Belt and Road to achieve economic policy coordination and carry out broader and more in-depth regional cooperation of higher standards; and jointly creating an open, inclusive and balanced regional economic cooperation architecture that benefits all." Further, it also contends that it "...aims to promote the connectivity of Asian, European and African continents and their adjacent seas, establish and strengthen partnerships among the countries along the Belt and Road, set up all-dimensional, multi-tiered and composite connectivity networks, and realize diversified, independent, balanced and sustainable development in these countries."

The *Vision and Actions* suggests: "Investment and trade cooperation is a major task in building the Belt and Road. We should strive to improve investment and trade facilitation and remove investment and trade barriers for the creation of a sound business environment within the region and in all the related countries.... Countries along the Belt and Road should enhance customs cooperation such as information exchange, mutual recognition of regulations, and mutual assistance in law enforcement..."

Belt and Road Routes

One can also cite numerous other factors that could have prompted China to come up with the BRI idea. One of them certainly appears to be the Trans-Pacific Partnership (TPP) proposal that the USA spearheaded in a big way in the late 2000s. Although it was touted as the 21st century gold standard free trade agreement, its strategic dimension was too obvious to be overlooked, for the most glaring was the exclusion of China from the TPP, the world's largest trading nation and the most important economic power in Asia. Beijing strongly suspected (with enough basis) that it was aimed at containing China and to downgrade its growing economic centrality.[2]

A pivotal step towards realizing the BRI objectives was the mammoth meeting held on 14-15 May 2017 in Beijing under the banner *The Belt and Road Forum for International Cooperation*. It was a mega show which drew 29 heads of state and government and representatives from more than 130 countries and 70 international organizations, prompting CNN to dub it as China's New World Order.[3] In the inaugural speech, President Xi claimed that the "Total trade between China and other Belt and Road countries in 2015-2016 has exceeded US$ 3 trillion, and China's investment in these countries has surpassed US$ 50 billion. Chinese companies have set up 56 economic cooperation zones in over 20 countries, generating some US$ 1.1 billion of tax revenue and 180,000 jobs for them." Further, he asserted: "China has engaged in multiple forms of financial cooperation with countries and organizations involved in the Belt and Road Initiative. The Asian Infrastructure Investment Bank has provided US$ 1.7 billion of loans for nine projects in Belt and Road participating countries. The Silk Road Fund has made US$ 4 billion of investment, and the 16+1 financial holding company between China and Central and Eastern European countries has been inaugurated. With a distinctive focus, these new financial mechanisms and traditional multilateral financial institutions such as the World Bank complement each other. A multi-tiered Belt and Road financial cooperation network has taken initial shape".[4]

If China goes ahead with the project as planned with huge investments, it will connect China with Asia, Africa, and Europe through a vast network of railways, roads, ports, and industrial parks. It is so huge that nothing of this kind has ever been undertaken. Little wonder that it has elicited assessments that vary from one extreme to another, with some hailing it as a boon due to its potential to dramatically improve the infrastructure in developing countries and thus contributing to its economic development while boosting trade and good returns for China;[5] others fear it is a kind of neo-colonialism that could force many small and poor countries into a Chinese debt trap.[6]

There is also a geopolitical dimension to what may seem to be purely a geo-economic initiative. Not everyone seems to be convinced that China is undertaking such a vast project not simply because of potential economic gains but certainly has vested geopolitical interests embedded. This assumption is based on the fact that China is seeking to alter the existing Indo-Pacific security order. It is challenging the US dominance and is spreading its political net across the region much more forcefully than ever before. It certainly does not want to go the Japanese way, that is, to become an economic superpower but remain a political pygmy. To buttress its geopolitical ambitions, China is gearing itself to become a major military power. Apart from the fact that it is the second-largest spender on defence after the USA—from less than US$ 140 billion in 2018, it has gone up to nearly $ 230 billion in 2018—China is fundamentally reorganizing its armed forces. While drastically reducing the overall number of military personnel, the emphasis now is on force multipliers and advanced technologies. Secondly, while reducing the overall importance of the army, the focus is increasingly shifting to building a formidable navy that can project power and operate in regions far from its shores. It is a long-term plan, and China still has a long way to go.

Maritime Silk Road

As noted, there is no question that the entire maritime environment in the Indo-Pacific region encompassing a vast region from India to Japan and from China to Indonesia is under the spotlight for a variety of reasons. This region is riddled with numerous island and maritime boundary disputes; the South China Sea exemplifies this. Perhaps the bigger issue is that this region is witnessing the rise of new great maritime powers such as China, India, and Japan. Both China and India, which had been historically continental powers, are gearing to emerge as maritime powers of consequence. Japan, which is primarily a maritime power that had preferred to live as a junior security partner of the USA since the Second World War, is taking unprecedented initiatives to beef up its sea power and acquire greater strategic autonomy. If the maritime balance of power is fundamentally shifting, the challenges posed by non-traditional security issues are increasing. From maritime terrorism, transnational crimes, piracy, natural disasters, sustainable development of oceanic resources, to the security of sea lanes of communication, all are becoming daunting that cannot be dealt with by any one country. If one takes the example of trade, according to the United Nations Conference on Trade and Development (UNCTAD) estimates, roughly 80 per cent of global trade by volume is transported by sea. Of that, 60 per cent passes through the Indo-Pacific. A third of global trade passed through the South China Sea.

A notable development resulting from growing trade and vibrant economic activity in East Asia is that the West Pacific Ocean and the Indian Ocean are getting closer, not merely geopolitically but even geo-economically. One cannot visualize the Asia Century without factoring in the Indian Ocean. China's interest stems from the fact that either in terms of economic prosperity or security the West Pacific Ocean is now intrinsically linked to the Indian Ocean. Comprising a third of the world's population and flanked by some of the economically vibrant regions, the Indian Ocean is already the second fastest-growing region in the world after East Asia. The combined GDP of the rim countries is likely to go up to more than US$ 10 trillion by 2020 from $ 5.7 trillion in 2010, which will be nearly 11 per cent of global output. The intra-regional trade, which stood at US$ 1.6 trillion in 2015, constituting over 13 per cent of global trade, is increasing rapidly, indicating growing markets and expanding economic opportunities. It is forecast that India and Southeast Asia, with a combined population of nearly 1.9 billion, are some of the brightest spots. Additionally, with its huge resource base, Africa will be the next frontier of growth, with the southern and eastern regions facing the Indian Ocean already becoming economically vibrant. Not to forget that the Persian Gulf will remain the principal source of energy for both Asia and

Europe for the foreseeable future. Further, more than half of the world's trade traverses through the Indian Ocean (out of which nearly two-thirds is by countries outside the region), indicating how important this ocean is to the rest of the world. So, it is not surprising that Beijing has come up with the MSR initiative.

The MSR has two major routes starting from the coastal ports of China extending to Europe crossing the South China Sea, the Malacca Strait, and the Indian Ocean, and the second connects to the South Pacific. Interestingly, a very comprehensive document was released exclusively on the MSR on 20 June 2017, soon after the Belt and Road Forum meeting took place entitled *Vision for Maritime Cooperation under the Belt and Road Initiative*. In contrast to the *Vision and Actions* document, besides the missing "Actions" part, the common threads that run through much of the MSR document are the blue economy, blue partnerships, and sustainable development through cooperation. Beijing appears keen to send the message across that the motive is not merely economic gains but to undertake joint efforts to reap the benefits of the oceans and seas in a cooperative and sustainable way. While underscoring its efforts to implement the UN 2030 Agenda for Sustainable Development in the field of coasts and oceans, it states that "China is willing to work closely with countries along the Road, engage in all-dimensional and broad-scoped maritime cooperation, build open, inclusive cooperation platforms and establish a constructive and pragmatic Blue Partnership to forge a 'blue engine' for sustainable development".[7] The *Vision* document outlines five principles: "Shelving differences and building consensus; Openness, Cooperation and Inclusive Development; Market-based operation and multi-stakeholder participation; Joint development and Benefit sharing".

As far as the framework is concerned, it advocates the theme of sharing blue space and developing a blue economy and that "China encourages countries along the road to align their strategies, further all-around pragmatic cooperation, and jointly build unobstructed, safe and efficient maritime transport channels. Together we will build platforms for maritime cooperation and develop the Blue Partnership, pursuing a path of harmony between man and the ocean, characterized by green development, ocean-based prosperity, maritime security, innovative growth and collaborative governance."

Further, the *Vision* avers that "Ocean cooperation will focus on building the China-Indian Ocean-Africa-Mediterranean Sea Blue Economic Passage, by linking the China-Indochina Peninsula Economic Corridor, running westward from the South China Sea to the Indian Ocean, and connecting the China-Pakistan Economic Corridor (CPEC) and the Bangladesh-China-India-Myanmar Economic Corridor (BCIM-EC)." Apart from the emphasis on 'Green development,' it also enumerates a number of steps for harnessing oceanic resources. Perhaps the most notable aspect of the Vision on Maritime Cooperation is its reference to maritime security. It asserts: "Maritime security is a key assurance for developing the blue economy. Efforts will be made to promote the concept of common maritime security for mutual benefits. Cooperation in maritime public services, marine management, maritime search and rescue, marine disaster prevention and mitigation, and maritime law enforcement will be strengthened in order to enhance capacities for minimizing risks and safeguarding maritime security."[8] An unusually heavy dose of emphasis on green and cooperative aspects appears probably to assuage concerns that might arise because of the massive MSR and also because the 'blue economy' is in vogue.

The question of how the MSR will unfold down the road is not easy to fathom at this stage, for there are growing concerns about Chinese investments and the likely debt burden they will impose, which have either resulted in scaling down some projects or completely cancelled. One of the most common beliefs is also that investments under MSR will yield geopolitical dividends. Once again, it is not easy to tangibly demonstrate the gains as recent events in Sri Lanka and the Maldives suggest where pro-China regimes were overthrown in the popular vote in part due to worries about China's rising economic influence.

India and the Maritime Silk Road

Except in the immediate aftermath of independence, India never seemed to have a cogent, long-term policy towards the Indian Ocean. However, it has been a different story ever since China has come into the picture, beginning from the mid-2000s. The Indian Navy has come out for the first time with a series of doctrine and strategy documents mapping areas of vital interest such as the 2004 *Indian Maritime Doctrine*, 2007 *Freedom to Use the Seas: India's Maritime Military Strategy*, and the most recent 2015 *Ensuring Secure Seas: Indian Maritime Security Strategy*. There has been a visible increase in India's diplomatic engagement with the Indian Ocean littorals. Further, New Delhi is also pursuing vigorous defence diplomacy vis-à-vis the rim countries.

As far as China's MSR is concerned, when the BRI was announced, India neither welcomed nor opposed it contending that Beijing had not provided sufficient details nor was it consulted in order for it to take a view (which is true) and that China had kept many things vague and unclear especially with respect to how it would execute it. India's disquiet about port-building projects in its neighbourhood was already palpable, and the grand MSR plan began to ring alarm bells louder, which was further aggravated by a hyperactive Indian media (which quite often goes overboard when it comes to China or Pakistan) that started painting alarmist scenarios.

Yet, it cannot be said that India is not concerned. China has begun its forays into the Indian Ocean at a time when New Delhi was gearing itself to establish its dominance for the first time in several centuries, especially after the USA had begun to gently nudge India to play a bigger security role in the region. Though Beijing claims that port-building and other activities were nothing but commercial, there are doubts that they could be potentially used for non-civilian purposes in the event of a crisis. Gwadar port, which also serves Pakistani interests, certainly will be a prime location for this.

Moreover, as noted, the PLA-Navy is becoming a major potent force with the acquisition of force projection capabilities such as aircraft carriers, a posse of attack and conventional submarines, long-range reconnaissance aircraft, and a large number of ocean-going platforms coupled with considerable sea-lift capabilities. China's assertive actions in the South China Sea and the East China Sea are also raising doubts about its intentions in the Indian Ocean. There is a growing feeling that China is using its financial muscle and economic diplomacy for geopolitical gains in countries around India.

Perhaps among all the issues that has riled India the most is the China-Pakistan Economic Corridor (CPEC) in which China is expected to invest more than US$ 50 billion. The CPEC purports to construct a vast network of modern transport and several energy projects, and special economic zones. The plan is to link Gwadar port (that China had built) with Kashgar city in China's Xinjiang Autonomous Region. India's strong opposition stems from the fact that the Corridor passes through the Gilgit-Baltistan region of Pakistan, which is a part of the area in the former princely state of Jammu and Kashmir, what India calls Pakistan-occupied-Kashmir and claims to be as its territory illegally occupied by Pakistan. It is felt that China has undertaken this project despite India's known stand, thus amounting to an endorsement of the Pakistani territorial claims.

The MSR initiative came at a time when India-China relations had been going through a rough patch. A series of developments in the past few years such as China's refusal to endorse India's membership in the Nuclear Suppliers Group, repeated blocking of the proposal to declare the Pakistan-based Masood Azhar-led Jaish-e-Mohammad as a terrorist outfit at the UN Security Council's sanctions panel, the 2017 Doklam standoff, etc., had frayed relations. Thus, the MSR proposal and a massive CPEC plan appeared to reinforce the viewpoint that China wanted to encircle India strategically.

India refused to participate in the high-profile BRI Forum for International Cooperation meeting held in May 2017 in Beijing to drum up support for the Initiative. One of the official reasons for not participating in the BRI Forum meeting is: "We are of firm belief that connectivity initiatives must be based on universally recognized international norms, good governance, and rule of law, openness, transparency and equality. Connectivity initiatives must follow principles of financial responsibility to avoid projects that would create unsustainable debt burden for communities.... No country can accept a project that ignores its core concerns on sovereignty and territorial integrity".[9]

India and the China-Pakistan Economic Corridor

It appears that the Chinese belatedly realized how important India's participation in the MSR was for its geostrategic location and its market. To placate Indian ire, the Chinese envoy to India went to the extent of suggesting that Beijing was ready to rename the CPEC and insisting that China "has no connections to or impact on sovereignty issues. Even we can think about renaming the CPEC". It is worth mentioning here that the Press Trust of India, on 11 May 2017 stressed that "China and India have had successful experience of de-linking sovereignty disputes from bilateral relations before." Foreign Minister Wang Yi also said that "If sovereignty alone was the issue, China could work around it as it had during the China-Pakistan border dispute of 1963, in which they agreed that all negotiations were subject to re-negotiation after the "settlement of the Kashmir dispute".[10] Yet, so long as the CPEC is part of the MSR, India is unlikely to participate in it, and that would be a major setback for China. If sovereignty is the issue for India, it is not clear how China can enlist the Indian backing by simply renaming the CPEC. In any case, there is no way Gilgit-Baltistan can be avoided if China's objective is to connect the Xinxiang region with the Indian Ocean.

For two reasons, China will find it very difficult to confront India in the Indian Ocean. One, the geostrategic location of India astride major trade routes is its biggest advantage. For any extra-regional power to be able to influence militarily in India's vicinity by taking on the Indian Navy, will be a tough proposition. Two, China's own geographical location surrounded by not so friendly countries. Moreover, it is involved in very tricky territorial disputes in the South China Sea, East China Sea, and the question of Taiwan. For China, dealing with these will be top priority rather than trying to project power into the Indian Ocean where both India and the U.S. are formidable military powers. The only support that the PLA Navy can count on in the event of a military conflict will be the Pakistani Navy, which can hardly be addressed as a major force to reckon with because of the Pakistani Army's complete domination (which it acquired more for political reasons). Thus, the Chinese Navy's ability to fight a war with India and win in the Indian Ocean from a short to mid-term viewpoint is doubtful. The others, such as Hambantota in Sri Lanka or Kyaukpyu deep-sea port in Myanmar or Chittagong port in Bangladesh that China is building, are unlikely to be used for military activities by China given their own equation with India and the perils of openly aligning with China. Even Gwadar has its own limitations in terms of using it as an alternative to the Indian Ocean sea trade routes, notwithstanding the CPEC connectivity development. Thus, China's critical reliance on the Indian Ocean and its own limitations to project power and handle Indian militarily in its backyard are realities that Beijing would be quite aware of.

It is also important to recognize that India-China relations are maturing even as they become more complex and multi-faceted. Their relationship is not a zero-sum game but has elements of both competition and cooperation. Both will try hard to ensure that the CPEC issue would not undermine an otherwise fairly comprehensive partnership that is steadily taking shape between the two. This is the reason why they periodically undertake the exercise of 'resetting' the relationship to keep it on an even keel. The April 2018 Wuhan India-China 'informal summit' meet is one such exercise. The meeting resulted in the establishment of a hotline between the two military headquarters to ensure that Doklam type incidents do not recur. The Wuhan impact could be seen when the Indian defence minister in a press conference affirmed that there was no tension between the navies of India and China in the Indian Ocean,[11] contrary to the dominant perception that full-blown rivalry was brewing. There is a growing realization that they need each other, and the nature of their relations will be a key aspect of the evolving Indo-Pacific order. Hence, Prime Minister Modi rightly pointed out: "No other relationship of India has as many layers as our relations with China...we have displayed maturity and wisdom in managing issues and ensuring a peaceful border.... I firmly believe that, Asia and the world will have a better future when India and China work together in trust and confidence, sensitive to each other's interests".[12] It is this that will govern the India-China relationship, including in the Indian Ocean.

By the time the second BRI forum meeting was held in April 2019, some discernible shifts could be seen. Among others, on two issues, Beijing appears to have considerable introspection on certain aspects of the BRI. One, China certainly has become more sensitive to the question of potential debt traps in countries where it is investing heavily. Two, unlike earlier, China is open to join hands with third parties in undertaking projects so that not only is the risk reduced but also to make them more transparent and put a check on the major criticism it was facing. New Delhi once again abstained from attending the meeting, but, surprisingly, the response to the BRI was muted compared to the previous meet. A number of problems that the Chinese economy is facing—a ballooning debt, rapidly enlarging non-performing assets, slowing growth to trade conflict with the USA under Trump—would certainly result in slowing down the pace of BRI projects and may even result in scaling down some of them, but the Initiative is unlikely to come to a halt. Beijing would also be mindful of alternative sources of funding for infrastructure emerging by countries such as India, Japan, and the USA, individually and jointly.

Conclusion

It needs to be recognized that China is emerging as a global power and, like all other rising great powers in the past, it too is trying to challenge the status quo and striving to create a new economic and security order that reflect its status. Invariably, it would disturb the existing equilibrium, and that may raise alarm and concern besides resistance by the established powers. That is a major reason why tensions are growing between the USA and China. As part of its efforts to realise its ambitions and expand its footprint, Beijing has come up with an extremely ambitious enterprise called the BRI. If all those projects that are envisaged under it materialize, then there is no question that China would be catapulted to become a truly global power. As far as India is concerned, the maritime prong of the BRI, the MSR, will pose a challenge in part because some of China's infrastructure projects are in close vicinity to India, and thus China would become a factor in the Indian Ocean. China has concerns in the Indian Ocean since more than 60 per cent of its trade, including critical crude oil, passes through this region. However, it would be an exaggeration to suggest that China will deploy its navy forward by acquiring a string of base facilities in the Indian Ocean Rim and challenge the Indian Navy. For China, the MSR serves its interests in many ways, the foremost being economic at a time when it is saddled with excess industrial capacity, especially in sectors such as cement and steel. The Chinese economy is in the midst of a major transition from export-led to increasingly consumption-led growth. It is also sitting on massive foreign exchange reserves of more than US$ 3 trillion, which need to be productively made use of and hence the need to explore business opportunities outside China. No other region requires massive infrastructure investments as much as the Indo-Pacific. Moreover, even as its economy expands rapidly, China also needs new markets for products, given that the developed Western and Japanese markets are stagnant. As China expands its economic footprint, it most likely would also yield geopolitical gains. Yet, given growing concerns about the debt burden, the Chinese investments might have imposed limitations on China's MSR ambitions. So, one has to wait and see how it eventually unfolds and what kind of implications it will have.

NOTES

1. Vision and Actions on Jointly Building Silk Road Economic Belt and 21st Century Maritime Silk Road (2015, March). National Development and Reform Commission, Ministry of Foreign Affairs, and Ministry of Commerce of the People's Republic of China. Xinhua. Retrieved March 29, 2015 from http://news.xinhuanet.com/english/china/2015-03/28/c_134105858.htm.
2. Now that President Trump has withdrawn from the TPP, the sting has been taken out and the Regional Comprehensive Economic Partnership (RCEP) that is being finalised in which China is the dominant player will take the centre stage.
3. CNN (2017, May 14). Retrieved 18 April, 2017 from http://edition.cnn.com/interactive/2017/05/world/chinas-new-world-order/
4. Xinhua (2016, January 13). China's Arab Policy Paper. Xinhua. Retrieved May 13, 2018 from http://www.xinhuanet.com/english/china/2016-01/13/c_135006619.htm
5. China encircles the world with One Belt, One Road strategy, https://www.ft.com/content/0714074a-0334-11e7-aa5b-6bb07f5c8e12
6. Larmer, Brook (2017, May 2). Is China the World's New Colonial Power? New York Times. Retrieved May 3, 2017 from https://www.nytimes.com/2017/05/02/magazine/is-china-the-worlds-new-colonial-power.html. Voices of concerns are growing from the Philippines to Cambodia and from Sri Lanka to Pakistan about Chinese debt trap. For instance, see Veasna Var and Sovinda Po (2017, March 18). Cambodia, Sri Lanka and the China debt trap. East Asia Forum, Retrieved March 23, 2017 from http://www.eastasiaforum.org/2017/03/18/cambodia-sri-lanka-and-the-china-debt-trap/
7. Vision for Maritime Cooperation under the Belt and Road Initiative (2017, June 20). Xinhua. Retrieved June 21, 2017 from http://news.xinhuanet.com/english/2017-06/20/c_136380414.htm
8. Interestingly, it *Vision* states the creation of "cooperative mechanisms for joint maritime law enforcement, fishery law enforcement, and anti-terrorism and anti-violence on the sea will be developed and improved." It lists out a number of new initiatives such as the launch of a Marine Science and Technology Cooperation Partnership Initiative, Centre for Marine Meteorological and Oceanographic Climate Data, the Marine Scholarship Program, conduct marine education and cultural exchange and so on.
9. Press Trust of India (2017th, May 11). To allay India's fears Beijing offers to rename China-Pak economic corridor. Retrieved May 12th, 2017 from http://www.hindustantimes.com/india-news/to-allay-india-s-fears-beijing-offers-to-rename-china-pakistan-economic-corridor/story-sR1eLvpvtZJkIcF6uU7moM.html
10. Press Trust of India (2018, May 2). India, China militaries to set up hotline after Wuhan meeting. Retrieved May 3rd, 2018 from https://www.thehindubusinessline.com/news/india-china-militaries-to-set-up-hotline-after-wuhan-meeting/article23744616.ece
11. Press Trust of India (2018, May 2). India, China militaries to set up hotline after Wuhan meeting. Retrieved May 3rd, 2018 from https://www.thehindubusinessline.com/news/india-china-militaries-to-set-up-hotline-after-wuhan-meeting/article23744616.ece
12. Modi, Narendra (2018). Keynote Address at Shangri-La Dialogue. Retrieved June 03, 2018

fromhttp://www.mea.gov.in/SpeechesStatements.htm?dtl/29943/Prime+Ministers+Keynote+Address+at+Shangri+La+Dialogue+June+01+2018

REFERENCES

CNN (2017, May 14). Retrieved 18 April 2017 from http://edition.cnn.com/interactive/2017/05/world/chinas-new-world-order

Larmer, Brook (2017, May 2). Is China the World's New Colonial Power? *New York Times*. Retrieved 3 May 2017 from https://www.nytimes.com/2017/05/02/magazine/is-china-the-worlds-new-colonial-power.html. Voices of concern are growing from the Philippines to Cambodia and from Sri Lanka to Pakistan about a Chinese debt trap. For instance, see Veasna Var and Sovinda Po (2017, March 18). Cambodia, Sri Lanka and the China debt trap. East Asia Forum, Retrieved 23 March 2017 from http://www.eastasiaforum.org/2017/03/18/cambodia-sri-lanka-and-the-china-debt-trap

Modi, Narendra (2018). Keynote Address at Shangri-La Dialogue. Retrieved 3 June 2018 from http://www.mea.gov.in/Speeches-Statements.htm?dtl/29943/Prime+Ministers+Keynote+Address+at+Shangri+La+Dialogue+June+01+2018

Press Trust of India (2017, May 11). To allay India's fears Beijing offers to rename China-Pak economic corridor. Retrieved 12 May 12, 2017 from http://www.hindustantimes.com/india-news/to-allay-india-s-fears-beijing-offers-to-rename-china-pakistan-economic-corridor/story-sR1eLvpvtZJkIcF6uU7moM.html

Press Trust of India (2018, May 2). India, China militaries to set up hotline after Wuhan meeting. Retrieved 3 May 2018 from https://www.thehindubusinessline.com/news/india-china-militaries-to-set-up-hotline-after-wuhan-meeting/article23744616.ece

Vision and Actions on Jointly Building Silk Road Economic Belt and 21st Century Maritime Silk Road (2015, March). National Development and Reform Commission, Ministry of Foreign Affairs, and Ministry of Commerce of the People's Republic of China. Xinhua. Retrieved 29 March 2015 from http://news.xinhuanet.com/english/china/2015-03/28/c_134105858.htm.

Vision for Maritime Cooperation under the Belt and Road Initiative (2017, June 20). Xinhua. Retrieved 21 June 2017 from http://news.xinhuanet.com/english/2017-06/20/c_136380414.htm

Xinhua (2016, January 13). China's Arab Policy Paper. Xinhua. Retrieved 13 May 2018 from http://www.xinhuanet.com/english/china/2016-01/13/c_135006619.htm

14

Maritime Silk Road and Infrastructure

Vijay Sakhuja

China's Maritime Silk Road has attracted international attention and is seen as both a symbolic and substantive representation of China's rising power potential in the 21st century. It is symbolised by high levels of technological sophistication and organizational efficiency in building ports, roads, and rail connectivity infrastructure in Africa, South, Southeast, and West Asia, and the Mediterranean Sea that has led to the integration of the regional economies with the rest of the world. The economic values of these infrastructure projects attract a high strategic premium given the ever-increasing international shipping, which has witnessed continuous growth for several decades. The Maritime Silk Road is also a portrayal of China's ability to provide fiscal resources to develop maritime infrastructure projects at home and overseas.

This chapter expounds on the 21st Century Maritime Silk Road (MSR) under the Belt Road Initiative (BRI) and highlights the infrastructure being developed in support of the Initiative. It briefly discusses the historical context of connectivity between Asia and other parts of the world and argues that the MSR is an attempt to recall the glorious period of Chinese connections with other civilizations of the world. Further, the MSR has come under international scrutiny and labelled '*debt-trap* diplomacy'; the paper argues that 'lend (money) and lease (infrastructure)' are old arrangements and have been in practice in modern times.

Historical Context: Continuity and Change

The history of the civilization of Asia is replete with examples of global and regional trading contacts as far as Europe through continental and maritime routes. The ancient 'silk route' running thousands of kilometres through the Tarim Basin, Kashgar, Ferghana Valley, Persia, Syria, and beyond over rugged mountainous terrain and vast deserts linked Asia with the Roman Empire and facilitated the movement of goods by caravans. Similarly, commerce was carried over the seas through the Indian Ocean, and goods such as silk, spices, porcelain, animals, etc., were traded. This resulted in a sophisticated and flourishing maritime enterprise that contributed to the growth of China, India, and Southeast Asia, and the Arab and the Persian world participated and benefitted from it.

China's maritime prowess was symbolized by the Song and Ming dynasties, and Zheng He, the greatest mariner of the time, undertook seven expeditions from 1405 to 1433 to the Indian Ocean for trade, projecting power, defeating challengers, and establishing spheres of influence.[1]

In current times, China is attempting to recall its maritime glory through the MSR that has a foundation in the ancient world.[2] It is harnessing the seas for a full realization of its position in the 21st-century international system and demonstrates to the international community that during ancient times, China was highly interconnected and globalized, and that the seas had shaped its destiny in significant ways, and continue to do so.

In his speech during the 16th China-ASEAN Summit in Bandar Seri Begawan, Brunei, in October 2013, Chinese Premier Li Keqiang put forward a seven-point proposal on China-ASEAN cooperation including reference to the MSR. Key issues of his speech included maritime cooperation to build the Maritime Silk Road of the 21st century in the fields of marine economy, maritime connectivity, marine environment protection, and scientific research, maritime search and rescue, and fishery;[3] this idea of maritime cooperation has now expanded to include not only the ASEAN member-states but also many African and Asian countries. Similarly, President Xi Jinping has stated that the BRI is rooted in the ancient Silk Road and "focuses on the Asian, European and African continents...all countries, from Asia, Europe, Africa or the Americas, can be international cooperation partners of the Belt and Road Initiative".[4]

From Home to Overseas

According to the State Oceanic Administration (SOA), China's maritime industry contributed significantly to the national GDP. In 2018, 'China's total maritime economy was pegged at 8.3 trillion Yuan ($ 1.2 trillion) and ranked 15th in the world for maritime economy size. China has become one of the world's major maritime economies after years of development. However, compared with developed countries, China still has a long way to go to become a leading marine power'.[5] Furthermore, 'maritime industries have become a new engine of the country's economy;' According to a report released by the Ministry of National Resources, 'the total output value of China's marine economy in 2018 grew 67 per cent year-on-year, accounting for 9.3 per cent of the total GDP and creating 36.89 million jobs.' The maritime economy has doubled every six years on average from 2001 to 2018, accounting for more than 9 per cent of the total economy for ten consecutive years.[6]

It is fair to say that after honing skills at home, China has developed the requisite capacity to build marine infrastructure overseas. In the last ten years, China has financed 600 projects in 112 countries; a majority of these are part of the BRI and include 41 pipelines and other oil and gas infrastructure, 203 bridges, roads, and railways, which create new ways for China to move its goods around the world, 99 power plants for nuclear, natural gas, coal and renewable which give China new markets for its construction and equipment companies".[7]

As the name suggests, the MSR has oceanic moorings and was conceptualised to develop maritime infrastructure in countries astride the route in Southeast Asia, South Asia, West Asia, and Africa. Several European countries also feature in the schema. These are finance, technology, and human resource-intensive projects and require a number of capabilities to conceptualize, execute and, above all, deliver on schedule.

Based on the national vision document for the development of the MSR, the State Oceanic Administration has announced that it will "promote the building of the 21st-Century Maritime Silk Road by enhancing bilateral and multilateral maritime cooperation with other countries."[8] In this context, Gwadar port in Pakistan, Hambantota in Sri Lanka, plans to develop the Sonadia port in Bangladesh, build a new deepwater port in Crimea, reconstruct the Sevastopol port, develop an industrial park near Jask port in Iran, and interest in developing the Kra Canal in Thailand are significant contributions to the MSR. These maritime nodes are connected to economic corridors such as the China-Pakistan Economic Corridor to connect Kashgar to Gwadar overlooking the Arabian Sea-Indian Ocean and the China Myanmar Economic Corridor (CMEC) from Kunming, the capital of Yunnan Province, with Kyaukphyu, a port town in Myanmar, overlooking the Bay of Bengal-Indian Ocean.

In commercial terms, it has been noted that China's 'One Belt, One Road' is valued at US$ 1.4 trillion and is set to make a bigger impact than the USA's Marshall Plan to rebuild post-war Europe.[9] Speaking at the opening ceremony of the Belt and Road Forum for International Cooperation in May 2017, Chinese President Xi Jinping stated that the aim of the BRI is to "complement the development strategies of countries involved by leveraging their comparative strengths"[10] and China has signed cooperation agreements with over 40 countries and international organizations and carried out framework cooperation on production capacity with more than 30 countries. Further, the "total trade between China and other Belt and Road countries in 2014-2016 has exceeded US$ 3 trillion, and China's investment in these countries has surpassed US$ 50 billion. Chinese companies have set up 56 economic cooperation zones in over 20 countries, generating some US$ 1.1 billion of tax revenue and 180,000 jobs for them."[11]

Lend and Lease: Recalling the Past

Leasing territory and developing maritime infrastructure is not a new practice, and in modern times, States have transacted such agreements with allies, partners, and friends to advance geopolitical, geo-economic, and geostrategic interests.[12] These have also involved leasing military hardware to allies and friends to be either returned on expiry of the agreement or gifted to them as a goodwill gesture to symbolize the practice of naval diplomacy.

For instance, in 1898, after the USA's victory in the Spanish-American War, Spain relinquished claims on Cuba and ceded sovereignty over Guam, Puerto Rico, and the Philippines to the USA.[13] The Cuban government agreed to lease three locations for use as naval or coaling stations, including the naval station at Guantanamo Bay. Subsequent lease agreements of 1903 and 1934 resulted in the USA being granted "complete jurisdiction and control over" so long as they remained occupied.

Another good example of the lend-lease approach is the May 15, 1940, agreement between President Franklin D. Roosevelt and UK Prime Minister Winston Churchill wherein the two leaders agreed to exchange 40 to 50 old US Navy destroyers for obtaining British naval and air bases in the Atlantic Ocean on lease[14] amid fears that a British defeat would bring Germans to US shores. The March 11, 1941, 'An Act to Promote the Defence of the United States' was approved by the Congress,[15] and the USA-Britain agreement resulted in US access to various British possessions (in Newfoundland, and many places in the Caribbean) for setting up naval or air bases, on 99-year rent-free leases.

President Roosevelt announced that "The United States should loan what articles were needed, as a man would loan his garden hose to help his neighbour put out a fire without reference to payment, but with the expectation that the hose itself would be returned."[16]

Similarly, during the Cold War, the Soviet Union negotiated with other countries a number of military access agreements. For instance, the Tartus base in Syria was offered to the Soviet Union in 1971 on a 74-year renewal agreement (49-year lease followed by a 25-year automatic extension).[17] One of the significant features of the agreement was that the 'facility will operate outside of Damascus' legal jurisdiction, and Syria will not interfere with any military activities related to its operation.'[18] Russia also leased an airbase in Western Syria for a period of 50 years.

In Vietnam, the Cam Ranh Bay served as a forward base for the Soviet Navy during the Cold War. The lease expired in 2004, and since then there have been speculations that Moscow is negotiating a deal with Hanoi for access to Cam Ranh Bay.[19] Likewise, in 1964, the Soviet Union set up the Lourdes listening post in Cuba, and according to Russian Military Intelligence (GRU), it was the "greatest single overseas asset" and "provided 60-70 per cent of all Russian electronic intelligence data on the United States".[20] After the Cold War, Russia abandoned the Lourdes facility due to financial constraints as Cuba was reluctant to reduce the annual rent of US$ 200 million for leasing the facility.

China has obtained long-term leasing rights to a number of ports and maritime spaces in the Indian Ocean and the Mediterranean Sea through agreements.[21]

Sl. No.	*Port*	*Lease Country*	*Lease Term (in years)*
1	Port of Chittagong	Bangladesh	NN
2	Colombo Harbour	Sri Lanka	35
3	Koh Kong new port	Cambodia	99
4	Darwin Port	Australia	99
5	Doraleh Multipurpose Port	Djibouti	NN/10
6	Al Dqum Port and Dry dock	Oman	NN
7	Port of Gwadar	Pakistan	40
8	Hambantota Port	Sri Lanka	99
9	Kuantan Port	Malaysia	99
10	Kyaukpyu Deep Sea Port	Myanmar	None
11	Maleka Gateway	Malaysia	99
12	Port of Mura	Brunei	60
13	Port of Pyra	Bangladesh	None
14	Port of Tanjun Priok	Indonesia	NN
15	Port Kelang	Malaysia	NN
16	Sittwe Port	Myanmar	NN

Sl. No.	*Port*	*Lease Country*	*Lease Term (in years)*
17	Sonadia	Bangladesh	NN
18	Feydhoo Finolhu Island	Maldives	50
19	Malaka Gateway	Malaysia	99
20	Piraeus Port	Greece	35

Conclusion

China's appetite for new port projects and deep pockets helps it aggressively push the MSR among many countries in the Indian Ocean, particularly the small island states, and win their support since they are constrained due to lack of expertise and finances. Many of these countries appear to be quite sanguine about Chinese support, notwithstanding the fear of a debt trap (Sri Lanka, Pakistan, the Maldives, Ethiopia, Kenya, and Malaysia) partly due to its ability to deliver quality products.

Further, lend-lease is not a new phenomenon, and major powers such as the USA and the Soviet Union have used it as a tool for maximizing national interests and also to support alliance partners and friends. As far as China is concerned, it is fair to argue that although it is a newcomer to the lend-lease club, it has a promising future. It is exercising economic diplomacy to carve for itself a leadership role as a regional and global stakeholder.

NOTES

1. Chiu Liang-Yeong, *Zhang He: Navigator, Discoverer and Diplomat*, (Singapore: Unipress, 2001).
2. "Work Together to Build the Silk Road Economic Belt and The 21st Century Maritime Silk Road", Speech by H.E. Xi Jinping, President of the People's Republic of China at the Opening Ceremony of The Belt and Road Forum for International Cooperation, 14 May 2017. Online available at http://www.xinhuanet.com/english/2017-05/14/c_136282982.htm (accessed 10 December 2019).
3. Foreign Ministry Spokesperson Hua Chunying's Regular Press Conference on 10 October 2013. Online available at http://kw.chineseembassy.org/eng/fyrth/t1086912.htm (accessed 10 December 2019).
4. "Work Together to Build the Silk Road Economic Belt and The 21st Century Maritime Silk Road", Speech by H.E. Xi Jinping President of the People's Republic of China at the Opening Ceremony of The Belt and Road Forum for International Cooperation, 14 May 2017. Online available at http://www.xinhuanet.com/english/2017-05/14/c_136282982.htm (accessed 10 December 2019).
5. Ni Hongzhang "Fast-growing maritime industries become new economic engine", online available at http://www.globaltimes.cn/content/1148546.shtml (accessed 30 November 2019).
6. Ibid.
7. Derek Watkins, K. K. Rebecca Lai & Keith Bradsher, "The World Built by China", online available at https://www.nytimes.com/interactive/2018/11/18/world/asia/world-built-by-china.html (accessed 20 November 2019).
8. "Vision for Maritime Cooperation under the Belt and Road Initiative", online available at

http://www.xinhuanet.com/english/2017-06/20/c_136380414.htm (accessed 25 November 2018). Also see "China Focus: China's maritime economy expands by 7.5 pct in recent five years", *Xinhua*, 21 January 2018.

9. For more details visit https://www.scmp.com/news/china/policies-politics/article/2000835/chinas-us14-trillion-one-belt-one-road-extends-beijings (accessed 20 November 2019).
10. "Full text of President Xi's speech at opening of Belt and Road forum", *Xinhua*, 14 May 2017.
11. Ibid.
12. Vijay Sakhuja, "China's Maritime Infrastructure Projects in the Indian Ocean : Lend and Lease Agreements", online available at https://www.vifindia.org/article/2018/april/03/china-s-maritime-infrastructure-projects-in-the-indian-ocean-lend-and-lease-agreements (accessed 30 November 2019).
13. "The Spanish-American War, 1898", online available at https://history.state.gov/milestones/1866-1898/spanish-american-war (accessed 26 March 2019).
14. "Lend-Lease and Military Aid to the Allies in the Early Years of World War II", online available at https://history.state.gov/milestones/1937-1945/lend-lease (accessed 26 March 2019).
15. "Transcript of Lend-Lease Act (1941)", online available at https://www.ourdocuments.gov/doc.php?flash=false&doc=71&page=transcript (accessed 26 March 2018).
16. Galen Varon, A Journey With America's Queen: A Tour Aboard USCGC STORIS (WMEC-38) The "Queen" of the Fleet (Raleigh: Lulu Press, 2013).
17. "Russia Moves Forward with Syrian Naval Base", online available at https://www.maritime-executive.com/article/russia-moves-forward-with-syrian-naval-base#gs.NSaL5qc (accessed 26 March 2019).
18. "Russia Moves Forward with Syrian Naval Base", online available at https://www.maritime-executive.com/article/russia-moves-forward-with-syrian-naval-base (accessed 24 November 2019).
19. "A Vietnam 'Base' for Russia?" online available at https://thediplomat.com/2016/10/a-vietnam-base-for-russia/ (accessed 24 November 2018). Also see "US navy returns to Cam Ranh Bay", online available at https://www.scmp.com/article/977291/us-navy-returns-cam-ranh-bay(accessed 24 November 2019).
20. "Russia to Abandon Bases in Cuba and Vietnam", *Jamestown Foundation, Monitor,* Volume: 7, Issue: 192, October 18, 2001.
21. Mohan Malik, "The China-India Nautical Games in the Indian Ocean", online available at https://www.macdonaldlaurier.ca/china-india-nautical-games-indian-ocean-part-one-mohan-malik-inside-policy/ (accessed 25 March 2019).

    (b) Mathieu Duchâtel and Alexandre Sheldon Duplaix , "Blue China: Navigating the Maritime Silk Road to Europe", online available at https://www.ecfr.eu/publications/summary/blue_china_navigating_the_maritime_silk_road_to_europe (accessed 25 March 2019).

15

The Maritime Dimension of China's Belt and Road Initiative: Implications for India

Shishir Upadhyaya

In 2013, Chinese President Xi Jinping announced the proposal for a Silk Road Economic Belt over land connecting western China to Europe across the Eurasian continent and a Maritime Silk Road stretching from the western Pacific across the Indian Ocean up to the Mediterranean. Together, the two proposals have now come to be known as the BRI. The BRI, in addition to many land-based projects, seeks to build and augment the maritime infrastructure along the sea routes in the Indo-Pacific region to improve maritime trade in the region and boost regional economies.[1] China had invited India along with other states to participate in this new venture. Although India objected to China's proposal, as the "Silk Road" passes through Pakistan occupied Kashmir (PoK), which is disputed by India, the then External Affairs Minister, Sushma Swaraj, during her visit to Beijing in 2015, stated that whilst India would not give a blanket endorsement to the BRI project, it would support the project where the synergies of the two countries met.[2]

The BRI spans at least 68 countries with an announced investment as high as $ 8 trillion for a vast network of transportation, energy, and telecommunications infrastructure linking Europe, Africa, and Asia.[3] The BRI infrastructure, when completed, will encompass a population of 4.4 billion people with a collective GDP of about $ 21 trillion (one-third of the global wealth) and connect every participating country on three continents, linking the world's top emerging markets.[4] The BRI will be funded by the Asian Infrastructure Investment Bank (AIIB), another Chinese initiative that has attracted support from 57 countries, including India.[5] When the silk route vision is fulfilled, then, as noted by an analyst, "all roads will quite literally lead to Beijing".[6] A National Bureau of Asian Research special report notes, "in many ways, the BRI looks very much like an effort to replicate on a region-wide scale China's development model of the past 30 years that led to such spectacular economic results".[7]

India and some others, including the USA, do not consider the BRI as benign. In this regard, the former US Secretary of Defence, James N. Mattis stated:

> I think in a globalized world, there are many belts and many roads, and no one nation should put itself into a position of dictating 'One Belt, One Road...the 'One Belt, One Road' also goes through disputed territory, and I think that in itself shows the vulnerability of trying to establish that sort of a dictate.[8]

For the BRI critics, the project is more about "strategic ambitions than commercial logic"[9] or an "insidious plot" by China for world domination where China strikes opaque deals and inflates the value of projects, leaving poorer countries in a "debt trap".[10]

Regardless of the actual or the stated motivation for the BRI, it is clear that the scope and the scale of the project, particularly its maritime dimension, could bestow China with powerful long-term strategic influence in the Indian Ocean region, which India would need to balance suitably. This chapter examines China's strategic engagements with various Indian Ocean regional states to assess the scope of Chinese maritime power in the Indian Ocean region covering South Asia, Southeast Asia, West Asia, and East Africa.

The first part looks at the major Chinese maritime and infrastructure projects under the BRI in key regional states along the proposed routes. Next, it provides an overall assessment of Chinese strategic influence in each of the sub-regions and also discusses the potential impact of the growing Chinese maritime power on India's position as a major regional maritime power and "net security provider".

China's Strategic Ties with Indian Ocean Regional States under the BRI

An overview of China's strategic relations with various Indian Ocean region states and the major infrastructure projects under the BRI is as follows:

Pakistan

At the centre of the Sino-Pakistan naval co-operation is the strategically important Gwadar Port in Balochistan province, developed as part of the China-Pakistan Economic Corridor (CPEC) under China's BRI. The port will be connected by rail and road to China, thus providing China an alternate route to the Indian Ocean. However, this venture is not without risks, and Pakistan will need to repay $ 40 billion to China over the next 20 years on the $ 26.5 billion investment.[11] In the case of a default in payments–not unlikely given Pakistan's economic situation–Pakistan would have to possibly forsake control of Gwadar Port to China, as witnessed in Sri Lanka and other countries. But is Pakistan worried about such an eventuality? Probably not. According to former Pakistani diplomat Husain Haqqani, the military-backed regime in Islamabad believes that a long-term or permanent strategic involvement of the Chinese would actually strengthen Pakistan's national security. It is likely that Gwadar could emerge as a Chinese naval base, although the extant security situation in Balochistan poses considerable risks.

Bangladesh

In 2016, Bangladesh officially joined the BRI following Chinese President Xi Jinping's visit to Dhaka. This event was dubbed as the beginning of "a new historical starting point" in China-Bangladesh relations.[12] During this visit, President Xi pledged $ 24 billion to Bangladesh in economic aid as lines of credit for 24 projects, and both the countries agreed to further co-operate in various areas, such as overland and maritime connectivity, infrastructure development, industrial capacity co-operation, energy and power, transportation, information, and communication technology, and agriculture.[13] China is currently engaged in the development of Chittagong port along with several other infrastructure projects. Notwithstanding the close Sino-Bangladesh ties, the Sheikh Hasina government seems to have taken care not to antagonise India, with whom Bangladesh has improved relations significantly over the last decade. Prime Minister Hasina recently stated that India does not have to worry about Dhaka's close ties with Beijing since their co-operation was only meant for the country's development.[14] In a recent development, ostensibly to placate India, the Bangladesh government cancelled a Chinese port project at Sonadia and awarded India a new port project at Payra closer to its coastline.[15] Besides Payra, India has also invested in Mongla and Chittagong ports, all of which have important economic and security implications for both countries.[16]

The Maldives

In September 2014, during the tenure of President Abdulla Yameen, who sought to foster close ties with China over India, Chinese President Xi Jinping visited the Maldives—the first-ever Chinese leader to visit the country. The Maldives signed up for the BRI and also passed a crucial land reform bill in the parliament that allowed foreign entities to procure land in the Maldives.[17] The land reform bill made it possible for foreigners to buy land in the Maldives provided they invested more than $ 1 billion and that 70 per cent of the land was reclaimed from the Indian Ocean. This paved the way for large-scale Chinese investments in the Maldives, which continued until the Yameen government was replaced by President Ibrahim Mohamed Solih. In 2018, former President Abdul Nasheed, who exposed the Yameen government, highlighted that China had acquired 17 islands in the Maldives.[18] Significantly, Chinese economic engagements included investments in tourism and large-scale infrastructure projects. It was reported that in 2015, over 360,000 Chinese tourists visited the Maldives, accounting for more than 30 per cent of the total visitors.[19] Key infrastructure projects include upgradation of Male international airport and the building of the China-Maldives Friendship Bridge, the Maldives' first sea-crossing bridge connecting Male with the islands of Hulhumale and Hulhule, where the country's international airport is located. Other important projects include the development of a port and an industrial zone on the northern-most Ihavandhippolhu Atoll and an ocean observatory facility, which could be a potential intelligence monitoring post at Makunudhoo in the north.[20] This is located about 720 km south of India's Lakshadweep Islands, overlooking the strategic Nine Degree Channel.

As a result of growing Chinese control over the Yameen government, Indo-Maldives maritime co-operation was adversely impacted. Subsequent developments such as the withholding of work permits of Indian workers by the Maldivian immigration authorities deeply infuriated New Delhi, damaging bilateral ties.

Under President Yameen, China's rapidly growing economic engagements and political influence with the Maldives also saw the country being pushed into a "debt trap", and India's relations with the Maldives were troubled. As a result of China's projects in the Maldives, the country's debt expanded from 73 per cent of the GDP in 2015 to around 109 per cent in 2018, making the Maldives one of the most indebted states to China.[21] Amidst protests from the opposition, Yameen tried to consolidate and strengthen his position, putting several dissidents in jail but was eventually defeated by Ibrahim Mohamed Solih in the 2018 elections. Indian Prime Minister Modi, in his first-ever visit to Male, attended the swearing-in ceremony of President Solih. President Solih has sought to repair the damaged relationship with India quickly, and during his maiden foreign visit after assuming office to New Delhi in December 2018 described India as the "closest friend" of Male.[22] India has pledged financial aid of $ 1.4 billion to help the Maldives repay its $ 3.2 billion debt to China.[23] New Delhi's swift offer for a bailout package obviously indicates that the support is not unfettered. Evidently, without India's economic aid announced in 2018, the Maldives could have defaulted on its debt and forced to hand over state assets to China. Overall, India's relations with the Maldives seem to be back on track, and the Solih government is taking urgent steps to improve ties with India, including revoking the land reform bill. But countering Chinese influence has proved to be an expensive proposition for India.

As flat, low-lying coral atolls, the Maldives is highly vulnerable to the impact of climate change and rising sea levels and is thus faced with a future that is considerably gloomier than almost all other Indian Ocean region states. It is obvious that the Maldives desperately needs international support to deal with the wide range of challenges facing it. For instance, in 2014, when the Maldives was overwhelmed by a water crisis following a major fire in the country's desalination plant, it reached out to India, China, the USA , and Sri Lanka for assistance. India was the first to respond, pressing into service five Air Force planes and two naval ships.[24] Pertinently, within days of India's assistance, China was also able to deliver over 1,000 tons of freshwater using civilian aircraft and a PLA Navy auxiliary ship.[25]

Although India, as the aspiring net security provider for the region, has conducted regular surveillance missions in the Maldivian EEZ in collaboration with the Maldivian Navy and also provided assistance whenever required, it may not always be in a position to bear complete responsibility for the security of the Maldives. Consequently, it would be difficult for India to justifiably dissuade the Maldivians, should desperate measures demand, from reaching out to China or other states for any support, including assistance from Beijing. It would, therefore, be in India's interests to facilitate alternate funding options for the Maldives and the Asia-Africa Growth Corridor (AAGC) led jointly by India and Japan to provide such an opportunity. At the same time, India must build its own maritime capacity in the Lakshadweep Islands to augment its regional presence and strengthen its security relationship with the Maldives.

Sri Lanka

Sri Lanka's strategic position overlooking the Indian Ocean shipping lanes makes it an important location along China's Maritime Silk Road, which Sri Lanka joined at the end of 2017. Beijing has, thus, been keen to expand its influence in

Colombo and has dramatically increased its financial investments in Sri Lanka to the tune of $ 5 billion.[26] Most of this funding was in the form of loans aimed at large-scale infrastructure development projects, such as the Hambantota port and airport and the Colombo port city and highways. According to certain analysts, Chinese investments in Sri Lanka have largely been "poorly-planned and frivolous" and have failed to stimulate the economy or generate any benefits for the citizens.[27] Whilst Chinese investments in Sri Lanka, particularly the development of the Hambantota port, were viewed with suspicion in India, they were generally acknowledged as part of Sri Lanka's post-war reconstruction efforts. However, in late 2014, under the Rajapaksa government, the visit of a PLA Navy *Song*-class conventional submarine and a Type-925 submarine support ship, *Changxing Dao*, which docked at the Chinese-run Colombo International Container Terminal (CICT) en route to the Gulf of Aden for anti-piracy operations, raised the alarm in New Delhi. The employment of a submarine for anti-piracy patrols by itself was considered an unreasonable and bizarre excuse by the PLA Navy and clearly seen as an attempt by China to "test the waters" in India's neighbourhood, maybe to ascertain how far Colombo could go to support a key investor. The idea of China gaining privileged access to Sri Lankan ports as a matter of routine unnerved New Delhi, and India, supported by the USA, is suspected by some to have orchestrated the fall of the Rajapaksa government in the 2015 elections.[28] The new government in Sri Lanka has made it clear that Chinese submarines are no longer welcome.

However, by December 2017, Sri Lanka was unable to repay its debts to China and, after protracted negotiations, formally handed over the port of Hambantota and 15,000 acres of land to China on lease for 99 years. In 2019, Sri Lanka faced a record debt of $ 5.9 billion to China and is still struggling to service its payments.[29] However, the Sri Lankan government maintains that the port will not be used for military purposes.

On balance, it appears that the scope and depth of India's multi-faceted and historical ties with Sri Lanka have provided New Delhi with significant strategic influence and political sway in Colombo, surpassing China's recent influence. India's "thoughtful" economic assistance programmes for Sri Lanka, though smaller than China's, are reported to have generated far greater benefits to the Sri Lankan people than the large-scale and sometimes infructuous infrastructure projects by Chinese companies. India has invested a total of $ 1 billion since 2003 and in 2013 committed $ 2 billion over five years in vital sectors, including transportation, telecommunications, health care, energy, banking, and tourism.[30] Moreover, as highlighted above, India has established a wide-ranging and exclusive security relationship with Sri Lanka, an area where China has had limited engagements.

Myanmar

Myanmar has had close strategic relations with China, particularly since the late 1980s, after the military regime took control. During this period, Myanmar faced isolation from all the Western powers and also India. However, China developed strong political ties with Myanmar and extended economic and military support, which helped the country tide over Western sanctions and diplomatic pressure at the United Nations.[31] Since 1988, China has been the largest supplier of military hardware and training to the rapidly expanding Myanmar armed forces under the military regime; military sales include fighter jets, missiles, guns, artillery, tanks, and various types of ships.[32] In 2011, following a period of internal political reforms that led to a rapprochement with the West, Myanmar was seen moving away from China and, during this period, it even suspended a major Chinese project for construction—the Myitsone dam. However, with the re-commencement of ethnic fighting in the Kachin and Northern Shan states, resulting in the Rohingya community crisis, Myanmar has come under international pressure. The country's military has once again been accused of human rights abuses and has been brought under US sanctions since 2017. However, as a Permanent Member of the UN Security Council (UNSC), China has used its veto power to resist West-led efforts to punish Myanmar. This has once again boosted Sino-Myanmar relations and helped to speed up various China-funded BRI projects, including the 1,700-km Myanmar-China Economic Corridor to connect China's Yunnan province with three economic centres in Myanmar (Mandalay, Yangon New City, and Kyaukpyu Special Economic Zone) through the Kyaukpyu deepwater port, the Kyaukpyu-Kunming high-speed railway, and natural gas pipelines.[33] Reportedly, the suspended Myitsone dam project is also likely to be awarded to China.[34]

Based on the above developments, it is evident that Myanmar is almost entirely dependent on China for economic and political support. Even though it has tried to reduce its financial dependence on China by re-negotiating some of the projects and diversifying its infrastructure funding with India, it is unlikely to break out of Chinese control in the near to mid-term.

Indonesia

China's relations with Indonesia were elevated to a comprehensive strategic partnership in 2013 and have further strengthened under the Jokowi government, with Indonesia joining the BRI and the China-led Asia Infrastructure Investment Bank (AIIB) in 2015.[35] For China, close relations with Indonesia are vital for the BRI's success, and Beijing has sought to promote strategic co-operation with Jakarta. In 2015, during the visit of President/Prime Minister Jokowi to Beijing, Chinese President Xi stated, "the 21st Century Maritime Silk Road, proposed by President Xi Jinping, and the Strategy of the Global Maritime Fulcrum initiated by President Joko Widodo are complementary".[36] However, Indonesia has been wary of the growing Chinese assertion in the South China Sea, where the Chinese Nine-Dotted Line claim overlaps with the EEZ of Indonesia's Natuna islands. In a bid to assert its sovereignty, in July 2017, Indonesia renamed the northern reaches of its EEZ in the South China Sea as the North Natuna Sea, and in 2018, it commissioned a military base in the Natuna islands located in Selat Lampa on the Natuna Besar island. Clearly, the new base is aimed at deterring any potential threat from China.

As a consequence of the disputes mentioned above, China-Indonesia relations are tinged with mutual suspicion, and engagements under the BRI have been relatively slow. The only major BRI ventures in Indonesia are a $ 6 billion high-speed rail project connecting Jakarta with the textile hub of Bandung and a $ 1.5 billion hydropower plant being constructed by the Chinese state firm, Sinohydro, in Sumatra.[37]

Indonesia has sought to balance its relations with China by concurrently promoting security co-operation with India. On the whole, the situation could work to India's advantage and India-Indonesia security ties are expected to expand in the near term.

Malaysia

China has accorded priority to building up its relations with Malaysia, a key ASEAN member and a claimant to some of the Spratly Islands in the South China Sea. In recent years, China-Malaysia relations have acquired greater momentum, fuelled by nearly $ 34 billion in loans for infrastructure mega-projects under the BRI, including a major rail link, a new "Forest City", and a port at Malacca. Moreover, annual bilateral trade since 2015 has crossed $ 56 billion.[38] Reportedly, in 2015, the Chinese President Xi Jinping told the visiting Malaysian Prime Minister Najib Razak, "China and Malaysia are good neighbours and friends that trust and respect each other", pointing to the development of China's BRI as an opportunity to deepen relations between the two countries.[39] Since then, China has become the largest foreign investor in Malaysia, moving ahead of the USA and Japan.

Under Najib Razak, defence co-operation between Malaysia and China was initiated with the signing of a defence co-operation agreement in 2015. The same year, the two countries carried out a large-scale combined exercise, "Peace and Friendship 2015" in the Straits of Malacca, involving all the three services.[40] Later, in November 2016, during his third visit to China since 2009, Prime Minister Najib signed 14 agreements with China, including one for the joint development of at least four Chinese-designed littoral combat ships.[41] This deal was Malaysia's first major defence acquisition from China and a clear sign of advancement in China-Malaysia relations under Najib Razak.

However, progress in Sino-Malaysia strategic relations has been stalled since 2018, when Mahathir Mohamad, who took over office from Najib Razak after a surprise parliamentary election victory, has sought to balance ties with China to avoid getting too close. Evidently, Najib was seen as being "too soft" on China, apparently since Beijing had afforded him personal assistance. Chinese investments had provided for a US$ 2.3 billion bail-out for the Malaysian state-owned investment firm, 1Malaysia Development Berhad (1MDB), which was mired in large outstanding debts and a political scandal involving Najib.[42] Clearly, Najib's ability to act tough with Beijing was restricted, and it was later reported that he "seldom criticised China, even as it sailed coast guard ships near Malaysian claimed waters," whilst investment ties flourished.[43] Under Mahathir Mohamad, Malaysia re-negotiated various BRI projects, and it is likely that some projects could be cancelled. Mohamad has probably been the first regional leader to publicly warn China against promoting "a new version of colonialism" by trying to expand their economic control over the poorer states in the region.[44] However, the government has stated that Malaysia will remain a part of the BRI even though it may limit Chinese investments. The new administration is also looking at alternate sources for funding, such as Japan. On balance, Chinese influence in Malaysia is expected to decline and could provide an opportunity for India to expand its strategic relationship with Malaysia.

Iran

China's relations with Iran were formally established in 1971 only after the US rapprochement with China. In later years, during the Iran-Iraq War, China was a key arms supplier to Iran. China's relations with Iran have progressively evolved, and Beijing sees Iran in the context of its own relations with the USA, leveraging "the Iran card" in its "negotiations with the United States over various issues. Based on this factor, China has adjusted its proximity or distance from Tehran."[45] Iran is a key supplier of crude oil to China, which, like India, had also received a waiver from the ongoing US sanctions. Currently, China is seeking closer ties with Iran since it could be a potential key player in the BRI. During the visit of President Xi Jinping to Tehran in January 2016, the two countries signed several agreements, including co-operation in the BRI, which included a proposed Iran-Iraq-Turkey land corridor connecting with Central Asia and Europe, nuclear energy, and a decision to increase trade tenfold to $ 600 billion in the next ten years.[46] However, following the imposition of fresh US sanctions, most projects, including the proposed Iran-Iraq-Turkey land corridor, are on hold.[47]

Iraq

Iraq's relations with China are based on their oil trade. China buys more than half of Iraq's oil, making it the second-largest supplier after Saudi Arabia. In 2014, when the Iraqi prime minister visited Beijing, Sino-Iraq relations were upgraded to a "strategic partnership", and President Xi Jinping pledged Chinese assistance in "energy, electricity, communication and infrastructure" projects in Iraq, which he linked with China's BRI,[48] including the proposed Iran-Iraq-Turkey land corridor mentioned above. However, given the prevailing security situation, most of these projects are yet to be activated.

Israel

China has close defence ties with Israel and has depended on it for modern military technology and hardware that it could not obtain from the USA or Europe. Over the years, Israel has emerged as a major arms supplier to China after Russia. Many of Israel's arms sales have come under pressure from the USA, notably the contract in 2000 for the Israeli built airborne early warning system, Phalcon, which could be installed on a Russian IL-76. Reportedly, China intended to procure four to eight systems at an estimated value of $ 1 billion, probably one of the largest defence deals by Israel.[49] However, it was cancelled due to objections raised by the USA. Israel has signed up for the BRI and awarded several infrastructure projects to Chinese companies, including the development of a new port in Ashdod.[50] Furthermore, under the BRI, by 2021, China is likely to gain privileged access to Israel's strategic Haifa port, which is periodically visited by US Navy ships. Already, China's Shanghai International Port Group has signed a 25-year contract for rights to operate the port.[51] The USA has evidently warned Israel that US Navy ship visits could be scaled down or stopped should China take over port operations. It remains to be seen how Israel responds to the USA.

Oman

Oman's relations with China were founded on energy trade but, in recent times, have been dominated by their rapidly expanded economic co-operation following Oman's decision to join the BRI. Oman's national strategy to diversify from an oil-dependent economy, as outlined in its Vision 2020, complements China's vision of the BRI. For China, the strategic location of Oman in the Arabian Sea makes it an important point along the Maritime Silk Road, and for Oman, the Maritime Silk Road provides a golden opportunity to emerge as a logistics, tourism, and business hub in the region, perhaps an alternative to Dubai. Chinese investments in Oman surpass other West Asian states, and a consortium of Chinese firms have invested over $ 10.7 billion in building a brand new industrial city in Duqm, situated 550 km south of the capital, Muscat.[52] The plan includes a special economic zone (SEZ) with a port and a wide range of other ventures, including an oil refinery, a methanol plant, a giant solar energy equipment manufacturing operation, an automobile assembly factory, an oil and gas equipment production site, a tourism zone, and a multi-million logistics enterprise.[53] In time, Duqm could become the first megacity in the Arabian Peninsula. Sino-Oman relations also include maritime co-operation, and PLA naval ships on anti-piracy patrols off the Horn of Africa have often utilised Port Salalah in Oman for operational turnaround. Overall, the convergence of strategic interests between China and Oman seems to indicate that their relationship will continue to flourish. It remains to be seen how Oman balances its own ties with India.

Qatar

Qatar is the second-largest natural gas provider to China, supplying more than one-fifth of its needs.[54] However, Qatar's diplomatic relations with China, which were first established in 1988, were slow to progress. It was only after 30 years that the two countries held their first strategic-level dialogue in Beijing to explore areas for co-operation, including an operational plan in the BRI.[55] As part of Qatar's "pivot" to China, perpetuated by the regional tensions, Qatar has invested its sovereign wealth fund in China and other countries, including India. In China alone, Qatari investments have surpassed $ 13 billion with a further investment of $ 15–20 billion planned in real estate and infrastructure over the next five years.[56] Reportedly, Qatar has also covertly procured the SY-400 short-range ballistic missiles from China.[57] Based on these developments, it is likely that Sino-Qatar relations would progress further, although China would take care to maintain a neutral position in the Qatar-Gulf rift. It is evident that the tensions between Qatar and other Gulf states would have an impact on India's bilateral ties and defence co-operation with Qatar, but India's good relations with all the other Gulf countries and the USA mean that India could continue with its strategic engagements albeit on a low key.

Saudi Arabia

China's relations with Saudi Arabia have rapidly grown in strength since the end of the Cold War in 1990, when Saudi Arabia officially established diplomatic relations with the PRC, breaking away from Taiwan. A key milestone was achieved in Sino-Saudi relations with the signing of the 1999 Strategic Oil Cooperation Agreement, creating a partnership between the world's largest consumer and an oil producer. The relationship received a further boost with the visit of King Abdullah to Beijing in 2006, his first-ever official visit abroad after succession to the throne. During his visit, the King signed a series of agreements covering not just the energy trade but also infrastructure and telecommunications. Saudi-China ties were elevated to a comprehensive strategic partnership following the visit of President Xi Jinping to Riyadh in January 2016, to include co-operation in economic, political, and military fields. Since 2016, Saudi Arabia has sought to diversify its economy as outlined in the Saudi Vision 2030 and has expressed interest in the BRI, which could potentially provide new opportunities for growth and investments.[58] In March 2017, during the visit of Saudi King Salman to Beijing, the two countries signed contracts valued at $ 65 billion covering energy, education, and technology, including an agreement to establish a manufacturing facility for China's CH-4 hunter-killer drones or unmanned aerial vehicle (UAV) having similar capabilities as the US MQ-1 Predator UAV.[59] The Chinese drone is already in use by several Gulf countries. Unconfirmed reports also indicate that a Chinese ballistic missile manufacturing and testing facility is being constructed inside Saudi Arabia.[60] Reportedly, a proposal by Saudi Arabia to fund certain projects under the China Pakistan Economic Corridor (CPEC) in Pakistan is under discussion, under similar lines as being pursued with India for projects in the Maldives. It seems clear that China-Saudi relations are poised to expand in the coming years as Saudi Arabia seeks to diversify diplomatic relations away from the USA, which have been tested following recent developments such as the murder of journalist Jamal Khashoggi by Saudi agents in Istanbul and the war in Yemen. This could pave the way for greater economic and strategic influence of China in the region. In comparison, for now, India's multi-dimensional relations with Saudi Arabia, including energy trade and contemporary defence co-operation, could be seen as progressing smoothly. Overall, it appears that Saudi Arabia is keen to balance its bilateral relationships with India and China whilst maintaining close ties with the USA.

The United Arab Emirates (UAE)

The UAE is home to one of the largest and busiest ports in the world and a gateway to Africa, the Middle East, and Europe, making it an important hub along the BRI. Bilateral relations with China were elevated to a comprehensive strategic partnership during the historic state visit of Chinese President Xi Jinping in July 2018, the first-ever visit by a Chinese head of state in 29 years to the Arab state.[61] Recent years have also seen a spate of visits by trade delegations from China, and currently, the "UAE is home to approximately 200,000 Chinese citizens and 4,000 trading companies". The annual trade between the two countries exceeds $ 50 billion, with a forecast of rising to $ 70 billion in 2020.[62] Furthermore, according to a study, the UAE provides a low-risk investment destination for China since the country has a high credit rating.[63] It is, therefore, evident that Sino-UAE economic ties are set to accelerate in the coming years. The lack of defence engagements with China suggests that growing economic ties may not translate into meaningful political or military influence that could impinge upon India's strategic relations.

Yemen

As a major trade partner in the Gulf region, China has significant economic interests in Yemen and has played a key role in resolving the conflict. In 2011, China as a member of the Group of Ten—comprising the five Permanent Members of the UN Security Council along with Saudi Arabia, Oman, Kuwait, the UAE, and the European Union—was closely involved in Yemen's political transition process. Later, after the political transition failed to bring stability and the Houthis seized control of Sanaa, China voted in favour of Security Council Resolution 2201, calling for an immediate withdrawal of the Houthis.[64] In March 2015, PLA Navy ships deployed on anti-piracy patrols off Somalia were diverted to Aden for the first-ever evacuation of Chinese nationals abroad. About 600 Chinese citizens and 225 foreign nationals were evacuated from Aden.

In 2017, when negotiations at the UN failed, China tried to "bridge the trust deficit between the Houthi-Saleh bloc and the UN". Although the talks were unsuccessful, China won praise from both sides.[65] Following the December 2018 ceasefire in Yemen, China has offered significant humanitarian aid for Yemen, and the Chinese Ambassador to Yemen, Ambassador Tian, stated: "China was willing to actively participate in Yemen's future economic reconstruction process, as it promotes the BRI in the region".[66] China's initiatives in helping to resolve a regional conflict may have won it respect in the region as an impartial negotiator and could pave the way for further diplomatic engagements.

Egypt

In comparison to India, China's relations with Egypt have expanded rapidly. Egypt's Suez Canal lies at the heart of China's Maritime Silk Road and, not surprisingly, China is currently the largest investor in the Suez Canal, where it is also developing a Special Economic Zone. China has been Egypt's largest trading partner since 2012, and its economic engagements have swelled considerably in recent years.[67] Following a relative decline in Egypt's relations with the USA and reluctance in Washington to supply arms, Cairo has sought to diversify its diplomatic engagements with Russia and China. In 2014, Egypt signed a $ 3.5 billion arms deal with Russia and a comprehensive strategic partnership with China. However, despite the upswing in Sino-Egypt relations, it is believed that China's economic investments in Egypt may not translate into political or military influence, given the leverages maintained by the USA and the role of other regional investors, notably Saudi Arabia and the UAE.[68]

Eritrea

Chinese interest in Eritrea has been growing since 2001 when China cancelled an outstanding debt and further committed several multi-million-dollar development projects. Eritrea is an important partner in China's BRI, and Port Massawa is a key point along the Maritime Silk Road through the Red Sea. Significantly, the President of Eritrea, Isaias Afewerki, who received his political training in 1967 under the Communist Party of China (CPC) trainers, is a good friend of China.[69]

Notably, Chinese projects in Eritrea include a large hospital in the capital city of Asmara, which was completed in 2006, and major power and port infrastructure projects, including a $ 400 million project by the China Harbour Engineering Company for the construction of a 70,000 tonne bulk cargo terminal and a 50,000 tonne multipurpose terminal, plus associated infrastructure at Port Massawa.[70] Other Chinese investments in Eritrea include major stakes in the mining of copper, zinc, gold, and silver. Overall, China has considerable economic and political influence in Eritrea.

Sudan

As Sudan's largest trading partner, China holds considerable sway over the country. Traditionally, Sudan has been one of the largest oil suppliers in Africa, and more than two-thirds of its oil is imported by China, which has invested heavily in its energy sector. China was also the largest supplier of arms to Sudan during the period of the civil war, going against UN sanctions that prohibited sales of arms and equipment to Khartoum's regime and rebels in Darfur.[71] In fact, in 2004,

China threatened to veto the UN Security Council Resolution 1564, which called for an oil embargo on Sudan and subsequently stalled other UN Security Council resolutions, condemning President Bashir and his regime's alleged war crimes in South Sudan, Darfur, and other areas.[72] China continued to stand with President Bashir even as he was wanted by the International Criminal Court for crimes against humanity and genocide.[73] Clearly, China's political and military influence in Sudan can only be expected to strengthen under the BRI.

Djibouti

Djibouti is a focal point along China's maritime road, where Chinese military and commercial interests converge. In August 2017, China commissioned its first overseas military base at Djibouti. A few months earlier, President Golleh had inaugurated the Chinese-built multipurpose port at Doraleh, a few minutes' drive from the naval base. Reportedly, the PLA Navy has exclusive authority to use one of the berths in Port Doraleh.[74] It is evident from these developments that China has planned and created a dual-use infrastructure that could serve both commercial and military purposes and, clearly, Chinese-built ports in the Indian Ocean region could also be potential naval bases. Other major Chinese projects in Djibouti include the Ethiopia-Djibouti electric railway–the first of its kind in Africa–completed at a cost of $ 4 billion and a $ 300 million-plus water pipeline system to transport drinking water from Ethiopia to Djibouti.[75] For a country with a GDP of around $ 1.8 billion, these projects indicate that it could be heading towards a "debt trap". As witnessed in Sri Lanka, a failure to repay its loans to China could entail the transfer of land and assets to China. This could potentially have huge security implications not only for India but significantly for the USA and others based in Djibouti.

Somalia

China is seen as playing a leading role in Somalia's development and has built over 80 infrastructural projects such as hospitals, stadiums, and roads. Somalia is supportive of the BRI, but given the current state of development and security in the country, it is unlikely that the country would play any significant role in the BRI in the near to mid-term.

Kenya

China-Kenya relations were upgraded to a comprehensive strategic cooperative partnership in recent years, and currently China is Kenya's largest trading partner and investor. A comprehensive strategic cooperative partnership implies defence co-operation, but no significant bilateral military co-operation has been noted.

Chinese investments have expanded rapidly since 2015, following Kenya's admission into the BRI. Kenya has contracted at least 14 projects with China worth $ 8.5 billion and also received grants and other investment projects–mainly in the manufacturing, construction, and hospitality sectors —valued at almost $ 1 billion.[76] China's flagship project in Kenya is the country's new 472-km Standard Gauge Railway or SGR, estimated to be worth $ 3.2 billion. The railway line has been planned to eventually connect land-locked African states, including South Sudan, eastern Democratic Republic of Congo, Rwanda, Burundi, and Ethiopia to Ports Lamu and Mombasa in Kenya, thence to the Indian Ocean.[77] It is expected that the rail link will facilitate future trade between the African states and also improve international trade. However, Chinese projects and investments in Kenya are not without problems and have caused resentment amongst the locals who have accused Chinese companies of unfair hiring practices and racial discrimination, leading to sporadic protests and attacks on Chinese workers. Further, a 2018 report by Kenya's Auditor-General had sparked fears that the Chinese debt could be unsustainable and possibly lead to the Chinese taking over Port Mombasa, although the Kenyan President later stated that there was no cause for alarm.[78] However, Kenya's debt to China has grown to more than half of its GDP, and the risk of a "debt trap" is assessed to be real.[79]

Tanzania

Tanzania maintains close strategic relations with China, from whom it has received significant defence assistance in the form of training, military hardware, and infrastructure. In 2018, Tanzanian President John Magafuli inaugurated a Chinese-built training centre for the Tanzania People's Defence Forces (TPDF) at Mapinga in Bagamoyo district, where, in 2014, China signed a contract to build a new mega-port and an economic zone under the BRI. The mega-project is expected to cost at least $ 10 billion. Since Tanzania could not raise the necessary capital, a part (undisclosed) ownership of the port has been handed over to China.[80] The Bagamoyo project includes railway lines stretching over 2,500 km, connecting the port with land-locked neighbours, which have also been awarded to a Chinese consortium.[81] The proximity of a large defence training centre to a mega port under Chinese ownership has given rise to speculation that Bogamoyo could be the next Chinese naval base in the Indian Ocean region when it commences operations by 2020.

Comoros

China was the first country to recognise the Union of Comoros after independence from France in 1975 and has now emerged as its primary partner over France.

Chinese assistance programmes to Comoros include medical and health support, infrastructures such as power plants, airports, stadiums, and schools.[82] Reportedly, China is also providing training for Comorian army personnel, including Mandarin-language classes. Evidently, China's interest in Comoros is based on the island's strategic location, which could serve as an intelligence-gathering base and help to control shipping along the Mozambique channel. Furthermore, the recent discovery of oil reserves near the islands provides a huge potential for economic exploitation. Regardless of Chinese motives, the Comorians appear to have largely welcomed their investments; the Comorian vice president once stated, "China tries to do all the best for us."[83] Clearly, Chinese influence in Comoros seems set to intensify in the coming years.

Madagascar

China's relations with Madagascar set it apart from all the other African states–possibly with the exception of South Africa–due to the presence of a large Chinese Diaspora estimated at over 60,000, much larger than the population of persons of Indian origin, which is about 20,000. Chinese labourers employed by the French had started arriving in Madagascar around mid-1800 and later established themselves as traders. Owing to the presence of a sizeable Sino-Malagasy community, the "new Chinese" who arrived in the 1990s were perceived to be less "foreign" in Madagascar than in other African societies.[84] Evidently, this has facilitated China's inroads into the Malagasy market. For China, Madagascar serves as "a bridge between the African continent and the BRI".[85] However, Madagascar's dilapidated infrastructure means China will have to build it up to suit the BRI. Currently, China is involved in building a deep-water port in the bay of Narinda, on Madagascar's north-western coast facing Mozambique, and a national highway connecting Antananarivo and Toamasina. Two major deals by China were the acquisition of iron ore mining rights and a 10-year deal for fishing rights in Madagascar's EEZ for $ 2.7 billion.[86] The fishing rights deal has been widely opposed by local fishermen. The mining rights were obtained during a period of political crisis when most countries would have preferred to stay away from Madagascar. A similar approach can be seen at other trouble spots in Africa and seems to suggest that China would be prepared to use force when required to defend its interests. However, wide-ranging Chinese investments in Madagascar, including the traditional vanilla trade, are increasingly being opposed by the locals, and it is possible that an internal backlash could jeopardise Chinese investments. Thus, the long-term sustainability of various Chinese projects is not clear. Pertinently, China's maritime co-operation with Madagascar has been limited except for a recent visit by PLA Navy ships deployed on anti-piracy patrols.

Apparently, China has preferred to maintain close bilateral security ties with Madagascar's neighbour, Comoros.

Mauritius

Mauritius has maintained friendly relations with China since its independence in 1968, helped by a sizeable Chinese Diaspora that has preserved former trading links. Chinese President Xi Jinping visited Mauritius in July 2018 and was given a grand reception. This was his first overseas trip after re-election in March 2018, and bilateral trade and investment under the BRI were the two main items for discussion. Mauritius seems to have taken care to limit Chinese engagements to trade and investments, not to antagonise India, and there was no talk of defence/ security co-operation with China. The two countries have signed a free trade agreement, and China recently overtook India as Mauritius' largest trading partner. It has also made several investments in infrastructure projects such as the upgradation of the Ramgoolam International Airport, health facilities, the Bagatelle dam, and a new sports complex.[87] Mauritius presents itself as the strategic "gateway" to Africa and a potential entrepôt along the Maritime Silk Road, but its small size, southerly location, proximity to the US Navy base at Diego Garcia, and very importantly, the strategic influence exercised by New Delhi could limit its actual importance for China. Therefore, Seychelles could probably be a more advantageous option for China.

Seychelles

Chinese economic engagements with Seychelles have grown significantly in the past decade. In 2006, the Seychelles President visited Beijing to secure a $ 4.5 million grant from the Chinese government.[88] Subsequently, in 2007, Chinese President Hu Jintao visited Seychelles at the end of his eight-African nation tour. He was the first-ever Chinese leader to visit the country.[89] Hu Jintao described Seychelles as "a shining pearl in the Indian Ocean". China has since invested in several multi-million-dollar projects, including constructing the National Assembly and the Supreme Court buildings. In 2011, following the visit of China's Defence Minister, General Liang Guanglie, who led a 40-member military delegation to Seychelles, China announced plans to set up a base in Seychelles to support its anti-piracy operations in the region.[90] As part of the developing ties, in 2014, China gifted Seychelles a patrol craft and two Y-12 aircraft for maritime surveillance.[91] Whilst China's new found military interest in Seychelles raised concerns in India, no noteworthy PLA Navy activity was observed in the region, and at the end of 2015, China confirmed its plans of setting up a base at Djibouti. In any case, the announcement by President Michel of an Indian naval base in

Seychelles had effectively put an end to speculation that Seychelles was moving closer to China. Nevertheless, China's economic interests in Seychelles remain, and during the visit of President Faure to Beijing in September 2018, the two countries signed an MoU for enhancing socio-economic and infrastructural development co-operation under the BRI.[92] India's diplomatic efforts to counter Chinese military influence in Seychelles seem to have paid off, but clearly it will have to persist with its efforts and also follow through with its economic and military commitments to ensure sustained political support and attention.

Mozambique

As noted above, China has already established close relations with the Comoros Islands and Madagascar; hence, promoting strategic relations with Mozambique assumes greater urgency and importance for India. China's early relations with Mozambique were framed by the membership of both the countries in the communist bloc. China had provided military assistance to the Mozambican Liberation Front (Frelimo) fighters during their independence struggle against the Portuguese. Post-independence in 1975, China played a key role in Mozambique's development under the Frelimo regime, although in the later years, Mozambique moved closer to the Soviet Union. During the Cold War, Mozambique was embroiled in a lengthy civil war which ended in 1992, and Mozambique transitioned to a democratic government in an election overseen by the United Nations. With the onset of peace, Mozambique became a "model of co-operation with Western countries and donors, after having adhered to the conditions and programmes presented by the Bretton Woods institutions in 1984".[93] China renewed its relations with Mozambique in 1997, although subsequent governments have not been able to "establish the same close connection as its predecessors did during the era of ideological solidarity".[94] Currently, China's ties with Mozambique are largely limited to the trade, investment in infrastructure, agriculture, and energy sectors. Bilateral defence co-operation that existed until a decade ago seems deficient with few exchanges except for a recent visit by the PLA Navy's hospital ship *Peace Ark*, which called at Maputo in November 2017. However, increasing Chinese investments in Mozambique under the BRI could once again help to expand Chinese influence in Mozambique.

South Africa

China has been South Africa's largest trading partner and investor over the past decade, ever since Sino-South Africa relations were elevated to the level of a comprehensive strategic partnership in 2010 when South African President Jacob Zuma made his state visit to Beijing. Direct investments from China to South

Africa in multiple sectors, including marine economy, mining, finance, manufacturing, and infrastructure, crossed $ 25 billion in 2017. In mid-2018, when President Cyril Ramaphosa visited Beijing at a time when South Africa was on the brink of an economic recession, China committed an additional $ 10 billion in investments.[95] As the largest economy in Africa and a co-chair with China of the Forum on China-Africa Cooperation (FOCAC), South Africa has also played a key role in supporting Chinese engagements in Africa. Pertinently, China's top five financial institutions have branches in South Africa. China's political and strategic co-operation with South Africa can be framed in the context of four important platforms, notably, FOCAC co-operation, BRICS grouping, the BRI, and the South-South co-operation.

In recent times, the two countries have moved forward to expand defence co-operation, steered by the China-South Africa Defence Committee. Following the eighth Defence Committee meeting between the South African military chief and his counterpart in Beijing in August 2018, a joint statement mentioned,

> China and South Africa will jointly promote the level of co-operation in defence affairs, and make positive contributions to the enrichment of the connotation of China-South Africa comprehensive strategic partnership in the new era as well as the maintenance of international and regional security and stability.[96]

Significantly, South Africa is increasingly being visited by PLA Navy ships and a PLA Navy Task Group of four ships called at Simon's Town in June 2018. Clearly, defence and maritime co-operation between the two countries are set to expand, and it is likely that China could leverage its influence over the South African government to play a larger role in the Indian Ocean regional institutions, such as the Indian Ocean Rim Association (IORA) and Indian Ocean Naval Symposium (IONS), currently dominated by India.

Overall Assessment of Chinese Strategic Influence in the Indian Ocean Region

Based on the scope and depth of Chinese relations with various countries in the Indian Ocean region, this section makes an overall assessment of Chinese influence vis-a-vis India, in the various sub-regions and the likely implications for India.

South Asia: This is a region of core interest to India. Evidently, India's strategic influence in Sri Lanka and the Maldives has considerably strengthened in recent times. India's defence ties with Bangladesh are also seen as evolving progressively, supported by the current Hasina government. However, Bangladesh is likely to remain dependent upon China for military hardware, and it is likely that China, having failed to counter India's influence in the Maldives and Sri Lanka, would seek to expand its security ties with Bangladesh, probably with support from Pakistan, to undermine India's emerging security ties. India's bilateral relations with Pakistan will continue to remain hostile in the foreseeable future, and the growing Sino-Pakistan nexus remains the greatest challenge to India's security in South Asia.

Over the last decade, Sino-India competition for influence in South Asia has intensified, and regional states, particularly the Maldives and Sri Lanka, caught in the geopolitical "tug of war", have witnessed greater interference in their domestic affairs from both the powers. In the long run, this Sino-Indian contest could restrict the agency of small states, not just in South Asia but the entire region to their own detriment and impact regional stability. Large Chinese investments flowing into small states have exacerbated the risk of "debt traps" and could potentially result in China taking over a country's strategic assets, as in the case of Sri Lanka. This has forced India to focus its economic and military resources to maintain close security relations within South Asia, matching even China's massive investments in Sri Lanka and the Maldives.

As India is a net security provider for the region, those states would expect it to increasingly meet their maritime security requirements. A similar strategy followed by Australia with respect to the Pacific Island countries involving the supply of the Pacific patrol boats and regular maritime surveillance missions has proven expensive and difficult to sustain in the face of growing Chinese economic and political influence. Thus, the Indian strategy to be the net security provider could face similar challenges in the future and possibly backfire on India in the long term. This could even provide China a chance to step in as a more dependable security partner.

Southeast Asia: India's relations with all the Southeast Asian states have expanded significantly since the 1990s, and the current level of security co-operation with most countries based on the various maritime engagements has never been better. India's relations with Indonesia, Myanmar, Singapore, Thailand, and Vietnam are particularly close, whilst relations with others are seen as improving. In comparison, China's security ties are sparse, although recent efforts aimed at improving defence co-operation such as the China-ASEAN combined exercise have been successful. Whilst the USA continues to be the largest contributor to security in the region, India's Act East policy and maritime security co-operation have also received support from the USA as it complements their strategic "pivot" to the Asia-Pacific region.

Support from the USA seems to have been an important factor in improving India's position in Southeast Asia. Also, India's relations with the regional states and other US allies in the Asia-Pacific region such as Australia, Japan, and South Korea, appear to be shaping up in conformity with the overall strategic interests of the USA in the Asia-Pacific.

A much-needed focus by the Indian government on improving civil, maritime, and military infrastructure in the Andaman Islands and other steps such as a new trilateral combined exercise in the Andaman Sea and plans for joint development of a naval base at Sabang, Indonesia, clearly suggest that India has larger strategic plans to expand its maritime influence in the region. These developments are expected to add force to India's political, diplomatic, and strategic efforts in Southeast Asia and increasingly impinge on Beijing's sphere of influence.[97] However, backing from the USA and continued support from the ASEAN states mean that India can expect to balance Chinese economic and political influence in the region with close maritime engagements.

West Asia: In comparison to India, which has historical ties and cultural affinity with the West Asian region, China is largely viewed as an "outsider". China's evolving relations with the West Asian states are generally seen in the context of its energy imports and the BRI that focuses on connectivity and trade co-operation stretching from China across Eurasia. Crucially, the land Silk Road and the maritime Silk Road crisscross each other in West Asia. China's investments in several major infrastructure projects in West Asia under the BRI seem to be driven purely by economic interests. Evidently, the question of a "debt trap" does not apply to the oil-rich Gulf states. In comparison, similar economic linkages with South Asian states such as Pakistan, the Maldives, Sri Lanka, and Bangladesh, which have a lower credit rating and carry significant investment risks, seem to be influenced by strategic considerations rather than economic interests, aimed at challenging India's regional influence.

For the West Asian states, China, as an emerging global power, could be a viable alternative partner to the USA, whose changing priorities under the Trump regime could lead to complications in the region. Thus, it is likely that China's deepening economic relations with the West Asian countries could translate into broad-based defence co-operation and political influence. China has also sought to leverage its bilateral relations with the West Asian states to carve a larger role for itself. For instance, in 2010, China, offered, although unsuccessfully, to mediate in a long-running island dispute between the UAE and Iran over the sovereignty of the Greater and Lesser Tunbs and Abu Musa islands located in the Persian

Gulf. Furthermore, it also played an important role during the negotiations in the Yemen conflict. As regard defence co-operation, until the 1980s, China was a key arms supplier to Iran, Iraq, and Saudi Arabia. Recent developments, such as the agreement for a UAV manufacturing facility in the Middle East, indicate that it could once again emerge as an important strategic weapons supplier, possibly as an alternative to the USA. Prior to the establishment of a logistics facility at Djibouti in 2017, China's naval engagements with the region were limited to ship visits as part of the ongoing deployment of the PLA Navy on anti-piracy missions. Oman, followed by Yemen, was the preferred destination for PLA Navy ships on anti-piracy missions. However, with the operationalisation of the naval facility at Djibouti, it is likely that the PLA Navy would be in a position to play a larger role in the region.

It is likely that China will continue to build up security relationships in the region and establish close security ties with Saudi Arabia and the UAE. It is also probable that China would leverage its strategic ties with Pakistan to strengthen its position in the region just as the USA leverages Pakistan's local knowledge to develop closer working relations with the Gulf Arab states. Ultimately, even though China may not dominate the region in terms of strategic influence, given the overarching control by the USA, it could certainly surpass India's sphere of influence. Essentially, this implies that India can no longer take for granted its historical influence in the region but must double its efforts to sustain and incrementally strengthen extant strategic ties with the regional states, particularly the Gulf Cooperation Council (GCC) countries. Pertinently, the Indian Navy already conducts combined naval exercises with two of the six GCC navies, notably Oman and the UAE, with naval exercise with the Saudi Navy under discussion. Thus, India could propose to expand the scope of its engagements to establish a formal partnership with the GCC and initiate combined naval exercises with the GCC navies.

East Africa: China's engagements with Africa go back long before the announcement of the BRI in 2013. Presently, China has become Africa's largest trade partner, and Africa is China's second-largest overseas construction project contract market and the fourth largest investment destination.[98] So far, China has completed over a thousand projects in Africa and built 6,500 km of railways, over 6,000 km of highways, more than 200 schools, 80 stadiums, dozens of government office buildings, and a large number of airports and ports, helping intra-Africa trade and integrating it with the global economy.[99] Contrary to the common perception that Chinese engagements with Africa are tantamount to neo-colonialism, the response of the African states has largely been positive, with the exception of a few local protests.[100] In December 2015, speaking at the China-Africa Forum in South Africa, Chinese President Xi Jinping announced a $ 60 billion package for development in Africa covering several areas, including infrastructure projects, health care, aid for drought-stricken countries, and thousands of scholarships for African students.[101] The Zimbabwean President, Robert Mugabe, praised the Chinese president and stated,

> Here is a man representing a country once called poor, a country which was never our coloniser. He is doing to us what we expected those who colonised us yesterday to do ... We will say he is a God-sent person.[102]

The continued acceptance of Chinese investments by African states over the past five decades is a sign that Chinese presence in Africa is seen "as that of a partner in economic development rather than an aspiring hegemon".[103] Clearly, China's influence in the region surpasses all others and is expected to intensify further, commensurate with the coming wave of investments under the BRI. It is obvious that increasing Chinese investments and presence of a growing worker population will invariably lead to greater Chinese influence in the region and also call for greater naval presence facilitated by the PLA naval base at Djibouti. Additional bases at Comoros and Tanzania with whom China's defence co-operation has intensified also seem likely. Obviously, these developments would support the PLA Navy in playing a larger role in the region.

Conclusion

In less than a decade, since 2009, when the PLA Navy first entered the Indian Ocean, China commissioned a full-fledged and fortified naval base at Djibouti in 2017, with additional facilities likely to come up in other African states and possibly in Pakistan. Clearly, China's assertive projection of maritime power compared to India's benign approach has accorded China "quick wins", and also led to significant political and economic influence. Over the next decade, it is expected that China will work towards consolidating its position in the wider region.

China already enjoys almost complete political and economic control in Pakistan and major influence in several East African states, specifically Comoros, Eritrea, Tanzania, and Djibouti, and significant economic influence in the Middle East. However, China has also realised the limits of its economic and political authority in strategic locations such as Sri Lanka, the Maldives, Mauritius, and the Seychelles, where India exercises considerable political clout. China's recent attempts to gain influence, particularly in Sri Lanka and the Maldives, were relatively short-lived, and India's leadership prevailed. Similarly, India has stepped up its diplomatic efforts in other countries, specifically Bangladesh, Myanmar, and Indonesia, to counter Chinese influence and establish closer strategic ties.

However, India's influence in several parts of the region appears to have diminished, particularly in East Africa, an area which was long seen to lie on the fringes of India's strategic interests, leading to general neglect of historical ties. Here, India appears to have ceded influence to China, and consequently, Chinese economic and political sway overshadows India's relations. Further, China's position in Africa has been strengthened by the new PLA Navy base in Djibouti.

In West Asia, the growing Chinese economic and political authority in the region poses a challenge to India's regional influence. However, India is presented with an unprecedented opportunity to improve overall relations, particularly with the Gulf Arab states and especially the UAE and Saudi Arabia, and proactive efforts could help to counterbalance China.

On balance, it is evident that the BRI will help China to expand and consolidate its strategic influence in the wider Indian Ocean region. Clearly, this will come at the cost of India's position as the regional leader, and India will need to strive hard to maintain its regional leadership.

NOTES

1. Abhijit Singh, "China's Maritime Silk Route: Implications for India," *Institute of Defence Studies and Analyses Commentary*, 28 July 2014.
2. "Narendra Modi changed India's 'attitude' towards Maritime Silk Road: Chinese daily," *The Economic Times*, 4 July 2016.
3. John Hurley, Scott Morris, & Gailyn Portelance, *Examining the Debt Implications of the Belt and Road Initiative from a Policy Perspective*, Centre for Global Development Policy Paper No. 121, March 2018, p. 1.
4. Nadège Rolland, "China's Silk Road," *The National Bureau of Asian Research Commentary*, 12 February 2015, p. 1.
5. Christopher Len, "China's 21st Century Maritime Silk Road Initiative, Energy Security and SLOC Access," *Maritime Affairs*, Vol. 11, No. 1, 2015, p. 8.
6. Ibid.
7. Erica Downs, Mikkal E. Herberg, Michael Kugelman, Christopher Len, & Kaho Yu, *Asia's Energy Security and China's Belt and Road Initiative*, NBR Special Report No. 68, Washington DC, November 2017, p. V.
8. "Many Belts and Many Roads," *CSIS*, 11 October 2017, available at https://reconnectingasia.csis.org/analysis/entries/many-belts-and-many-roads/html
9. Ibid.
10. Stephen China, "BRI Debt Trap: An Unintended Consequence?" *The ASEAN Post*, 9 October 2018.
11. "Pakistan to Pay China $40b on $26.5b CPEC Investments in 20 Years," *Tribune*, 26 December 2018.

12. Sultana Yasmin, "The Changing Dynamics of China-Bangladesh Relations," *The Daily Star*, 11 November 2018.
13. Ibid.
14. "India has Nothing to Worry about China-Bangla Ties: Sheikh Hasina," *The Economic Times*, 21 February 2018.
15. "India to Develop Payra Port in Bangladesh," 5 June 2016, available at http://www.newscast-pratyaksha.com/english/india-develop-payra-port.html
16. "India has been an Enthusiastic Cheerleader for Sheikh Hasina and Promises to do More in the Coming Five Years," *The Times of India*, 5 January 2019.
17. "Maldives Foreign Land Ownership Reform Bill is Approved," *BBC*, 23 July 2015.
18. David Brewster, *Between Giants: The Sino-Indian Cold War in the Indian Ocean*, Ifri Centre for Asian Studies, Paris, December 2018, p. 19.
19. Darshan. M. Baruah, "Modi's Trip and China's Islands: The Battle for the Indian Ocean," *The Diplomat*, 11 March 2015.
20. Ibid., pp. 18–19.
21. Brewster, *Between Giants*, p. 19.
22. "India is the Closest Friend of the Maldives: President Ibrahim Mohamed Solih," *The Hindu*, 16 December 2018.
23. Brewster, *Between Giants*, p. 19.
24. "Maldives Water Crisis: India Transports 1,000 Tonnes of Fresh Water to Male," *NDTV*, 7 December 2014.
25. "China Follows India, Rushes Water to Crisis-hit Maldives," *The Economic Times*, 7 December 2014.
26. Sameer Lalwani, "China's Port to Nowhere," *Foreign Affairs Snapshot*, 8 April 2015.
27. Ibid.
28. "Former Sri Lankan President Mahinda Rajapaksa Blames India for his Election Defeat," *DNA*, 13 March 2015.
29. "Lanka Struggling to Prepay Record Foreign Debt: PM," *The Times of India*, 11 January 2019.
30. Lalwani, "China's Port to Nowhere".
31. Ye Htut, "'Myanmar-China Relations in 2018: Enter the Dragon' by Ye Htut," Institute of Southeast Asian Studies-Yusof Ishak Institute, 5 January 2018.
32. Garver, *Protracted Contest*, pp. 260–270.
33. Nian Peng, "China and Myanmar's Budding Relationship," *East Asia Forum*, 24 August 2018.
34. Nan Lwin, "China's Six Belt and Road Projects in Myanmar to Watch in 2019," *The Irrawaddy*, 24 January 2019.
35. Prashanth Parameswaran, "China and Indonesia under Jokowi: Show Me the Money," *The Diplomat*, 28 January 2015.
36. Shannon Teizzi, "Indonesia, China Seal 'Maritime Partnership'," *The Diplomat*, 27 March 2015.
37. Wilda Asmarini & Maikel Jefriando, "Indonesia asks China for special fund under Belt and Road: ministers," *Reuters*, 3 July 2019.
38. Euan Graham, "Dominoes in the South China Sea," *Lowy Institute Commentary*, 1 November 2016.
39. Shannon Tiezzi, "Can China Rebuild Its 'Special Relationship' with Malaysia?" *The Diplomat*, 18 November 2015.
40. Sumathy Permal, "China and Malaysia's First-ever Joint Military Exercise is an Important Strategic Move," *The Star*, 28 September 2015.
41. Graham, "Dominoes in the South China Sea".
42. Prashanth Parameswaran, "Is China Now Malaysia's Largest Investor?" *The Diplomat*, 13 January 2016.

43. Ralph Jennings, "Malaysian PM Shows Signs of a Bolder Stance on South China Sea," *Voice of America*, 25 June 2018.
44. "Mahathir Mohamad Warns against 'New Colonialism' during China Visit," *Financial Times*, 20 August 2018.
45. Mahmoud Pargoo, "What Does Iran Really Think of China?" *The Diplomat*, 7 November 2018.
46. "Iran's Leader Says Never Trusted the West, Seeks Closer Ties with China," *Reuters*, 24 January 2016.
47. "Embracing the BRI Ecosystem in 2018," *The Deloitte Insights*, 12 February 2018, available at https://www2.deloitte.com/insights/us/en/economy/asia-pacific/china-belt-and-road-initiative.html
48. Shannon Tiezzi, "China and Iraq Announce Strategic Partnership," *The Diplomat*, 23 December 2014.
49. "Israel and US Clash over Spy Plane Sale to China," *The Guardian*, 20 April 2000.
50. "China's Belt and Road Initiative: What's in it for Israel?" *The Jerusalem Post*, 10 January 2018.
51. Ilan Berman, "Israel's Dangerous Dalliance with China," *The Wall Street Journal*, 13 January 2019.
52. Amar Diwakar, "Oman's Coastline Is the Next Stop on China's Belt and Road," 19 December 2017, available at https://emerge85.io/Insights/omans-coastline-is-the-next-stop-on-chinas-belt-and-road/html
53. Wade Shepard, "Why China is Building a New City Out in the Desert Of Oman," *Forbes*, 8 September 2017.
54. Iqtait, "China's Rising Interests in Qatar."
55. "Qatar, China Hold First Round of Strategic Dialogue," *The Gulf Times*, 12 December 2018.
56. Ibid.
57. Ibid.
58. "China Wants Saudi as Key Belt and Road partner," *Arabianindustry.com*, 11 July 2018, available at https://www.arabianindustry.com/construction/news/2018/jul/11/china-wants-saudi-as-key-belt-and-road-partner-5952245.html
59. "Chinese Drone Factory in Saudi Arabia first in Middle East," *South China Morning Post*, 27 March 2017.
60. "Rocket-Engine Test Stand at Secret Saudi Missile Base Resembles Chinese Design, Experts Say," *South China Morning Post*, 27 January 2019.
61. "UAE, China Expand Trade, Cultural Relations Following Xi's Visit," *Xinhua*, 25 September 2018.
62. "A New Era Beckons for UAE-China Relations," *Arabian Business*, 27 July 2018.
63. John Hurley, Scott Morris, and Gailyn Portelance, *Examining the Debt Implications of the Belt and Road Initiative from a Policy Perspective*, Centre for Global Development Policy Paper 121, March 2018, pp. 6–8.
64. Chang, *China and Yemen's Forgotten War*, p. 2.
65. Ibid.
66. Ibid., p. 4.
67. David Wood, "Egypt Loves China's Deep Pockets," *Foreign Policy*, 28 August 2018, p. 2.
68. Ibid., p. 4.
69. "Eritrea Profile–Leaders," *BBC*, 1 May 2014.
70. "China Commits Millions in Aid to Eritrea," *Tesfanews*, 3 May 2013.
71. Phillip Manyok, "Oil and Darfur's Blood: China's Thirst for Sudan's Oil," *Journal of Political Sciences & Public Affairs*, Vol. 4, No. 1, 28 January 2016, pp. 3–4.
72. Ibid.
73. "Beijing Defends Sudan President Bashir's Presence at China-Africa Summit," *Agencia EFE*, 3

September 2018.

74. Monica Wang, "China's Strategy in Djibouti: Mixing Commercial and Military Interests," *Council on Foreign Relations*, 13 October 2018.
75. Ibid.
76. Sanne Wass, "Kenya & China: A love-Hate Relationship?" *Global Trade Review*, 1 August 2018.
77. "Will Kenya Get Value for Money from its New Railway?" *BBC*, 8 June 2017.
78. Embassy of the People's Republic of China in the Republic of Kenya, "Issue of Takeover of Mombasa Port by China is Pure Propaganda: Kenyan President," 2 January 2019, available at http://ke.china-embassy.org/eng/zkgx/t1626610.html.
79. "Will Kenya Get Value for Money from its New Railway?" *BBC*, 8 June 2017.
80. "Construction of US $10bn Bagamoyo Port in Good Progress," *Construction Review*, 12 September 2018.
81. "Tanzania Awards $9b in Rail Projects to China," *China Daily*, 5 June 2015.
82. "Why is China Investing in the Comoros," *CBS News*, 12 November 2014.
83. Ibid.
84. "For 'One Belt, One Road,' China Casts Madagascar as a 'Bridge' to Africa," *World Political Review*, 2 May 2017.
85. Ibid.
86. "Fishermen Oppose $2.7 bn Deal Opening Madagascar to Chinese Fishing," *Asia Times*, 10 November 2018.
87. "Mauritius and Africa must Avoid Chinese Debt-trap," *New Delhi Times*, 14 August 2018.
88. Kamlesh Agnihottri, "Chinese Quest for a Naval Base in the Indian Ocean–Possible Options for China," *National Maritime Foundation Commentary*, February 2010.
89. "Seychelles Welcomes Chinese President," *The Seychelles Weekly*, 9 February 2007.
90. "China to Open Military Base in Seychelles," *The Times of India*, 12 December 2011.
91. "Seychelles Receives Patrol Vessel Donated from India," *Defence Web*, 5 February 2016.
92. "Seychelles and China Sign Agreements as President of Island Nation Continues Visit," *Seychelles News Agency*, 3 September 2018.
93. Paula Cristina Roque, *China in Mozambique: A Cautious Approach Country Case Study*, South Africa Institute of International Affairs Occasional Paper No. 23, January 2009, pp. 1–3.
94. Ibid.
95. "China Offers to Help South Africa Out of Its Economic Recession," *The South African*, 14 August 2018.
96. Tom O'Connor, "China and South Africa Deepen Military Ties Amid Anger over Trump's White Farmers Comments," *Newsweek*, 24 August 2018.
97. Baladas Ghoshal, *China's Perception of 'Look East Policy,' and Its Implications*, Institute of Defence Studies and Analyses Monograph Series No. 26, New Delhi, October 2013, pp. 70–75.
98. "Foreign Ministry Spokesperson Hua Chunying's Regular Press Conference," Ministry of Foreign Affairs, People's Republic of China, 28 January 2015.
99. Embassy of the People's Republic of China in the Republic of Mauritius, "Speech at the Symposium on Public Diplomacy and China-Mauritius (Africa) Relations by Gong Yufeng, Chargé d'affaires of the Embassy of China in Mauritius," 12 April 2018, available at http://www.ambchine.mu/eng/sgxw/t1550450.html
100. Alvin Cheng-Hin Lim, "Africa and China's 21st Century Maritime Silk Road," *Asia-Pacific Journal*, Vol. 13, Issue No.1, March 2015, p. 2.
101. "Africa: China Pledges $60 Billion to African Development," *Al Jazeera*, 4 December 2015.
102. Ibid.
103. Ibid.

SECTION V

DIGITAL BRI

16

Belt and Road Initiative (BRI): Towards Connectivity and Control

Ajey Lele and Kritika Roy

China's Belt and Road Initiative (BRI) has become the most coveted topic since its announcement in 2013 by President Xi Jinping in Kazakhstan. The BRI concept is a reincarnated version of the age-old Silk Trade Route that included a huge network of strategically located trading posts, markets and, thoroughfares designed to streamline the transport, exchange, distribution and storage of silk and goods.[1] Today, this concept has been extended to include digital, space and aviation mediums besides land and sea routes.

The recently concluded second BRI forum in April 2019 based on the theme "Shaping a Brighter Shared Future" highlighted the opportunities and outcomes of the initiative that could be reaped by the world. This forum was also important as it focused more on ameliorating the concerns regarding China's debt trap and unsustainable means of expansion. In this context, programs like "Debt Sustainability Framework", "Beijing Initiative for the Clean Silk Road" and the "Green Silk Road Envoys Program" were announced for the participating nations. In addition, weightage was given to incorporating digital and emerging technologies in the initiative that is: promoting the concept of the digital Silk Road. Although, much deliberation was not done on the space and aerospace

The authors have published a paper on a similar subject which is available at https://idsa.in/occasionalpapers/china-digital-bri-op55, accessed 30 December 2019.

part of the BRI, nonetheless, one cannot be ignorant of the growing expansion in these areas.

The BRI is an initiative that is made in China and made for China. It can also be defined as a collective term that binds together all the Chinese projects within China as well as those that are across the globe. This chapter analyses the developments in digital, space and aerospace mediums so as to understand the nature of the Chinese footprint and intent of Chinese investments.

China's Rationale for Pursuing the BRI Objective

The Belt and Road initiative comes as a response to many of the challenges that China has been facing for some time like China's structural overcapacity problem and the issue of plummeting demand. Additionally, the BRI has also been commensurate with China's ambition of enhancing self-reliance, promoting economic cooperation and expanding global footprints.

Connectivity and global influence has been the mainstay of the BRI.[2] Additionally, it was seen as a tool to meet economic targets and expand China's market beyond its borders, thus solving a massive overcapacity problem that the country was facing for a while. Overcapacity not only makes a country's financial system more vulnerable but also increases debt levels. By the later part of 2012, the rate of the capacity utilisation of China's shipbuilding industries, electrolytic aluminium, steel, flat glass, and cement, was all less than 75 per cent, inducing severe implications like increasing non-performing assets, declining profits, and mass unemployment. In 2013, guiding opinion, which advocated an active expansion of the external market, was laid down by the State Council as a solution.

To add to this, China has already been increasing its global influence on a bilateral basis. For instance, China invested in projects with countries along the South Asian Region, particularly in Sri Lanka (Hambantota), Myanmar (Kyaukpyu), Bangladesh (Chittagong), and Pakistan (Gwadar). Additionally, China provided capital for initiatives like building shipping facilities, constructing deepwater ports, naval bases, and pipeline projects in many of these countries. China's foray into the South Asian region and its investment in different sectors has been termed as "string of pearls" which neatly folds under the larger ambit of China's BRI. Moreover, China has been strengthening its trade ties with various nations across the globe in different sectors. This brings into reality the fact that going forward, these ties may act as leverage for China to forward its ambition of officially constituting BRI among nations.

Digital, Aviation and Space Silk Road

Digital Silk Road

In the 21st century, Information and Communication Technology (ICT) has emerged as a lifeline for all sectors from education to medical sciences to business and national security. It has truly revolutionised the world, made it faster and brought it closer. Since the last decade, Chinese policy has increasingly backed high technology industrialisation and has promoted an innovation-driven economy. A Digital Silk Road is believed to play a "pioneering" and "fundamental" role in these ambitious and interrelated goals.

For China, digitisation is an opportunity to elevate its domestic market, economic growth and expand its footprints globally. The size of China's digital economy has surged from 15 per cent of GDP in 2008 to 33 per cent in 2017, mainly driven by the integration of ICT with traditional sectors.[3] China's Ministry of Foreign Affairs, the National Development and Reform Commission (NDRC), and the Ministry of Commerce came out with a White Paper in 2015 that specifies that,

> "[China] should jointly advance the construction of cross-border optical cables and other communications trunk line networks...and create an information Silk Road...build bilateral cross-border optical cable networks at a quicker pace, plan transcontinental submarine optical cable projects, and improve spatial (satellite) information passageways to expand information exchanges and cooperation".[4]

China is in the midst of a long-term restructuring that has seen the decline of low-end industries and the emergence of higher-value factories like Chinese internet giants, robotics, etc. The country's venture into ambitious national initiatives such as "Made in China 2025" aims to guide the country's industrial modernisation and break its dependence on foreign technology and an initiative like "Internet Plus" is a guideline to amalgamate emerging technologies like Cloud computing, big data and IoT (Internet of Things) within various trades and businesses.[5] China's initiative to make inroads in its digital economy will soon become new drivers of job creation by 2025. China has forged ahead in fields such as next-generation IT (Information Technology); in fact, Chinese companies like Huawei and ZTE are set to gain global dominance in the roll-out of 5G networks. There is a growing and complex alliance being formed between the state and its home-grown Internet companies in building a "digital silk road", with a multi-faceted aim to mitigate industrial overcapacity, facilitate corporate China's global expansion, support the internationalisation of the renminbi, construct a China-centered transnational network infrastructure, and promote an Internet-enabled "inclusive globalisation".

The rise of Chinese Internet giants and e-commerce markets in both the domestic and global markets has added impetus to the policy discourses on building the "digital silk road" which furthermore has implications for both BRI and non-BRI countries.

Air Silk Road

It is common knowledge that the focus of the BRI is towards developing overland and maritime infrastructures. There is an important but less discussed element to this gigantic initiative, and that is of the investments getting made (and planned for the future) in the aerospace sector. This section and the next section discuss the aspects of investments being made in the aviation and space sectors.

Li Jiaxiang, Administrator of Civil Aviation Administration of China (CAAC) during 2015, had proposed that all BRI countries (including China) adopt a proactive, more liberal and flexible aviation policy for an active, orderly and progressive approach to liberalisation. According to him, China will train 500 personnel for the B&R countries, through exchange, training or as international students. Also, it was mentioned that China would support ICAO's (International Civil Aviation Organization) safety support partnership program to provide safety support to B&R countries. China is the world's second-largest aviation power after the USA (United States of America). The international expansion planned under the BRI has the potential of reshaping the global aviation industry.

Before discussing China's investments in this sector, it is important to point out that during the 21st century, the aviation industry's centre of gravity has shown an eastwards movement. The Asia-Pacific region is emerging as a major nerve centre for this industry and handles almost 50 per cent of global aviation traffic. On the other hand, pockets of West Asia (Middle East) have also shown growth in terms of handling aviation traffic. It is here that smaller states like the UAE (United Arab Emirates) and Qatar have emerged as major hubs for providing global aerial connectivity. All this indicates that the market is already ripe in the region and now China is trying to expand it further under the BRI, both in the passenger traffic and air cargo sectors.

China is ensuring that it would deal with various subsets of the aviation industry from infrastructure development to expanding the business of Chinese airlines to leasing aircraft to manufacturing aircraft and ground infrastructure and accommodating additional international freighter flights. The basic idea is to make brand "China" as a popular global aviation brand.

The Belt and Road Big Data Report (2017) circulated by the State Information

Centre mentions that by the end of May 2017, direct air routes had connected 26 provincial regions in China (84 per cent of the total number), with 43 countries along the extended Belt and Road, with 240 new air routes opened in 2016. Major airports in cities like Shanghai, Beijing, Guangdong, Sichuan and Fujian have the most air links. Additionally, some 113 additional international air routes are being operated since 2017-18, connecting countries along the Belt and Road. Significant airport and infrastructure investment has already occurred, and the majority of investors are attracted fundamentally by Western Europe, and then by openings in the east of that continent where cargo rather than passenger facilities are getting erected to take advantage of a comprehensive road network. In addition, some small airports there have been courted by several Chinese operators and investors. China also has an interest in professionally managing airport operations for other states.

Major projects are being undertaken in Central Asian States like Kyrgyzstan, Kazakhstan and a few others. Also, there are projects that are underway in Iran, Turkey, Russia, Belarus, Poland, Germany and the Netherlands. These are mainly either airport development projects, terminal up-gradation, other infrastructure expansion or building of new airports.

Aviation is emerging as an important sector of cooperation between China and the European Union (EU). In May 2019, the European Commission and China signed important agreements to develop aviation between Europe and China. One agreement is a bilateral civil aviation safety agreement (BASA), and the other is a "horizontal" aviation agreement. It allows any airline from the EU to fly to China from any EU member-state. For example, Air France could operate flights to China from some Italian or German airports. Also, China and the EU have much to offer to each other in the arena of the aircraft manufacturing industry setup. For Airbus, China is a major market, and almost 25 per cent of all Airbus aircraft operate in China. In March 2019, Airbus and China Aviation Supplies Holding Company signed an agreement for the sale of 300 aircraft to Chinese companies. China also hosts some Airbus production and research centres (one of Airbus' main research centres is located in Shenzhen). Since 2008, some Airbus A320 aircraft are being assembled in Tianjin. In April 2019, the first Airbus H135 helicopter assembly line was inaugurated in Qingdao. The Chinese domestic airline market is anticipated to triple between 2017 and 2037. The BRI is expected to further accelerate the development of air traffic between China and countries along the new Silk Roads.

The BRI has already started benefiting the Chinese aviation industry. Agencies like the China Eastern Airlines (one of the three major state-owned air transport groups in China) are projecting major growth for the future. In particular, air travel to BRI partner-states is already showing an increase. The Shanghai-based China Eastern has been building the Aviatic Silk Road and opened more than 100 routes to around 50 cities and 20-plus countries. China Eastern and the Guangzhou-based China Southern are expected to make major investments towards developing new airports in an effort to enhance their position in the Beijing market.

At present, Chinese airline expansion through the BRI is found in a relatively gradual fashion. However, there is much of interest in this area of the BRI globally. Also, Chinese companies like Alibaba are showing tremendous interest in making investments in projects related to airport development. All in all, the BRI is expected to make the aviation industry boom significantly.

Space Silk Road

Space is another sector in which China has made huge advances during the last few years. Today, China is recognised as one of the leading players globally in the space arena. Chinese scientists were the forerunners of primitive rockets back in the year 900, though they only launched their first Long March rocket in 1970 on the back of Soviet technology, and sent a human into space in 2003.[6] At present, China is making fast progress in the outer space area. It has a very successful moon program, and at present their Lander-Rover system is collecting observations from the surface of the moon. They have various other programs, including one for the establishment of a space station in the near future. This section debates various aspects of China's space program, which are BRI specific.

Connectivity is the key to BRI strategy, and hence there is a greater relevance for China's satellite-based technology which provides PNT (Positioning, Navigation and Timing) inputs. It was realised that for any connectivity, be it in water, road, rail or air, there is a requirement of such a PNT system. It is likely that this need could have been instrumental towards formulating the idea on the Space Silk Road. This concept was introduced in 2014 by the International Alliance of Satellite Application Services (ASAS). The Space Silk Road aims at creating an entire range of space capabilities including satellites, launch services, and ground infrastructure and at supporting related industries and service providers to go global.[7]

China's space agenda is normally perceived as a maze within a maze. However, for the last two decades or so, China has been a lot open towards discussing its space agenda. To date, they have published four White Papers (2000, 2006, 2011, and 2016) on space aspects providing various details of their present and proposed space projects. However, possibly these could be only projects which China wants the rest of the world to know and not the others. China has developed assets for meteorology, remote sensing, earth observation, communication, and navigational. The 2016 White Paper identifies various fundamental policies with regard to international space exchanges and cooperation. The paper also states that China is keen on 'strengthening bilateral and multilateral cooperation which is based on common goals and serves the Belt and Road Initiative.'

Zheng He (1371-1433), a Chinese mariner, is known to have explored much of the world for China. He is known to have undertaken seven major expeditions and be responsible for establishing Chinese trade in new areas and credited with opening up of the Maritime Silk Road. The ancient Chinese invented astronavigation and Zheng is known to be the first user of this technique during his various expeditions. The location and direction of his fleet were estimated by observing the stars and constellations, such as the Big Dipper, the Southern Cross, and the Lyra constellation. Living on the northern hemisphere, the Chinese on land also used to navigate by spotting the Big Dipper.[8] The Chinese word for the Big Dipper is 'BeiDou'. The modern-day satellite-based navigational system introduced by China, which is also known to have a major role in the conceptualisation of BRI is termed as BeiDou.

The BeiDou navigational system (BDS) has generated interest globally owing to its quality and China's systematic management of the entire project. At present, China intends to have a 35-satellite system for providing a global network for positioning, navigation, and timing services. This is an all-weather system and is in line with the needs of the country's national security and economic and social development.[9] This system is at the heart of the entire BRI project and is often termed as the "digital glue"[10] binding together BRI participants and known to be playing a major role in taking the BRI forward.

China Satellite Navigation System

China started exploring satellite navigation technology in the late 1960s. However, owing to various technical difficulties and lack of funding, particularly during the Cold War era, China had not made much progress towards developing such a system. Based on the 'Twin-Star' regional navigation theory, they tested the satellite positioning system on two DFH-2A communications satellites. This test showed that the precision of the Twin-Star system was comparable to the publicly available signals of the American Global Positioning System (GPS).[11]

Following this, government approval for the development of the satellite navigational system was granted during 1993–94. BeiDou/BeiDou-1 was China's first regional navigational system and was developed by the China Academy of Space Technology (CAST).[12]

As per the China National Space Administration (CNSA) and CSNO (China Satellite Navigation Office), the development of the Chinese global navigation system is to be carried out in three phases.[13]

1. Phase-I is BeiDou Navigation Satellite Demonstration System, which has been established in the period 2000-2003. The experimental BeiDou navigation system consisted of three satellites.
2. Phase-II is the regional BeiDou navigation satellite system covering China and neighbouring regions by 2012. By 2014, the system will be ready to initially offer high-precision positioning and navigation services to the Asia-Pacific region.
3. Phase-III is the BeiDou navigation satellite system to be established completely and provide global service by 2020.

China is planning to have a 35-satellite global navigational network by 2020. BeiDou supports both global worldwide services and regional services. The global services are further sub-divided into two other services: Open Service and Authorized Service. The Open Service is similar to the GPS (Global Positioning System) and Galileo is free and open to all users worldwide. The system is designed to provide a position accuracy of 10 metres, a timing accuracy of 50 ns and a velocity accuracy of 0.2 metres per second. While the Authorized Service aims at ensuring high reliable use even in complex situations and is expected to provide military-grade signals, for regional use, there are wide-area differential services and short message services.[14] The entire system is expected to be dynamic in nature. As the number of satellites increases, obviously the nature of services provided would improve. Some structural changes are also expected owing to the emergence of new technologies and based on the performance of the system.

The Beidou Phase III system comprises the migration of its civil Beidou-1 or B1 signal from 1561.098 MHz to a frequency centred at 1575.42 MHz—the same as the GPS-L1 and Galileo-E1 civil signals—and its transformation from a quadrature phase-shift keying (QPSK) modulation to a multiplexed binary offset carrier (MBOC) modulation similar to the future GPS-L1C and Galileo-E1. The Phase-II B1 open service signal uses QPSK modulation with 4.092 megahertz bandwidth centred at 1561.098 MHz. The existing (as in May 2019) Beidou constellation spacecraft are transmitting open and authorised signals at B2 (1207.14 MHz) and an authorised service at B3 (1268.52 MHz). Real-time, stand-alone Beidou horizontal positioning accuracy was classed as better than 6 metres (95 per cent) and with a vertical accuracy better than 10 metres (95 per cent).

Table 1[15] is based on various sources available on the Internet and gives a broad idea about various navigational system-related launches.

Table 1: Summary of Satellites

Block	*Launch Period*	*Satellite launches*			*Currently in orbit and healthy*
		Success	*Failure*	*Planned*	
1	2000-2006	4	0	0	0
2	2007-2014	20	0	0	16
3	2015-present	37	0	7	37
	Total	61	0	7	53

Last update: February 28, 2021.

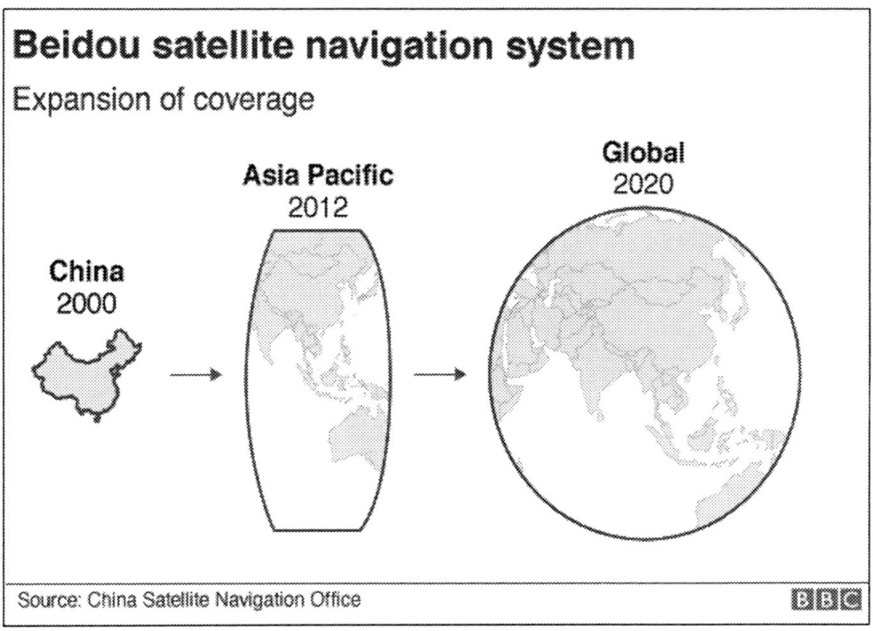

BeiDou has a significant user base in China. More than 6.17 million commercial vehicles are known to be using it. In particular, public transportation systems like buses, taxis, etc., are dependent on this system. There are 35,000 postal and express delivery vehicles and 80,000 buses in 36 cities depending on China's BDS and some 370 public service ships across the country. At present, the reach of BDS is possibly covering more than 50 countries with an approximate population of around 3 billion people. The system is also used in indigenous civilian aircraft.[16]

The BeiDou could be said to have applications beyond standard navigational inputs. It has been widely used for communication, marine fishery, hydrological monitoring, weather forecasting, surveying, mapping and geographic information, forest fire-prevention, time synchronisation for communication systems, power dispatching, disaster mitigation and relief, emergency search and rescue, and other fields.[17] The BRI member-states would have all these services available.

China is trying to plug in BDS with other global satellite systems to provide free use in search-and-rescue services around the world. It has been recognised by the International Civil Aviation Organization, International Maritime Organization and the 3rd Generation Partnership Project. (3GPP is a standards organisation that develops protocols for mobile telephony). The BDS has already been used in the Safe City Project in Phongsaly in northern Laos. It is used to maintain public security and position police forces and emergency vehicles. The BDS is expected to make the applications of the BeiDou system tailored to suit customers' needs. It can provide diverse and innovative services. For example, accurate positioning can be used in driving tests and overhauling tracks of high-speed railways. This system is expected to also have significant utility in arenas like disaster management. It would help to monitor landslides and dam deformations using accurate positioning. It is broadly argued that the capabilities of the BDS would be only limited by imagination.[18] There appears to be much attraction amongst BRI states for the acquisition of this system.

Space Silk Road[19]

A comprehensive evaluation of the Digital Silk Road is closely linked to China's activities in space. As part of the initiative, the country provides not only Internet connectivity but also satellite launches. Thus, the "Space-based Silk Road" is likely to encompass many powerful communications satellites and high-resolution remote-sensing satellites.

The Institute of Space & Earth Information Science (ISEIS) of the Chinese University of Hong Kong (CU) has signed an agreement with Dong Fang Teng Fei (DFTF, a subsidiary of the Beijing Xiangzhi company) during 2014 to join the "Space Silk Road" for developing global satellite services. To further international services for Chinese satellites, important aerospace enterprises and research institutes like the China Great Wall Industry Corporation, China Satellite Communication Co. Ltd., etc. have come together to form an International Alliance of Satellite Application Service (ASAS) in August 2014 and have initiated the "Space Silk Road" program to coordinate international cooperative research in space-based satellite technology for the 'Silk Road Economic Belt' strategy.

There are some projects, mostly at the bilateral level, which are not clearly identified as projects under the BRI umbrella. However, it appears that such projects would be part of (official or unofficial) the BRI mandate. Some projects could be said to have begun before the initiation of the BRI and now could be supported under BRI policies.

The most startling example today is of Argentina. Here one project has sparked broad international media interest. This is a 50 million USD Chinese-funded satellite and space mission control centre in the country's Patagonia region that had a role in landing a Chinese Rover on the far side of the moon in January 2019. The bilateral agreement was signed in 2012 (only in 2016, was the non-military clause been added) and gives Argentina access to antenna time at the control centre. However, there is no evidence that there are any scientific benefits for Argentina from this project. The project is run in a very secretive fashion and commoners, visitors and media have no access to the site. Also, no information about the nature of work being done is shared with the outside world.

In South Asia, Pakistan is an important partner for China in its Space Silk Road project. The science and technology relationship between Islamabad and Beijing dates back to the 1970s and has typically involved China's assistance in technology transfers, undertaking joint projects and in training. In recent times, the cooperation between the two countries has deepened and widened owing to the China-Pakistan Economic Corridor (CPEC), a flagship BRI project. They are planning to expand and deepen their collaboration in the areas of new and emerging technologies such as nanotechnology, biotechnology, and information and communications technology. Space is also one area which is getting a lot of attention. China has already launched satellites for Pakistan, and recently a remote sensing satellite was launched in 2018. Now, there is a proposal to cooperate in human spaceflight with the aim of sending a Pakistani astronaut into orbit by 2022. Their cooperation also extends to space security efforts in multilateral forums.[20]

By connecting industries and infrastructure projects along the BRI, China's satellite navigation and communications system hopes to dominate the new digital infrastructure in BRI space. As new ideas for space-based Internet services emerge, China is well ahead of the curve. Google, Amazon and SpaceX are all developing projects to provide broadband services around the world through networks of satellites numbering hundreds.[21]

China's space ambition neatly folds into the technological requirements of developing BRI countries. Control of the high ground of space would allow domination of the Earth because if information is the basis of 21st-century power, space is the domain through which that information will flow. While China presents these dramatic advances as part of its effort to promote space and digital connectivity through international cooperation, there is no mistaking its implications on all fronts, be it geopolitical, technological, foreign policy, or geostrategic.

Implications for India

India has been a staunch critic of China's multi-dimensional BRI, more so, because the initiative tends to overlook India's "sovereignty and territorial integrity". Especially with the 'string of pearls' theory coming into the realm of reality, New Delhi does fear being sidelined in its own region. This brings forth a necessity to dwell on the likely implications of not being a part of the initiative. Additionally, India's intent of staying away from the BRI needs to be backed by strong foreign policy objectives and strategy. Today, digital, air and space mediums are the major facilitators of economic growth and strategic benefits.

The Indian Space Research Organization (ISRO), ranks fifth in the world and has a record of launching the most satellites.[22] India has launched various types of satellites (ranging from Earth observation to strategic surveillance), rockets (capable of placing satellites in different types of orbits), space telescopes and undertaking deep space and planetary missions. ISRO also envisages sending humans into space in a couple of years from now.[23] Every mission in the space domain has been a technological challenge and has been accomplished with a high degree of self-reliance and capability, despite many international technology embargoes.[24] This is evident in the success of Mission Mangalyaan.[25]

India has been able to explore outer space more economically, but it has also become self-reliant and assists many nations in their space projects. India launched the South Asian Satellite to boost regional communications and improve disaster links amongst its six neighbours that have helped the country to carve a unique place in space diplomacy.[26]

Although India is making strides in the space sector, it substantially lags in the other two dimensions, especially with regard to innovation or the manufacture of digital and aviation equipment. Nonetheless, the country is vouching for advanced technologies like 5G, quantum computing and AI, especially for its Smart Cities endeavours. In order to set a roadmap for the rollout of 5G, the Government of India had set up a high-level forum which, in its report, suggested the early allocation of the 5G spectrum, increasing the quantum of spectrum available, and lowering its pricing. The panel had also suggested three initiatives—

attracting global 5G conference events to India, setting up national 5G events, and the creation of a comprehensive programme to develop India-specific 5G applications. Moreover, the country has repeatedly stated its ambition of "not missing the 5G" bus.[27]

India is also laying the foundation for advances in many emerging technologies, although it still has a long way to go. A model similar to that of space could be used for promoting digital and aviation diplomacy. However, the major challenge has been the lack of the manufacturing sector. Much of the infrastructure for these technologies would most likely rest upon either technology imports or on equipment made by foreign vendors in India. Nevertheless, the country has a huge market that could be used as economic leverage to achieve strategic objectives. Control over investments provides the Indian state with an economic tool to attain political and strategic objectives. The Indian government must keep this in mind while framing rules attracting foreign investment and regulating the participation of foreign firms in any sector.

Even technology collaboration should be given serious consideration wherein technology giants of different nations could be invited to build capacity in India. This will give a positive push to "Make in India" and the "Digital India" movements. However, India would need to lay down its own laws on data integrity, encryption, and access for law enforcement to electronic data, the Internet of Things and digital payments to ensure security as well as development.

The country can help facilitate alternative paths of growth for its immediate neighbours by leveraging its links with its extended neighbourhood. This should be done in ways that are transparent and mutually beneficial—in contrast to Chinese projects that are seen as debt-traps and one-way roads to Beijing's domination. This will help re-imagine a joint destiny of growth for India and its immediate neighbours, which will build more sustainable relationships and make the neighbours partners in India's growth.

Conclusion

The Belt and Road Initiative is a mercurial concept laid out by China that has a life of its own. This initiative is different from the original concept of the Silk Route in the sense that the 21st Century Silk Route encapsulates all the mediums of connectivity under a single umbrella. Such an endeavour would not only facilitate the passage for economic growth but would also act as a conduit to export China's model of the economy (Beijing Consensus) and cyber governance. There are several long-term benefits of the BRI that China may enjoy later in the decade.

Many of these digital projects are looked upon as blessings by developing countries as they cater to the needs of the economically weaker countries and offer cost-effective products for the local populace. China does have a knack of understanding the local needs. For instance, it is building ICT infrastructure for many African countries. In Myanmar, in 2017, less than 1 per cent of the population had broadband access. Now, the country's Minister of Transport and Communication is operating with Huawei to bring in 5G broadband services by 2025, thereby overleaping many generations of mobile networks.[28] China is also aiding in space projects of various developing nations. It has helped Ethiopia to launch its first satellite in September 2019.[29] In January 2018, China gave 550 million USD to Nigeria for the purchase of two satellites from Chinese manufacturers which were to be launched in the next two years. Even Brazil has collaborated with China to launch a jointly developed satellite to monitor the Amazon rainforest.

However, the behaviour of nations is often guided by national interests as underscored in the realism school of thought. China's development approach is driven by a desire to have equitable, high-quality growth with more focus on self-reliance, especially with the rise of unilateralism and trade protectionism. Such advancement is defined by a ruthless willingness to innovate and experiment, by a lively defence of national borders and interests, and by the increasingly thoughtful accumulation of tools of asymmetric power projection.

The scale of Chinese state support for emerging and space technologies undermines the ability of many states to compete fairly either within China or in third markets. It is known by many players that first-mover advantage in deployment will create new revenue streams from the expanded use of the IoT and other 5G-enabled technologies, and so enable faster advancements in a country's development. This will also enable China to set standards of technologies that are still in the pipeline. In 2015, the Chinese leadership set up a "Special Leading Small Group on the Major Project of Standardization along with the BRI project" to coordinate the idea of "first develop then regulate".[30] Currently, China is the only country ahead of the UN's International Telecommunication Union's "2020 5G development schedule". Chinese experts are leading the way in the 5G group of the International Organization for Standardization (ISO) (also called 3GPP). It has been estimated that China is the leader in the standardisation of 5G, the Internet of Things, and block chain technology. The standard-setting process is crucial as it will determine not just how networks would be built but also how money flows between participants in the technology ecosystem.

Besides, China being the leading supplier of ICT, space and aviation infrastructure and services, it would mean sufficient leverage for it to manipulate the policy options of those states as it would control the vital capabilities that support their economic growth. In 2018, a report titled "The Rise of Digital Authoritarianism" accused China of being the front runner of abusers of Internet freedom, and also blamed it for exporting its "techno-dystopian" model to other nations.[31] Egypt, for instance, has been drawing heavily from China's model of cyber governance.[32] In 2018, the country passed a cybercrime law that infringes on the individual's rights in the name of national security.[33] China has hosted a two-week-long seminar on "Cyberspace Management" for officials of countries along the BRI, besides conducting sessions on its systems of surveillance and censorship for media officials from Morocco, Libya, and Egypt.[34] Promoting its own model of cyber governance (that is, sovereign cyberspace) enables China to protect its own critical information infrastructure from unwanted cyber intrusion and foreign data access. At the same time, controlling data would allow the country to monitor enterprises and citizens to enforce compliant and conformist behaviour.

The idea of the "Digital, Air and Space Silk Road" is almost nearing reality. On 29 May 2015, the China Satellite Global Services Alliance (CSGSA) and the International Trade Centre (ITC) jointly held the 2nd China Satellite Global Services International Cooperative Talks where international experts discussed the construction of the Space Silk Road. With an increase in global aviation traffic in general and an increase in traffic in the region owing to the Belt and Road network, a rise in the safety demands of civilian airlines is expected. The disappearance of Malaysia Airlines flight MH370 and the shooting down of flight MH17 over Ukraine highlights the need for a more comprehensive satellite network to provide additional and real-time information about aircraft positions.

The existing black box in aircraft provides information only after a mishap (provided it is found undamaged). China wants to use the Space Silk Road system to create a live-feed "black box" which would provide constant global coverage of all air, shipping and overland routes. The system is also expected to enable planes and satellites to communicate with each other. China proposes to use the Beidou navigational network as one of the important components in this system. Obviously, all this would require an addition to the civilian aircraft equipment inventory adding relevant transmitters, receivers, data storage equipment, etc. This could generate additional business too.

Seamless Internet connectivity and digital infrastructure backed by emerging technologies would be essential for the success of space BRI as there could be issues with aircraft and ships passing through areas covered by different satellite signals. The leading satellite company in China, China Satellite Communications, has plans to launch new satellites using Ka-band frequency (offering higher speeds and requiring a smaller satellite dish for operations) that will envelop the BRI region in the near future.

With data becoming the new-age goldmine, there would always be a potential threat of cyber espionage and 'back doors'. China has often been accused of cyber-plots to steal intellectual property. An article titled "Chinese Hackers Target Universities in Pursuit of Maritime Military Secrets" described more than two dozen universities suffering data breaches related to maritime technology with military applications. Universities, which often lack security controls, are often subject to cyber-attacks.[35] Huawei has also been accused of stealing trade secrets, and countries have been encouraged not to use Huawei's 5G technology, alleging it contains 'back doors' for the Chinese government.

Additionally, China's control over a vast amount of data is the most obvious strategic risk. By controlling data flow, China can understand markets better, identify and eliminate local competitors, and carry out commercial research and development, thus limiting the capacity of regional players to reap the economic benefits of data produced in the region. This may lead to "data colonialism" or "data authoritarianism",[36] that is, in the near future economic power and international favouritism shall be reaped by those who would control the data.

The mighty three Silk Roads in the digital, air and the space mediums are set to remake the whole landscape of international development, economics and society and, by extension, politics. A new World Bank Group study has also promoted the BRI stating that it could "speed up economic development and reduce poverty for dozens of developing countries; but it must be accompanied by deep policy reforms that increase transparency, improve debt sustainability, and mitigate environmental, social and corruption risks".[37] Improving connectivity will allow information exchanges, bring about "mutual benefit and win-win cooperation" and realise the long nurtured "Chinese dream", according to a White Paper of the Chinese government.

Dependency on economic growth does reduce the timeline for growth and prosperity. However, development of any kind needs to be based on reciprocal and transparent cooperation. There is a need for states to take an approach where they exercise maximum oversight on Chinese developments within the country. When a security system is being set up, it is important to change the password. It is vital for developing countries to build and ascertain secure supply chains. It is also pertinent to minimise the risks by testing and verifying the security aspects of imported equipment and safeguard balanced reciprocal conditions with regard to China. At the same time, it is necessary to devise effective and autonomous policies to ensure the system of effective checks and balances. Another important move has to be towards data localisation rather than allowing the data to be stored in other countries where it is susceptible to attack and misuse. The BRI is like candy given to placate children. However, excess candy may lead to rotting of the teeth. So there always needs to be an effective mechanism to control and check these developments lest the implications are too big to control!

NOTES

1. "About the Silk Road," *United Nations Educational, Scientific and Cultural Organization,* see https://en.unesco.org/silkroad/about-silk-road, accessed 15 March 2019.
2. Frank Holmes, "China's Belt and Road Initiative Opens Up Unprecedented Opportunities," *Forbes*, 4 September 2018.
3. Longmei Zhang & Sally Chen, "China's Digital Economy: Opportunities and Risks, "*IMF Working Paper,* January 2019.
4. "Vision and Actions on Jointly Building Silk Road Economic Belt and 21st-Century Maritime Silk Road," National Development and Reform Commission, (NDRC) People's Republic of China, March 2015, see http://en.ndrc.gov.cn/newsrelease/201503/t20150330_669367.html
5. See https://www.ctamericas.com/chinas-internet-plus-future/
6. Visit https://time.com/5623537/china-space/, accessed 26 December 2019.
7. "China`s Space Silk Road," *Medium,* May 25, 2018, see https //medium.com/@beltandroad/china-s-space-silk-road-4e09721543a6, accessed 12 March 2019.
8. "China's BeiDou navigation system to serve B&R countries," *Xinhua News Agency,* 16 November 2018, see https://eng.yidaiyilu.gov.cn/qwyw/rdxw/71826.htm, accessed 15 May 2019.
9. "China's BeiDou Navigation Satellite System," White Paper, 16 June 2016, see http://www.china.org.cn/government/whitepaper/2016-06/16/content_38681076.htm, accessed 12 February 2019.
10. "China's 'One Belt, One Road' Takes to Space," *The Wall Street Journal,* 28 December 2016, see https://blogs.wsj.com/chinarealtime/2016/12/28/chinas-one-belt-one-road-takes-to-space/ accessed 12 February 2019.
11. 'BeiDou Experimental Satellite Navigation System', see http://www.astronautix.com/craft/beidou.html, accessed 30 June 2019.
12. Ajey Lele, "Autonomy in Satellite Navigation Systems: The Indian Programme", *Indian Foreign Affairs Journal* Vol. 9, No. 3, July–September 2014, 240-254.
13. "CNSS," *eoPortal Directory*, see https://directory.eoportal.org/web/eoportal/satellite-missions/content/-/article/cnss, accessed 11 May 2019.
14. "BeiDou Services," *esanavipedia*, see https://gssc.esa.int/navipedia/index.php/BeiDou_Services, accessed 8 May 2019.
15. https://en.wikipedia.org/wiki/BeiDou, accessed 25 December 2019.
16. "10 BeiDou satellites to be launched by China this year," *Geospatial World,* February 2019, see https://www.geospatialworld.net/news/10-beidou-satellites-to-be-launched-by-china-this-year/, accessed 16 May 2019.
17. Rui C. Barbosa, "Beidou-3 navigation satellite launched on Long March 3B," *NASA Spaceflight.com,* 20 April 2019, see https://www.nasaspaceflight.com/2019/04/beidou-3g2q-navigation-long-march-3b/, accessed 10 May 2019.

18. "China's BeiDou navigation system to serve B&R countries," *Xinhua News Agency*, 16 November 2018, see https://eng.yidaiyilu.gov.cn/qwyw/rdxw/71826.htm, accessed 15 May 2019.
19. This section is based on author's earlier work available at https://idsa.in/idsacomments/silk-road-initiative-via-aerospace_alele_211015, accessed 16 May 2019.
20. "Space Silk Road: Pakistan And China Enhance Space, Science And Technology Cooperation," *Spacewatch Asia Pacific*, see https://spacewatch.global/2018/11/pakistan-and-china-enhance-space-science-and-technology-cooperation/, accessed 28 April 2019.
21. C. Rajamohan, "Raja Mandala: A silk road for the heavens," *The Indian Express,* 23 April 2019, see https://indianexpress.com/article/opinion/columns/india-china-silk-route-beijing-belt-and-road-initiative-big-earth-data-5689184/ accessed 8 May 2019.
22. https://www.socialcube.in/isro/
23. Dinesh C. Sharma, "Space Race 2.0: ISRO now Stands at the Cusp of Next Change," *DownToEarth*, 6 May 2019, see https://www.downtoearth.org.in/news/science-technology/space-race-2-0-isro-now-stands-at-the-cusp-of-nextchange-64257
24. Ibid.
25. Ajey Lele, "Mangalyaan's Mars Orbit: One Giant Leap for India, One Small Step for Mankind," *The Wall Street Journal,* 24 September 2014, see https://blogs.wsj.com/indiarealtime/2014/09/24/mangalyaans-mars-orbit-one-giantleap-for-india-one-small-step-for-mankind/
26. South Asian Satellite to boost regional communication, Press Information Bureau, Government of India, 7 May 2017, see https://pib.gov.in/newsite/printrelease.aspx?relid=161611
27. Navadha Pandey, "India's Game Plan to Switch on 5G Connections," *LiveMint,* 4 October 2018, see https://www.livemint.com/Industry/Kf4PMD5CxQMB5AKR6gBcEP/Indias-game-plan-to-switch-on-5Gconnectionhtml, accessed 24 September 2019.
28. Chan Jia Hao, "China's Digital Silk Road: A Game Changer for Asian Economies," *The Diplomat,* 30 April 2019, see https://thediplomat.com/2019/04/chinasdigital-silk-road-a-game-changer-for-asian-economies/
29. https://www.aljazeera.com/ajimpact/ethiopia-launches-satellite-china-191220064331417.html
30. Kristin Shi-Kupfer & Mareike Ohlberg, "China's Digital Rise," *Mercator,* Institute for China Studies, April 2019, see https://www.merics.org/sites/default/files/2019-04/MPOC_No.7_ChinasDigitalRise_web_4.pdf
31. Emily Dreyfuss, "The Internet Became Less Free In 2018. Can We Fight Back?" *Wire,* 26 December 2018, see https://www.wired.com/story/internet-freedomchina-2018/
32. Tin Hinane El Kadi, "The Promise and Peril of the Digital Silk Road," *Chatham House,* June 2019, see https://www.chathamhouse.org/expert/comment/promise-and-peril-digital-silk-road
33. Tin Hinane El Kadi, "The Promise and Peril of the Digital Silk Road," *Chatham House,* June 2019, see https://www.chathamhouse.org/expert/comment/promise-and-peril-digital-silk-road
34. Abdi Latif Dahir, "China is exporting its digital surveillance methods to African governments," *Quartz Africa,* November 2018, see https://qz.com/africa/1447015/china-is-helping-african-countries-control-the-internet/
35. See, https://www.iotworldtoday.com/2019/05/01/made-in-china-2025-plan-still-controversial-in-the-west/
36. Yuval Noah Harari, "Who Will Win the Race for AI?" *FP Global Thinkers,* 2019, see https://foreignpolicy.com/gt-essay/who-will-win-the-race-for-ai-unitedstates-china-data/
37. "Success of China's Belt & Road Initiative Depends on Deep Policy Reforms, Study Finds," The World Bank, 18 June 2019, see https://www.worldbank.org/ en/news/press-release/2019/06/18/success-of-chinas-belt-road-initiativedepends-on-deep-policy-reforms-study-finds, accessed 24 September 2019.

17

China's Digital Belt and Road Initiative: Emerging Concerns

Arun Vishwanathan

The ambitious Chinese government project of connecting China to the countries and economies in Europe, South America, Asia, and Australia popularly known as the Belt and Road Initiative (BRI) was announced in 2013 during the visit of Chinese President Xi Jinping to Central Asia and South East Asia. During the September 2013 visit to Kazakhstan, President Xi, speaking at Nazarbaev University, spoke about "jointly building the Silk Road Economic Belt...which will open up the transportation channel from the Pacific to the Baltic Sea and to gradually form a transportation network that connects East Asia, West Asia, and South Asia".[1]

In October 2013, during a visit to Indonesia, President Xi spoke at the Indonesian Parliament about the "21st Century Maritime Silk Road...supplying each other's needs and complementing each other's strengths, to jointly seize opportunities and meeting challenges for the benefit of common development and prosperity".[2] The Silk Road economic belt forms the overland component of this project while the Maritime Silk Road forms the maritime component of this project. The project is also known by alternative names which include Belt and Road Initiative (BRI), One Belt, One Road (OBOR), and the Chinese name for the initiative namely, *yidaiyilu*.[3]

With the emergence of China as a global power, the BRI has enormous historical significance for the Chinese. This is indicated by the fact that the Chinese President announced such an important pet project of the Chinese government during his visits to Kazakhstan and Indonesia. During the reign of the Han dynasty, the historical Silk Road connected China to countries like India, Pakistan, and Afghanistan in South Asia as well as the Central Asian countries like Kyrgyzstan, Tajikistan, Turkmenistan, and Uzbekistan to European countries. It was to underline this historical connection that President Xi Jinping announced the project during his visit to Central Asia and South East Asia.

Given the importance attached to the initiative and the plan to complete the entire project by 2049—on the occasion of the 100th anniversary of the establishment of the People's Republic of China—a policy framework paper was prepared for the BRI at the apex level with the authorisation of the State Council. The Ministry of Foreign Affairs, Ministry of Commerce, National Development and Reform Commission all were part of the paper which was entitled "Vision and Actions on Jointly Building Silk Road Economic Belt and 21st Century Maritime Silk Road" released in March 2015.[4]

The centrality of the Belt and Road Initiative (BRI) for the Chinese establishment and top leadership can be gauged from the fact that during the 19th National Congress held in 2017, the BRI was incorporated into the Chinese constitution. The amendment stated that the BRI furthered "the principle of achieving shared growth through discussion and collaboration, and pursuing the Belt and Road Initiative".[5] President Xi views the BRI as his legacy and speaking at the first Belt and Road Forum in 2017 he underlined the importance of the BRI in changing existing relations between countries stating that "...exchange will replace estrangement, mutual learning will replace clashes, and coexistence will replace a sense of superiority...the initiative would boost mutual understanding, mutual respect and mutual trust among different countries".[6]

Connectivity is one of the major hallmarks of the BRI project. This has taken the shape of trans-continental railway lines linking China to Europe, roads and highways, deep-water ports, energy pipelines, and many such associated projects. Beijing has been steaming ahead with the project with over 120 countries signing cooperation agreements with China and becoming part of the BRI initiative. The Chinese have invested more than US$ 100 billion in infrastructure-related projects which form part of the BRI.[7] However, interestingly, the geographical scope of the project continues to expand from traditional routes with historical significance to projects which have economic, strategic significance like the maritime passage to Europe via the Arctic.

In addition to physical connectivity, the State Council-authorised Framework and Vision document for the BRI also pushed for digital connectivity. The report outlining its plans for a future digital BRI stated, "We should jointly advance the construction of cross-border optical cables and other communications trunk line networks, improve international communications connectivity, and create an Information Silk Road. We should build bilateral cross-border optical cable networks at a quicker pace, plan transcontinental submarine optical cable projects, and improve spatial (satellite) information passageways to expand information exchanges and cooperation".[8]

The various components and spread of existing and planned BRI projects across the globe are graphically depicted in an excellent map by the *Mercator Institute for China Studies* (Figure 1).

However, the Initiative has had its share of significant pushback both from the USA and also from India which did not send an official delegation to both the major Belt and Road Forums held in 2017 and 2019. However, this pushback is part of a larger concern about China's continued rise, which is no longer seen as 'rising peacefully'!! This chapter will deal with these concerns about the Chinese BRI project in subsequent sections. After providing an overview of the BRI project and its evolution and broad plans, the chapter will move on to highlight the plans under the Digital BRI or what is also known as the Digital Silk Road.

Tracing the Evolution of Digital BRI

The foundation for the digital connectivity component of the Belt and Road Initiative, also known as Digital BRI, was laid in the framework Vision Document which was sanctioned by the State Council and released in March 2015. As mentioned in earlier paragraphs, the Vision Document laid out three major elements of the Digital BRI Initiative. This included the following:

1. International cross-border optical cables and other similar communication networks which were aimed at improving international communications connectivity,
2. Participation of Chinese hardware and software companies in the digitisation of the BRI initiative with the supply of networks, telecommunications, and related equipment and spread Chinese cyber norms and,
3. Improving spatial (satellite) information passageways to expand information exchanges and cooperation.

Additional details about the Digital BRI program became available following

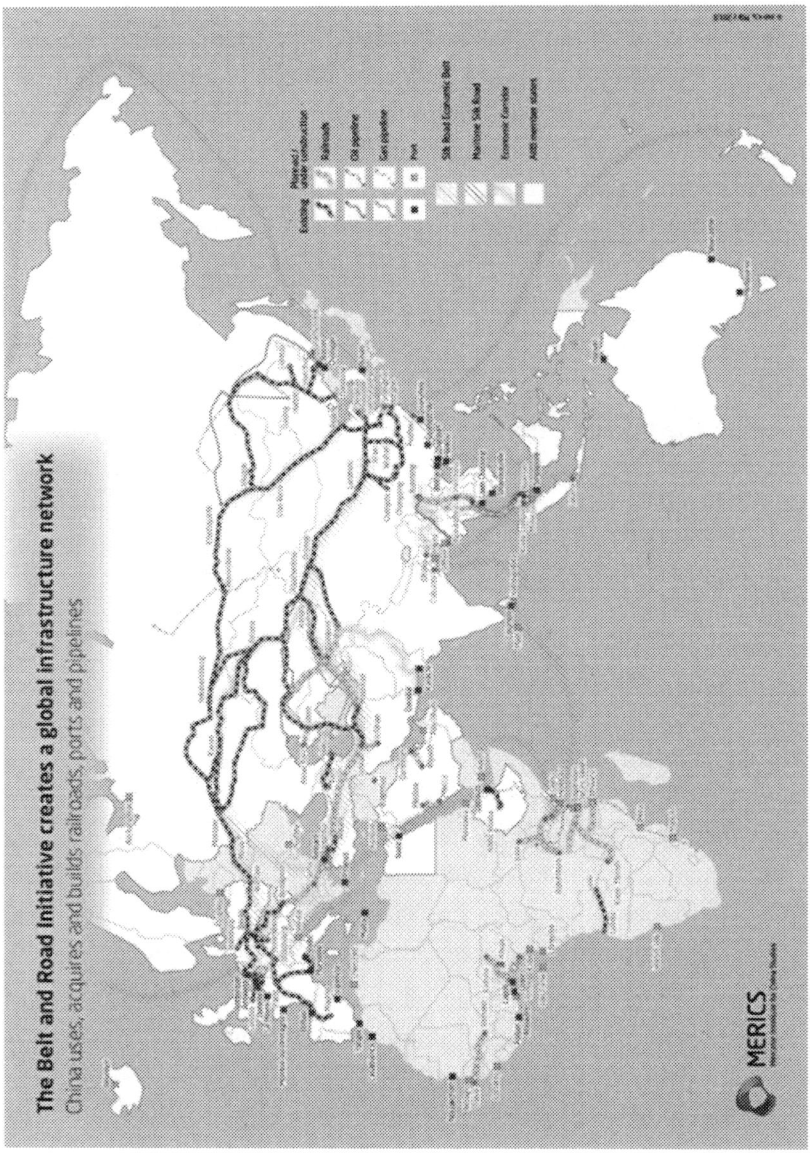

Figure 1: Global Infrastructure Network Planned under the Belt and Road Initiative[9]

the release of the Vision Framework document in March 2015. The digital connectivity element of the overall BRI project too received constant support from President Xi. The State Administration of Science, Technology, and Industry for National Defence and the National Development and Reform Commission (NDRC) jointly came up with a guideline paper in November 2016 to facilitate the construction of the above-mentioned digital connectivity networks and its key facilities.[10]

Speaking at the First Belt and Road Forum for International Cooperation (BRF) in May 2017, President Xi Jinping emphasised: "on information facility connectivity but also on information sharing", He stressed on the need for "innovation-driven development" and the need to pursue cooperation in "frontier technological areas such as digital economy, artificial intelligence, nanotechnology, and quantum computing, and to advance the development of big data, Cloud computing and smart cities".[11] The statement makes it very clear that the Chinese leadership is quite focussed on harnessing the opportunity presented by the BRI project to foster the development of emerging technologies in the digital domain to ensure Chinese dominance in it in the coming years and decades.

The Chinese have been backing their ambitions with adequate funding to push for the BRI projects. While it has been estimated that the Chinese have spent an estimated US$ 100 billion on infrastructure-related BRI projects,[12] they aim to spend an equally large sum towards developing capacities and capabilities in the digital BRI domain. The Mercator Institute for China Studies estimates that Chinese entities have spent close to US$ 17 billion on completed digital BRI projects encompassing the laying of undersea optic-fibre cables, e-commerce, and mobile payment projects and the like.[13] However, given the lack of reliable data, the actual figure could be much higher.

The Chinese Artificial Intelligence (AI) Strategy, which was released by the State Council in August 2017, outlines a Chinese whole-of-government approach in the field of artificial intelligence. The strategy plans to increase the Chinese AI industry from the existing worth of around RMB 10 billion (US$ 1.5 billion) to RMB 400 billion (US$ 60 billion) by 2025 and become a global "premier innovation centre" on AI by 2030 with a net worth of RMB 1 trillion (US$ 150 billion) by 2030.[14]

The document outlines the importance of Artificial Intelligence (AI) for economic development and social construction. The document describes AI as the "core driving force for a new round of industrial transformation, [which] will advance the release of the huge energy stored from the previous scientific and technological revolution and industrial transformation, and create a new powerful engine, reconstructing production, distribution, exchange, consumption, etc., links in economic activities".[15]

Equally important for the Chinese is the use of AI for maintaining social stability amongst its population, for decision-making, to provide early warning for planning social security operations, disaster relief, and possibly also for monitoring its population in general and dissidents in particular. The 2017 strategy document states:

> "The widespread use of AI in education, medical care, pensions, environmental protection, urban operations, judicial services, and other fields will greatly improve the level of precision in public services, comprehensively enhancing the people's quality of life. AI technologies can accurately sense, forecast, and provide early warning of major situations for infrastructure facilities and social security operations; grasp group cognition and psychological changes promptly; and take the initiative in decision-making and reactions—which will significantly elevate the capability and level of social governance, playing an irreplaceable role in effectively maintaining social stability."[16]

Another significant policy announcement about Digital BRI was made by President Xi Jinping at the National Cyber Security and Informatization Work Conference in Beijing on April 20–21, 2018. Placing the context of the announcement is equally important given the fact that the Chinese cyberspace authorities had been recently upgraded to a commission from a central leading group. It was against this backdrop that President Xi who is also the Chair of the Central Commission for Cyber security and Informatization (also known as the Central Cyberspace Affairs Commission), outlined the top-level priorities for the country in the domain. President Xi stressed the importance of indigenous innovation in becoming a cyber superpower in the coming years and spoke of the opportunity that was presented to China in the domain of:

> "...informatisation development, strengthen online positive propaganda, safeguard cyber security, promote breakthroughs in core technologies in the information area, give rein to the guiding role of informatisation in economic development, strengthen civil-military integration in the cyber security and informatisation domain, actively participate in international cyberspace governance processes".

The speech by the Chinese president lays out the major focus areas of the Chinese in the digital domain which focus on the development of Internet infrastructure, development of associated technologies indigenously, pushing digital economy, cyber security, and push for fostering international cyberspace governance. The next section of the article will look at the geographical areas and the focus of the Digital BRI project followed by the concerns which have been raised about the program across the globe.

Spread and Focus of Chinese Digital BRI Project

As outlined in the above paragraphs, the initiation of the digital BRI program can be traced to the Vision Framework document released by the State Council in March 2015. Over the past five-odd years, we have seen the rapid growth of the Chinese BRI Initiative across the globe. Similarly, the digital BRI Initiative encompasses digital connectivity in the form of global crisscrossing optic fibre cables carrying voice and data, mobile telephony networks, digital and e-payment infrastructures, artificial intelligence, surveillance equipment, and technology as well as space-based satellites providing imaging, positioning as well as many other services to BRI-partner countries. The Chinese are supplying or bundling many of these technologies as part of the 'smart shipping' or 'smart cities' projects that they are pushing across various corners of the globe. The BRI has spread across various parts of Asia starting from South East Asia to South Asia to Central Asia, to the Middle East, Europe as well as various parts of Africa and Latin America.[17] Figure 2 from the Mercator Institute for China Studies highlights the various aspects and the geographical spread of the digital BRI program launched by the Chinese.[18]

Cross-border Submarine and Terrestrial Fibre Optic Cables and Data Centres

A very significant component of the Chinese BRI project is the submarine and terrestrial fibre optic cables and data centres that it has either constructed or been planning as part of the BRI project. The majority of international data traffic, whether voice or data, is transmitted through underwater fibre optic cables which crisscross the world. As most of these undersea cables are controlled by the USA, China is using this opportunity to change the status quo.

It is against this background that it sought to use the BRICS grouping to push for an undersea fibre optic cable network supported by the group's members; this, however, did not get much traction due to the concerns of the other members with data security. China also sees the laying of overland and undersea fibre optic cables as an economic opportunity, especially in landlocked countries in Central Asia, Africa, among others. Once these countries have good Internet connectivity, Chinese e-commerce companies like Alibaba and JD.com find it easier to access those markets. This is a point that will be dealt with in subsequent paragraphs.

China has been working on undersea and terrestrial fibre optic cables for

Figure 2: Digital Silk Road[19]

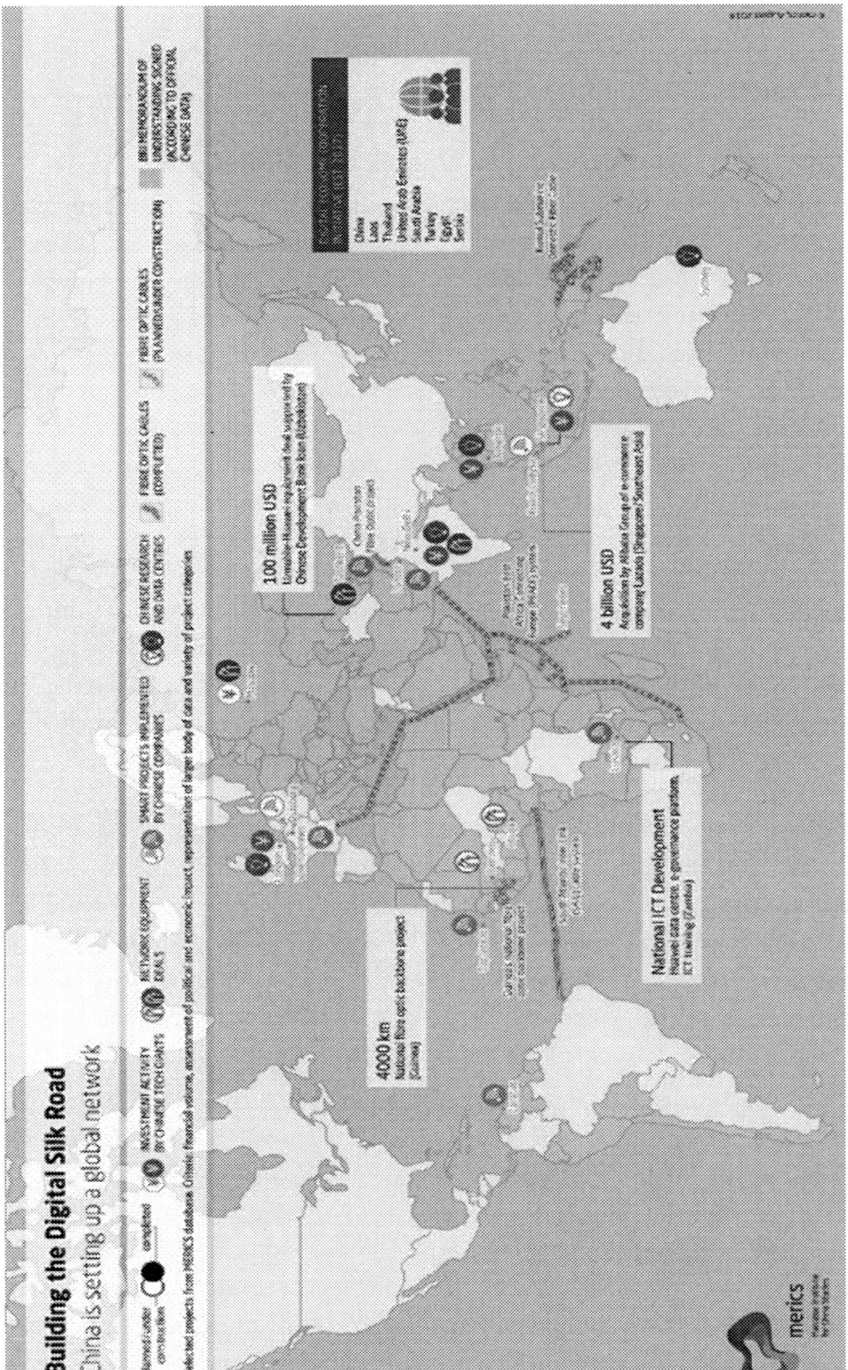

many years before the launch of the digital BRI Initiative. Sanchita Basu Das (2017) notes that as far back as 2006, Chinese private players ZTE and Huawei were asked to put in place the fibre-optic network in Afghanistan and Tajikistan. Similarly, Chinese companies have partnered with Russia to work on the world's longest Trans-Europe Asia cable link, and the Europe-Russia-Mongolia-China network, the TransEurasian Information Superhighway, and the Diverse Route for European and Asian Markets.[20] In 2014, Chinese telecom majors, China Telecom, China Mobile, and China Unicom, jointly worked on the SeaMeWe-5 submarine cable connecting South East Asia, the Middle East, and West Europe.[21] These companies have also been working together to build a "China-ASEAN Information Harbour" and they also own the Southeast Asia-Japan as well as the Asia Pacific Network-2 fibre optic cables.

China has also been working on the fibre optic cable network in Pakistan as part of the China-Pakistan cooperation under the CPEC which Beijing plans to extend to Central Asia and Europe.[22] To cater to the landlocked Central Asian region, China has signed agreements with Tajikistan, Kyrgyzstan and Afghanistan to put in place the Silk Road Fibre Optic Cable project.[23] Chinese telecom major Unicom has also put in place the 6,000-km South Atlantic Inter Link (SAIL) fibre optic cable network connecting Cameroon port of Kribi to Fortaleza in Brazil at an estimated cost of US$ 136 million.[24] Sen Gong et al. note that the Huawei Corporation has put in place "more than half of the wireless towers, 70% of the Long-Term Evolution (LTE) mobile broadband network, and more than 50,000 km of the optical cable network in over 50 countries in Africa".[25] The Mumbai-based Gateway House researcher, Chaitynya Giri, has put out an interesting map (Figure 3) detailing the expanding Chinese global telecom empire.[26]

Andre Wheeler, writing in *Silk Road Briefing,* estimates that with all these efforts China either owns or is assisting with the building of approximately 30 per cent of existing cables in Asia and a 54 per cent share of planned cables. Globally China, therefore, owns or supplies 11 per cent of the existing cables and 24 per cent of the planned cables.[27] With these efforts, it is shortly likely to break the global stranglehold of the USA over cross-border fibre optic cable networks.

A major area of focus highlighted by the "Made in China 2025" policy unveiled by Premier Li Kiqiang in 2015 was on developing, implementing, and developing an ecosystem around 5G technologies. The policy aims to transform China into a technological powerhouse in 10 strategic sectors within a decade. They include New Information Technology, Numerical Control Tools, Aerospace Equipment,

Figure 3: 5G Mobile Technology and Cellular Wireless Infrastructure

High tech Ships, Railway Equipment, Energy Saving, New Materials, Medical Devices, Agricultural Machinery, and Power Equipment.[28]

As Chinese companies enjoy the first-mover advantage in 5G over American and European companies, they are aggressively pushing for adoption of their equipment, standards, and technology across mobile and cellular networks in various parts of the globe. This is given the Chinese understanding that once Chinese 5G equipment and standards are adopted, it will be very hard for other companies to penetrate these markets given the prohibitively high capital cost and time required in switching over and replacing these technologies and equipment.

5G technologies are touted as the next big thing, given their ability to support greater bandwidth and carry more data and voice, and more reliability and support connectivity between various Internet of Thing (IoT) devices and systems. To this end, large amounts of money and manpower have been invested by Chinese government companies like the China Telecom, China Unicom, and China Mobile as well as private firms and Chinese government-supported firms like Huawei and ZTE into developing 5G technologies.

Besides South Korea, which has about 10 per cent of its country's networks on 5G technologies already, China is the only other country that is rapidly setting up 5G networks. The Chinese plan to set up more than half a million 5G base stations with tens of thousands being added every week in its bid to secure its leadership position in 5G as well as boost the sagging domestic economy.[29] This is part of the "new Infrastructure" campaign that China has launched to boost domestic growth and link IoT technologies with the economy. Huawei has won contracts worth US$ 4 billion for 5G rollout across China since the beginning of 2020. Scott Bicheno, writing for *Telecoms.com,* has estimated that Huawei and ZTE between them have won almost 88 per cent of the massive US$ 170 billion (1.2 trillion Yuan) joint tender floated by China Telecom and China Unicom for 5G rollout across mainland China.[30] At a time when the global economy has slowed down due to the COVID-19 pandemic, Chinese companies like Huawei and ZTE are relying on domestic growth to come out of the first economic contraction in several decades.[31]

As Ajey Lele and Kritika Roy point out in their IDSA Occasional Paper on the issue, Chinese companies are the global leaders (Figure 4) on 5G patents with 2,386 patents as compared to 1,388 filed by LG and 1,353 filed by Samsung. Lele and Roy point out that Huawei has invested over US$ 600 million for R&D in 5G technologies since 2009.[32]

Figure 4: Top Companies in Declared 5G Patents[33]

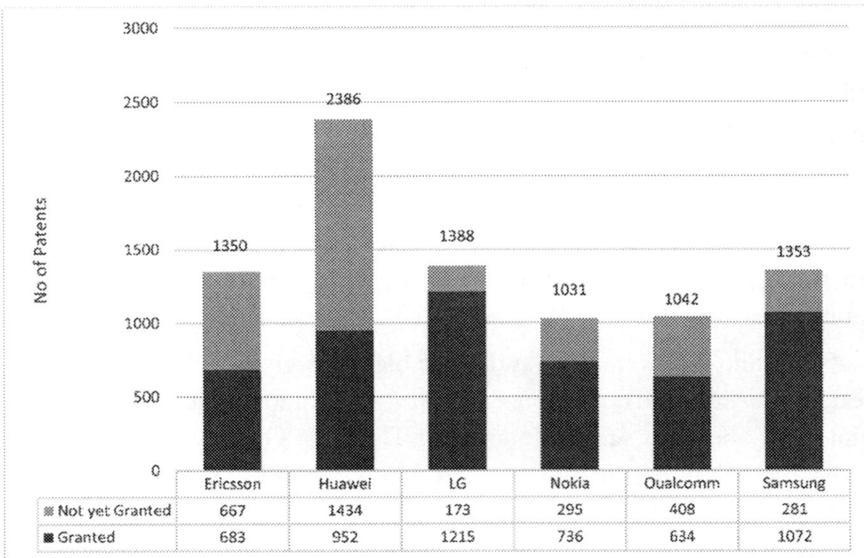

Another important stakeholder in the BRI and Chinese push for overseas investment is the Chinese state-backed banking institutions. These include the China Development Bank (CDB), Industrial and Commercial Bank of China (ICBC), China International Trade and Investment Corporation (CITIC), China Export and Credit Insurance Corporation (CECIC), Sinosure, and the China Export-Import Bank. These companies have been spearheading the Chinese push for infrastructure development and connectivity projects in foreign shores.[34] In some cases, it has been noticed that after receiving funding from these institutions, Chinese companies are chosen to execute the contracts. This makes one wonder whether there is a *quid pro quo* in such funding by the Chinese banking institutions.

One such case was the credit line of US$ 2.5 billion extended by the Industrial and Commercial Bank of China and the China Development Bank to the Indian telecom major, Bharati Airtel, to modernise its telecommunication equipment. Following this, the Indian telecom major selected Chinese telecom equipment companies like Huawei and ZTE to supply the network and telecom equipment to execute its projects. MERICs point out that Russia's Rostelecom also received US$ 600 million in part to purchase Huawei and ZTE equipment.[35]

Digital Economy, Digital Payment, and Cross-border e-commerce in BRI Countries

One of the important threads that run across the various projects unveiled under the Chinese BRI and the digital BRI program is bolstering Chinese economic growth and support to its own companies. As part of the "Made in China 2025" and "Internet Plus" initiative, the Chinese have been pushing for deploying e-commerce, payment gateways, and infrastructure in various parts of the globe ranging from Africa, parts of Asia, South East Asia, etc. This is done with the specific aim of allowing Chinese companies to tap these rather 'virgin' markets whose immense economic potential is yet untapped.

China is globally the second-largest retail market with sales of US$ 5.8 trillion in 2019. China's e-commerce market has grown at a phenomenal compounded annual growth rate of 120 per cent between 2003 and 2011.[36] The Chinese are trying to expand this successful business model overseas by introducing preferential duty rates and allowing international companies to sell goods to Chinese customers through Chinese e-commerce websites without holding a business licence. Between 2015 and 2018, Deloitte estimates that cross-border e-commerce turnover from China has grown at a rate of about 76 per cent.[37] In 2019, the total export value of the cross-border e-commerce players in China amounted to about 94.4 billion yuan which is a substantial increase from around 56.1 billion yuan in 2018. China's leading cross-border e-commerce retailer, AliExpress, had about 150 million overseas buyers in 2018.[38]

Chinese e-commerce conglomerates like Alibaba and JD.com would then ride on the strength and availability of these robust digital payment and internet platforms and expand their e-commerce operations in these countries. As K. Brown and A. Burjanadze write, such cooperation to put in place ICT, digital payment networks led to larger sales by the Chinese e-commerce giants. The availability of shipping and overland freight connectivity as a result of the BRI project also helped the supply chain and allowed companies to ramp up their capacity in these new markets in a very short time.[39]

As Hong Shen notes, it is a part of taking leadership in this sector that Jack Ma, co-founder of the Chinese conglomerate, Alibaba, proposed an Electronic World Trade Platform–an electronic equivalent of the WTO—in 2016. This proposal immediately received support from the Chinese government and was incorporated in the G20 Leaders Communique at the Hangzhou Summit.[40] The BRI program, which improves connectivity and access to markets and the digital BRI, which puts in place Internet connectivity, mobile, and e-payment platforms fosters cross-border growth of e-commerce by Chinese companies. Given the fact that cross-border sales account for only around 2.2 per cent of Chinese online retail sales, the leadership is aware of the huge potential for long-term growth in this sector.

Chinese Plans for a 'Space Silk Road'

The concept of a Space Silk Road was introduced by the Chinese in the 2014 International Alliance of Satellite Application Services (ASAS) and aims to put in place satellites, launch services, and ground infrastructure which would provide positioning, navigation, and timing inputs necessary for the many connectivity projects via rail, shipping, and telecommunications that the BRI seeks to put in place.

The mainstay in the Chinese Space Silk Road is the BeiDou satellite navigation system, the first of which was launched in 1993-94. The China National Space Administration (CNSA) and the China Satellite Navigation Office (CSNO) have put in play a three-phase plan to provide global coverage with a 35-satellite strong BeiDou constellation by 2020. The Chinese have already met this objective in 2019 as the BeiDou navigation system has 40 satellites in orbit. As Ajey Lele and Kritika Roy point out, the open services provided by the BeiDou are similar to the GPS and Galileo navigation systems and are available free of charge to all users worldwide. The BeiDou network can be used for multiple applications ranging from communication, fishery, hydrological monitoring, weather forecasting, and mapping. However, the authorised services on the BeiDou network are more reliable and accurate and are only available for limited use by the military and other such users.[41] The success of the program can be seen from the fact that 30 BRI nations have now signed for the BeiDou navigation network.[42]

Another ambitious project which is part of the Space Silk Road project of the Chinese is the Hongyan constellation of 320 low-orbit communication satellites. The project is being spearheaded by the Chinese Academy of Space Technology, which is a subsidiary of the China Aerospace Science and Technology Corporation (CASC). These satellites would provide two-way, real-time data globally. China claims that these satellites will provide broadband access to 200,000 users, voice connectivity to two million users, and IoT coverage to 10 million users in China and BRI countries. The first of the satellites was launched in 2018 and once the pilot demonstration of nine satellites is successful, the Chinese plan to put in place about 60 satellites in orbit by 2023 and the entire satellite constellation of 320 satellites by 2025.[43]

The state-owned China Aerospace Science and Industry Corporation (CASIC) has plans to put into orbit a low-earth orbit (LEO) commercial communication satellite constellation made up of 156 satellites called Xingyun. The first two satellites of the Xingyun constellation were launched in May 2020.[44] With these proliferated constellations of satellites, China seeks to put in place redundancies for its military and civil applications and also put in place a new space architecture that was earlier only available to a few space-faring countries like the USA and Russia.

Growing Concerns about Chinese BRI and Digital BRI Projects

The Belt and Road Initiative is an attempt by the Chinese to fuel its economic growth by pushing trade, investment, physical and digital connectivity across the world. Involving over 65 countries across the globe, the BRI is much bigger than the post Second World War Marshall Plan, which covered only 18 countries. Another important statistic that highlights the massive nature of the Initiative is that the BRI projects have received a direct investment of around US$ 1,280 billion.[45]

In September 2013, when Chinese President Xi Jinping announced the BRI Initiative speaking at the Nazarbaev University in Kazakhstan, many met it with scepticism and disbelief. It was not clear how such a large project would be physically and financially sustainable over a long period. However, as Andre Wheeler points out, "the BRI represents a significant shift in global trade, laying the foundations for a paradigm shift in supply chain and logistics management".[46] As Wheeler correctly points out, the BRI was an attempt by the Chinese also to achieve greater economic heft with the integration of sea-based and land-based transportation and logistics routes as well as creating a supporting infrastructure like ports, dry ports, and special economic zones along these routes. This was part of the Chinese plan to "regain its lost economic glory" by 2049 marking the anniversary of a century of Chinese Communist Party rule.

It was gradually that the nature and scope of Chinese plans and ambitions underlying the Belt and Road Initiative (BRI) became apparent despite the concerns and pushback and the project began.

One of the areas that have been receiving a lot of attention in recent months is the 5G standard for telecommunication networks. As the Chinese have taken the lead and are pushing for adoption of its standard and equipment across the globe, Huawei managed to tie up 5G contracts with 91 countries at the beginning of 2020. However, as the risk of having Chinese operators managing their telecom networks became apparent to countries, many began to pull out of such contracts.

Countries and telecom operators that have expressed reluctance or are averse to allowing Chinese 5G operators to install equipment or have access to their telephone or communication networks include the USA, Spain, Germany, Brazil, United Kingdom, India, Canada, Australia, France, South Korea, Greece, Japan, among others.[47] Mobile operators in these countries are choosing Ericsson and

Nokia, among other mobile network equipment vendors over Chinese companies given the apparent risk they perceive in having Chinese companies having access to their sensitive data and networks.

Another area of growing concern is the Chinese BeiDou navigation satellite constellation. As China wishes to replace the USA's Global Positioning System (GPS) with the BeiDou system, many countries are worried about the national security implications that they could have especially as the BeiDou system will be based on China's own military tracking requirements.[48] Similar concerns have been voiced about voice and Internet data being streamed across the globe on Chinese fibre optic cables.

The question that one should be asking is whether in the long term it would be possible for countries to resist the Chinese offers given that many a time they come bundled with sweet financial and other incentives for the countries' leaders. In case the international comity of nations is not able to provide an alternative to the Chinese, it is unlikely that countries will be able to resist Beijing's overtures especially as their equipment is much cheaper and is offered with 'soft', even though unsustainable, financial loans. A broader question we need to ask ourselves is whether we are just replacing the technological and digital 'domination' by the USA of yesteryears with a future world that will be dominated by the People's Republic of China. As of now, for many countries across the globe, this is a future that is far from being palatable.

NOTES

1. Jinping Xi, "President Xi Jinping Delivers Important Speech and Proposes to Build a Silk Road Economic Belt with Central Asian Countries," *Ministry of Foreign Affairs of the People's Republic of China*, 7 September 2013, https://www.fmprc.gov.cn/mfa_eng/topics_665678/xjpfwzysiesgjtfhshzzfh_665686/t1076334.shtml
2. Jinping Xi, "Speech by Chinese President Xi Jinping to Indonesian Parliament," *ASEAN-China Centre*, 3 October 2013, http://www.asean-china-center.org/english/2013-10/03/c_133062675.htm
3. For the purpose of this essay and to avoid any confusion due to the use of various terms for the project, the author will use Belt and Road Initiative (BRI) throughout, apart from where it is there in original statements and reports which are being quoted.
4. National Development and Reform Commission, Ministry of Foreign Affairs, People's Republic of China, and Ministry of Commerce, People's Republic of China, "Vision for Maritime Cooperation under the Belt and Road Initiative," *The State Council, The People's Republic of China*, March 2015, http://english.www.gov.cn/archive/publications/2017/06/20/content_281475691873460.htm; National Development and Reform Commission, Ministry of Foreign Affairs, People's Republic of China, and Ministry of Commerce, People's Republic of China, "Vision And Actions On Jointly Building Silk Road Economic Belt And 21st Century Maritime Silk Road" (Beijing: The State Council, The People's Republic of China, March 2015), https://eng.yidaiyilu.gov.cn/qwyw/qwfb/1084.htm

5. "'Belt and Road' Incorporated into CPC Constitution," *Xinhua*, 24 October 2017, http://www.xinhuanet.com/english/2017-10/24/c_136702025.htm
6. Jinping Xi, "Full Text of President Xi's Speech at Opening of Belt and Road Forum," *Xinhua*, 14 May 2017, http://www.xinhuanet.com//english/2017-05/14/c_136282982.htm
7. "Mapping the Belt and Road Initiative: This Is Where We Stand," *MERICS-Mercator Institute for China Studies*, 7 July 2018, https://merics.org/en/analysis/mapping-belt-and-road-initiative-where-we-stand
8. National Development and Reform Commission, Ministry of Foreign Affairs, People's Republic of China, and Ministry of Commerce, People's Republic of China, "Vision And Actions On Jointly Building Silk Road Economic Belt And 21st Century Maritime Silk Road".
9. "Mapping the Belt and Road Initiative."
10. State Administration of Science, Technology and Industry for National Defence and National Development and Reform Commission, "Guidelines for Facilitating the Construction of Spatial Information Passageways and Application along the Belt and Road Route," November 2016, http://www.ndrc.gov.cn/zcfb/zcfbqt/201611/t20161123_827548.html
11. Jinping Xi, "President Xi Jinping's Keynote Speech at the Opening Ceremony of the International Cooperation Forum of Belt and Road Initiative.," *Xinhua*, 14 May 2017, http://www.xinhuanet.com/world/2017-05/14/c_1120969677.htm
12. "Mapping the Belt and Road Initiative."
13. MERICS, "Networking the 'Belt and Road': The Future Is Digital," *MERICS-Mercator Institute for China Studies*, 28 August 2019, https://merics.org/en/analysis/networking-belt-and-road-future-digital
14. State Council of People's Republic of China, "Full Translation: China's 'New Generation Artificial Intelligence Development Plan' (2017)," *New America*, 1 August 2017, http://newamerica.org/cybersecurity-initiative/digichina/blog/full-translation-chinas-new-generation-artificial-intelligence-development-plan-2017/; Krzysztof Koz³owski, "BRI and Its Digital Dimension: Twists and Turns," *Journal of Science and Technology Policy Management* 11, No. 3 (2018): 313, doi:10.1108/JSTPM-06-2018-0062
15. State Council of People's Republic of China, "Full Translation."
16. Ibid.
17. Andre Wheeler, "China's Digital Silk Road (DSR): The New Frontier in the Digital Arms Race?," *Silk Road Briefing*, 19 February 2020, https://www.silkroadbriefing.com/news/2020/02/19/chinas-digital-silk-road-dsr-new-frontier-digital-arms-race/
18. MERICS, "Networking the 'Belt and Road': The Future Is Digital," *MERICS-Mercator Institute for China Studies*, 28 August 2019, https://merics.org/en/analysis/networking-belt-and-road-future-digital
19. MERICS, "Networking the 'Belt and Road': The Future Is Digital," *MERICS-Mercator Institute for China Studies*, 28 August 2019, https://merics.org/en/analysis/networking-belt-and-road-future-digital
20. Sanchita Basu Das, "OBOR's Digital Connectivity Offers Both Benefits and Risks," ISEAS Perspective, ISEAS Perspective (Singapore: ISEAS Yusof Ishak Institute, 4 August 2017), 4.
21. Kerry Brown and Anna Burjanadze, "The Digital Silk Road: Upgrading the '16+1' Cooperation?" in *China and the New Silk Road: Challenges and Impacts on the Regional and Local Level*, (eds) Harald Pechlaner et al. (Springer, 2020), 139–40.
22. Shen Hong, "Building a Digital Silk Road? Situating the Internet in China's Belt and Road Initiative," *International Journal of Communication*, 12 (2018): 2692.
23. Ajey Lele and Kritika Roy, *Analysing China's Digital and Space Belt and Road Initiative*, IDSA Occasional Paper 55 (New Delhi: Institute for Defence Studies and Analyses, 2019), 16.
24. Ding Qian, "China Breakthroughs: SAIL Ahead on South Atlantic Cable Network," *CCTV*

English, May 7, 2017, http://english.cctv.com/2017/07/05/ARTITi0QntQhXqvZoN4dwobj 170705.shtml
25. S. Gong, J. Gu, & F. Teng, "The Impact of the Belt and Road Initiative Investment in Digital Connectivity and Information and Communication Technologies on Achieving the SDGs," K4D Emerging Issues Report (Brighton, UK: Institute for Development Studies, 2019), 6, https://assets.publishing.service.gov.uk/media/5c86628940f0b6369b76a372/K4D_Emerging_Issues_-_BRI_Investment_Part_A-final.pdf
26. Giri Chaitanya, "Mapping China's Global Telecom Empire - Version 2," *Gateway House*, 2 August 2018, https://www.gatewayhouse.in/china-global-telecom-tentacles/
27. Wheeler, "China's Digital Silk Road (DSR)."
28. "Made in China 2025," Backgrounder (Institute for Security and Development Policy, June 2018), https://isdp.eu/content/uploads/2018/06/Made-in-China-Backgrounder.pdf.
29. Anjani Trivedi, "China Is Winning the Trillion-Dollar 5G War as It Integrates Internet with Real Economy," *The Print*, 13 July 2020, https://theprint.in/opinion/china-is-winning-the-trillion-dollar-5g-war-as-it-integrates-internet-with-real-economy/459633/.
30. Scott Bicheno, "Huawei and ZTE Win 88% of Joint China Telecom/Unicom 5G Tender," *Telecoms.Com*, 28 April 2020, World, https://telecoms.com/503971/huawei-and-zte-win-88-of-joint-china-telecom-unicom-5g-tender/
31. "Shunned by U.S., Huawei Winning China's $170 Billion 5G Race," *Bloomberg Quint*, 23 April 23, 2020, https://www.bloombergquint.com/business/shunned-by-u-s-huawei-winning-in-china-s-170-billion-5g-race.
32. Lele and Roy, *Analysing China's Digital and Space Belt and Road Initiative*, 21–22.
33. Muzammil Hassan and Aman Kumar, "Explorations of 5G Standards and Preliminary Findings on Essentiality by Amplified and GreyB," 2 June 2020, https://www.greyb.com/5g-patents/
34. Executive Research Associates Pvt. Ltd., "China in Africa: A Strategic Overview" (Executive Research Associates, October 2009), 77, https://www.ide.go.jp/library/English/Data/Africa_file/Manualreport/pdf/china_all.pdf; Muyang Chen, "Beyond Donation: China's Policy Banks and the Reshaping of Development Finance," *Studies in Comparative International Development*, 2020, doi:10.1007/s12116-020-09310-9
35. MERICS, "Networking the 'Belt and Road' - The Future Is Digital."
36. Richard Dobbs *et al.*, "China's e-Tail Revolution: Online Shopping as a Catalyst for Growth" (McKinsey Global Institute, March 2013), 11, https://www.mckinsey.com/~/media/McKinsey/Featured%20Insights/Asia%20Pacific/China%20e%20tailing/MGI_China_e%20tailing_Full_report_March_2013.pdf
37. "China Cross-Border e-Commerce Trends for 2020," *Agency China*, 14 January 2020, https://agencychina.com/blog/china-cross-border-e-commerce-trends-for-2020/
38. Yihan Ma, "China: Cross-Border e-Commerce Retail Export Value 2019," *Statista*, 17 September 2020, https://www.statista.com/statistics/1173365/china-cross-border-ecommerce-retail-export-value/
39. Brown and Burjanadze, "The Digital Silk Road: Upgrading the '16+1' Cooperation?" 143.
40. Hong, "Building a Digital Silk Road? Situating the Internet in China's Belt and Road Initiative," 2693–94.
41. Lele and Roy, *Analysing China's Digital and Space Belt and Road Initiative*, 29–30.
42. Wheeler, "China's Digital Silk Road (DSR)."
43. John Sheldon, "China's New Space Race: First Satellite of CASC's Hongyan LEO SATCOM Constellation To Launch By End Of 2018," *Space Watch Global*, 23 November 2018, https://spacewatch.global/2018/11/chinas-new-space-race-first-satellite-of-cascs-hongyan-leo-satcom-constellation-to-launch-by-end-of-2018/
44. "Xingyun-2 01, 02 (XY-2 01, 02)," *Gunter's Space Page*, accessed 12 October 2020, https://space.skyrocket.de/doc_sdat/xingyun-2.htm.

45. K.C. Fung *et al.*, "Digital Silk Road, Silicon Valley and Connectivity," *Journal of Chinese Economic and Business Studies* 16, No. 3 (2018): 2, doi:10.1080/14765284.2018.1491679
46. Wheeler, "China's Digital Silk Road (DSR)."
47. "World Waking up to China's True Intentions to Dominate 5G: US Official," *Mint*, 26 June 2020, https://www.livemint.com/news/world/world-waking-up-to-china-s-true-intentions-to-dominate-5g-us-official-11593171649885.html
48. Brown and Burjanadze, "The Digital Silk Road: Upgrading the '16+1' Cooperation?," 143–44.

SECTION VI

COVID-19 AND BRI

18

Impact of COVID-19 Pandemic on China's Belt and Road Initiative

Sitakanta Mishra

Introduction

Debating the geostrategic repercussions of the Coronavirus pandemic at this juncture is undoubtedly secondary compared to the concerns for the health safety issues of the entire humanity. However, the pandemic has generated considerable strategic tremors that may usher in a new world order with an alteration in the current global power hierarchy. Whatever it may be, with the onset of the pandemic, neither the world is the same any more, nor will it remain the same post-pandemic. Besides the health crisis, the pandemic's ugly face is clearly visible in the economic sphere the world over. While G-20 nations have entered a staggering situation, supply chains and manufacturing of goods and services across the world have been disrupted. According to the World Trade Organization (WTO), "world trade is expected to fall by between 13% and 32% in 2020 as the COVID-19 pandemic disrupts normal economic activity and life around the world".[1] Besides, construction and engineering projects are being impacted severely in every corner of the world. Work has stopped along the China-Pakistan Economic Corridor (CPEC);[2] Cambodia's Sihanoukville Special Economic Zone has come to a standstill; the Payra coal power plant in Bangladesh has been delayed, and projects across Indonesia, Malaysia, and Myanmar are stuck in holding patterns.[3] Especially, the pandemic seems to have given "a body blow to China's landmark initiative–the Belt and Road Initiative (BRI)—with most of the 142 recipient nations now seeking to renegotiate the deal",[4]

Speculations on the impact of the COVID-19 pandemic and BRI's fate have given rise to a dyadic debate: one side arguing the pandemic's long-term negative impacts on it, and definite disruption of the project. Many even view the risk of the spread of the virus along the BRI, and the success of the project may be lost forever; in contrast, proponents of BRI visualize increasing importance of the BRI though a temporary slowdown is inevitable. Like it or not, the BRI serves a number of China's core domestic, economic, and geopolitical interests; therefore, China cannot afford to lose this geopolitical instrument at any cost; reportedly, it has taken some extra measures to bring the project back on track after it managed to control the pandemic within. Before passing any value judgment on the BRI's fate, one must know that it is not an ordinary infrastructure project; it is an umbrella initiative with multiple stakeholders, having tremendous geostrategic importance. The project's success or failure could "reconfigure relationships, reroute economic activity, and shift power within and between states".[5]

The sections that follow, therefore, attempt to fathom the impact of the COVID-19 pandemic by understanding the nature of the project, various angles and magnitude of impact, and finally, China's response in dealing with the likely impacts on the BRI. In the end, a prognosis is made to argue that the BRI, COVID-19 pandemic, and the current global economic situation–all seem to be testing times for China's global leadership resolve. The pandemic-generated public health crisis and consequent response will lay bare China's great power leadership aspirations. Whether it will emerge successful or not, and to what extent, is a matter of conjecture.

The Impact Angles

The impact of COVID-19 on the BRI is speculated from various angles. First, "more than 133 countries have initiated restrictions on the entry of Chinese personnel and those who have recently visited the country.... Thousands of Chinese workers have either been stuck in China, unable to return to project places after they went home for Spring Festival, or stuck in quarantine".[6] Second, disruptions of supply chains have occurred as "cities across China are shut down, and factories sit idle".[7] Third, as China has to deal with the virus outbreak at home and divert resources to stabilize the domestic economic situation, BRI projects might not get the priority investment and attention that it used to receive earlier. Fourth, as the global economy sinks into recession, BRI partner-countries, especially "frontier markets, are unlikely to take on fresh debt to finance new projects in the near term".[8] Fifth, and more importantly, for a multilateral mega project like the BRI to succeed, 'a pliable world' is a prerequisite which the Coronavirus pandemic has shattered. Even if China overcomes the pandemic and refocuses on the project, it "can only involve itself abroad to the extent that it is welcome". [9]

Moreover, resistance to BRI has also been gradually building up. For the Belt and Road, "perhaps the most significant COVID-19 casualty is the world's enthusiasm for the kind of connectivity and dependence that China promotes".[10] In an op-ed in the *South China Morning Post*, Daniel Russel says that "accepting a degree of Chinese influence, along with funding and infrastructure, is one thing; accepting pathogens is quite another." However, "COVID-19 will not be fatal to the Belt and Road, but...the disease's fast and lethal spread will cause governments to rethink the risks attached to ever more integration and economic dependence on their giant northern neighbour".[11] Already, shortages in demand have caused problems for countries that took BRI loans; for example, Sri Lanka. More-developed BRI countries are also likely to face demand challenges; one such example is Italy. Given the weakening of the global economy, Beijing will have to shoulder more financial costs and new ways to divert more trade to BRI routes if it wants the BRI to make significant headway in the near term.[12] Rather than only allowing borrowing countries to defer payments on their BRI loans, as Felix K. Chang (a senior fellow at the Foreign Policy Research Institute) suggests, "China may have to restructure or forgive far more of them. China may also need to find ways to divert more trade to the BRI. Finally, China could help create demand by dropping its import barriers and encouraging other countries to export goods to it".[13]

For these and other reasons, one would believe that the BRI will be negatively impacted by the COVID-19 pandemic. There is no denying the fact that part of the project is halted and China has to absorb short-term impacts though Chinese officials have been at pains to assure the world that the virus will not have "any negative impact" on Belt and Road projects.[14] They offer assurances that the adverse economic impact is only temporary, and on 2 March 2020, the China Development Bank said it would provide low-cost loans to affected Belt-and-Road-related companies.[15] The report "BRI Beyond 2020" by Economist Corporate Network, supported by Baker McKenzie and Silk Road Associates, shows that the ripple effects of COVID-19 are affecting the nature, pace, and scope of China's BRI activity in Africa, mostly for the short-term.[16] According to the *Asia Times*, the disease's fast and lethal spread will cause governments to "rethink the risks attached to ever more integration and economic dependence on its giant northern neighbour".[17] All these speculations and the Chinese responses, though, indicate a definite short-term impact; the larger question that this chapter enquires into is 'will COVID-19 be fatal to the BRI'?

The Nature of BRI

To fathom the exact repercussions of the pandemic on the BRI, one needs to first understand the nature of the BRI, the terms and conditions of investment, and management of the project resources. At the outset, "(the) BRI is an umbrella initiative which covers a multitude of investment projects designed to promote the flow of goods, investment, and people".[18] Over 70 countries have already signed up for the project; most of them are developing countries with the weakest credit ratings in the world. But BRI loans are not foreign aid but investment plans in the host country. As the global economy sinks into recession, BRI countries, especially frontier markets, are unlikely to take on fresh debt to finance new projects in the near term. With the onset of the pandemic, there are shortages, may be temporary, in demand, causing problems for countries that took BRI loans.[19]

Even if China manages to convince its partners to continue the projects already initiated, the restriction on the movement of men and material from China is a concern. According to the Chinese National Immigration Agency, more than 133 countries have initiated restrictions on the entry of people from China and those who have recently visited the country. Consequently, the supply chain that sustains the project construction process is disrupted. Therefore, it is evident that the progress of projects will hit a roadblock due to the ongoing pandemic.

Since the 2008 financial crisis, China has become the centre of the global economy. But the coronavirus has broken the boundaries of globalization and halted economic growth globally, which in turn has disturbed "the conditions the Belt and Road needed for success.... If China faces a de-globalising world hostile to its ambitions where Chinese labour and investment are met with unease and suspicion, the Belt and Road is dead".[20] Essentially, there are four direct reasons caused by the pandemic for which the BRI is perceived to be in a bad shape. They are: (1) The financial crisis within China and in partner countries; (2) Global supply chain disruption; (3) Fear of spread of virus along the BRI; and (4) Lack of demand in partner countries. Deconstructing each of these factors would reveal the extent to which the BRI would be affected.

First, the financial crisis within China and in partner countries. The COVID-19 outbreak has severely weakened China's economic performance. "China faces a drawn-out struggle to revive an economy that suffered its biggest contraction since possibly the mid-1960s. The world's second-largest economy shrank by 6.8

per cent from a year earlier in the quarter ending in March 2020".[21] First, "the likely devastating impact on the world economy has hurt China's economy significantly" through lower demand for Chinese products, and disrupted global supply chains in which China's economy is deeply embedded and heavily dependent.[22] Second, domestic manufacturing units are affected by the lockdown leading to disruption in production and supply. Third, the disruption in global value chains and "the reconfiguration of multinationals' production facilities away from China, have ominous ramifications for the Chinese economy's long-term prospects".[23]

Fourth, the diversion of resources for managing the pandemic may result in an economic resource crunch for developmental project investment. It is argued that "the economic fallout and the volume of investments needed to shore up China's health infrastructure and resuscitate the damaged SME sector will divert resources from belt and road projects." According to a Heritage Foundation study, even before the virus struck, China's foreign investments were down by 41 per cent in 2019.[24] Daniel Russel, in an op-ed in the *South China Morning Post,* says that "as China faces a credit crunch from a recession, state-owned enterprises will be motivated to sell or withdraw from risky projects overseas".[25] Despite all these, it is difficult to imagine that Beijing will back away from the BRI.

Further, Daniel Russel, in a study titled "Navigating the Belt and Road" (June 2019) by the Asia Society Policy Institute (ASPI) has highlighted the already crippling problems of financial, environmental, and political sustainability in Belt and Road projects.[26] He categorically mentions that

> "Beijing is seeking to multilateralise the BRI and open it up to the international public and private investors. The challenge is that commercial banks, MDBs, and private international financiers will not invest in a project that has not been adequately de-risked or is not designed to be financially viable. The use of public money through government-backed insurance or Chinese development bank financing, which provides implicit or explicit government guarantee, has created a moral hazard in which 'easy money' leads Chinese developers to take outsize risks or pursue unprofitable projects. This has led to financial losses, political backlash, environmental damage, and other adverse outcomes".[27] If this is to be believed, the pandemic and consequent economic downturn will further deteriorate the BRI's financial status. But will China allow such a situation to unfold? Will China be a muted spectator of its dream geostrategic vision fading? It would be unrealistic to argue that there would be no impact. As Bee Chun Boo rightly says, "The COVID-19 epidemic definitely has a dampening effect on BRI activities as Chinese companies focus their resources and efforts on dealing with the various types of the impact caused by such epidemic".[28]

It would be fair to assume that the effects will likely be relatively short term; in some cases, the BRI activities have been gradually resumed. Reportedly, the foreign sellers and partners are adjusting their deal timetables to make allowances for the impact caused by the pandemic. Ben Simpfendorfer, CEO of Silk Road Associates, explains that "the BRI will remain a priority for China, but it will affect the Chinese government's short-term and long-term response to COVID-19, because shortfalls in China's health sector, and the economic fallout for the country's financially challenged SME sector, will divert official attention and resources away from the BRI over the next 12 months and potentially longer. This may mean reduced investments in BRI's smaller, less critical markets where the opportunities to connect such investments to the global supply are limited. For example, Central Asia, Sub-Saharan Africa, and Eastern Europe will accordingly see a short-term dip in BRI-related activity in comparison to Southeast Asia".[29]

1. ***Supply Chain Disruption:*** The first casualty of the COVID-19 pandemic is the supply chains (both men and material) as cities across China shuts down, factories remain idle, and people are under quarantine. The BRI projects are predominantly reliant on Chinese, rather than local, materials and supplies, but "the COVID-19 crisis has hampered China's as well as global manufacturing supply chains that used to feed the BRI projects. China's shuttered factories not only need workers to be released to resume normal output but also need restored supplies of raw materials and active truckers and shipping ports to deliver their goods abroad".[30] "The global shipping industry was slowed to the point that more tonnage of container ships was idled around the world now. This has had a quick impact throughout the BRI", where major projects have been delayed because they simply cannot get the supplies they need out of China.[31]

Reportedly, the Jakarta-Bandung high-speed railway in Indonesia that depends on China for half of their construction materials has been halted.[32] "The nickel and cobalt projects of Tsingshan Holding Group, GEM Co. Ltd. and Zhejiang Huayou Cobalt—worth a combined $ 11 billion—have been disrupted due to the coronavirus".[33] It is also feared that the Batang Toru dam could miss its scheduled completion date. In addition, the required labour force is not available as "thousands of Chinese workers have either been stuck in China, unable to return to work after they went home for the Spring Festival, or stuck in quarantine." Construction of a 510-megawatt dam in the Batang Toru rainforest in Indonesia has ground to a halt as its Chinese workers have been unable to get around a ban on flights from China.[34]

> A break on the flow of Chinese labour is a major factor in these disruptions. China has repatriated its citizens working in different countries, "which will

grind other BRI projects to a halt. At the recipient country level, more than 130 countries around the world have placed entry restrictions on Chinese citizens or individuals travelling from China. The Chinese government has lobbied BRI countries, including the Solomon Islands and Pakistan, to ease these travel restrictions. The longer that Chinese workers are unable to return to projects overseas, the longer the projects will languish incomplete, and some may be abandoned altogether".[35]

2. *Fear of Spread of Virus along the BRI:* Criticism and accusations are advanced against the BRI as it might spread the virus. The BRI projects are essentially infrastructure projects, mainly undertaken by Chinese state-owned enterprises (SOEs) where Chinese labourers are employed; therefore, there are chances that they could introduce the virus into the regions where these projects are undertaken.[36] Also, it is alleged that the increased volume of human traffic using the infrastructure could get affected. Hence as a protective step, passenger tickets along the Trans-Siberian and all other passenger routes through the Belt & Road into Kazakhstan and Russia were closed since early January 2020.[37]

There is some scepticism also about the spread of virus along the BRI. While it is true that thousands of Chinese workers have been posted overseas to work in infrastructure projects, they are extremely well protected from the local communities, says Chris Devonshire-Ellis. In an op-ed in the *Silk Road Briefing*, (21 April 2020), Chris says that the Chinese SOEs working overseas and deploying Chinese labour typically house them in temporary accommodation or camps. They are monitored, not allowed access to local amenities, and essentially corralled. Chinese food and drink are provided, and all necessities catered for. Apart from the occasional senior manager, one simply does not see Chinese workers from overseas mixing with the local population. Besides,—these workers are typically on 6-12 month deployments—none of them were in China when the outbreak began in Wuhan. Many of them later returned to China, leaving just a small number of admin and security staff behind.[38] On the other hand, some partner countries are determined to continue business as usual. For example, "the government of Pakistan is in full consultation with the government of China as well as companies working on the CPEC projects.... Pakistan's government has taken effective measures to provide full protection to the Chinese workforce working on CPEC. In addition, the Chinese workers who are returning to Pakistan have to undergo double quarantine system for their safety as well as the safety of other workers".[39]

It cannot be established that through the BRI, the pandemic has spread or likely to spread. Had there been any transmission of the virus from China along the Belt & Road, it would have spread from Eastern China towards the West up to Russia, which shares a 4,209-km border with China. Yet, that is not what has happened. Rather infections among the returned Russian holidaymakers from Italy and Europe have been reported. China now has a new cluster of infections around places bordering Russia. These are returning Chinese workers from Suifenhe, a wholesale goods market town close to the Russian border, who have returned home to China in order to escape the virus and lockdown in Moscow.[40]

So, it is difficult to prove that the BRI helps to spread the virus to the West. But cross-border infections from returning nationals to their respective countries remain a considerable threat, and a "likely "second wave" of COVID-19 might come from returnees who have not been properly registered, monitored, and quarantined".[41] Undoubtedly, challenges still persist, but one would imagine that China will share its experience of battling COVID-19 with other BRI countries for a speedy recovery and thereby resume BRI activities early.

3. ***Lack of Demand in Partner Countries:*** The pandemic-generated economic crisis in the BRI partner countries has resulted in shortages in demand. This is no boost for infrastructure projects; rather, partner countries find themselves in a 'debt trap.' In addition, many "partner countries find excessive reliance on Chinese labour" troublesome as it reduces the projects' benefits to them and generates social tensions and other problems. "The heavy reliance of BRI projects on imported Chinese labour, inadequate local employment opportunities, weak safeguards for workers' rights, and lack of training programs are widespread complaints in Southeast Asia".[42]

Whether China is pursuing "debt trap diplomacy" or not, the result is the same. This is widely perceived even before the pandemic proliferated. The most widely known case is that of Sri Lanka. The BRI-financed port at Hambantota in Sri Lanka has able to attract only a tiny number of ships. Low revenue generation led to non-payment of interest on loans. As a result, Sri Lanka was forced to give a Chinese port operating company a 99-year lease and 15,000 acres of land around it so that Colombo could repay its Chinese creditors.[43] A similar fate could befall Djibouti and its strategic port near the Horn of Africa, as the country's debt to China has spiralled to over 100 per cent of its annual GDP.[44] In April 2020, reportedly, "Zambia was considering offering its copper mines to its Chinese creditors in exchange for debt deferral or forgiveness".[45] In Bangladesh, the transport minister warned that a Chinese funded "billion-dollar bridge project was under threat. In Nigeria, a major rail project was put on hold. Pakistan's planning and development minister said the US$ 62 billion CPEC faced delays.

Indonesia's investment minister has also announced delays for the Jakarta-Bandung high-speed rail project".[46]

The more developed BRI countries are also likely to face demand challenges. For example, Italy, which experienced a rapid spread of the pandemic, was the first European country to join the BRI in early 2019. Italy's economy had already been struggling under a huge debt burden. Such developments make partner countries feel insecure and cautious about BRI projects. Unless Beijing shoulders more financial costs of the projects in these challenging times, BRI projects in the worst-affected countries will not make any significant headway in the near term. China needs to help create demand in partner countries "by dropping its import barriers and encouraging other countries to export goods to it" besides restructuring, or forgiving, the loans, if necessary, instead of allowing only deferred repayments, to prove its genuineness.[47] It has to help divert more trade to BRI routes to boost the utility of the projects, thereby attracting demand for new projects.

Ground Realities

There is no doubt that COVID-19 has severely impacted the BRI as much of it has been shut down since the outbreak of the pandemic. Work has stopped along the CPEC, on Cambodia's Sihanoukville Special Economic Zone, and the Payra coal power plant in Bangladesh, whereas projects across Indonesia, Malaysia and Myanmar are stuck. Although about 60 per cent of China's small and medium-sized companies have resumed operations due to gradual control over the pandemic in China, there is no doubt that it has proved to be an upheaval.[48, 49]

Certainly, the pace of resumption of BRI projects will depend on the speed of China's containment of the virus and the broader economic recovery, and supply chains coming back to normal. Many hold that "the occasional epidemic here and there is simply something that the Silk Road—ancient and new—has always had to contend with".[50] Meanwhile, the pace of digital BRI activity has ramped up, despite challenges to manufacturing and supply chain activity, as have investor interest in Chinese tech companies and the general healthcare industry.[51]

One must keep in mind that the BRI has become central to China's foreign policy and Xi Jinping's political status and legacy; it was even written into the constitution of the Chinese Communist Party side by side with "Xi Jinping Thought".[52] This assimilation of Chinese political identity, economic interest, and grand strategy means that the BRI is here to stay. Over the years, "not only have the BRI projects increased in number, value, and geographic scope across more than 70 countries worldwide, but also it serves a number of China's core domestic, economic, and geopolitical interests."[53] China is building an alternative world order, and the BRI serves as an instrument in facilitating Chinese access to strategic places of the world, a definite attribute of a superpower. As an umbrella initiative, which covers a multitude of investment projects designed to promote the flow of goods, investment, and people, the new connections fostered by the BRI could "reconfigure relationships, reroute economic activity, and shift power within and between states".[54] China's vision of the BRI as a globe-spanning trade network—one that put China at its centre—will not be allowed by the current Chinese dispensation to be inscribed in history as "China's Chernobyl moment", certainly not due to a pandemic.[55]

Chinese officials have been at pains to assure the world that the virus "will not have any negative impact" on BRI projects.[56] They have offered assurances that the adverse economic impact is only temporary. Yet, the authorities are aware that the outbreak is causing difficulties for overseas projects. On 2 March 2020, the China Development Bank said it would provide low-cost loans to affected Belt-and-Road-related companies.[57]

The Counter Narrative

As a counter-narrative to the gloomy introspection by European and US analysts since the outbreak of the virus, many argue that the BRI bloc of countries has a rather big and bold future. This assertion is based on the premise that the BRI goes well beyond infrastructure projects to a broader trade, investment, and economic growth strategy. Connectivity and corridor infrastructure is just one aspect of the BRI, which is certainly not immune to occasional vagaries. In fact, the BRI is not just odd infrastructure collaboration. "China and 63 core BRI partner countries account for nearly 50 per cent of the world's population and 30 per cent of the global economy. Over the next five years, many of the BRI countries are also expected to outperform the global average in terms of economic and population growth rates".[58]

Misperceptions regarding the BRI are all-pervasive as the information shared is scanty. It is alleged that details of the BRI memorandums of understanding (MoUs) are not publicly available. While the government continues to maintain and regularly update its official Belt and Road portal, the vast majority of its content is focused on official speeches or trade statistics rather than information regarding project contracts. This has culminated in many biased assertions and the spread of negativities regarding the BRI. For example, the assertion of resource crunch is widely asserted but in fact, ill-founded: less than 13 per cent of Chinese ODI is in BRI countries, of which nearly 65 per cent goes to South-east Asian countries (based on 2017 data).[59] This suggests that "despite the government's emphasis on the BRI as a cornerstone policy, reality lags behind the rhetoric, with the BRI still playing a small and limited role in China's engagement with the world."[60] Second, the euphoria that the BRI is a massive global undertaking, and may not sustain in the wake of the global pandemic, needs to be viewed with a pinch of salt. Despite the broadening of participation in the BRI, trade and investment linked to the BRI is still concentrated in Asia, and especially in the ASEAN (Association of South-east Asian Nations) region. China's major trading partners among the BRI countries are Vietnam, Singapore, and Malaysia, and further deepening of economic relationships between China and these ASEAN markets after 2020 is expected.

If closely observed, one can see how China is utilising the pandemic crisis to its advantage by offering crisis leadership and help partner-countries through an aggressive "COVID diplomacy". For example, China has used COVID-19 diplomacy to speed up BRI projects in Myanmar. On 6 May 2020, the Chinese Ambassador, Chen Hai had a meeting with Deputy Minister for Planning, Finance and Industry Set Aung of Myanmar regarding "the implementation of the China-Myanmar Economic Corridor (CMEC) project—which falls under the BRI—as an attempt to push such projects through".[61] China, amid its own slowdown, may face BRI partner-countries defaulting on debts, cancelling or renegotiating BRI agreements, or lowering the priority of the BRI to focus on arresting the pandemic and its impacts. But China's state-owned banks are still awash in cash. China can unilaterally benefit from the economic struggles of BRI partners, which may open the way to snapping up distressed assets or strategically repositioning existing BRI projects during or after the crisis.[62]

This path will not be opted by China as its image has been hampered enough involving the Hambantota project in Sri Lanka a few years ago. Rather, China seems to have adopted a more generous strategy and hinted at a shift in its BRI project strategy amid growing concerns about debt repayments from many partner-countries. China's Premier, Li Keqiang, at the start of the National People's Congress (NPC), said recently that China "will focus on quality in the joint pursuit of the BRI".[63] China seems to have chalked out a financial assistance package that included grants, interest-free loans, and preferential loans for debt relief. Chinese authorities feel that "simply waiving debtors' obligations as some countries or organizations have called for is not going to be effective as a solution. If any debtors encounter difficulties to pay on time, there may be tailored plans including rescheduling or China increasing funding to help related projects resume operation and return profits".[64] Rather, they suggest repayments "by multiple financial or other approaches, such as China adding grants to help bring projects back to life, conducting debt-to-equity swaps, or hiring Chinese firms to assist operations".[65]

After initial speculations in the wake of the pandemic, some countries have come out openly supporting the BRI project and reassuring their collaboration with China. For example, Greece has reasserted that Greece-China cooperation under the BRI will undoubtedly progress with strong momentum to the benefit of both sides. Greek authorities have categorically said that COVID-19 will not harm Greece-China relations. Adonis Georgiadis, Greek Minister of Development and Investment, said in a written statement to *Xinhua* that "We believe in the ties between the two countries. We appreciate China as a true friend of Greece and a significant investor in our country.... All our investment plans continue normally, and we are waiting for our Chinese friends to continue with even greater momentum".[66] The Greek minister also expressed his admiration for the way in which the Chinese government has dealt with the pandemic.

Besides its geostrategic objectives, the BRI is "a 'soft power' vanity project to burnish China's international image. The Chinese leadership views the BRI as a way of both legitimising China's model of governance and economic development to the rest of the world, and positioning China as the leader of (an) alternative new world order".[67] Therefore, China would go to any extent to save face and position. In April 2019, analysts at Rhodium Group in Hong Kong attempted to assess the financial viability of China's BRI and revealed surprising facts. As per their study, particularly in Africa, China has renegotiated 22 loans worth $ 32 billion, and the Group suspects that around two dozen cases of debt forgiveness, especially to African countries, are not in the public domain.[68]

This is not to argue that the pandemic will not have any adverse impact on the BRI. Chinese foreign minister Wang Yi has admitted in May 2020 that "the impact of COVID-19 on the Belt and Road cooperation is temporary and limited. COVID-19 will only strengthen and re-energise Belt and Road cooperation and open up new possibilities".[69] China now sees an opportunity in the global health crisis in the form of re-launching the Health Silk Road (HSR), a component of the BRI. "Beijing has wanted to shape public health governance since 2015, and the HSR allowed it an opportunity to launch the initiative globally. This helps China keep the BRI relevant, as well as gain control of a global narrative that has so far blamed them for obfuscation and misinformation".[70]

A Prognosis

The two opposing narratives on the viability of the BRI are convincing. Which narrative would be closer to reality is too early to conclude. Nevertheless, there are genuine concerns of the BRI partner-countries regarding project financing and sustainability. In the extreme, if the global economic slowdown lingers, it may push them into a debt trap. Therefore, China needs to pursue crisis control measures with fresh impetus for the project. But as a strong counter-narrative, as argued by the Australian geopolitical expert Digby James Wren, the BRI has "the potential to drive the post-COVID-19 global economic recovery and reconstruction in somewhat the same way that the American Marshall Plan (did) after the end of World War II".[71] If the BRI with new impetus is successfully executed, the post-pandemic period would see the ushering of a new world order centred around China.

If one buys a positive narrative, the prerequisite to realize it is the existence of a 'pliable world.' The pandemic has generated enough apprehension, insecurities, and scepticism among the partner countries, which would certainly hinder any enthusiastic response to BRI projects in the foreseeable future. The rejuvenation of the BRI depends on how efficiently and quickly China can help allay such fears of the partners. Unless and until the pandemic is controlled the world over, prospects of the BRI becoming a favoured global connectivity project cannot be realized. But it is clear that the pandemic will linger, and the world has to live with it for some time. Therefore, the idea that the BRI project would resume with full force post-pandemic would be a misnomer. Countries would take some time to settle the course with the pandemic and rethink their terms with the BRI. Meanwhile, China will have to find ways to bail out its partners in difficulty. This is in no way the end of, or the death of, the BRI. Rather it has a long future unless there is a domestic political upheaval in China, as many would presume.

To conclude, the BRI has entered its sixth year and has been portrayed primarily as a foreign strategy directed by a powerful leader. The Chinese domestic public no longer asks serious policy questions like what are the driving forces, who are the policy supporters, and what interest groups are involved in the BRI process.[72] "Inside China, it is hard to detect overt signs of any wavering in support for the BRI pronouncements from top Chinese leaders. But beneath the surface, there is growing unease in China about BRI."[73] In the wake of the pandemic, there is some muted domestic public dissonance on BRI funding and management. "With the country feeling an economic squeeze, fighting a trade war with the USA, and facing criticism from nations receiving BRI funds, Chinese sceptics, including academics, economists and the business community, are quietly asking if their government is putting its scarce resources to the right use",[74]

There are no official announcements on Beijing's priority involving Xi Jinping's BRI dreams. But the BRI has been projected as Xi's signature foreign policy agenda to build traditional and digital infrastructure around the world worth $ 1 trillion to ensure that Beijing reaps many of the benefits. Most BRI infrastructure contracts are given to Chinese companies, and most projects rely overwhelmingly on Chinese labour and supplies. Meanwhile, China's foreign exchange reserves were approaching $ 4 trillion; therefore, it seems brilliant to use some of the foreign exchange to invest in infrastructure. [75] Coupled with the use of Chinese contractors, materials, and funds, the BRI could also help solve China's excess capacity problem in its steel, cement, and construction industries. Financially it sounds lucrative for Chinese domestic stakeholders as well. But as an offshoot, the BRI has also created "significant foreign dependencies upon China".[76] The COVID-19 pandemic might worsen this dependency, but efficient management of this situation would establish China's superpower credentials.

Put together, the questions on the prospects of the BRI, winning over the COVID-19 pandemic, and dealing with the global economic crisis seem to be posing a stringent testing time for China's global leadership resolve. Response to all these will lay bare China's great power leadership aspirations. It is too soon to say precisely how the pandemic will change the broad contours of Chinese foreign policy, but it has already highlighted some of the frailties of the BRI, which may prove to be temporary.

NOTES

1. WTO, Press Release, "Trade set to plunge as COVID-19 pandemic upends global", economy, visit https://www.wto.org/english/news_e/pres20_e/pr855_e.htm, 8 April 2020.
2. "China-Pakistan Economic Corridor work stopped", visit https://www.deccanchronicle.com/world/neighbours/310120/china-pakistan-economic-corridor-work-stopped.html, 20 January 2020.
3. Keith Zhai & Matthew Tostevin, "Coronavirus slows China's Belt and Road push", visithttps://www.reuters.com/article/us-china-health-silkroad-idUSKBN20C0RF
4. "Coronavirus deals a body blow to China's grand global influence plans", visit https://www.business-standard.com/article/international/coronavirus-deals-a-body-blow-to-china-s-grand-global-influence-plans-120050400661_1.html, 4 May 2020.
5. Vinod Saighal, "What virus could mean to China's BRI vision", https://www.thestatesman.com/opinion/virus-mean-chinas-bri-vision-1502892208.html, 25 May 2020.
6. Wade Shepard, "Coronavirus Outbreak Puts Belt And Road Projects On Hold, For Now", https://www.forbes.com/sites/wadeshepard/2020/02/29/coronavirus-outbreak-puts-belt-and-road-projects-on-hold-for-now/#525a12966a2f, 29 February 2020.
7. Ibid.

8. "Global Covid-19 Pandemic A Significant Short-Term Hit To China's Belt And Road Ambitions", visithttps://www.fitchsolutions.com/infrastructure-project-finance/global-covid-19-pandemic-significant-short-term-hit-chinas-belt-and-road-ambitions-08-04-2020, 8 April 2020.
9. Luka Ivan Jukic, "Coronavirus May Kill China's Belt and Road Initiative", visit https://www.insideover.com/economy/coronavirus-may-kill-chinas-belt-and-road-initiative.html, 8 April 2020.
10. Daniel Russel, "The Coronavirus Will Not Be Fatal for China's Belt and Road Initiative but It Will Strike a Heavy Blow", visit https://www.scmp.com/comment/opinion/article/3075624/coronavirus-will-not-be-fatal-chinas-belt-and-road-initiative-it, 19 March 2020.
11. Ibid.
12. Felix K. Chang, "Lack of Demand: The Coronavirus Pandemic and China's Belt and Road Initiative," visit https://www.fpri.org/article/2020/04/lack-of-demand-coronavirus-pandemic-belt-and-road/, 20 April 2020.
13. Ibid.
14. Russel, op cit, 10.
15. "China Development Bank to support belt and road companies hit by coronavirus-Xinhua", visit https://www.reuters.com/article/health-coronavirus-china-belt-and-road/china-development-bank-to-support-belt-and-road-companies-hit-by-coronavirus-xinhua-idUSB9N2AM006, 2 March 2020.
16. "BRI Beyond 2020", visit at https://www.bakermckenzie.com/-/media/files/insight/publications/2020/03/bribeyond2020_part_2.pdf?la=en#:~:text=BRI%20beyond%202020%3A%20Partnerships%20for,and%20wrote%20the%20report%20independently, January 2020.
17. Bertil Lintner, "China virus infects Myanmar Belt and Road plans", visit https://asiatimes.com/2020/02/china-virus-infects-myanmar-belt-and-road-plans/, 5 February 2020.
18. China Power Team. "How will the Belt and Road Initiative advance China's interests?" see https://chinapower.csis.org/china-belt-and-road-initiative/, 8 May 2017.
19. Op cit., 8.
20. Luka Ivan Jukic, "Coronavirus May Kill China's Belt and Road Initiative", see https://www.insideover.com/economy/coronavirus-may-kill-chinas-belt-and-road-initiative.html, 8 April 2020.
21. "Coronavirus | China's economy in worst downturn since 1960s", see https://www.thehindu.com/news/international/coronavirus-chinas-economy-in-worst-downturn-since-1960s/article31370073.ece, 17 April 2020.
22. Sarah Tong & Li Yao, "How Much Will the Chinese Economy Be Damaged by COVID-19?" see https://www.brinknews.com/how-much-is-the-chinese-economy-going-to-be-damaged-by-covid-19-coronavirus/, 12 May 2020.
23. Ibid.
24. "Coronavirus will not be Fatal for Belt & Road but it will strike a Heavy Blow", see https://www.beltandroad.news/2020/03/20/coronavirus-will-not-be-fatal-for-belt-road-but-it-will-strike-a-heavy-blow/, 20 March 2020.
25. Russel, op cit., n. 10.
26. Daniel R. Russel & Blake Berger, "Navigating the Belt and Road Initiative", see https://asiasociety.org/sites/default/files/2019-06/Navigating%20the%20Belt%20and%20 Road%20 Initiative_2.pdf, June 2019.
27. Ibid., p. 14.
28. Op cit., n. 16, p. 2.
29. Bee Chun Boo, Martin David & Ben Simpfendorfer, "How will COVID-19 affect China's

Belt and Road Initiative?", see, https://www.weforum.org/agenda/2020/05/covid-19-coronavirus-disrupt-chinas-bri/, 4 May 2020; Michael Evans, "The Impact of COVID-19 on China's Belt and Road Initiatives in Africa", see https://www.bakermckenzie.com/en/newsroom/2020/03/bri-africa, 31 March 2020.

30. Dipanjan Roy Chaudhury, "Covid-19 pandemic puts brakes on Chinese projects", see https://economictimes.indiatimes.com/news/international/world-news/covid-19-pandemic-puts-brakes-on-chinese-projects/articleshow/75017723.cms, 6 April 2020.
31. Kirk Lancaster, Michael Rubin, and Mira Rapp-Hooper, "What the COVID-19 Pandemic May Mean for China's Belt and Road Initiative, see https://www.cfr.org/blog/what-covid-19-pandemic-may-mean-chinas-belt-and-road-initiative, 17 March 2020.
32. Shepard, op cit., n. 6.
33. Ibid.
34. Ibid.
35. Lancaster, op cit., n. 33.
36. Chris Devonshire-Ellis, "Did China Spread The Coronavirus Along The Belt & Road Initiative?", see https://www.silkroadbriefing.com/news/2020/04/21/china-spread-coronavirus-along-belt-road-initiative/, 21 April 2020.
37. Ibid.
38. Ibid.
39. Irfan Ali, "Impact of Covid-19 on CPEC, see, https://moderndiplomacy.eu/2020/06/15/impact-of-covid-19-on-cpec/, 15 June 2020.
40. Devonshire-Ellis, op cit., n. 37.
41. Ibid.
42. Daniel R. Russel and Blake Berger, "Navigating the Belt and Road Initiative", see https://asiasociety.org/sites/default/files/2019-06/Navigating%20the%20Belt%20 and%20 Road%20 Initiative_0.pdf, June 2019.
43. Maria Abi-Habib, "How China Got Sri Lanka to Cough Up a Port", https://www.nytimes.com/2018/06/25/world/asia/china-sri-lanka-port.html, 25 June 2018.
44. Chang, op cit., n. 12.
45. Ibid.
46. Russel, op cit. n. 10.
47. Chang, op cit., n. 12.
48. Lankaster, op cit., n. 32.
49. Shepard, op cit., n. 6.
50. Ibid.
51. Baker McKenzi, "Understanding How COVID-19 Alters BRI", see https://www.bakermckenzie.com/-/media/files/insight/publications/2020/03/covid19-bri-short-report.pdf?la=en
52. Douglas Bulloch, "A New Era: Xi Jinping Lays Out His Plans For The Future Of China", see https://www.forbes.com/sites/douglasbulloch/2017/10/29/a-new-era-xi-jinping-lays-out-his-plans-for-the-future-of-china/#683cdc086a66, 29 October 2017.
53. Russel and Burger, op cit., n. 43.
54. Saighal, op cit., n. 5.
55. Liubomir K. Topaloff, "Is COVID-19 China's 'Chernobyl Moment'?" see, https://thediplomat.com/2020/03/is-covid-19-chinas-chernobyl-moment/, 4 March 2020.
56. Russel, op cit., n. 10.
57. "China Development Bank to support belt and road companies hit by coronavirus-Xinhua", see https://www.reuters.com/article/health-coronavirus-china-belt-and-road/china-development-bank-to-support-belt-and-road-companies-hit-by-coronavirus-xinhua-

idUSB9N2AM006, 2 March 2020.

58. Op cit., n. 16.
59. Ibid.
60. Ibid.
61. Shah Suraj Bharat, "Is China Deploying COVID-19 Diplomacy to Speed BRI Projects in Myanmar? see https://thediplomat.com/2020/05/is-china-deploying-covid-19-diplomacy-to-speed-bri-projects-in-myanmar/, 20 May 2020.
62. Jason Tower & Jennifer Staats, "China's Belt and Road: Progress on 'Open, Green and Clean?', see https://www.usip.org/publications/2020/04/chinas-belt-and-road-progress-open-green-and-clean, 29 April 2020.
63. Ananth Krishnan, "China suggests shift in BRI approach amid debt concerns", see https://www.thehindu.com/news/international/china-suggests-shift-in-bri-approach-amid-debt-concerns/article31660841.ece
64. Ibid.
65. Ibid.
66. "Greece-China cooperation under BRI will progress despite COVID-19 pandemic: officials, experts", see http://www.xinhuanet.com/english/2020-05/30/c_139099374.htm, 30 May 2020.
67. Why is there so much furore over China's Belt and Road Initiative? see https://asiapacific.anu.edu.au/news-events/all-stories/why-there-so-much-furore-over-chinas-belt-and-road-initiative, 2 June 2020.
68. Elliot Wilson, "China: End of the Belt and Road?", see https://www.euromoney.com/article/b1lx4xdjgghf3z/china-end-of-the-belt-and-road, 4 June 2020.
69. "Wang Yi: COVID-19 only to strengthen, re-energize BRI cooperation", see https://news.cgtn.com/news/2020-05-24/Wang-Yi-Coronavirus-to-strengthen-and-re-energize-BRI-cooperation-QKOTpIJpkc/index.html, 24 May 2020.
70. Deep Pal, Rahul Bhatia & Suchet Vir Singh, "Health Silk Road—How China plans to make BRI essential in Covid-hit South Asia", see https://theprint.in/opinion/health-silk-road-how-china-plans-to-make-bri-essential-in-covid-hit-south-asia/439603/, 11 June 2020.
71. Abhishek G. Bhaya, "BRI to lead post-COVID-19 'Marshall Plan' for global recovery", see https://news.cgtn.com/news/2020-04-11/BRI-to-lead-post-COVID-19-Marshall-Plan-for-global-recovery-Pyun62Fl7y/index.html
72. Min Ye, "Domestic politics of China's Belt and Road Initiative", see http://www.theasanforum.org/domestic-politics-of-chinas-belt-and-road-initiative/, 17 June 2020.
73. Minxin Pei, "Will China let Belt and Road die quietly?", see https://asia.nikkei.com/Opinion/Will-China-let-Belt-and-Road-die-quietly, 15 February 2019.
74. Ibid.
75. Ibid.
76. Lankaster, op cit., n. 32.

Index

*